EFFECTIVE METHODS OF EDP QUALITY ASSURANCE
2nd Edition

EFFECTIVE METHODS OF EDP QUALITY ASSURANCE
2nd Edition

William E. Perry

QED Information Sciences, Inc.
Wellesley, Massachusetts

Library of Congress Catalog Number: 87–29136
International Standard Book Number: 0-89435-196-6

Printed in the Unites States of America.
88 89 9 8 7 6 5 4 3 2 1

Library of Congress Cataloging-in-Publication Data

Perry, William E.
    Effective methods of EDP quality assurance.

    1. Electronic data processing—Quality control.
2. Quality assurance. I. Title.
QA76.9.E95P48   1987   005   87-29136
ISBN 0-89435-196-6

Contents

List of Figures

Figure   *Page*

Figure   *Page*

Tables

Foreword

Is there any significant product that is not subject to a quality assurance operation? Automobiles, airplanes, buildings, refrigerators and television sets must pass tests assuring quality. Computer programs are equally significant works; however, each is different and considered more a work of art than an engineered product.

Programmers did not graduate from the same schools that produce the makers of products. Engineering students learn how to document their work. They learn production methods, testing, and project management. Programmers, I having been among the earliest, majored in mathematics, music, history, and accounting. We didn't know about engineering matters and, therefore, became cottage craftsmen and artists in the absence of the disciplines that transformed other crafts and arts into engineering.

Finally, only in recent years have programming and programmers been forced into the discipline necessary to economically produce the most complex structures known to man — computer programs. Software engineering, structured programming, and quality assurance are emerging in spite of the fact that our universities and colleges still have not advanced to producing software engineers.

The more advanced software-producing organizations are finally realizing the need for formalized life-cycle standards and practices. Quality assurance, one important step in the life cycle, is recognized by these organizations as necessary for quality software. An independent testing of programs designed and documented so that they may be formally tested before entering productive use has been found essential — something engineers knew about at least a hundred years ago.

Effective quality assurance requires competent programmers to work in this speciality. We need test programmers or quality assurance programmers just as we have these specialities in engineering. They must be given an identity, stature, and a career path of continued growth of the specialty. A body of knowledge, formal methods, tools, and techniques are needed.

May this book be a significant contribution to the advancement of software engineering practices and quality assurance in particular.

Donn B. Parker
Menlo Park, CA
1987

Preface

The rapid growth of computer technology during the past twenty years has had a substantial impact on organizations. During that time, data processing departments have placed their effort on expanding the use of the computer and discovering new applications. Progress has been substantial during these twenty years, but so have the problems. Data processing, once held in awe by most people, has now become the scapegoat for many organizational problems.

Management's attempt to control the computer has been directed at the symptoms rather than the problems. Management has established elaborate approval procedures for new applications. Users of the computer are charged for that use so that they are aware of, and are charged for, the cost of their applications. Management has frequently slowed the use of new technology by vetoing plans to install new equipment until it has been proven by several years of use.

Many of the problems associated with data processing applications can be attributed to the lack of an orderly installation process, properly supervised from inception through installation.

The emergence of quality assurance groups in data processing is an attempt by data processing management to reduce these problems. In manufacturing operations, the quality control function began decades ago. Data processing, being a production department for office operations, can use quality practices to perform the same function in EDP that quality control does in a manufacturing operation.

This book provides data processing organizations a methodology for implementing a quality control (QC) and quality assurance (QA) function. Guidance is provided for establishing, staffing, and promoting quality assurance. QC is presented as a function that continually reviews systems throughout the systems development life cycle. The book explains the techniques and methods for performing those reviews. A quality control/quality assurance manual prepared by a major organization is included in Appendix A. The review methods and techniques given in book, together with a how-to-do-it manual, provide organizations with all the materials they need to build and develop an effective quality function in data processing.

One responsible for implementing and/or operating a quality assurance function must understand the critical difference between quality assurance and quality control. Many QA groups actually practice QC; and parts of this book reflect that practice. However, even though it may be necessary to practice QC initially, it is a poor practice. See Chapter 1, The Critical Difference Between Quality Control and Quality Assurance, for a discussion of the difference between QA and QC.

William E. Perry
Orlando, Florida
1987

Part I

THE QUALITY ASSURANCE
FUNCTION

Chapter 1
QUALITY ASSURANCE: AN ESSENTIAL ELEMENT OF ELECTRONIC DATA PROCESSING

Data processing technology continues to outpace systems analysts' ability to build well-controlled and easily maintainable applications. Data processing personnel continue to search for techniques to improve the quality of computerized applications. One such technique is the quality assurance (QA) function. For the last 20 years, data processing departments have been forming quality assurance groups within their domain at a steady rate.

The general function of these groups is threefold: 1) to ascertain compliance to the approved methods of building applications; 2) to assure a reasonable level of performance; and 3) to assure that the goals of the organization, and especially those of the system user, are satisfied. These goals can best be accomplished by establishing a quality-oriented EDP environment.

Organizations continually quest for quality products. Similarities abound between the problems of manufacturing a product and producing a computerized application. The early success of American industry hinged on its ability to consistently produce products of high quality. Those organizations that were able to maintain high quality were able to dominate their industries. The formation of a QA function provides data processing management with an additional degree of confidence that the computerized applications will be well controlled and easily maintainable.

Organizations that achieve high quality in their products first establish an acceptable level of quality and then build a mechanism that assures this level is maintained. In manufacturing that mechanism is known as quality control. The quality control group works with the manufacturing departments to assure that the desired level of quality is maintained. Quality control includes more than an evaluation of the end product. It begins with the examination of the raw materials and continues throughout the manufacturing cycle.

Data processing organizations must equate their function to manufacturing a product in order to see the need for a quality control function. Data processing must assume the responsibility of determining an acceptable level of quality, and then establish the mechanism— quality assurance function— to determine that level is maintained. If you, the data processing professional, say, "My product is hand crafted and it's a one-of-a-kind type product, so it cannot be measured and compared against a standard," QA has little chance of success in your organization. On the other hand, if you say, "My skill is finding better ways to perform work, but the end product can be measured and evaluated against a standard," then the QA function can perform a very viable service for you.

Many companies are now using or considering the use of structured design and structured programming techniques to improve the quality of their systems. These techniques go hand in hand with the quality assurance function. The two disciplines are compatible and mutually supportive. The use of structured techniques provides the standardization and documentation by which QA can measure. Conversely, it appears in practice that successful implementation of structured methods requires some form of QA function to ensure the proper use of the new techniques.

Quality assurance is a step along the path of evolution of data processing from an art to a science. A successful quality assurance function requires that standards be established against which quality can be measured. The function should be advisory to data processing personnel with its clout coming from management support.

WHAT IS QUALITY?

The dictionary defines *quality* as an attribute or characteristic that is associated with something. Thus quality cannot be universally defined but, rather, must be defined for the item in question. Quality becomes a stated list of attributes and characteristics. In a data processing environment quality must be defined by the organization. Definitions may vary significantly from one organization to another. For one organization a well-built Model T Ford is quality, while to another organization it is a fully loaded Cadillac. Quality cannot be built into a product, or measured, until it is defined. Most data processing organizations have only begun to address what high-quality computerized applications are. Thus, the first task of EDP quality assurance may be to define what is meant by quality in the organization.

WHAT IS QUALITY ASSURANCE?

Data processing professionals are no different from other employees of their organization. They want to do a good job and be amply commended and rewarded for that job. The problem faced by data processing personnel is that their technology is not well understood, so if the application they build "works," few people, if any, know whether they did an outstanding job or just a satisfactory job. A means to evaluate the caliber of their work is needed.

The QA function has the primary responsibility of determining if the users' needs have been adequately satisfied. But the needs of the user must be viewed in proper perspective with the needs of other users and the overall goals of the organization. It is important that the data processing systems support the objectives and goals of the organization. Figure 1.1 illustrates the evaluation objectives of a QA function.

QA evaluates systems prior to their implementation. This includes both the building of new systems and enhancing existing systems. As a means of determining if the users' needs are being satisfied, QA evaluates three areas.

1. **Goals.** Does the system achieve the objectives of both the user and the total organization? The goals of the organization come first, and the goals or requirements of the user second. Should the requirements of the user conflict with the goals of the organization, it is important for QA to point out this conflict. The goals of any one user should be in harmony with the goals of other users.

2. **Methods.** Are standardized methods utilized in performance of the data processing function? These methods are manifested as policies, procedures, standards, and guide-

lines.   The QA function will evaluate compliance to these methods of performing work.

3. ***Performance.*** Have the systems analysts optimized the use of computer hardware and software when implementing applications? Optimization involves skilled systems design, the use of proper programming and systems techniques, as well as the best use of the available hardware and software.

Figure 1.1 **EVALUATION OBJECTIVES**

Individuals appointed to a QA function work with systems analysts and programmers to achieve these objectives. This does not give QA the responsiblity for systems design. The group should take on the role of a counselor as opposed to the role of a policeman. Differences of opinion are settled by management decisions.

Figure 1.1 illustrates that standards are extremely important in satisfying users' needs. Methods should not interfere with goals, nor should methods reduce performance. Goals should not override performance, and so on. However, it is only through standards that the proper balance among goals, methods, and performance can be achieved. If the department fails to set standards, systems programmers will set them. Far too often, data processing management relinquishes the setting of standards to programmers— and later reprimands them for poor performance.

EXAMPLES OF AVOIDABLE PROBLEMS

The following are examples of unsatisfactory applications that have cost organizations large amounts of money. The systems were designed by experienced data processing personnel. They are cases where the existence of a QA function could have saved the data processing department embarrassment and the organization money.

Example 1. A large manufacturing company was designing an on-line order entry system to replace a batch-oriented system. Under the existing system, all orders for a day were processed in a batch overnight. The sales organizations were notified the next morning of stockouts, delays in delivery, and other information pertinent to the execution of the order.

The new on-line order entry system would give the sales office the necessary information immediately. Thus, sales representatives could confirm with customers (while taking the order) shipment dates, method of shipment, stockouts, and so on. The systems designers ran preliminary tests on the equipment, and built an extensive application costing several hundred thousand dollars. When the application was coupled with the vendor's software, however, the resulting performance degraded to the point that the response time was unacceptable at the sales location test site. This caused the data processing department to divert systems programmers to the function of building a specialized message switching system. After expending many thousands of dollars on additional programming effort, the decision was finally reached that the desired performance was unachievable.

A QA function challenging performance by questioning the ability of technology to produce the desired response times would have alerted data processing management to the problem many months and several hundred thousand dollars sooner than when the inability was actually discovered.

Example 2. A sales organization established an operating standard limiting program modules to 64K in order to create the proper job mix in a multitask environment. A systems designer building a new system realized that the 64K limitation would degrade performance significantly. By increasing the program's module size to 180K, the designer was able to eliminate several passes of a large file. As this was a frequently run system, the designer argued that the exception was warranted, and proceeded to build the application using the 180K module limit. The application was complete and tested before the operations personnel realized the desired standard had been exceeded. They let the system run nonetheless. But whenever the new application ran, the normal mix of work could not be run. This meant that while the designer's application achieved a higher level of performance, the net result was less throughput at the computer center during the day.

Example 3. A large job order manufacturing organization designed a production control system to handle the entire process. The system was designed so that the engineering department would enter the bill of materials necessary for a job. From that, the system would explode the subcomponents listed into their bill of material. The computer system would then determine schedules, order raw material, and issue the paperwork on the appropriate date. The net result was each work station would be given a daily list of jobs that were to be completed that day, together with the location of the parts. As status was reported using data terminals, the computer would adjust schedules to be reflected in the next day's work. The success of the system was dependent upon the correct entry of information from the shop floor. The system was designed by engineers. When the machine operators were asked to prepare computer input, the job was beyond their capabilities. To remedy this situation, the organization put data entry clerks on the shop floor. Since the machine operators' pay was used for calculating incentive payroll, they could no longer control the work they did to assure maximum incentive pay. Thus, rather than reporting actual production, the operators reported production that guaranteed them maximum pay. Within six months, the organization scrapped the new system and reverted to the manual paperwork system.

This is an example where the systems designer clearly overengineered the system for the people it was designed to assist. Again, a QA group challenging the usability of an application would have alerted management of this potential problem during the systems design phase. The type of changes that could have been incorporated in the initial system would have been done, thus saving the organization the several hundred thousand dollars required to build another system that the machine operators could utilize.

Example 4. A user department in a life insurance company wanted a change made to an application. The change was extremely complex but would have simplified some operating procedures in the user department. The systems designer performed an evaluation and determined it was uneconomical to make that particular change. At the same time the systems programmers were converting from one version of an operating system to another. The change cost about $14,000, for which no economic justification was made.

In this situation it is difficult to evaluate which of the two decisions was correct. Were the goals of the organization relegated to second place and the desires of the data processing operation put first? If that $14,000 had been spent to satisfy the requirement of the user, would the overall functioning of the organization have been better? A difficult pair of questions, but a QA group could have provided a much needed independent viewpoint.

QUALITY ASSURANCE OBJECTIVES

The QA group works with the systems designer in designing new systems and enhancements to existing systems. In this process, QA evaluates goals, methods, and performance. The quality assurance group performs those functions that the data processing manager might do personally if time permitted. Figure 1.2 outlines the elements that make up the objectives of QA.

Under **goals,** the QA reviews each system to determine that

1. The system meets the needs of the user department(s) and other users.
2. The system is consistent with the needs of other users. One system does not infringe on the rights of other systems users.
3. The goals are consistent with the objectives of the organization. In all cases, the organization's objectives should have a higher priority than the goals of one user.
4. The goals of the system meet the EDP department objectives. If there is a conflict, resolve it before implementing the system.

5. The goals of the system are consistent with industry and government requirements.   Where either the industry or government has set requirements for data processing systems or this specific application, those requirements need to be incorporated into the system.

6. The system complies to the intent of management (i.e., controls are adequate) and the system is auditable.

GOALS	METHODS	PERFORMANCE
Meets user needs Consistent with needs of other users Consistent with organization objectives Meets EDP department objectives Consistent with industry and government requirements Controlled and auditable	The system was implemented using organization and EDP department: Policies Procedures Standards Guidelines	The system design is: Economical Effective Efficient

Figure 1.2 **ELEMENTS OF QA OBJECTIVES**

Under **methods**, QA reviews systems to determine that the system being implemented is using the organization and EDP department's:

1. *Policies.* The broad-based course of action selected by the organization.

2. *Procedures.* The particular methods outlined by the organization to accomplish objectives.

3. *Standards.* Rules set up by the organization for the measure of quantity or quality of work.
4. *Guidelines.* Recommended methods for performing work.

Under **performance**, QA reviews systems to determine that the design is

1. *Economical.* The system is to be performed in the way that requires the least cost.
2. *Effective.* The system will accomplish the results desired with minimum effort.
3. *Efficient.* The system as designed maximizes the use of people and machines.

While these terms sound somewhat synonymous, each requires a different evaluation of the system. *Economical* means dollar considerations. *Effectiveness* brings in the criteria of time and ease of performing the task. *Efficiency* considers such things as whether or not all or parts of the system should have been computerized, or whether it could have been done more efficiently manually.

WHY IS A QUALITY ASSURANCE GROUP NEEDED?

Experience has shown that the best time to influence the design of systems is in the earlier stages of development. Once the design of a system has been determined, it is costly to make significant changes. Adjustments during and after the programming stage tend to be more fine tuning than modifications of any magnitude. Figure 1.3 illustrates that while the majority of the cost of developing a system occurs after programming has commenced, the ability to influence the design is inversely proportional to the cost.

Management tends to become involved in the system when the cost becomes significant and the dates of implementation approach. Thus, we have the paradox of management's influence and concern coming at the point in the systems development life cycle where they are least able to influence the systems design.

The establishment of a QA function provides management with a degree of confidence that an independent, technically trained group is monitoring the goals, methods, and performance of applications from the beginning of the project. This relieves data processing management of personally performing this function.

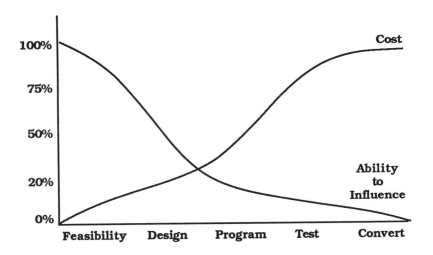

Figure 1.3 **COST OF PROJECT VERSUS QA's ABILITY TO INFLUENCE**

Challenges Facing the EDP Manager

The EDP manager is faced with some unique problems in the performance of the data processing mandate. Figure 1.4 illustrates those challenges facing the EDP department which the establishment of a QA group would help solve. The solutions are discussed in the later chapters of this book.

The data processing manager is responsible for a highly technical function that interfaces with most operating groups within the organization. In most highly technical departments, the manager is able to contain the technical aspects of the function within the department. This is not true in the data processing organization, since other departments and groups within the organization use and rely upon the result of EDP systems. This puts the EDP manager in an influential and responsible role in most departments within the organization.

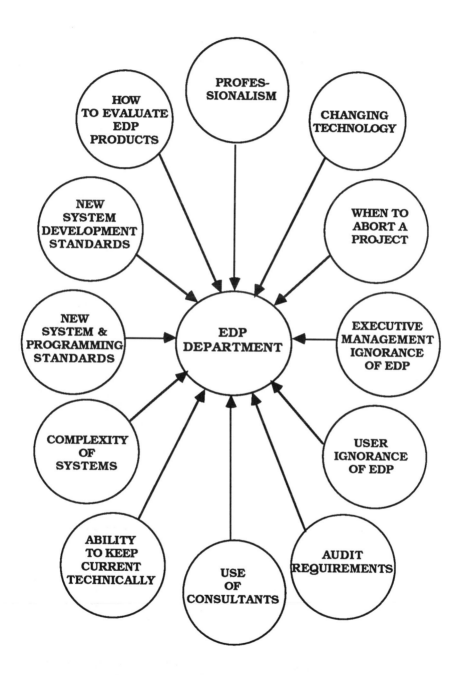

Figure 1.4 **CHALLENGES OF THE EDP DEPARTMENT**

Some of the unique challenges facing an EDP department relate specifically to the technical aspect of data processing. An independent evaluation group such as QA can assist the EDP manager in dealing with these challenges.

Changing Technology. Vendors continually offer new data processing hardware and software. This continual modification by vendors may obsolete existing systems and cause a significant percentage of data processing resources to be expended just to stay current with technological changes. The value of making many of these changes is rarely examined. Technology tends to trap organizations into continuing with one vendor's line of hardware and software.

When to Abort a Project. Once a data processing system is under development, it is rarely stopped unless a major disaster is pending. Few organizations have the proper criteria and information to make an early judgment as to when system development should be stopped on an uneconomical project or one that is running into technical difficulties.

Executive Management Ignorance of EDP. Few members of executive management have a detailed knowledge of the technical aspects of data processing. However, these same individuals are required to make decisions regarding the future of data processing. Too frequently, decisions are made on intuition as opposed to facts. Many of these decisions inhibit DP effectiveness because there appears to be distrust on the part of many members of executive management over economic evaluations of data processing proposals.

User Ignorance of EDP. Frequently, users of data processing have minimal technical knowledge of data processing. This puts them in a position of having to accept recommendations by data processing systems designers. The systems designers, in turn, have little knowledge of the needs and requirements of the user. Thus, while it may be technically feasible to provide the user with desired features in an application, neither the user nor the systems designer can properly match needs with technical capacity of data processing to satisfy those needs.

Audit Requirement. Auditors are becoming more active in evaluation of computer applications. Unfortunately, many of these auditors are not technically qualified to perform the evaluations they are making. This places an additional burden on the data processing department to technically support the auditor. Failure to support the audit effort may result in having to respond to management about audit comments for which the goals are desirable but for which the technology does not permit economical achievement.

Use of Consultants. No one individual in data processing can be knowledgeable on all aspects of designing and implementing a computer application. Ideally, consultants should be used as needed to assist in solving technical problems. Unfortunately, few organizations provide the systems designers access to a consultant.

Ability to Keep Current Technically. All members of the data processing department, especially management, have difficulty in keeping technically current in their field. As data processing systems become more segmented, this problem accelerates. Although it was possible 10 years ago for one person to implement an entire system, it now takes a group of individuals to perform the same function. Data processing management, because of its technical lag, has difficulty in assessing the adequacy of new ideas in system design and the adequacy of new hardware and software systems under consideration.

Complexity of Systems. As systems become more integrated, they become more complex. Chains of systems now flow through entire organizations. One transaction, such as an order, can trigger numerous transactions to be automatically generated by the computer system. Thus, the development of one system can affect the operation of many other systems. It now becomes necessary for a systems designer to comprehend fully the impact of a new system, or enhancement to an existing system, on all the systems affected by that development.

Few Systems and Programming Standards. Systems and pro-gramming work remains basically an art. Without standards, systems designers and programmers can innovate in ways which facilitate errors and incur high maintenance costs on computer-ized applications.

Few Systems Development Standards. The development process itself in most organizations remains a highly skilled craft. Individuals personalize applications so that each one is developed in a unique manner. The development process too frequently is one that meets the personal requirements of the lead systems designer. This uniqueness of the development process has led to executive management's reluctance to rely on EDP–proposed costs and schedules. There have been too many cost overruns and schedule extensions in implementing data processing applications.

How to Evaluate EDP Products. When hardware is purchased, software obtained, or applications built, it is difficult for management to evaluate the product. The lack of standards tends to make each product unique. Because of the time required to get data processing products operational, requirements and environments change during that process. Thus, economic evaluations and objectives stated in the proposal often change sufficiently by the implementation date to make evaluations difficult.

Professionalism. Many individuals within the data processing department are more loyal to the data processing profession than to the organization that employs them. Their divided loyalty can cause them to be more concerned about the technical aspects of data processing than meeting the needs of their own organization. This misplaced professionalism causes reluctance on the part of data processing professionals to use "canned" systems. They would rather specify and develop "personalized" systems, which may not be in the best interest of the organization but are technically valuable for the personal improvement of the data processing professional.

WHEN IS A QUALITY ASSURANCE FUNCTION NEEDED?

A recent study by the American Petroleum Institute showed that member companies having an EDP quality assurance function staffed that function at the ratio of 1 QA person per 40 systems designers and programmers. The survey indicated that the staffing rate was expected to increase to 1 QA person for each 15 systems designers and programmers in the near future. This is not an ideal to strive for but a needed staffing level for the function to be fully effective. The staffing ratios suggested by the API study appear to be in line with the ratios in other industries that have adopted the QA concept.

The staffing ratios indicate that when a data processing department has 10 or more systems designers and programmers, they need one full-time-equivalent to perform the quality assurance function. At fewer than 10 systems designers and programmers, the function should still be performed but would probably be done on a part-time basis. For example, a department of six would require half a full-time-equivalent position to perform the QA function. Six systems designers and programmers should be considered the entry point to add the QA function.

If your organization has its major financial systems computerized, QA takes on even greater importance. If any of the following questions can be answered affirmatively, the EDP department should seriously consider adding the function:

- Does the department have six or more systems designers or programmers?

- Are any of the organization's major financial systems computerized?

- Is the total data processing budget over $250,000 per year?

WHO SHOULD STAFF THE FUNCTION?

The QA function staff should be as knowledgeable in data processing as the senior systems analysts and designers in the department. If the function is not staffed by the best people in the data processing department, it will be ineffective. Designers who are having their systems reviewed must have respect for the individuals performing the review. Likewise, DP management must have respect for those performing the reviews if they are to support the reviewers' recommendations.

Assignment to the QA group can be done in one of three ways: full-time, part-time (in addition to the individual's regular assignments), or as a training mechanism for personnel in the data processing department. Those assigned to the group for training need not be in lead positions in the group.

Individuals assigned to the group should be expected to spend a considerable amount of time (8–12 weeks per year) maintaining their technical proficiency. This proficiency can be maintained through courses, conferences, and on-the-job training.

OPERATION OF THE QUALITY ASSURANCE FUNCTION

The QA function should be charged with the task of looking at all new data processing applications as well as major enhancements to existing applications. With limited resources available, it is important that the personnel in the group optimize its resources. The method that has proved effective is to have the group establish checkpoints at various key points in the EDP systems development life cycle. These checkpoints, which are illustrated in Figure 1.5, are the feasibility study, design, programming, testing, and conversion.

Checkpoints are of two kinds: 1)   the point at which advice and counsel from the QA function will be most beneficial for the systems designers, and 2) points when the group can evaluate the status of the system being implemented. Status checkpoints serve as an independent evaluation when DP management or user management need to decide whether to commit more resources to continue the project.

During each of the five key phases in the systems development life cycle, QA interacts one or more times with the project development team. At the end of most of these checkpoint reviews (discussed in detail in later chapters), the QA person or group will make a report to management. The report may be either oral or written, and may be given to an appropriate level of management. Management will then take any action it feels is warranted.

THE CRITICAL DIFFERENCE BETWEEN QUALITY CONTROL AND QUALITY ASSURANCE

Quality is an attribute of a product that is either present or absent. For example, a quality attribute of a program is the job number. It is either present or absent. If present, the program is a quality program as far as job number is concerned; if it is absent then we say the program has a defect.

The role of quality control is to measure products against a standard or attribute like a job number to determine if it is there. The purpose of quality control is to identify defects and have them corrected so that defect-free products will be produced. Quality control is limited to looking at products. It is a function that should be performed by the workers. Tasks such as systems reviews and software testing are quality control tasks.

Quality assurance is a function that manages quality. It sets up quality control, but normally does not perform the actual quality control work of inspecting products. Quality assurance uses the results of quality control to evaluate and improve the "processes" that produce the products. Thus we see that quality assurance works with the processes, and quality control works with the products.

The quality dilemma that quality assurance people face is that they cannot properly do their job of working with the processes until

1.   the processes are established (standards and procedures);

2.   quality control has been installed in the processes to provide quality assurance groups information on product defects.

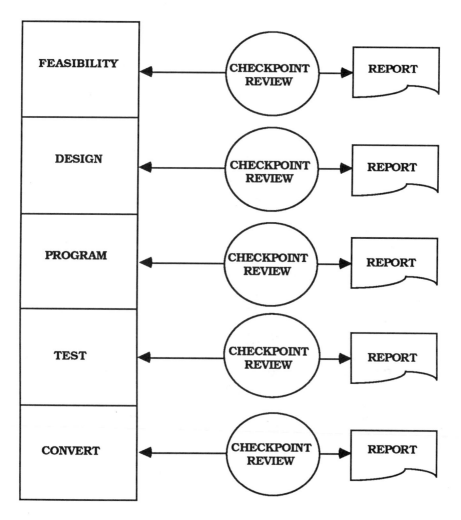

Figure 1.5 **OPERATION OF QUALITY ASSURANCE FUNCTION**

Until formal process are established and utilized, and quality control exists in those processes, many quality assurance groups will spend their time establishing process (standards and procedures) and performing quality control activities such as system development reviews. The purpose of reviews should be twofold for quality assurance groups: first, to help the projects by performing quality control for them, but second and more important, to learn how to do quality control so the QC process can be formalized and turned over to the projects.

In this book a lot of material is devoted to quality control activities, but they are labeled *quality assurance tasks*. The intent is to assist quality assurance groups in setting up quality control. However, the QA group should turn over all QC tasks to the projects or involved workers as quickly as those QC tasks can be perfected, documented, and the workers trained in how to perform those activities.

SUMMARY

QA groups are being established within data processing departments to provide management with an independent evaluation of the goals, methods, and performance of new systems under development and enhancements to existing systems. The function should be staffed with individuals as knowledgable in data processing as the EDP department's senior personnel. When a data processing department exceeds six systems analysts/programmers, it should consider establishing this function. It can be staffed by full-time individuals, or by means of additional assignments for personnel in the data processing department. QA operates by conducting reviews at predetermined checkpoints. The basis of these checkpoint reviews is to assist the project team in systems design and to provide management with an independent evaluation of the system at that point in time. This independent evaluation will help data processing management make a decision whether or not to provide additional resources to complete the project.

Chapter 2
ROLE OF A QUALITY ASSURANCE GROUP

From the time a project commences until it becomes operational, there is a wide range of possible solutions. Data processing department management wants assurance that DP systems are traversing the best solution path. The design of systems must satisfy both the users' needs and the proper utilization of technology. The role of quality assurance is to steer project development in the right direction. Its role is fourfold. The first is to assist the organization in developing the standards and guidelines necessary to build competent systems. Second, QA should review the adequacy of and adherence to general controls, such as the operating procedures and program change procedures. Adequate general controls will assure a proper environment in which to develop and operate systems. Third, QA should provide technical advice to the project team. Fourth, it must review the development of all applications to assure compliance with organization's goals, methods, and performance criteria.

QUALITY ASSURANCE FUNCTIONS

In the American Petroleum Institute study on the quality assurance function mentioned in Chapter 1, one of the questions asked was "What duties are being performed by the quality assurance group in your organization?" The duties and percentages of responses are listed below.

Duties Performed	% of Responses
Review system controls	92
Develop control standards	92
Review systems design for completeness	85

Duties Performed (cont'd)	*% of Responses (cont'd)*
Assure documentation is complete	85
Provide technical advice	85
Recommend specific controls	77
Develop systems and programming practices	77
Review for conformance with systems test plan	77
Assure that systems and programming practices are being followed	69
Review for conformance to systems design	69

Among the other duties listed by respondents to the questionnaire were review economic justification, review operating and development cost, validate resource availability, and education. This information will be of value when the charter for QA is developed.

Because QA is organizationally a part of the data processing department, its primary role and function should be supportive of the data processing function. The group is an extension of the responsibilities of the data processing manager. It assumes part of the role currently performed by data processing line management. The role of QA is fivefold. Figure 2.1 illustrates this role. The role is illustrated as a pyramid because each segment of the role builds upon the previous segment.

Analyze EDP Errors

Most of the problems and concerns in a computerized environment are readily available in the form of documented or identified errors or problems. Analyzing these problems can provide the basis for improving the quality of the EDP environment. For example, if the major cause of program "hang-ups" is inadequate space allocation, providing a solution to this problem will improve programmers' performance, and thus improve quality.

Some quality assurance groups spend as much as half their effort tracking errors and analyzing them. This involves examining errors as they occur, pinpointing correction responsibilities, making sure that correction actually occurs, as well as looking for long-range solutions to the problems.

Some quality assurance groups issue an "error alert" report for common errors. An error alert serves two purposes. First, it helps programmers avoid repeating the same error, and second, it

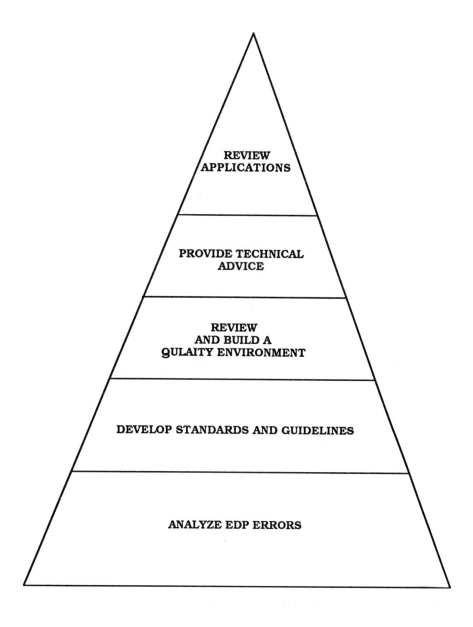

Figure 2.1 **ROLE OF A QUALITY ASSURANCE GROUP**

publicizes the fact that the quality assurance group is providing a positive service to all systems analysts and programmers.

Develop Standards and Guidelines

Developing standards and guidelines for the organization's data processing is a fundamental QA role. Obviously, if the organization already has satisfactory standards and guidelines, the group need not develop them. However, few data processing departments have adequate standards and guidelines for the development, implementation, and operation of data processing systems.

The types of standards and guidelines that are needed include the following.

- *System development process standards.* The steps and methods by which an organization approves, implements, and enhances computerized applications.
- *Documentation standards.* The types and contents of documentation that will be produced as a result of developing computerized applications.
- *Programming standards.* The methods and procedures that programmers will follow in designing, coding, documenting, and testing programs.
- *Control standards.* The methods by which computer system and programs will be controlled.
- *Operating standards.* The procedures that must be followed to place programs into production and operate programs in a production mode.
- *Hardware and software standards.* The types of hardware and software packages that will be used by the organizations and those features within software that will be utilized during operation. The standards should include the methods by which hardware and software can be modified or changed.
- *Performance standard.* The level or criteria to be achieved in doing work.

Review and Build a Quality Environment

QA should review the general controls in an operating environment and determine whether they are adequate and whether they comply with general controls. The organizations' standards and guidelines form the basis for developing general controls. Without detailed standards, it becomes difficult to enforce general controls. A review of the general controls can be done either as a special review or when a specific application is being reviewed. This review becomes a mechanism to provide data processing management on compliance to general controls.

Examples of General Controls:

- Segregation of duties between various functions as outlined in department charters, job descriptions, and an organization's policies and procedures
- Policies and procedures for budgeting projects, reporting status, and scheduling work
- Policies and procedures for following an organization's standards and guidelines

Provide Technical Advice

There are three main areas in which project teams need advice: 1) understanding the intent and meaning of an organization's policies, procedures, standards, and guidelines; 2) determining the best method for using the organization's hardware and software; and 3) assessing the impact of the application being developed on other applications currently in operation or under development. Project teams have a full-time task getting their projects operational. The intent of project personnel is to do the best possible job, but their time is limited. In the three areas just listed, the project team will utilize the knowledge of the team members. However, the project team does not have time to do much exploration of the unknown. It is in this area that QA members can provide assistance to the project team.

The technical assistance QA provides takes two forms. The first is answering specific requests by the project team: this can be an interpretation of a standard, advice requested on how best to accomplish some part of the project requirements, or merely a general discussion on various approaches. The second is advice volunteered by QA members where they feel it is needed. This advice can be the result of personal experiences utilizing good techniques and understanding where the project team is violating standards or policies of the organization. It often takes the form of suggestions on how to avoid problems or reduce efforts.

Whether or not a project team accepts the QA group's technical advice is dependent upon good personal relationships between QA and the project team. If a trusting relationship can be fostered so the project team knows QA is working toward the betterment of the project, the advice will be well received.

It is important that QA not try to capitalize on providing this advice. If the project team accepts recommendations and QA claims credit for these recommendations, the future effectiveness of the QA group will be diminished.

REVIEW APPLICATIONS

The primary purpose of QA is to review applications. The earlier functions provide the base for the application review. For example, the review includes compliance to organization standards, guidelines, general controls, and good data processing practices. If QA has played an active role in the development and review of criteria, they will be more adept in assessing compliance.

The QA review comprises six parts:

1. Review the system under development for
    a. technical competence of design,
    b. adequacy of internal controls,
    c. cost/benefit analysis of the system,
    d. satisfying needs of users.
2. Determine that the systems development project is consistent with the plans and goals of the data processing department, other applications, and the organization.
3. Determine that the system under development is in compliance with the organization's policies, procedures, standards, and guidelines.
4. Determine that the system under development makes effective and economic use of the organization's hardware, software, and other resources.
5. Determine that the plan for testing the system is adequate.
6. Determine that the plan for converting from one system to another or placing the new system into production is adequate.

PROJECT APPLICATION EVALUATION OBJECTIVES

This chapter began by discussing how QA helps steer the systems development project to the best solution. Next we reviewed the types and importance of controls. Last, we talked about the primary role being to review the systems application underdevelopment. Now, let's look at what specific objective should be achieved in each QA area (i.e., goals, methods, and performance) during each of the systems development life cycle phases prior to implementation (i.e., feasibility study, design, program, testing, and conversion). Figure 2.2, Evaluation Objectives, lists the objectives by system development life cycle phase.

Criteria for Evaluating Goals

When QA reviews an application system under development, they should verify that the goals of the EDP department, organization, and user are being achieved. For systems development life cycle phases, QA must make judgments on the following criteria.

1. *Feasibility phase.* The user goals are realistic. The project goals are achievable. The project goals are compatible with the goals of the organization and goals of the EDP department.

2. *Design phase.* The design specifications will achieve the project goals.

3. *Program phase.* The program specifications will accomplish what was specified during the system design phase.

4. *Testing phase.* The implemented system achieves the goals specified during the design phase.

5. *Conversion phase.* The conversion to the new system can be achieved without any loss of control over data and processing.

Criteria for Evaluating Compliance

One of the major functions performed by QA is verifying compliance to the organization's policies, procedures, standards, and guidelines. During each phase of the systems development life cycle, QA should assure the following:

1. *Feasibility phase.* The feasibility study has evaluated all the project criteria and the justification for implementing the project is in accordance with the organization's standards and procedures.

SDLC PHASE / QUALITY ASSURANCE AREA	FEASIBILITY	DESIGN	PROGRAM	TESTING	CONVERSION
Goals	Goals are realistic, achievable, and compatible with organization goals	System design achieved goals	Program design achieves goals	Goals are met	Controlled conversion
Methods	Justification standards	Systems standards	Programming standards	Testing standards	Conversion standards
Performance	System is cost-effective	Optimizes people and machines	Optimizes hardware and software	Meets systems criteria	Economical conversion

Figure 2.2 **EVALUATION OBJECTIVES**

2. *Design phase.* The project is designed in accordance with the organization's standards and guidelines in such a manner that it can be programmed, operated, and maintained by the normal procedures of the organization.

3. *Programming phase.* The coding of programs will be in accordance with the standard methods of programming.

4. *Testing phase.* The testing of the programs and systems is adequate and done in accordance with the standards and guidelines of the organization.

5. *Conversion phase.* The conversion is adequate and performed in accordance with the standards and guidelines of the organization.

Criteria for Evaluating Performance

The QA group should evaluate the efficiency, effectiveness, and economy of the systems design. Even if performance is not a specific objective, the group would be negligent if they did not make a professional judgment about performance. The QA group's evaluation of performance of a computerized application should include ascertaining the following:

1. *Feasibility phase.* The proposed system is cost-effective. This includes both the   proposed design as well as whether or not the application should be computerized.

2. *Design phase.* The proposed design optimizes the use of people and machines.   People perform those functions for which they are best suited, and machines perform those functions for which they are best suited.

3. *Program phase.* The implementation of the design specifications through programming optimizes the use of hardware and software.   (Are there any preprogrammed packages that could be used more economically to achieve the specification requirements?)

4. *Testing phase.* The implemented systems meet those criteria of performance objectives outlined in the feasibility and design phase.

5. *Conversion phase.* The conversion should be performed in the most economical manner. Because conversion is a one-time function, it may be more economical to do a manual conversion than to develop the computer programs necessary to make the required changes. Obviously, each conversion has to be analyzed as if it were a new computerized application being studied, designed, programmed, and tested.

QUALITY ASSURANCE GROUP TASKS

Within the role of QA are various tasks that may or may not be performed by QA. It is important that the role and tasks be established and known before to the group becomes active. If the charter is well understood by all interested parties, the probability of success increases greatly. When the tasks they are given become a source of debate or argument because they are not understood by project teams or users, the group can spend more time justifying and explaining its role than actually performing its task.

Chapter 1 discussed many of the challenges facing the EDP department and the fact that QA can help the data processing department to meet those challenges. Figure 2.3 reviews the challenges and the role QA can perform in helping the EDP department with them. The challenges are categorized according to the four parts of the role of QA. Understanding these tasks and how they relate to the challenges of the EDP department will prove helpful in establishing the charter.

Listed below is a brief explanation of how QA can help the EDP department meet some of their challenges:

1. *Changing technology.* The quality assurance group works with new systems and new technology and must keep current in that technology to perform their function. Becoming knowledgeable, they can help other members in the EDP department, including management, keep current by discussing new technology in staff meetings, through writing papers, and personal counseling.

2. *When to abort a project.* By making evaluations at the end of each phase of the system development life cycle, the quality assurance group can advise data processing management when projects are in trouble. This early warning mechanism enables management to make informed decisions about aborting projects.

3. *Executive management ignorance of EDP.* An independent technical assessment of data processing applications and controls will give executive management additional assurance as to whether or not they are making proper decisions.

4. *User ignorance of EDP.* The quality assurance group can challenge both the user and the project team regarding whether or not the system meets the user's needs and requirements. These requirements are both those specified in the system and those that should be specified in the system.

5. *Audit requirements.* The auditors have requirements for computer data and a need to assess the adequacy of internal controls. Many auditors are unable to perform these tasks due to lack of data processing knowledge. The quality assurance group, once they understand audit requirements,

ROLE	EDP DEPARTMENT CHALLENGE	QUALITY ASSURANCE TASKS
Review Application	When to abort a project	Evaluates system in all phases
	Executive management ignorance of EDP	Provides executive management with a technical assessment
	User ignorance of EDP	Ascertains user requirements are met
	Audit requirements	Ascertains audit requirements are met
Provide Technical Advice	Changing technology	Knows current technology
	Use of consultants	Acts as internal consultant
	Ability to keep current technically	Acts as a technical consultant to systems analysts
	Complexity of systems	Knows many system
Review and Build a Quality Environment	How to evaluate EDP products	Evaluates EDP products
	Build a quality environment	Counsel EDP management
Develop Standards and Guidelines	Few systems and programming standards	Helps set standards
	Few system development standards	Helps set standards
	Professionalism	Evaluates quality of work
Analyze EDP Errors	Know type of problems	Quantify problems
	Know cost of problems	Identify problems
	Know magnitude of problems	Determine cost of problem

Figure 2.3 **TASKS OF A QUALITY ASSURANCE FUNCTION**

can ascertain that those requirements are met in new applications.

6.   *Use of consultants.* Because the QA group will be current technically and will work on a wide variety of projects, its members will be able to act as internal consultants to members in the data processing department on technical problems.

7.   *Ability to keep current technically.* The use of the quality assurance concept will give the data processing manager some assurance that the implementation of new systems will utilize the most current technology. This is because QA can act as a technical consultant to the systems analyst, thus relieving the analyst of some of the pressure of having to maintain technical proficiency in all aspects of data processing.

8.   *Complexity of systems.* The interrelationships of systems make it difficult for any one systems analyst to comprehend some of the problems they can cause. The QA group working with many systems will be able to ascertain that the totality of systems mesh into an integrated network of systems. The use and enforcement of structured techniques will further help the QA group in identifying and qualifying these interrelationships.

9.   *Few systems and programming standards.* Where standards are missing, the quality   assurance group can help set them. Their experience in working with many systems   puts them in an ideal position to help set standards.   The use of structured programming helps overcome the programming "art" syndrome and provides standard programming practices against which work can be measured.

10.   *Few systems development standards.* Where standards are missing, the quality assurance group can help set them. Their experience in working with many systems puts them in an ideal position to help set standards. The implement- ation and enforcement of structured design techniques provides an excellent vehicle for the development of work- able standards.

11.   *How to evaluate EDP products.* The quality assurance group understands the needs of many systems and has an appre- ciation for the current technology. This background puts

them in an ideal position to evaluate EDP products, both hardware and software.

12. *Professionalism.* After evaluating many computer applications over a period of time, the quality assurance group will be in a position to evaluate the technical aspects of the systems designer's and programmer's work. This will help the data processing manager assure upper management that the organization is getting good value for its data processing dollars.

The tasks listed are representative of the many tasks that can be performed by a quality assurance group. Projections state that systems will assume an even greater portion of an organization's business procedures. This increasing reliance on data processing mandates the need for a group to assure quality in data processing systems applications.

ESTABLISHING THE QUALITY ASSURANCE CHARTER

When QA is formed, a charter for the group should be established. The charter should be circulated to those organizations that will come in contact or use the services. This will eliminate all misunderstandings of what the group is authorized to do.

The following process is recommended to establish a charter:

1. Organize a task force to establish a draft charter. The task force should comprise
   a. the probable manager of the quality assurance function,
   b. the manager or assistant manager of the data processing department,
   c. one or more project leaders,
   d. one or more key users of data processing applications,
   e. the manager or assistant manager of computer operations,
   f. the general auditor or EDP audit manager of the organization,
   g. a member of executive management (suggest this individual be chairman of the task force).

2. Have each task force member fill out a worksheet rating the potential tasks (from very important to very unimportant)

that could be performed by a quality assurance group. Figure 2.4 is such a worksheet. (This will be explained in a later section.)

3. Score the tasks in accordance of the rating given by those completing the worksheet (the scoring method will be expained in the section discussing the worksheet).

4. List the tasks in priority sequence based on their score. Then, using the material contained in the remainder of this book, estimate the amount of resources required to accomplish each task.

5. Determine with management consent the amount of manpower that will be allotted to staff the quality asurance function.

6. Incorporate into a charter those tasks that can logically beaccomplished with available resources. Add as an appendix to the charter those tasks (in sequence) that should be accomplished when time becomes available or additional resources are added.

Following this process will result in drafting a realistic charter for the group. The charter will have those tasks considered to be most important by the task force. This does not exclude the use of judgment on the part of the task force to move items around once the priority listing has been established. It does have the advantage of approaching the problem from a scientific viewpoint.

Once the charter has been drafted, it can then be reviewed by various members of management to obtain their concurrence or recommendations. This gives the process another critique which assures that management's concerns will be addressed by the quality assurance group.

Quality Assurance Group Role Worksheet

The worksheet shown in Figure 2.4 provides a listing of QA tasks. The tasks are categorized by the four major roles of QA. The individuals on the quality assurance task force should rate each of these tasks according to their own personal beliefs.

Where individuals have some specific reaction to a task that they feel needs clarification, they should complete the Comments section. These worksheets, when complete, show how the individual members of the task force see the role the QA group is to perform. Space is available to add tasks the individual feels should be performed by the group.

Because the individual members of charter-drafting task force come from different disciplines, they will probably assign different rankings to the tasks. This is healthy because it allows the different groups associated with data processing to provide input about this important function.

Scoring the Quality Assurance Tasks. Once each member of the task force has completed the Quality Assurance Group Role Worksheet, a consensus of viewpoints must be reached. A Task Score Worksheet (Figure 2.5) is provided for this purpose. One Task Score Worksheet should be prepared for each task in Figure 2.4 (a total of 54 worksheets). For that task, the total number of times "very important" was checked should be inserted in the "Number of Times Checked"/"very important" checked block. Likewise, the same is done for "important," "neither important nor unimportant," "unimportant," and "very unimportant." For each of these ratings, multiply the number of times checked times the constant listed on the worksheet. For example, for the "very important" rating, the number of times checked is multiplied by 5 to arrive at a score. When the score for each of the five ratings has been determined, they should be added together to arrive at a total score. The score will be an algebraic number which can be either plus or minus.

The Task Score Worksheet should then be resequenced so that the highest score is on top and the lowest score on the bottom. The rank should then be filled in from 1 through 54, with rank number 1 being the highest score, and rank 54 being the lowest score. Once they have been ranked, an estimated man-days per year needs to be determined as a requirement for accomplishing this task. When the number of days per year equals the available resources for the quality assurance function, the accomplishable tasks have been determined. The tasks should then be drafted into a charter.

The charter is the authority provided the group to accomplish its function. The charter provides it the authority to act. It should have three sections:

1. *Scope of work.* The general area in which the group will operate, together with the responsibilities and authority allowed to group, listed in general terms.

2. *Role.* A discussion of each one of the four potential parts of the QA role: a) review applications, b) provide technical

ROLE ELEMENT	QUALITY ASSURANCE TASK	RATING					COMMENTS
		Very Important	Important	Neither Important nor Unimportant	Unimportant	Very Unimportant	
REVIEW APPLICA-TION	**GOALS**						
	1. Determine if project goals are realistic						
	2. Determine if project goals are achievable						
	3. Determine if project goals are compatible with EDP Dept. Goals						
	4. Determine if project goals are compatible with Organization goals						
	5. Determine if project goals are compatible with other systems						
	6. Determine if system design will achieve project goals						
	7. Controls ensure compliance with the intent of management						
	METHODS						
	8. Determine if program design will meet system specifications						
	9. Determine if testing plan is adequate						
	10. Determine if conversion plan is adequate						
	11. Determine if compliance with project justification standards						
	12. Determine if compliance with system standards						

Figure 2.4 **QUALITY ASSURANCE GROUP ROLE WORKSHEET**

ROLE ELEMENT	QUALITY ASSURANCE TASK	RATING					COMMENTS
		Very Important	Important	Neither Important nor Unimportant	Unimportant	Very Unimportant	
	13. Determine compliance with programming standards						
	14. Determine compliance with control standards						
	15. Certifying system prior to their attainment of production status						
	16. Reviewing the adequacy of security						
	17. Verify system is on time and within budget						
	18. Recommend specific controls						
	19. Determine compliance with documentation standards						
	20. Determine compliance with testing standards						
	21. Determine compliance with conversion standards						
	PERFORMANCE						
	22. Determine that the system is cost-effective						
	23. Determine that the system optimizes people and machines						
	24. Determine that the system optimizes hardware and software						
	25. Determine that the testing procedures are efficient						

Figure 2.4   **QUALITY ASSURANCE GROUP ROLE WORKSHEET (cont'd)**

ROLE ELEMENT	QUALITY ASSURANCE TASK	RATING					COMMENTS
		Very Important	Important	Neither Important nor Unimportant	Unimportant	Very Unimportant	
	26. Determine that the conversion procedures are efficient						
	27. Measure hardware performance						
	28. Measure software performance						
PROVIDE TECHNICAL ADVICE	1. Advise on the use of hardware						
	2. Advise on use of software						
	3. Advise on system design						
	4. Advise on program design						
	5. Advise on use of controls						
	6. Advise on test procedures						
	7. Advise on conversion procedures						
	8. Advise on EDP department standards and guidelines						
	9. Advise on user department standards and guidelines						
	10. Advise on organization standards and guidelines						
	11. Advise users on data processing capabilities						
	12. Advise executive management on data processing capabilities						
	13. Advise data processing management on data processing capabilities						

Figure 2.4 **QUALITY ASSURANCE GROUP ROLE WORKSHEET (cont'd)**

ROLE ELEMENT	QUALITY ASSURANCE TASK	RATING					COMMENTS
		Very Important	Important	Neither Important nor Unimportant	Unimportant	Very Unimportant	
	14. Advise on intersystem interfaces						
REVIEW AND BUILD A QUALITY ENVIRON- MENT	1. Review organization structure						
	2. Review job descriptions						
	3. Review system standards						
	4. Review programming standards						
	5. Review documentation standards						
	6. Review testing standards						
	7. Review conversion standards						
	8. Review budget and cost procedures						
	9. Review system change procedures						
	10. Review supervisory procedures						
	11. Review operating procedures						
	12. Review quality of technical work						
	13. Meet regularly with DP management to review problems						
	14. Train EDP personnel						
	15. Monitor project status						
DEVELOP STAND- ARDS AND GUIDE- LINES	1. Develop and/or improve justification standards						
	2. Develop and/or improve system standards						

Figure 2.4 **QUALITY ASSURANCE GROUP ROLE WORKSHEET (cont'd)**

ROLE ELEMENT	QUALITY ASSURANCE TASK	RATING					COMMENTS
		Very Important	Important	Neither Important nor Unimportant	Unimportant	Very Unimportant	
	3. Develop and/or improve documentation standards						
	4. Develop and/or improve programming standards						
	5. Develop and/or improve testing standards						
	6. Develop and/or improve conversion standards						
	7. Develop and/or improve hardware standards						
	8. Develop and/or improve software standards						
	9. Develop and/or improve purchased application standards						
	10. Develop and/or improve operating standards						
	11. Develop and/or improve system development process standards						
	12. Develop and/or improve performance standards						
ANALYZE EDP ERRORS	1. On call to study all errors						
	2. Issue error alerts for common problems						
	3. Quantify errors and issue regular error reports						
	4. Develop recommendations/solutions for identified errors						

Figure 2.4 **QUALITY ASSURANCE GROUP ROLE WORKSHEET (cont'd)**

TASK:

SCORE CALCULATION:

RATING	NUMBER OF TIMES CHECKED	SCORE
VERY IMPORTANT		x5 =
IMPORTANT		x3 =
NEITHER IMPORTANT NOR UNIMPORTANT		x0 = 0
UNIMPORTANT		x-3 =
VERY IMPORTANT		x-5 =

TOTAL SCORE

RANK

ESTIMATED DAYS/YEARS
TO ACCOMPLISH

Figure 2.5 **TASK SCORE WORKSHEET**

advice, c) review general controls, and d) develop standards and guidelines.   If the task selection process does not include any tasks for one part of the role, eliminate that part. In that case, the charter only describes those parts of the role that will be performed by the group.

3.   *Tasks.* Under each part of the role, the tasks to be performed should be briefly listed.

The group charter will be a job description for the quality assurance group. It will be more detailed than some organization department charters, but this is necessary because it will be a new function to most organizations.   The charter serves three purposes. It outlines the responsibility of the group. It specifies the authority given the group in each aspect of its role. It educates the quality assurance group and other interested parties about the QA mandate. And, finally, it asserts that management expects high quality in data processing applications.

Figure 2.6 exemplifies a typical charter and can be used as a model for building a charter for a quality assurance group. The Appendix at the end of this chapter is a work plan developed by a quality assurance group to support its charter.

QUALITY ASSURANCE COSTS

The primary function of the quality assurance group is to review new applications. Time expended for other elements of the role supports this systems review function. The charter of the group, if established according to the criteria provided in this chapter, will give a breakdown of effort between application review and the other potential elements of the role.   In an ideal situation, this would be 70% for system reviews and 30% for all other tasks.

Next, what is needed is a method of dividing up the amount of effort that will be expended on each application being reviewed. Figure 2.7 suggests such an allocation of effort. The figure divides the time among the five phases of the system development life cycle where the QA should be involved (feasibility, design, programming, testing, and conversion).

The cost of quality assurance ideally should be included in the estimated project costs. If it is included as a line item in a project's budget, it should range somewhere between 2.5 and 5% of the total project cost. For example, if a project costs $100,000 to

QUALITY ASSURANCE CHARTER

It is the policy of the data processing department to provide a quality assurance group as a means of improving the quality of computerized applications. The manager of data processing is assigned the responsibility for the quality assurance function and will see that:

1. Applications are reviewed at the appropriate times to determine if they meet the needs of the user; are developed according to policies, procedures, standards and guidelines; and are implemented in a technically competent manner.
2. The results of these reviews are made available to user and data processing management.
3. The project team makes satisfactory disposition, within 30 days, of any recommendations resulting from a quality assurance review.

The manager and staff of the quality assurance function shall have full, free, and unrestricted access to all the information, records, and personnel of the project under review.

Specifically the manager of quality assurance shall be responsible for execution of the following tasks:

1. During application reviews the QA manager shall determine if:
   - Project goals are achievable
   - System design will achieve project goals
   - Program design will meet system specifications
   - Testing plan is adequate
   - Conversion plan is adequate.
   - There is compliance with all development standards
2. Developing and/or improve standards and guidelines for:
   - System standards   - Documentation standards
   - Programming standards   - Testing standards
   - Conversion standards
3. Reviewing general controls:
   - Quality of technical work
4. Providing technical advice on:
   - System design   - Program design
   - Test procedures
   - Conversion procedures   - EDP department standards
                                    and guidelines

Figure 2.6 **A TYPICAL QA CHARTER**

DEVELOPMENT PHASE	% OF QA TIME EXPENDED	% OF TOTAL PROJECT COST	
		Minimum	*Ideal*
Feasibility	10%	.25%	.5%
Design	40	1.00	2.0
Programming	30	.75	1.5
Testing	10	.25	.5
Conversion	10	.25	.5
	100%	2.5%	5.0%

Figure 2.7 **QUALITY ASSURANCE COSTS AND EFFORT**

implement, then between $2,500 to $5,000 should be allocated for the quality assurance aspect of that project. The minimum level to be effective is 2.5% of the project costs, and ideally 5% of the project costs should be allocated.

The early part of the design process is where the application can be most readily influenced. If the QA group spends the largest percentage of its time during the design phase of the system, it can make the greatest impact on that system. The time expended in the programming, testing, and conversion area is one of checking compliance to design specifications and organizations' policies, procedures, standards, and guidelines.

SUMMARY

EDP quality assurance is accomplished by a fourfold role: first, to develop standards and guidelines; second, to review general controls; third, to be a technical advisor on EDP matters; and fourth, to review applications. The first three segments of the role support the fourth.

The application review is spread out over five phases of the systems development life cycle. These phases are feasibility, design, programming, testing, and conversion. The review in each phase has three objectives. These are to determine that organization, user and EDP department goals are (or will be)

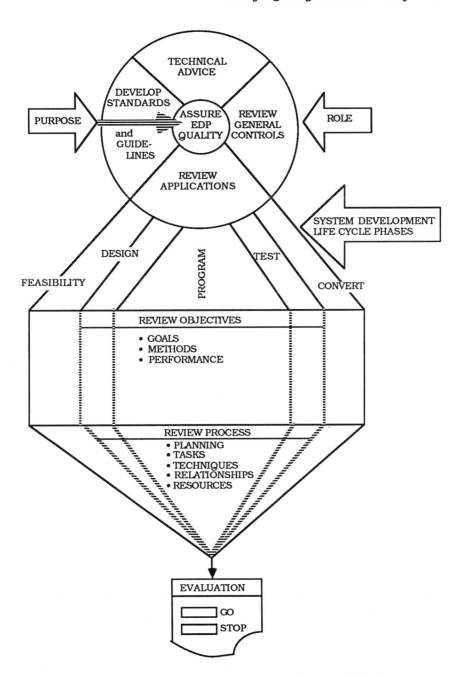

Figure 2.8. **THE QUALITY ASSURANCE FUNCTION**

achieved; to determine compliance with standards, policies, procedures and guidelines; and to assure reasonable performance. These objectives are achieved through a review process. This process starts with planning, and includes tasks agreed upon by management. In the execution of these tasks, the quality assurance group uses various techniques and resources. Much of the success of the group is dependent upon establishing good working relationships with data processing personnel. At the end of each phase, the quality assurance function will make a judgment on whether or not the project should continue through the next phase. Figure 2.8 illustrates the function.

Strong management support is essential if the function is to succeed. One method of obtaining this support is to get management agreement and support of a function charter that spells out the group's authority and responsibilities.

Appendix:
QUALITY ASSURANCE WORK PLAN

I. SCOPE

It is the policy of the Information Systems organization to provide a Quality Assurance function as an internal means of maintaining the quality and effectiveness of applications, facilities, and services provided by Information Systems (I/S) to assure National Steel Corporation will be a world class producer of quality products recognized for excellence.

A primary purpose of the Quality Assurance function is to assure that adequate Information Systems policies, standards, and guidelines exist in accordance with the Company's strategic direction. The major emphasis is on the measuring and monitoring of the internal development and operational process at appropriate times ensuring quality systems and reduced business risk.

In defining the scope of quality assurance, the following should be highlighted:

1) The Quality Assurance function will establish reviews procedures from an internal Information Systems perspective for evaluating all Information Systems areas to assure through reviews that systems are being designed, implemented, and operated according to Information Systems policy, standards, and/or guidelines.

2) Reviews of operational systems will determine the effectiveness of, and adherence to, policy standards and design criteria related to overall controls and security features.

3) Quality Assurance reviews will frequently be conducted on Information Systems (I/S) policies, procedures, standards, and/or operating guidlines without respect to a specific system. The internal coordination of these procedures and standards from one (1) internal Information Systems group to another will be reviewed for effectiveness.

Through the utilization of reviews Quality Assurance will be able to identify the processes that require changes to assure the production of quality products. However, the quality of products produced by Information Systems is the responsibility of the individual or team of individuals who are assigned to perform the task necessary to produce these products. The formalization of the Quality Assurance Program and the implementation of a Quality Assurance Review Program does not alter this responsibility. For this reason, the Quality Assurance Program will continue to be functionally decentralized. The areas of New Development, Data Administration, Systems Support, Process Control, Computer Sciences, Information Centers, and Telecommunications will continue to have primary responsibility for executing and if necessary, developing Quality Assurance activities.

Responsibility

Quality Assurance is responsible for the following functions:

   1)   *Establish Quality Assurance Systems Review Guidelines*

Quality Assurance will develop guidelines to determine which systems requires Quality Assurance review. Selection of which systems require reviews will be primarily based upon the significance of the application to business objectives, operations, strategic plans, and business risk.

Quality Assurance reviews examining the adherence to established Information Systems' (I/S) policies, procedures, standards, operating guidelines, and Quality Assurance guidelines relative to specific projects will be conducted on a scheduled basis.

   2)   *Assist in Development of Annual Quality Assurance Review Plan*

Quality Assurance will assist Information Systems departments in developing an annual Quality Assurance Review (QAR) plan. This Plan should address all areas of Information Systems: Development, Maintenance, Operations, Process Control, Data Base, Information Center, and Management Services.

Selecting from the annual planned objectives of each area (Development, Maintenance, Operation, Process Control, Information Center, Data Base, and Management Services) within Information Systems, Quality Assurance will coordinate its review objectives with the appropriate Information Systems management to confirm the Department's Annual Quality Assurance Schedule. On a quarterly basis, the schedule is reviewed with Information Systems management and updated.

In conducting systems development reviews, a phased approach will be followed. A review will be conducted at the completion of each of the following phases:

- System Requirements:
  - User Requirements
  - System Definition
  - Advisability Study
- System Design:
  - Preliminary Design
  - Detail Design
- System Programming:
  - Program Design
  - Programming/Program Testing
- Implementation Phase:
  - Implementation Planning
  - System Test/Start-up Preparation
  - Operation Turnover

Quality Assurance will have reasonable access to all the information, records, and personnel of the project or activities under review. Certain sensitive information may require user approval for access during the review process. Information Systems will determine the need for user approval prior to the start of the review.

Formal reports regarding accuracy of the findings and the achievability of recommendations will be agreed to by both Quality Assurance and the Information Systems area involved.

Quality Assurance will follow-up to ensure that all recommendations have planned implementation dates and are completed.

3) *Standards Reviews*

Quality Assurance develops and maintains programs/plans for conducting Quality Assurance reviews to assure the adequacy of Information Systems policies, procedures, standards, operating guidelines and Quality Assurance guidelines.

All Information Systems quality assurance guidelines, policies, procedures, standards, and operating guidelines in effect will be utilized by Quality Assurance as the base from which to conduct their reviews.

As well as using this information as a base, there is an inherent responsibility or Quality Assurance to recognize and report the need for change. Recommendations will be provided to the appropriate Information Systems group's management for approval and implementation.

Policies, procedures, standards, and operating guidelines maintained and utilized by these groups are subject to review and recommendations provided by Quality Assurance.

4)   *Coordination-Audit*

Upon notification by internal audit of EDP-related audit reports and findings relative to Information Systems, the Quality Assurance function will review the recommendations as they relate to Information Systems (I/S) policies, standards, and guidelines.

When applicable, Quality Assurance will review proposed changes/improvements to policies and standards with Information Systems management. A final report will be issued and the changes/improvements will be implemented by the responsible Information Systems area.

5)   *High Risk Review*

Annually, key operational systems will be selected either Commerical or Process Control by Quality Assurance for review to determine adherence to standards, procedures, operating guidelines and quality guidelines.

One measure of selection would be based on the volume and frequency of incidents requiring corrective action. Also, Data Center, Information Systems, and User Management can request a review based on their perspective of the system's condition.

Acting in a consultative capacity, Quality Assurance will perform these reviews to evaluate that Information System procedures, standards, and guidelines are being followed.

Included in these operational reviews will be the examination of contingency planning and file/data retention to guarantee adequate backup provisions.

6)   *Security Standards*

Quality Assurance will interface with the data security officer through periodic meetings to share in the establishment of uniform Information Systems safety and security standards and guidelines.

In response to Information Systems management requests, review of computer centers and/or systems development departments will be performed. The review will cover existing safety and security operational and maintenance elements within the facility. Recommendations will be made to enhance protection and control through new or revised procedures or additional physical protection devices.

7)   *Strategic Plan Reviews*

Strategic planning responsibilities within Information Systems will necessitate inventory-type operational reviews to gain an insight into the current systems environment. Identification of the need to upgrade hardware and/or software to be in line with future planning due to technology or standardization will be recommended.

8)   *Quality Improvement Programs*

This function will coordinate the development implementation of Information Systems Quality Councils and Quality Circles. These functions will create the avenue to implement Quality Process improvements which guarantees Quality products.

9)   *Establishing Quality Measuring Programs*

The function of these programs should be to acertain whether quality is being achieved, and if not, why not. Once the "why not" has been identified, the processes can be changed to prevent those types of problems from recurring. This measurement cycle (i.e., identify a problem, identify the cause of the problem, change the process to correct the problem, and the remeasure) will bootstrap quality. Over time, quality will increase significantly if this remeasurement cycle is pursued.

10)   *Managerial Review*

Quality Assurance will review the general management processes to confirm the compliance to corporate and departmental policies procedures and quality guidelines.

II. REVIEW POINTS

The following list of milestones indicates the subphases that require a Quality Review at their completion, the general identification of the Evaluators, and the typical composition of the review group. Because of the substantial diversity in types of systems that are built, it is impossible to specify the job titles of individuals who will play these roles. It is assumed that the reader will be able to directly translate the generalized descriptions shown in this list with the job titles and names of individuals who will best perform the required functions on his or her particular project.

The General Manager I/S, and the appropriate System General Manager are understood to always be ex officio members of any review group.

User Requirements

Purpose:	To determine the adequacy of the team's understanding of the current system and to evaluate the user requirements as defined.
Evaluated by:	Key User Supervisors Key Systems Development Person-Analysis Project Control Administrator Quality Assurance
Reviewed by:	Manager Information Systems Systems General Manager

Systems Definitions

Purpose:	To evaluate the system as proposed by the team; to agree to the procedures and assumptions to be used if an advisability study is deemed necessary.
Evaluated by:	Key User Supervisors Project Control Administrator Quality Assurance
Reviewed by:	Manager Information Systems Systems General Manager

Advisability Study

Purpose:	To review the results of the advisability study; evaluate the scope, costs, and associated benefits of each alternative.
Evaluated by:	Key User Supervisors Data Base Administration Key Systems Development Person-Analysis Project Control Administrator Quality Assurance
Reviewed by:	Key User Managers Manager, Information Systems Systems General Manager Sponsor

Preliminary Design

Purpose:	To ensure that the preliminary design satisfies the user requirements; evaluate the feasibility of the design and the potential technical issues (i.e., Data Base design, teleprocessing requirements, etc.)
Evaluated by:	Key User Supervisors Key Systems Development Person-Design Data Base Administration Operations Representative Project Control Administrator Quality Assurance
Reviewed by:	Systems General Manager Manager, Information Systems Sponsor

Program Design

Purpose:	To perform a technical review of the subsystems and programs to identify potential inefficiencies, cumbersome program designs; conformance to design standards.
Evaluated by:	Key Systems Development Person-Programming Operations Representative Project Control Administrator Quality Assurance

Reviewed by: Manager, Information Systems
                Systems General Manager

Programming/Program Testing

Purpose: To ensure that programs have been adequately
                tested and the test results provide an adequate
                level of confidence; review run procedures and
                conformance to programming standards.

Evaluated by: Key Systems Development Person-Programming
                Operations Representative
                Project Control Administrator
                Quality Assurance

Reviewed by: Systems General Manager
                Manager, Information Systems

Implementation Planning

Purpose: To ensure that areas of potential impact within
                the system and external to the system such as
                job descriptions, work flow, conversion plans,
                etc. are adequately covered in the
                implementation plans; review the system test
                plan.

Evaluated by: Key Users
                Key Systems Development Person
                Operations Representative
                Systems Support Representative
                Project Control Administrator
                Quality Assurance

Reviewed by: Systems General Manager
                Manager, Information Systems

Systems Test/Start-Up Preparation

Purpose: To evaluate the system to be turned over to
                operations to ensure adequate operating instruc-
                tions and documentation.

Evaluated by: Operations Manager
                Systems Support Manager
                Project Control Administrator
                Quality Assurance

Reviewed by: Systems General Manager
                Manager, Information Systems

III. PROJECT SELECTION PROCEDURES

Division Management of Information Systems identifies which project or areas are to be reviewed by the Quality Assurance Review Function. Some of the factors which may be used in making these determinations are

- Financial Application
- Statutory Requirements
- Exposure to Loss
- Application History
- Effort to Develop Application
- Time Span to Complete Project
- Expected Number of Application Programs
- New Hardware Technology
- New Software Technology
- User Involvement
- Internal Audit Involvement
- Skill Level of Project Team
- Availability of Quality Assurance Review Resources
- Risk Factory

IV. QUALITY ASSURANCE REVIEW AND ASSESSMENT PROCEDURES

A. Purpose

The purpose of this section is to outline the established guidelines and procedures which govern the conduct of Quality Assurance Review function, Management function, and the project team during the review process.

B. Responsibilities

1. *Quality Assurance*
- Develops detailed Quality Assurance review plan for the project.
- Gathers, conforms, and validates information needs to prepare Quality Assurance assessment reports.
- Prepares and publishes Quality Assurance assessment reports.

2. *Management*
- Reviews Quality Assurance assessment reports.

- Responds to recommendation and requests prepared by Quality Assurance review function.

3. *Project Team*
- Assists in developing detailed Quality Assurance Review plan for project.
- Assists in gathering and providing Quality Assurance review function with information needs for Quality Asssurance Assessment Reports.

C.   **Concept**

The Quality Assurance Review Program is founded upon the principle that a review of Quality Assurance activities based upon agreed checklist and review procedures will lead to improved quality and a better product.   It is not to be construed as a restrictive procedure or an effort to direct department efforts.   Quality Assurance Reviews should be approached with a spirit of assistance relying ultimately upon close cooperation and mutual professional confidence.

D.   **Procedures**

1. *Preliminary Review Procedure*

The purpose of this procedure is to initiate the Quality Assurance Review Processes for projects which are selected for review.   This procedure occurs prior to the first Quality Assurance Review for the project.

Responsibility	*Action*
Quality Assurance	a) Notifies Information Systems Project Leader of a schedule for Quality Assurance Kickoff Meeting
I/S Project Leader	b) Acknowledges schedule for Kickoff Meeting, may suggest different date.
	c) Coordinates with his/her project manager on Q.A. Kickoff Meeting.

Responsibility	*Action*
	d) Provides Quality Assurance with a copy of project request and any other information that would help Quality Assurance understand the project.
Quality Assurance	e) Conducts Kickoff Meeting.
	f) Provides copies of Quality Assurance Review Checklist to Project Team Member(s).
	g) Reviews Overview of project as provided by Project Team Member(s).
	h) Develops schedule* for first Quality Assurance Checkpoint Review.

2.   *Recurring Review Procedure*

The purpose of this procedure is to outline the processes which will be followed in developing Quality Assurance Assessment Reports. This procedure occurs at each Quality Assurance Review point within the project.

I/S Project Leader	a) As soon as available, provides Quality Assurance with tangible item(s) to support each item on the checklist prior to Quality Assurance Checkpoint Review.
Quality Assurance	b) Conducts a schedule Quality Assurance Checkpoint Review.

---

* Quality Assurance Reviews are to be scheduled at a number of key checkpoints in the project life cycle.

Responsibility	*Action*
	c) Reviews items on Quality Assurance Review Checklist and tangible items.
	d) If applicable, develops schedule* for subsequent Quality Assurance Reviews.
	e) Prepares preliminary Quality Assurance Assessment report for this review point.
	f) Discusses preliminary review point assessment report with Information Systems Project Leader.
	g) Discusses preliminary review point assessment report with Project Leader's Manager.
	h) Discusses preliminary review point assessment report with Project Leader's Director.
	i) Prepares finalized Quality Assurance Review/Checkpoint Assessment Report.
	j) Sends finalized Quality Assurance Review Checkpoint Assessment Report to Project Leader and Project Leader's Manager, and Director.

---

* Quality Assurance Reviews are to be scheduled at a number of key checkpoints in the project life cycle.

Responsiblity	*Action*
I/S Project Leader of Quality Assurance	k) Suggests modification to improve Quality Assurance Quality Assurance checklists for subsequent review checkpoint(s) for this project.
Quality Assurance	l) Reviews and obtains approval of proposed modification to Quality Assurance Checklists Leader, Project Leader's Manager and Project Leader's Director.
	m) Makes approved modification to subsequent Quality Assurance Checklist(s) for this project.
	n) Provides modified Quality Assurance Checklist to Project Leader and appropriate Information Systems Management Staff.

3.   *Final Review Procedures*

The purpose of this procedure is to identify opportunities to improve quality which may have been overlooked in the review point Assessment Reports. This procedure occurs after the last scheduled review point in the project.

Quality Assurance	a) Upon completion of the project an overall Quality Assurance Assessment Report will prepared for Information Systems Division Management.

Chapter 3
DEVELOPING THE QUALITY ASSURANCE FUNCTION

The quality assurance function can be initiated by executive data processing or internal auditing management. Once established, the QA group should report directly to the data processing manager. This high-level reporting assures the QA group of the authority and independence needed for success. There are four methods of staffing the function: 1) a full-time staff; 2) a combination of full-time and part-time personnel; 3) a perm-anent committee of data processing personnel; 4) a special task force to be established each time a review is undertaken.

The individuals staffing the function should be as skilled as the senior data processing personnel. The function will be more successful with a small number of highly skilled people than a large number of people with minimal data processing skills. The individuals in the group should be objective, naturally inquisitive, "take charge" type persons, and able to devote the necessary time to the successful fulfillment of the function. Last, it is important that the individuals in the group believe QA is necessary.

The key to success is strong management support. This support should be threefold: first, the function should be adequately staffed with highly skilled people; second, the function should be given the authority necessary to fulfill their responsibilities; and third, management must be supportive of recommendations. While this does not mean that all recommen-dations must be accepted, it does mean that they must be seriously considered and adopted if valid.

HOW TO GET STARTED

Normally QA groups are initiated by data processing departments. However, internal audit groups are beginning to become
the prime instigator in the establishment of the function.
If a data processing department has six or more systems analysts,
a major computerized financial system, or a budget over $250,000
per year, a QA function should be seriously considered.
       To establish QA in an organization, the initiating group
should:

1.   *Prepare a preliminary report.* The report should state the
     advantages and disadvantages as well as costs and expected
     benefits.

2.   *Establish a task force.* The objective of the task force would
     be to perform one or two quality assurance reviews.   The
     task force should comprise senior EDP personnel. The pre-
     liminary report should recommend the establishment of
     this task force.

3.   *Make final recommendations to management (after a test
     review).* This report should summarize the results of the
     task force quality assurance review.   It should contain a
     recommendation regarding how the group should be staffed,
     its authority and responsibilities, its organization struc-
     ture, to whom the group will report, and the methods of re-
     porting findings.

       Each organization needs to do some experimentation as to
how such a group can be most effective for them. Creating a task
force to perform one or two quality assurance reviews enables
this experimentation to occur. It is also low in cost, and does not
commit the organization to the formal establishment of a group
until some firsthand review experience can be gotten.
       The report recommending the establishment of QA should
be sent to the individual to whom the data processing manager
reports. If the request is initiated by the data processing department, they should solicit internal audit support and vice versa. It
would be unwise for internal auditing to propose such a function
without having data processing management support.

ORGANIZATIONAL STRUCTURE

The higher in the data processing structure the quality assurance
function reports, the better the probability of success. The level of

reporting is also indicative of management support. High-level reporting provides a degree of independence for the group because they can deal with other functions on an equal basis.

Within organizations the function is typically situated in one of three spots. First, in some companies it reports to the manager of systems. Second, it may be organizationally a coequal of the four major segments of data processing (operation, control, systems, and programming). Third, it may be a staff function reporting directly to the EDP manager. The recommended organizational structure is reporting as a staff function to the EDP manager. (See Figure 3.1.)

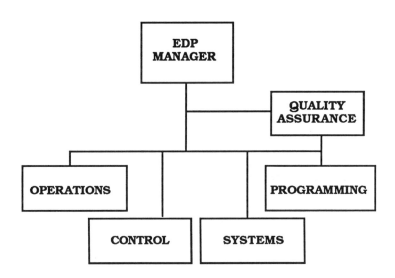

Figure 3.1 **SUGGESTED EDP DEPARTMENT ORGANIZATION**

Such a structure offers several advantages. It will receive the attention of the EDP manager. The QA manager need not be involved in the day-to-day functioning of the department as do other first-line managers. It is organizationally independent of all other aspects of the data processing department. And, finally the manager of quality assurance does not have to be in the same pay bracket as   other first-line managers in the data processing department.

The group will be in contact with other departments within the organization. The two most frequently contacted departments will be the user department and the internal audit department. In addition, QA personnel will be in meetings with and sending reports to executive management from time to time. Very early in discussions on a proposed system, executive management may desire an independent viewpoint on the feasibility and probability of success of the system. The QA is ideally suited to provide this type of advice.

QA should be heavily involved in major data processing decisions. However, keep in mind that the decisions will be made by data processing management, not by QA. The role played by QA is that of advisor to the EDP manager. This advisory role adds another reason for having QA as a staff function reporting to the data processing manager. The advisory role is more suited to a staff function than a line function.

STAFFING ALTERNATIVES

Most organizations initiate QA with a task force that is organized for the purpose of reviewing one or more data processing systems. The task force should comprise of leading EDP systems analysts and programmers. It should include the leading candidate for manager of the quality assurance function.

Three additional staffing alternatives are being used by various organizations. Ideally, a full-time staff should be available to perform quality assurance reviews. However, if an organization does not desire to make this commitment to the function, two other alternatives are available. These are a combination of full- and part-time personnel, and the establishment of a permanent committee of reviewers to perform quality assurance reviews. Figure 3.2 outlines the advantages and disadvantages of each alternative.

Task Force Method

The task force staffing method is most appropriate prior to the formalization of the QA function. This approach can also be utilized by the data processing manager whenever a review of a new system is desired. However, using the task force staffing method may mean there is no continuity between reviews. Each task force will tend to develop its own methods and procedures for the review. In addition, the task force members may have trouble finding sufficient time to perform the review properly if other tasks are competitors for their time.

There are advantages to the task force concept. Such a group can be uniquely developed for each review. The data processing manager can analyze problem areas in a new system and assign task force members with an appropriate background for these areas. In addition, it is a good training assignment for systems designers because it puts them in a position of analyzing the competency of systems design. The experiences learned from participating on a task force can be immediately implemented in the day-to-day work of the systems analyst.

STAFFING METHOD	ADVANTAGES	DISADVANTAGES
FULL-TIME STAFF	1. Continuity of reviewers 2. Commitment by managment to function	1. Cannot add specialized knowledge 2. Losing touch with practice
COMBINATION FULL TIME AND PART TIME	1. Continuity of function 2. Specialized knowledge can be added	1. Competition for time of part-timers 2. Full-time members lose touch with practice
PERMANENT COMMITTMENT	1. Continuity of function 2. Continuity of reviewers	1. Competition for reviewer's time 2. Committee not as authoritative as full-time group.
SPECIAL TASK FORCE FOR EACH REVIEW	1. Can build a group specialized for each 2. Can be used as a training assignment	1. No continuity between reviews 2. Competition for reviewers' time

Figure 3.2 **QUALITY ASSURANCE STAFFING ALTERNATIVES**

Full-Time Staff Method

The utilization of full-time staff has major advantages. First, it provides a continuity of reviewers. This is important to the data processing manager because the manager will know that all reviews are performed by the same methods. Another major advantage is the visible management support of the function by the assignment of full-time personnel. The task force concept could give the appearance of a lack of management confidence in the project team on a specific project. When task forces are assembled for only a limited number of projects, data processing personnel may question the motives of management for forming these task forces.

When full-time staffing is used, the competency of the review group is limited to the knowledge of the full-time staff. A task force can add specialized knowledge for specialized projects, but a full-time staff normally operates using the personnel available. In addition, it becomes difficult for full-time reviewers to maintain technical proficiency with current practice. It requires a special effort on the part of individuals to remain current with technology.

Permanent Committee Method

A step up from the task force approach is the formation of a permanent committee to perform reviews. The main difference between a permanent committee and a task force is the continuity of individual reviewers. A task force will be convened for the purpose of reviewing one system. A permanent committee will be convened for the purpose of reviewing many projects.

The permanent committee has the advantage of continuity of reviewers and continuity of the function. The permanent aspect of the committee says to project managers that their projects will be reviewed. It's not a hit or miss proposition dependent upon the whims of the EDP department manager. The fact that the function will be permanently established is indicative of a higher degree of management support than a specially convened task force.

The disadvantages of a permanent committee parallel those of the task force. These committees traditionally are part-time assignments for committee members. This means they have current work assignments competing for their time. As the intensity of the work assignment increases due to approaching target dates, individuals have less time and less desire to work as members of a review team.   Also, it is still a committee.   A committee can never be as authoritative as a function staffed with full-time personnel.

Full-Time and Part-Time Combination

Another staffing approach is to staff with one or more full-time personnel augmented by part-time personnel.   The part-time personnel would fill out the review team to achieve the desired staffing level and expertise needed.   The organization should begin by selecting one person as a full-time quality assurance manager.

Having one full-time member, the function gains continuity of purpose.   A strong manager of the function will help assure that the part-time people perform their function.   When the part-time staffers for the function feel torn between assignments, the full-time manager of quality assurance can work with other first-line managers to assure that the part-time members fulfill their obligations.

By utilizing part-time members, the group is able to add specialized knowledge where necessary.   This has proven to be an excellent mechanism for improving the work.   The full-time manager must insist on having only the best people assigned during the formative stages.   It is extremely important the first series of reviews demonstrate unequivocally the value of the QA function.   This does not mean that the function has to find major flaws in the system under review but, rather, that the assessment must prove accurate during the next phase of development of that application.

CHARACTERISTICS OF QUALITY ASSURANCE CANDIDATES

Obtaining the right individuals for the group is essential if it is to be successful.   The characteristics that make a good systems analyst/programmer are not sufficient to assure that that same individual will be successful in the quality assurance group.   The ability to review the work of others and to convince them there are better methods to perform their work takes some unique skills in dealing with people.   QA reviewers must be respected for their technical ability and have a good talent for communicative and persuasive abilities.

The key member in the group is the manager.   It is within this individual that we must look for all the traits necessary in a quality assurance reviewer. Others who are members of the group can succeed with only a subset of the desired characteristics if the manager is a very strong individual. Thus, we first must describe the manager of quality assurance.

The successful QA staff member must have

- A thorough understanding of data processing systems design and programming. The individual should be as knowledgeable in these skills as those being evaluated.

- An objective view so that the individual can distinguish between different methods of accomplishing a task that will produce acceptable results, and differences in quality of the methods where the results will not be the same.

- Leadership and take-charge personalities as reviewers will be working independently on special assignments. They cannot expect a lot of advice and guidance in performing their work. Therefore, the reviewers should be self-starters who will pursue assignments with interest and enthusiasm.

- An inquisitive nature because many of the problems and concerns to be uncovered in the review are not intuitively obvious. Thus, the individual who is a good reviewer needs to have the instinct to pursue leads and to put together bits of information that individually are meaningless but in total document the problem.

- An understanding of controls because any review of an application must include an internal control review.

- An ability to communicate both orally and in writing because much of the success of an individual in quality assurance can be ascribed to the ability to communicate needs and problems to project personnel. The more effective he or she is in communicating with data processing personnel, the more successful he or she will be in getting their ideas accepted.

- An ability to write reports. As the quality assurance reviewer must be able to transfer concerns and recommendations into written reports. Much of his or her success in having formal recommendations implemented will be dependent on the reviewer's ability to communicate the information to management through written reports.

In addition, the individual should be personally convinced of the importance of quality assurance and must be willing and able to devote the necessary time.

You should be able to perceive from this description that the quality assurance function is heavily people-dependent. The importance of getting the right individuals cannot be overemphasized.

DEVELOPING THE QUALITY ASSURANCE FUNCTION

The development of a QA function entails establishing an organizational structure for the group, obtaining the support of interested parties, building a staff, and establishing the steps or procedures under which the function will operate. The staffing of the structure encompasses development of job descriptions. Support for the function is needed from project leaders, project personnel, executive management, and internal auditing. The steps and procedures are the methods by which a group will conduct reviews.

Organizational Structure

The QA function should report directly to the data processing manager as a staff function. The individual in charge of the function should be the manager of quality assurance. Most organizations begin the function with one individual. Four other positions could logically be established within the function when it grows in size—three QA analysts and a secretary.

The individuals filling the technical positions must be highly skilled data processing personnel. The approximate salary ranges necessary to obtain individuals with necessary skills would be

- Quality assurance manager, $27,000 – $40,000
- Senior QA application review analyst or consultant, $25,000 – $32,000
- Quality assurance staff analyst, $22,000 – $30,000

Staffing the Quality Assurance Function

Regardless of whether the staff for the group is full-time or part-time, the qualifications needed for success are the same. To obtain better understanding of the job requirements, see the job descriptions in Figures 3.4, 3.5, 3.6 and 3.7. Each has five items of information:

1.   Job title — the name of the position.

2.   Report to — the individual in the organization's structure to whom this job reports.

3.   Function — general description of what the position should accomplish.

4.   Responsibilities and duties — those specific tasks that the individual is responsible to accomplish.

5.   Qualifications — the education, experience, and traits the individual should possess.

Job descriptions are designed to assist organizations in setting up positions for their own QA function. They can be used "as is" or modified to meet the special needs of your organization. Note that if only one position is established (i.e., quality assurance manager) that job description should include the responsibilities and duties of a senior quality assurance analyst. This is because the analyst job description contains the elements of the quality assurance review, while the manager job description is more supervisory oriented.

Figure 3.3 illustrates the structure of a mature QA group. The function would be headed by a manager. Reporting to the manager would be the quality assurance staff and the senior quality assurance application review analyst(s). As the workload and responsibility of the group grows, quality assurance analyst(s) and a secretary could be added. If the quality assurance manager was the only individual in the group, he would perform the functions of both the manager and the senior quality assurance analyst job.

If the function of the group entails highly technical aspects of data processing, one or more quality assurance consultants could be added to the group to provide this expertise. For example, if the QA function has responsibility for selecting and advising on operating systems features, this consultant could work with project and operating personnel on all aspects of operating systems as well as assisting in project reviews and the setting of standards. Such a consultant would be on the same level as a senior quality assurance analyst.

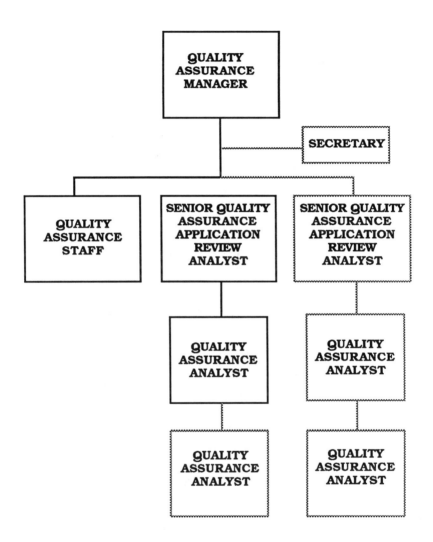

Figure 3.3 **SUGGESTED QUALITY ASSURANCE GROUP STRUCTURE**

JOB DESCRIPTION
QUALITY ASSURANCE MANAGER

REPORTS TO: Data Processing Manager

FUNCTION: Assists the data processing manager in implementing the quality assurance policy. Determines quality assurance objectives, establishes long-range goals and develops an operating budget for the group. Plans and assigns units of work, sets performance objectives, motivates, counsels and develops staff to achieve performance and work objectives. Interviews and evaluates qualifications of job applicants.

DUTIES AND RESPONSI-BILITIES: The quality assurance manager is responsible for:

1. Establishing quality assurance policy for all computer systems and computer operations of the company and directing the group in carrying out the policy.
2. Establishing the general criteria for reviews for EDP systems to determine what should be evaluated and when.
3. Promoting quality assurance concepts throughout the EDP department by issuing guidelines and providing instruction.
4. Providing consultation to EDP personnel and users as necessary.
5. Conducts quality assurance reviews acting as a senior quality assurance analyst.
6. Deciding on and reporting to the data processing manager failure by project teams to respond in a reasonable time to systems recommendations.
7. Providing continuing research on how to review and improve the quality of EDP systems.

QUALIFICA-TIONS: Candidate must have a bachelor's degree in either business or computer science with specialized knowledge in all facets of computer systems development and operations. Should have 10 years in computer systems or programming. The individual in this position should possess a reasonable ability in writing, speaking, and dealing with people.

Figure 3.4

JOB DESCRIPTION
SENIOR QUALITY ASSURANCE ANALYST

REPORTS TO: Quality Assurance Manager

FUNCTION: Reviews EDP systems to determine that goals will be achieved, methods followed and performance is satisfactory. In this respect, develops control standards and guidelines for EDP systems, and functions as a central source of knowledge on technology and standards for all EDP personnel. Supervises Quality Assurance assignments of the group to ensure system maintains a satisfactory level of quality, that systems will function efficiently, and that the systems will operate in accordance with established procedures.

DUTIES AND RESPONSI-BILITIES: The senior quality assurance analyst is responsible for:

1. Directing system reviews.
2. Evaluating and approving work and reports of quality assurance analysts.
3. Reviewing system during the feasibility, design, programming, testing and conversion phases. Advises data processing management of problems uncovered by this review.
4. Reviewing general controls. Advises data processing management of weaknesses.
5. Advising project team on EDP design and programming technology.
6. Developing EDP standards and guidelines.
7. Negotiating differences regarding systems implementation between assigned Quality Assurance Analysts, systems designers, and user departments.

QUALIFICA-TIONS: Requires intensive knowledge of the systems of the organization, the policies, standards, and procedures of the organization as well as the long-range goals and its philosophy with respect to advances in computer technology in order to insure that policy and established procedures are adhered to. Requires intensive knowledge of review techniques as well as a broad knowledge of computer systems and programming. Individual should have five years' systems and programming experience.

Figure 3.5

JOB DESCRIPTION
QUALITY ASSURANCE CONSULTANT

REPORTS TO: Quality Assurance Manager

FUNCTION: Within the entire electronic data processing environment, the incumbent provides any highly technical assistance necessary to assist project personnel in the performance of their function.

DUTIES AND: The quality assurance consultant is responsible for:
RESPONSI-
BILITIES
1. Advising and assisting project personnel with *details* in the use of new solutions for systems and program development.
2. Assisting the group in evaluating highly technical aspects of systems and program design.
3. Participating in the review of applications being developed to provide assistance in advancing system design approach.
4. Maintaining liaison with equipment manufacturers and software firms to keep abreast of trends in data processing.

QUALIFICA-   A bachelor's degree in computer science and considerable
TIONS: data processing experience is necessary. Incumbent should have at least five years of systems development and programming experience and excellent knowledge of computer programming and operating systems.

Figure 3.6

QUALITY ASSURANCE SUPPORT STAFF

As quality assurance groups mature many put more emphasis on establishing an environment in which quality can flourish and less effort needs to be spent on reviewing individual applications. Experience has shown that by reviewing a single application the most quality assurance can do is improve that application; however, by creating an environment encouraging quality, all

---

JOB DESCRIPTION
QUALITY ASSURANCE ANALYST

REPORTS TO: Senior Quality Assurance Analyst

FUNCTION: The incumbent assists in the performance of reviews of data processing systems.

DUTIES AND RESPONSIBILITIES: Under direct supervision, incumbent assists in the performance of reviews of the feasibility, design, programming, testing, and conversion efforts for new or modified computer systems. Incumbent may assist in the development of guidelines and standards. The incumbent assists in the preparation of formal reports of reviews. Any discrepancies and problems discovered during the review are referred to a higher level quality assurance analyst.

QUALIFICATIONS: In many cases, the individuals in this classification work independently and must have demonstrated the ability to exercise considerable initiative when conducting reviews as well as a minor degree of analysis and good judgment in making recommendations to improve systems. Requires the capability for assuming limited responsibility for the work performed as well as for the preparation and presentation of the audit report. Requires the ability to work on several assignments simultaneously. Individual should have three years of systems and programming experience.

Figure 3.7

applications can be improved. This also places quality assurance in a position where its contribution to the data processing function is more recognizable.

To establish a quality environment the QA function draws together those functions in the data processing department that support and improve quality systems. The purpose of putting all these support functions under the QA manager is to direct and coordinate their efforts in order to maximize quality. The support functions that are placed under the QA manager direct and coordinate their efforts in order to maximize quality. The support functions that are being placed under QA include the following (note that no one organization has included all of the following with their QA function).

- Error tracking
- Development of EDP application standards
- Development of software standards
- Authorization of deviations from standards
- Development of control standards
- Design of system controls
- Training of data processing personnel
- Tracking of production projects
- Performance analysis
- Hardware selection
- Software selection

Support Needed for a Successful QA Function

Part of the function of QA is to develop good working relationships with project personnel, internal auditing, and management. The support is necessary because QA operates as an advisory group. This advisory capacity of the group should be developed in a friendly environment as opposed to a hostile environment.

The day-to-day functioning of the group is with data processing personnel. This relationship is one of inquiry and discussion of future plans and alternatives under consideration. It is important for the QA reviewer to obtain honest and frank discussions with the project personnel. If a good working relationship has been achieved, these discussions will occur. On the other hand, if the project team is uncertain of the reviewer's motive, the working relationship will become very formal and the reviewer will have difficulty in obtaining the type of information needed. No information is volunteered and questions are answered in the briefest possible manner. Chapter 6 will discuss ways of building a good relationship.

Quality assurance and internal audit have some overlapping responsibilities. Properly established, the functions of the two groups should be complementary. The QA group is more qualified to evaluate the technical aspects of systems. On the other hand, internal audit is more qualified to comment on the adequacy of internal controls. Working together they can make a very strong team.

The function performed by QA could be performed by a highly technical competent internal audit group. However in practice, internal audit does not have the time or talent necessary to do a thorough quality assurance review. Without the available time and technically trained personnel, internal audit is either shortcutting these reviews or eliminating them altogether. Studies have shown that very few internal audit groups are involved in the systems design phase of new applications. QA should reach agreements with internal audit as to which aspects of data processing application reviews each will perform. There is more needed than the two groups can do combined, so reaching a logical division of work should not prove difficult. Chapter 12 will discuss this relationship with internal audit in detail.

The goals to which QA is dedicated will be supported by management. It is the method by which they are accomplished for which quality assurance needs the support. Quality assurance should primarily look to data processing management for support. However, support is also needed from user department management. Data processing management can help obtain user management support by explaining the role and responsibilities of QA.

Quality assurance should solicit support from data processing management to:

1. Provide the function with a sufficient number of competent personnel.

2. Provide the function with the authority necessary to carry out their responsibilities. This will assure the group of access to project information and personnel.

3. Have their recommendations considered and adopted. This can primarily be achieved through management interest and review of quality assurance reports, and a review by the project teams of the plan of action based on those recommendations.

Steps in Performing the Function

The QA group executes seven steps in the process of performing a review of an application under development. These steps include:

1. *Planning the review.* Developing plans and schedules to perform the review.

2.   *Preliminary review.* Gathering information necessary as background before commencing the formal review process.

3.   *Feasibility review.* Studying the feasibility results.

4.   *Design review.* Analyzing of the system design and assessing whether that design satisfies the goals of the application.

5.   *Program review.* Checking compliance to standards and design criteria.

6.   *Testing review.* Determining whether the system meets design criteria.

7.   *Conversion review.* Determining that the conversion process is well controlled.

The constraints of the review steps are illustrated in Figure 3.8. Note that the step result in a "go" or "no go" recommendation. This necessitates that QA has gathered enough information at the end of each of the reviews to recommend to management whether or not to proceed to the next phases of the project.

One constraint is the role or authority of the QA function. The function can do no more than authorized. The second constraint regards the QA methods and procedures which limit how and what the QA function does. QA is guided by two sets of procedures. The first is the standards, guidelines, policies, and procedures of the organization, which is supplemented by the technical advice they can offer the project team. The second is the policies and procedures of the QA group itself. These are the methods by which the function operates. These quality assurance group procedures will be discussed in detail in Chapters 4–10.

OBJECTIVITY

QA is asked to evaluate the competence and performance of their peers. This is especially difficult in QA groups that use part-time personnel.

Imagine for the moment yourself a member of QA group. You are assigned to the group on either a part-time basis or short-term assignment. You are assigned to review project X, headed by a person for whom you have worked in the past, and may again in the future. During the quality review process you note several items that may be potential problems in the future.

However, you are not completely sure. The project leader assures you they will be handled at some time in the future. You must now prepare a report for the project leader's supervisor. Judging the facts you have gathered, you believe the project will have some difficulty in achieving its objectives and meeting the schedule. On the other hand, the project leader had told you the problems will be handled in the future. You realize you may well be working for this leader in the next few months. What would you put in your report?

There is no easy answer to this question. Certainly a long-term assignment to QA improves one's objectivity. This does not assure that the long-term person will be independent, nor the short-term person overly influenced by the prospect of future assignments. However, it does raise a question that needs to be addressed by data processing management.

One of the steps that can help improve independence is having QA personnel report individually and confidentially to the data processing manager on areas of concern.   This has benefit to the QA members, but also has the effect of shifting some of their work responsibilities back to the data processing manager.

Other steps that can be taken to improve the independence of the QA group are:

1.   Making long-term assignments to the quality assurance group

2.   Guaranteeing that a quality assurance reviewer will not be assigned to a project leader whom that individual has reviewed during the last X months

3.   Using the most senior personnel in the data processing department to perform the quality assurance function

Those organizations using structured techniques will find that if the QA review is based on objective evaluation against the structured format imposed by the techniques, fewer personal implications of peer review have to be considered.

SUMMARY

Data processing management should assume primary responsibility for establishing the QA function.   Once established, data processing management should support that

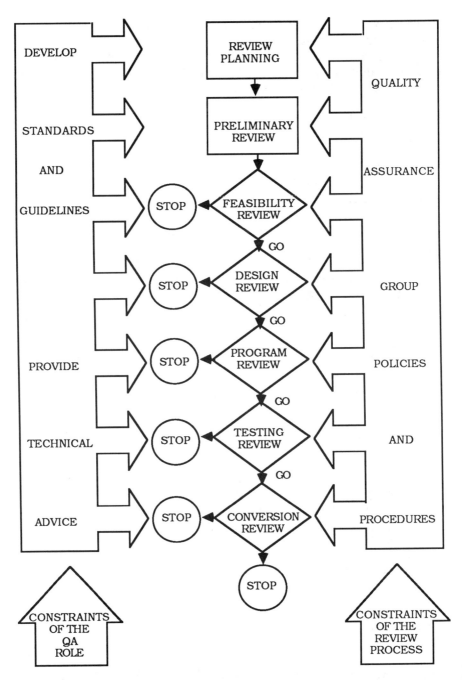

Figure 3.8 **CONSTRAINTS OF THE QUALITY ASSURANCE REVIEW PROCESS**

group with a sufficient number of competent personnel, provide the group with the authority it needs to perform their function, and then determine that the group's recommendations are being given serious consideration by the project team. Recommendations from the group should be adopted unless there are very valid reasons for not implementing them.

When QA is being developed, there are four areas that require consideration: 1) the organizational structure of the group; 2) the caliber, method, and quantity of staff for the group; 3) soliciting support from management, users, and internal auditing; and 4) developing the procedures and methods by which the group will operate. Management should closely monitor these areas and provide what guidance they can to ascertain the developing group gets off to the best start possible.

Independence of QA personnel should remain a continual concern of data processing management. It is in its best interest that the group maintain as much independence as possible. Data processing management should take those steps necessary to affirm its support for an independent function.

Part II

PLANNING THE QUALITY ASSURANCE FUNCTION

Chapter 4
SYSTEMS REVIEW PRIORITIES: ALLOCATING QA TIME

Ideally, QA is charged with reviewing all systems. As a practical matter it is rarely staffed sufficiently to review all systems in the appropriate depth. Therefore, some method is needed to assign priorities so as to allot the available review time among systems needing review.

This chapter will discuss the methods that can be used for selecting applications for review. A scientific approach based on four criteria is recommended. The criteria are the type of application, the complexity of the application, the technology being utilized to implement the application, and the people involved in specifying and implementing the system.

This approach assists in developing a plan for which applications to review and how much time should be expended on that review. The planning methodology calls for allocating 80% of the available review time, and leaving the remaining 20% as a contingency for special assignments and explaining the implications and solutions to problems associated with previous reviews.

METHODS OF SELECTING APPLICATIONS FOR REVIEW

After the QA is established, the next step is determining work priorities. One of the major criteria of success is in finding a good answer to the time allocation question. Without a plan for allocating resources, the work of the group can be dissipated in low-priority tasks.

One quality assurance manager practices saying "no" in front of the mirror so that he can turn down these requests. It is very easy to spend an hour or two trying to be a good guy.

Unfortunately, hours have the tendency to mount into days and weeks over the course of a year.

Five Common Methods for Selecting Applications for Review

QA groups tend to make choices in one of five ways:

1. *Intuition.* The manager selects those applications which he or she believes to be in need of review. Under this method, the manager will have a "feel" as to which application is most likely to cause problems for the organization. Both the application and the amount of time allocated to its review are at the prerogative of the manager.

2. *Directed.* Management of the data processing department directs what applications to review. This direction can either be application by application, or a set of criteria (all telecommunication applications, for example) that instructs QA as to which application should be reviewed.

3. *Reactive.* In this approach, the group becomes involved with applications as they begin to develop problems. Again, it can be each application individually or by some criteria (i.e., 10% over budget or 90 days late) that causes involvement.

4. *Planned judgment.* Using judgment, QA will select which applications they will review and for how long. The primary difference between judgment and intuition is the planning effort involved. Judgment implies an evaluation of alternatives. Intuition considers each application individually.

5. *Planned scientific.* A mathematically oriented approach to selecting applications based on a predetermined set of criteria. Mathematical values will be assigned as a result of analysis of each criterion. The mathematical summing of the individual criterion will result in a numerical value that can be used in assigning priority.

Of the five approaches, the planned scientific is the most objective. The other four tend to be subjective evaluations. This scientific approach has proven very successful in those organizations whose management is scientifically oriented. On the other hand, in organizations where management runs the organization by "the seat of their pants," such an approach may run into opposition. Utilizing the planned scientific approach, the manager can provide documented explanations as to why resources have been assigned to reviews of specific applications.

The five methods for selecting applications are generally in conflict with one another (see Figure 4.1). It is difficult to work by more than one of these methods at a time.

The remainder of this chapter is oriented toward the planned scientific approach to selecting applications for review. However, if your quality assurance group uses one of the other approaches, the criteria and methodology can still prove helpful in your application selection process.

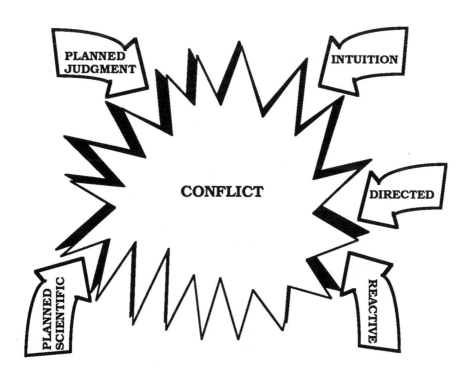

Figure 4.1 **METHODS OF SELECTING APPLICATIONS FOR REVIEW**

RATING CRITERIA

Experience has shown four general categories of concern for computerized applications. These can be restated as categories for rating (or evaluating) applications for review.

1. *Type of application.* The function or area that is being computerized. Examples would be payroll, accounts receivable, inventory, budgeting, demand deposits, and unearned premium reserves. One can consider software systems such as database managers, telecommunications systems, or bill or material processors, as types of applications.

2. *Complexity of applications.* The difficulty in computerizing and the amount of resources involved in building the application. Evaluation of complexity varies from person to person and installation to installation. What may be complex for a small computer installation may be a simple application to a large organization. Thus, complexity will be related to the size of the organization and skill of the personnel.

3. *Technology.* Problems with technology may be either hardware- or software-related. Most problems come from technology not previously utilized by the organization. When new hardware and software is involved in an application, it becomes more difficult to implement. This is due to the learning experience of individuals with those new products. There is also a correlation between the time the product has been on the market and difficulty in using it. When a product has been time-tested, its implementation is not as difficult as with a product newly introduced to the marketplace.

4. *People.* The skill, temperament, control orientation, dedication, and time available for the project all influence the type of job that can be performed by a specific individual. The complexity of current technology necessitates the team approach to developing a new application. These criteria are magnified by the number and backgrounds of individuals participating on the project team.

TYPE OF APPLICATION

The major criteria for determining if a system should be reviewed lies in the nature of the role of that application in the organization. Obviously, applications that control the assets of an organization are those of greatest concern. The higher the percentage of assets controlled, the greater the concern. The three aspects of types of applications that need to be evaluated are financial applications, statutory requirements, and exposure to loss.

Financial Applications

In merchandising organizations, the invoicing systems probably control the greatest percentage of resources. Next is the purchasing application, followed by the payroll application. It is thus the financial systems that merit the highest priority for review.

Statutory Requirements

Many data processing applications provide data to governmental agencies. This is especially true of regulated industries. In all industries, systems such as payroll interface with several governmental agencies. Invoicing systems that collect sales tax can interface with agencies of one or more states. Because of the necessity for correct reporting to governmental agencies, together with potential penalties for wrong information, extra time and effort is warranted on these systems. The larger the number of agencies involved, the greater the exposure of the organization.

Exposure to Loss

Computer applications are subject to exposure to loss. This exposure can be due to errors and omissions on the part of careless or dishonest employees or acts of sabotage on the part of disgruntled employees, and losses due to penetration by outsiders. Better than 95% of all losses will be those associated with employees of the organization. Therefore, undue effort should not be put on losses associated with outside individuals. The more liquid the assets of the organization (cash, readily salable inventory, etc.) the higher the exposure to loss. This factor needs to be considered in the evaluation criteria for reviewing applications.

COMPLEXITY OF APPLICATION

The complexity of an application will vary depending on the type of installation and the skill of data processing personnel. Complexity can be measured by many different criteria. The ones to consider are

1.   Application history
2.   Effort to develop application
3.   Time span to complete project
4.   Expected number of application programs
5.   Number of databases updated

Application History

The nature of certain applications seems to make them complex to operate. A study of the history of an application provides some insight as to the complexity of operation. Another means of measuring complexity is the number of errors and problems that have occurred. This can be determined by a study of the history of an application. Analysis of past events will provide us with some indication of future trends.

Effort to Develop Application

The effort to develop an application needs to be measured in man-months of effort. This is the best common denominator for systems development effort. Again, the skill of people within an organization will affect the effort needed to develop a typical application.

Time Span to Complete Project

If a project team has sufficient time to complete a project, it can be done as an orderly process. When the project team is pressured to do its work on a crash basis, the individual pieces must be compressed, subjecting the project to error. While it can be argued that too much time results in a poor use of resources because the project team will use the available time inefficiently, too little time usually has more problems associated with it.

Expected Number of Application Programs

The larger the number of programs included in an application—whether utilities or applications—the greater the complexity of the system. The longer the chain of programs, the more times data is passed, the greater the number of interfaces, and the more spread out the logic. These all add to the complexity of the system.

Number of Databases Updated

Application programs interact with files that will be retained and updated the next time a transaction is processed or the application run. The greater the number of files updated, the greater the complexity of the system.

Technology

The type of technology utilized by the project team affects the difficulty in developing the application. When an organization is using time-tested hardware and software, the implementation is facilitated. When the newer technologies are utilized, the systems analysts and programmers have the dual problem of understanding the application and the supporting hardware and software technology. When systems problems occur, it may be difficult to pinpoint whether the problem is application or technical in nature. Unfamiliarity with the technology greatly increases the probability of problems. Technology can be divided into hardware technology and software technology.

Hardware technology has progressed from card batch systems through on-line disk systems with telecommunication. As systems move through that progression, the complexity increases geometrically.

Today, software appears to be causing more difficulty technically than hardware. Special-purpose packages designed exclusively for an organization (an advanced release from a vendor of a new software package, or a routine that was specially developed by a vendor for a particular application) may be the most difficult to utilize. Once systems analysts and programmers have mastered a particular piece of software, additional applications using that software are much easier to implement.

PEOPLE

The skill level of the project team is a major ingredient in success for data processing applications. Three parties are involved in the development of most applications: users, internal auditors, and the project team.

The rating criteria described in this chapter can rate each of these groups independently. However, if the groups work together amicably, the probability of success increases greatly. Unfortunately, this is a difficult factor to rate. Therefore, the rater is cautioned that if known personality or departmental conflicts exist the effectiveness of that party could be lessened because of this conflict.

User Involvement

Organizations that have a history of successful data processing applications attribute much of their success to user involvement. The amount of user involvement can be considered one of the keys to success. An important criterion is the time user personnel have available to contribute to development of an application. It is helpful, but not necessary, for user personnel to have a strong technical understanding of data processing. If they fully understand the application and have a strong desire to understand data processing, that should suffice.

Internal Audit Involvement

Internal auditors can play a major role in systems development if they are technically competent regarding data processing. Many of the functions that might normally be performed by a quality assurance group can be performed by internal audit if they are involved in the application development cycle. This relationship between quality assurance and internal auditing will be discussed in detail in Chapter 15.

Skill of the Project Team

The technical competence of the project team is a major element in the success of an application. When systems analysts and programmers are experienced and competent, the probability of success increases tremendously. Quality assurance personnel must seriously assess the effectiveness of the project team and adjust their involvement with the project accordingly. The skills needed by the project team are the same skills that are considered important for a good quality assurance analyst.

OTHER SELECTION CRITERIA

The proposed criteria are provided as an example of this method of selecting applications. These criteria are oriented toward a financial organization, such as a bank or insurance company. Nonfinancial organizations may have to revise these criteria.

The success of using a mathematical process to select applications for review depends upon how closely those criteria correlate to risk. If the criteria are good predictors of problems, the selection process will be successful. It may be necessary to experiment with different criteria prior to identifying those criteria that have a high correlation to risk.

Additional criteria for selecting applications for a quality assurance review include

- Age of the application
- Skill of user personnel in working with computerized applications
- Visibility of application system
- Type of logic (difficult, average, easy)
- Need for security
- Need for privacy
- Number of people on the project

RATING INDIVIDUAL APPLICATIONS

Each new application or major enhancement to an existing application should be rated by the quality assurance group. The rating should be done in conjunction with the group's normal planning cycle. This planning cycle may be either monthly, quarterly, or yearly. The objective of rating individual applications is to determine the group's workload over the next planning period—that is, to establish a work priority scheme.

Assumptions and Caveats

The use of the proposed work prioritizing scheme is based on certain ideal assumptions and caveats. These include:

- An inventory of all computer systems (AISs)—operational, under development, or undergoing major change—is maintained,
- The inventory may not be complete due to user development or system changes made outside the system development process.
- To use the priority scheme, certain minimal information is required or the assessment of the system may not be valid.

- The full priority scheme would most easily be performed by EDP groups in order to enlist multiple perspectives, especially where resources are known to be a concern.

- Management in the organization must agree that risk can be evaluated by a standardized scheme.

- Users should always be consulted in the risk evaluation to ensure appropriate assumptions, and to assure maximum effectiveness.

- Judgment is still needed!

Within this framework of assumptions and caveats the entire EDP work plan can then be developed. To the degree these assumptions differ from the reality of the organization's SDLC environment, the work planning methodology should be adjusted.

EDP Planning/Prioritization Process

The risk evaluation performed as part of the work priority scheme must be done within the context of the entire EDP planning process. There are elements of the process that need to be considered prior to the risk evaluation (such as non-discretionary requirements) and other elements that require consideration afterward (such as resource constraints). Figure 4.2 and the following paragraphs present a suggested model for the entire prioritization process.

Nondiscretionary Reviews

As can be seen from the model in Figure 4.2, the review planning and prioritization process starts with front end qualifiers that must be considered by the auditor prior to making decisions with respect to which system(s) should be reviewed. These front end qualifiers consist of nondiscretionary factors which are beyond the reviewer's control. These nondiscretionary factors include, but are not limited to the following:

- External directives (laws, regulations, OMB circulars, and EDP standards);

- Internal directives and priorities (contractual requirements; requirements, standards, and policies of audit and data processing organizations; upper management directives)

- Business/organizational environment unique to the organization (effect of economy on organization, budget of organization, and technology available to or used by organization);
- Factors unique to the organization (presence and strength of quality assurance and security functions, management and control philosophy, structure, and policies)
- Geopolitical environment (public concern and politics)
- Resource constraints and economic health (dollars, time, expertise, training, tools, and techniques)
- Known problems with the system, from current logs or previous evaluations and audits (nature and magnitude of problems)
- Evaluations and audits planned by management
- Reviewer's institutional knowledge of the organization's universe of systems

After all of the front end qualifiers have been considered, it may be that the entire review plan is dictated by the nondiscretionary work. That is, external directives, internal directives, and/or resource constraints may require that certain audits be performed and these required reviews may use up the limited audit resources available. In this case, the priority scheme may still be useful for determining audit approaches and where to focus efforts.

If, on the other hand, additional review resources are available for discretionary reviews, the risk evaluation of the work priority scheme can be used to identify and rank the systems in greatest need of audit coverage. Ultimately, back end qualifiers may need to be considered for the discretionary reviews.

Risk Evaluation Levels and Dimensions

The work priority scheme expresses the risk concerns in terms of two levels and five dimensions.

Level I
   1. Criticality and mission impact

Level II
   2. Size/scale/complexity
   3. Environment/stability

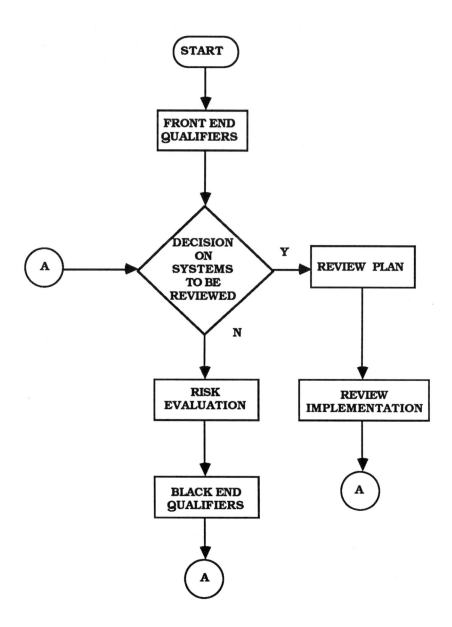

Figure 4.2 **EDP PLANNING/PRIORITIZATION PROCESS**

4. Reliability/integrity
5. Technology integration

Each dimension is defined as a related set of characteristics which can measure or estimate the amount of risk posed by that dimension to a failure of the system. The chief concern of each dimension can be stated in the form of a question as follows:

1. What is the impact or criticality of the system to the organization? A poorly developed or controlled system that is mission critical could jeopardize the basic operational or programmatic effectiveness; therefore, an impact/critical system commands audit attention. The larger the impact, the more important it is to audit.

2. How complex is the system? (This includes size considerations.) The more complete the system, the more difficult is communication and control, and consequently, the higher the risk of failure. The greater the chance for failure, the more important it is to review the system.

3. How stable is the system internally (structure) and externally (environment)? The less stable the system, the more difficult it is to develop procedures for communication and control, the greater the chance for failure, and the greater the need to review.

4. How reliable is the system and the information it processes and generates? That is, what is the chance of the system failing or the data being wrong? The answer to this question is obtained by looking at the controls in the system (integrity controls) and prior review experience. The less reliable system and data, the more chance for failure and the need to review.

5. How well is the technology integrated into the organization? The more poorly the system technology is integrated with the skills of the staff and the standards and procedures of the organization, the more chance for failure and the greater the need to review.

The overriding risk is criticality and mission impact. Systems with significant impact easily take precedence over all other dimensions in allocating EDP review resources. Because criticality and mission impact is so crucial, the work priority scheme assigns it to its own level. The two-level work priority scheme permits a high amount of flexibility depending on organizational need since it can be applied in any degree of detail required. For example, the results of Level I ranking may be adequate to prioritize all audit work, based on available time and resources. If additional ranking characteristics are necessary, the more detailed Level II can be used to further prioritize review work. A two-level review, additionally, enables the auditor to purge from consideration those systems which will definitely not be reviewed, for any number of reasons. Environment and resource issues enter here. The two-level work priority scheme follows in outline form, identifying the five dimensions and their related characteristics. (Note that the same characteristic may be used in more than one dimension because the question asked will be different.)

LEVEL I

Mission Impact/Strategic Value/Organization (Business) Criticality and Sensitivity Factors

- criticality of the system to the organization's mission
- criticality/sensitivity of the system to the well-being, safety, or interest of the general public/clients/consumers
- criticality/sensitivity of data and information
    competitive advantage
    confidence of the public in program/department
    privacy/confidentiality/security issues
- materiality of resources controlled by system
- fraud potential
- life cycle costs of system (people and dollars)
    development cost budget
        people
        dollars
            hardware
            software
            facilities
    operating cost budget
        people
            data processing/systems (including training)
            users (including training)
        dollars
            hardware (CPU, peripherals, terminals,
            telecommunications)
                acquisition

operation

software

acquisition

maintenance

supplies

facilities

configuration change control

- degree of dependence on AIS
- criticality of interfaces with other systems and external organizations

A Level I review, outlined above, provides a "first cut" at the total audit universe. This initial review will identify critical systems that require audit coverage. The additional dimensions to be reviewed in Level II should be used to rank these critical systems to find those most deserving of discretionary review coverage.

LEVEL II

System* Size/Scale/Complexity

- size of user area impacted
- number/complexity of interfaces/relationships with other projects or systems
- complexity of AIS technology (network size, communication needs, system configuration, degree of centralization, nature of transaction coupling mechanisms, nature of security)
- size/complexity of system

size of system budget

development costs

maintenance/operation costs

number/complexity of different inputs

number/complexity of unique files

number/complexity of unique outputs

number/complexity of logical files (views) system will access

number/complexity of major types of on-line inquiry

number of source documents maintained/retained

number/complexity of computer programs

---

* The term "system" is used in place of "project" to signify the entire AIS life cycle and the possibility of review at any point in the development process or operations.

          complexity of programming language
          complexity of system configuration
          number of human elements interfacing
          number of decision levels
          number of functions by devices
          number, types, and complexity of transactions
          number of external organizations impacted

- nature of interactions with external organizations

System Environment/Stability

- organizational breadth (interfaces, dependencies, system configuration)
- management involvement/commitment
- project management approach and structure
  configuration management program
  management efficiency and effectiveness
- specificity of, agreement on, and support for user requirements
- confidence in estimates—both cost and time—premising make-or-buy decisions, vendor selection, system testing/validation, etc.
- number of vendors/contractors involved
- newness of function/process to user
- problems associated with current system performance and/or system development effort
- existence/scope of data processing standards, policies, and procedures, especially systems development life cycle methodology and documentation requirements
- availability of evidence—document and report preparation and maintenance for entire system life cycle (test/validation/certification results, operations manual, system specifications, audit trails, exception reporting)
- quality and completeness of documentation
- general controls
  physical access controls
  environmental controls
  communication controls
  management controls environment
  document controls
  system change and test/validation/certification controls
- ongoing concern issues/organization effect (will mission objectives be met in a timely manner?)

interruption tolerance
ability to maintain performance
unsatisfactory system performance (adverse consequences from degradation or failure)
unsatisfactory system development completion
unsatisfactory conversion
- labor relations (salary parity, hours, fringe benefits, etc.)
- project team (management and staff effectiveness and training)
- organizational and personnel changes (frequency, magnitude, and number)
- functional requirements changes (frequency, number, and magnitude)
- technical changes (frequency, magnitude, and number)
- factors affecting cost/economic/budget climate
- availability and adequacy of back-up and recovery procedures

Reliability/Integrity

- hazards/risks to information system (data, hardware, communications, facilities)
- general controls
    environmental (e.g., physical access controls, natural hazards controls)
    management
- applications controls
- availability and adequacy of audit trails
- quality and quantity of automated error detection/correction procedures
- availability and adequacy of back-up and recovery procedures
- completeness, currency, and accuracy of documentation for audit
- prior reviews
- auditor judgment (intuitively obvious)

Technology Integration

- makeup of project team in relation to technology used (number, training, and experience)
- applicability of the data processing design methodologies and standards to the technology in use

- pioneering aspects (newness of technology and/or technological approaches used in this information system for application and organization)
- technical complexity of information system (interrelationships of tasks)
- user knowledge of DP technology
- margin for error (i.e., Is there reasonable time to make adjustments, corrections, or perform analyses before the transaction is completed?)
- utilization of equipment (tolerance for expansion)
- availability of automated error detection/correction procedures
- completeness, currency, and accuracy of documentation for implementation/maintenance/operation (e.g., operations/maintenance manuals)
- amount of hard-copy evidence

RISK SCORING: APPLICATION OF THE WORK PRIORITY SCHEME

Implementation of the Scheme

For the scheme to be of use to the EDP auditor, an analysis approach for risk scoring must be employed using the dimensions and characteristics. The rest of this section describes *one possible approach* that could be used. User experience will undoubtedly lead to modifications and improvements in the application of the scheme. If the EDP reviewer for some reason does not wish to use the scoring methodology, he or she could still keep the dimensions and their characteristics in mind when performing a less formal review.

Suggested Scoring Approach for Each Risk Dimension

The method of ranking and rating suggested here as a simple approach commensurate with the softness of the data available. Each dimension of the scheme should be treated and ranked separately, with scores then combined. Criticality/Mission Impact, the Level I dimension of the proposed scheme, would be analyzed first. The procedure is as follows.

First, the n characteristics *within a dimension* are ranked according to their importance to that dimension. The rank number of characteristic i is $I(i)$ and ranges from 1 to n, with n

correlated with the most important characteristic.   For operational systems one can use discriminant analysis applied to equal sets of known system failures and successes to obtain this ranking.   For developmental system a consensus view of audit management can be used, ideally obtaining sponsor or/user input.

Second, the rank, $I(i)$, is then converted to an importance weighting factor, $W(i)$, that is normalized to 20.   (The reason for selecting 20 is explained later.   This means that the sum of the weighting factors for the characteristics within a dimension is set to 20 (or normalized to 20).   Since each of the five dimensions has a different number of characteristics and we wish to treat the dimensions as equals, normalization will guarantee that the risk score range for each dimension will be the same.

The normalization factor, F, is the number which converts the rank $I(i)$ to the weighting factor $W(i)$ The relationships are

(1) $$W(i) = F \times I(i)$$

(2) $$\sum_{i=1 \text{ to } n} W(i) = \sum_{i=1 \text{ to } n} F \times I(i) = 20$$

Solving equation (2) for F, we find

(3) $$F = \frac{20}{\sum_{i=1 \text{ to } n} I(i)}$$

and substituting for F in equation (1) yields the importance weighting factor $W(i)$ for characteristic i:

(4) $$W(i) = \frac{20}{\sum_{i=\text{ to } n} I(i)}$$

Third, each characteristic is rated with respect to the risk of occurrence. One of the following risk ratings, $R(i)$, is assigned to characteristic i.

$$R(i) = 3 \text{ (for High Risk)}$$
$$R(i) = 2 \text{ (for Medium Risk)}$$
$$R(i) = 1 \text{ (for Low Risk)}$$

These ratings can be assigned by the auditor, again with user assistance if appropriate.

Finally, a dimension risk score (DRS) for the dimension of risk is obtained by multiplying the importance weighting by the risk rating of the characteristic and summing over the characteristics for that dimension. The equation for this is the following:

$$DRS(j) = \sum_{i=1\,to\,n} W(i) \times R(i)$$

where i = characteristics 1 to n

$W(i)$ = importance weighting for characteristic i
$R(i)$ = risk rating for characteristic i
$DRS(j)$ = dimension j's risk score, j = 1 to 5

The risk score for each of the five dimensions will range from 20 to 60 using these importance weighting and risk rating number assignments.

First Order System Risk Score

After completing a Level I review for an organization's universe of AISs, using the analysis scheme, the QA analyst can use the Criticality/Mission Impact dimension risk score as a first order approximation to a system risk score. Since these risk scores have all been normalized to the same number (20), it is possible to compare these risk scores across AIS and eliminate from further consideration AISs having a low risk with respect to Criticality/ Mission Impact.

Risk Level II Review Considerations

If it is decided that the more detailed Level II review is appropriate and affordable, one must decide upon a sequence for reviewing the remaining dimensions of the high risk, critical AISs. While there is no single "correct" way to do this, it might be appropriate to consider the following.

Since the Environment/Stability risk dimension includes the organization's general controls, including the strength and security functions throughout the SDLC (of both systems and major enhancements to existing systems), it may be most useful to review this dimension first in a Level II review. These general controls would heavily affect the need for review coverage as well as the scope and expertise necessary in that coverage. The EDP auditors could confidently reduce their scope and related testing of applications if they could rely on the organization's general controls and the safeguards these various review functions provide in the the SDLC process. Any ranking or prioritizing of the elements in the work priority scheme, beyond the overriding factors described above (i.e., external influence and mission criticality), could *not* be reasonably accomplished without a survey of the organization's general and applications controls and without an institutional knowledge of the organization, its SDLC process, and any facts and circumstances affecting system development activities. The characteristics in all four Level II dimensions should be weighted and rated in the light of such background information, and the dimension risk score, DRS, obtained for each of the four Level II dimensions.

The Second Order System Risk Score

As a second order approximation one can treat the dimensions as equal contributors to the risk score for the AIS as a whole. Under this assumption the system risk score, (SRS) is then a simple sum of the five dimension risk scores, (DRS).

$$(5) \qquad SRS = \sum_{j = 1 \text{ to } 5} DRS(j)$$

Since DRS(*j*) can range from 20 to 60, SRS will range from 100 to 300. The choice of 20 for the sum of the weights of the characteristics within a dimension is arbitrary and was made in order to place SRS in a reasonable range for comparing one system's risk score to another's.

An Example

It may be a useful exercise to go through an example of the arithmetic involved. Assume we wish to calculate dimension risk scores and system risk scores for two AISs. To simplify matters we shall assume small numbers of characteristics for each dimension. Dimension 1 has four characteristics, dimension 2 has three characteristics, dimension 3 has five characteristics, dimension 4 has three characteristics and dimension five has 2 characteristics. The importance ranking

$I(i)$ and the risk ratings $R(i)$ are obtained from audit management and the auditor respectively. The rest of the numbers in Tables 4.2 and 4.3 are calculated using equations (1) – (5). (Table 4.1 is a practice template of the table to assist the reader in learning the methodology.)

Using dimension 1 as a first order system risk score, we find AIS 1, with DRS = 42, is more at risk than AIS 2, with DRS = 38. We obtain the second order risk score by adding the five dimension risk scores for each AIS. Using these numbers, AIS 1 with SRS = 191.4, is again more at risk than AIS 2, with its SRS = 180.0. Only experience with the method will enable the reviewer to obtain more refined interpretations of the calculations.

SYSTEMS ENHANCEMENTS IN THE REVIEW PROCESS

Systems are enhanced (or modified) under different circumstances. These enhancements can be categorized as follows:

*   *Emergency changes.* Changes to systems that must occur before the application can run, usually within 24 hours or less.
*   *Software system changes.* Changes to systems that must be modified because of changes in vendor-supplied software, such as operating systems, compilers, sorts, etc. These changes normally do not affect the application's processing rules and can be made independent of the application programs.
*   *Short duration changes.* Changes for known errors or problems. Do not cause the system to "hang up" or produce unusable results, but must be corrected quickly. The change is normally installed within two weeks.
*   *Scheduled changes.* Changes to the systems that are known in advance and can be implemented on an orderly basis. The usual duration is 10 to 90 days.
*   *Major enhancements.* Changes of a substantial nature that can follow the procedures utilized in the building of new applications.

All major enhancements should be considered for review. These can be handled like any other new application because of their size. This type of change encompasses the largest single block of systems development and programming resources in many organizations.

Emergency changes and software system changes should probably not be reviewed by the quality assurance group. What should be reviewed in these cases are the procedures that control these types of changes. Without strong controls over changes of these types, unauthorized changes could be made, or major systems problems occur because of lack of control.

The questionable type of enhancements for review are those of short duration and scheduled changes. To determine QA involvement in these types of changes, the group should first determine the amount of data processing resources being utilized, and second, the exposure to the organization by making one of these types of changes to an application. Obviously, if it is an extremely sensitive application, QA should be involved. Application rating sheets will prove helpful in making this determination. For example, QA may ask each systems analyst to complete one of the application rating sheets (see Figures 4.3 and 4.4) for each short duration or scheduled change. The group can then pick a cutoff point. For example, if the score equals 75 or higher, the quality assurance group will become involved.

RESPONDING TO SPECIAL REQUESTS

Successful QA groups will receive a substantial number of requests for special assignments. There is value in responding to these requests if time is available. It is suggested that 20% of available review days be allocated to these types of requests. However, the manager of quality assurance should make a special effort to determine that no more than the allotted time is utilized for these types of requests.

When the requests exceed the amount of time allocated for them, the manager of quality assurance should discuss this situation with the manager of data processing. It is important to emphasize the primary objective for establishing the quality assurance group. If these objectives are subverted by satisfying special requests, the manager of quality assurance should not honor the requests.

SUMMARY

QA groups can have their efforts directed in a variety of ways. The method of direction can affect the effectiveness of the function.

Those groups that are most successful are those that achieve the objectives for which they are established. In order to do this, the groups must plan the use of their resources.

The resources can be allocated by determining which applications are in most need of review, and then allocating the available resources to satisfy those needs. This chapter has provided a methodology to make this allocation. Once the allocation has been made, the manager of quality assurance may still need to exert judgment because certain systems will need extra effort due to unique problems.

One cannot overemphasize the importance of setting objectives for the group and then developing a plan to meet those objectives. Data processing is a very orderly, methodical process. To operate successfully in that environment, the quality assurance group must develop very orderly, methodical plans.

AIS _____

DIMENSION	*I(i)*	*F*	*W(i)*	*R(i)*	*W x R*	*DRS(j)*
DIM 1 C(1) C(2) C(3) C(4)						
DIM 2 C(1) C(2) C(3)						
DIM 3 C(1) C(2) C(3) C(4) C(5)						
DIM 4 C(1) C(2) C(3)						
DIM 5 C(1) C(2)						

SRS _____

Table 4.1 **PRACTICE TEMPLATE FOR RISK SCORING OF AN AIS**

AIS ___1___

DIMENSION	$I(i)$	F	$W(i)$	$R(i)$	$W \times R$	$DRS(j)$
DIM 1						
$C(1)$	2	2	4	1	4	
$C(2)$	1	2	2	2	4	
$C(3)$	4	2	8	2	16	
$C(4)$	3	2	6	3	18	
	10	—	20	—	42	
						42.0
DIM 2						
$C(1)$	3	10/3	10	1	10	
$C(2)$	2	10/3	20/3	2	40/3	
$C(3)$	1	10/3	10/3	3	10	
	6	—	20	—	33.3	
						33.3
DIM 3						
$C(1)$	4	4/3	16/3	3	16	
$C(2)$	2	4/3	8/3	2	16/3	
$C(3)$	5	4/3	20/3	1	20/3	
$C(4)$	1	4/3	4/3	2	8/3	
$C(5)$	3	4/3	4	3	12	
	15	—	20	—	42.7	
						42.7
DIM 4						
$C(1)$	1	10/3	10/3	3	10	
$C(2)$	3	10/3	10	3	30	
$C(3)$	2	10/3	20/3	1	46.7	
	6	—	20	—	46.7	
						46.7
DIM 5						
$C(1)$	1	20/3	20/3	2	40/3	
$C(2)$	2	20/3	40/3	1	40/3	
	3	—	20	—	26.7	
						26.7

SRS ___191.4___

Note:
1st Order SRS (Range = 20 to 60) = DRS(1) = 42.0.
2nd Order SRS (Range = 100 to 300) = SRS = 191.4.

Table 4.2 **DIMENSION RISK SCORES AND SYSTEM RISK
SCORES FOR AIS 1**

AIS ___2___

DIMENSION	$I(i)$	F	$W(i)$	$R(i)$	$W \times R$	$DRS(j)$
DIM 1						
$C(1)$	4	2	8	3	24	
$C(2)$	2	2	4	1	4	
$C(3)$	1	2	2	2	4	
$C(4)$	3	2	6	1	6	
	10	—	20	—	38	
						38.0
DIM 2						
$C(1)$	2	10/3	20/3	3	20	
$C(2)$	1	10/3	10/3	1	10/3	
$C(3)$	3	10/3	10	2	20	
	6	—	20	—	43.3	
						43.3
DIM 3						
$C(1)$	5	4/3	20/3	3	20	
$C(2)$	3	4/3	4	1	4	
$C(3)$	1	4/3	4/3	2	8/3	
$C(4)$	2	4/3	8/3	1	8/3	
$C(5)$	4	4/3	16/3	3	16	
	15	—	20	—	45.4	
						45.4
DIM 4						
$C(1)$	1	10/3	10/3	2	40/3	
$C(2)$	3	10/3	10	1	10	
$C(3)$	2	10/3	20/3	3	10	
	6	—	20	—	33.3	
						33.3
DIM 5						
$C(1)$	2	20/3	40/3	1	40/3	
$C(2)$	1	20/3	20/3	1	40/3	
	3	—	20	—	20	
						20.0

SRS ___180.0___

Note:
1st Order SRS (Range = 20 to 60) = DRS(1) = 38.0
2nd Order SRS (Range = 100 to 300) = SRS = 180.0

Table 4.3 **DIMENSION RISK SCORES AND SYSTEM RISK
SCORES FOR AIS 2**

Application Name	Rating	% Review This Period	Adjusted Rating	% Total of all Ratings	Review Days

Figure 4.3 **ALLOCATING REVIEW TIME BY APPLICATION WORKSHEET**

Application Name	Rating	% Review This Period	Adjusted Rating	% Total of all Ratings	Review Days
FIRST	90	60%	54	27%	40.5
SECOND	80	40%	32	16%	24
THIRD	70	20%	14	7%	10.5
FOURTH	60	100%	60	30%	45
FIFTH	50	80%	40	20%	30

Figure 4.4 **ALLOCATING REVIEW TIME BY APPLICATION WORKSHEET**

Chapter 5
QUALITY ASSURANCE REVIEW OF AN APPLICATION SYSTEM

This chapter will examine what QA should do when reviewing an application. The "what" will be subdivided into goals, methods, and performance. In order to appreciate system problems, we will examine the reasons why some data processing applications are not successful.

The QA group is an aid to the data processing manager in solving the business problems of the organization. This objective must remain paramount as it performs its tasks. The QA group should undertake its review by a top-down approach, starting with management considerations: First, will the goals of the system solve the business problem? Second, are the methods in accordance with the organization's method of doing work? And third, will the data processing tasks be performed at a reasonable cost? The review approach is supportive of evaluating these three management considerations.

It is because quality assurance groups in different organizations perform different tasks, that this chapter discusses goals, methods, and performance independently. Most groups begin evaluating methods. It is only after they have achieved this successfully that they expand to review of goals and performance.

REVIEWING COMPUTER SYSTEMS APPLICATIONS

The QA review is a peer group activity. This means the project manager is reviewed by other project managers. The reviewers may be organizationally in a QA group, but they are part of the data processing department. Frequently the reviewers are good friends of the individuals being reviewed.   The context and framework of the review must be taken from this perspective. The questions and procedures undertaken in the review must be fair, approved by supervisors, and in the best interest of the project being reviewed.

The QA group should have established a charter prior to undertaking reviews. The object of the charter is to define the scope of work undertaken during the review. The scope can involve goals, methods, and performance.

The easiest way to begin the QA function is to review methods. However, keep in mind that the objective of a computerized application is to solve a business problem. Even the best designed computer system in the world, developed exactly in accordance with the organization's methods of doing work, is a failure if it doesn't solve the business problem.

The business problem must be analyzed from the viewpoint of the user. Listed below are examples of typical business problems in four industries.

Banks. Should the bank make a loan to a specific individual and for what purposes?

Insurance. Is an individual insurable for the coverage being requested?

Retail. Should a customer be extended the amount of credit being requested?

Government. Is a recipient eligible for the service being requested?

It is apparent that these are not computer problems; they are business problems. The computer may or may not be utilized in solving a business problem. Too frequently,computer systems personnel come to believe that all business problems can be solved with the computer. This leads us back to the three areas of quality assurance illustrated in Figure 5.1.

The goals of a system should be aimed at solving a specific business problem. If QA is involved in goal review, then it needs to seriously consider whether or not the computer is the best mechanism to solve the business problem. The QA group normally becomes involved when the computer is being considered as an aid or solution to the business problem. In these cases, its function is to determine if the computer can assist in solving the business problem.

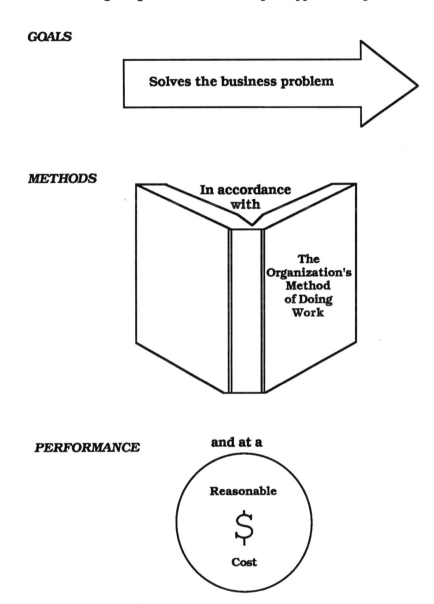

GOALS

Solves the business problem

METHODS

In accordance with

The Organization's Method of Doing Work

PERFORMANCE

and at a

Reasonable

$

Cost

Figure 5.1 **QUALITY ASSURANCE AREAS**

The main thrust of the review will be to determine that the methods utilized in the computer system are in compliance with the organization's methods. This includes all the policies and procedures (standards) of the organization that affect the application under review. They need to consider the policies and procedures of the area being computerized as well as methods of the data processing department. For example, if the system being computerized is a bank's demand deposit system, the rules within the application should be consistent with the demand deposit department's policies and procedures, and consistent with banking regulations.

Some groups become involved in performance. Quality assurance personnel are employees of the organization and should be concerned with the overall well-being of the organization. Even where performance is not an integral part of their function, they should be alert to gross negligence, sloppy work, and poor performance. Obviously, a cursory review does not entail a performance review but, rather, a broad judgment between good and bad performance. The quality assurance reviewer has an obligation to make data processing management aware of poor performance. This may be done formally or informally, but it should be done. A detailed performance review is a complete and time-consuming task.

Companies that have adopted the team approach to design and programming have found that poor performance by an individual is usually detected early by the team.

SYSTEMS FAILURES

Many data processing departments prominently display the motto "If you must make a mistake, make a new one." This indicates that most people can accept mistakes the first time, but lose their tolerance if the same error is repeated. People who progress in organizations tend to learn from their own and others' failures. Failing to meet an objective or a goal can be a very frustrating but good educational experience.

Prior to commencing the discussion on how to review computer applications, let us first learn from the mistakes of others. An analysis of the literature on data processing over the past 20 years provides us some insight as to why systems have failed. It would be nicer to reverse this and discuss the traits that make systems succeed, but it is more difficult to isolate a specific success characteristic.

We will examine systems failures by categorizing them three ways: first, the reasons why systems failed to meet their goals; second, the reasons why project teams failed because of inadequate or unused methods; and third, reasons why systems failed to meet a desired level of performance. These should be studied and referred to continually as the QA group becomes involved in the review of a new application system.

Reasons for Failure to Achieve Goals

The system goal is to solve the business problem. Listed in Figure 5.2 and briefly explained below, are actual reasons why organizations failed to achieve their goals:

Lack of Knowledge by Users about Computer Capabilities and Limitations. Users know what is needed to solve their business problems, but frequently do not know whether those problems can be solved on the computer. In instances where they make unrealistic demands for computer systems, or fail to use the power of the computer, the installed application never realizes the potential possible when the user has a good comprehension of computer capabilities.

Computer Personnel Specify the System. Computer personnel neither have the responsibility for the accuracy and completeness of the processing by the system, nor an understanding as to what is needed to make the system successful. Unfortunately, many users abdicate their systems specification responsibility. Computer personnel tend to specify systems that work well on the computer, but may not be easy to set in practice. Frequently, these systems are overengineered for the caliber of people using the system in the performance of their daily work.

User's Fear of Loss of Control of the System to EDP Department. The user and the EDP department may develop adversary positions, particularly when the computer application encompasses the work of two or more departments. When users feel that the implementation of the system may result in a loss of responsibility or power to the data processing department, their objectivity and desire for success may be lost.

Lack of Interest by User Management. Without interest by user management, user personnel may not devote the necessary time and effort to making the system successful. If those responsible for the system detect a lackluster attitude by their management toward the system, it may lessen their desire to make the system successful.

Lack of Interest by Company Management. Top management lack of interest makes the implementation priority questionable. Either or both the user and data processing department may decide to let this system slide in lieu of other projects for which there is more management interest. The lack of motivation that results from lack of interest by user management occurs on the part of all involved when top management lacks interest.

Unwillingness to Accept Responsibility for the System Because It Belongs to the Other Guy. The "It's not my system" syndrome is a major cause of system failure. This was especially true in the early days of data processing when users assumed data processing to be responsible, and data processing assumed the user to be responsible. In many of these cases, the wrong person (the programmer) made systems decisions. This is one of the primary reasons current literature emphasizes the need for user involvement and responsibility.

SYSTEM GOAL: Solve the business problem.

Causes of Goal Failures:

- Lack of knowledge by users about computer capabilities and limitations
- Computer personnel specify the system
- User's fear of loss of control of the system to EDP department
- Lack of interest by user management
- Lack of interest by company management
- Unwillingness to accept responsibility for the system because it belongs to the "other guy"
- Organizational disputes over responsibilities
- Wrong application being developed
- No long-range systems plan

Figure 5.2 **SYSTEMS FAILURES — GOALS**

Organizational Disputes over Responsibilities. Many systems encompass the work and responsibilities of two or more departments. When these functions become consolidated into one system, it may be difficult to pinpoint organizational responsibility. Either both departments may feel responsible for a particular function, or neither department may assume responsibility. Top management should step in and resolve these organizational responsibility disputes as early as possible in systems development process.

Wrong Application Being Developed. Many times the application being developed does not solve the business problem. It provides interesting information, information that may be helpful, and even information that is useful, but not at the proper time or in the proper format. For example, if the business problem is to determine whether or not an individual is insurable, but the data processing system does not contain the necessary attributes to make that decision, it has not been successful at solving the business problem.

No Long-Range Systems Plan. The objective of a systems plan is to make sure all the individual applications will fit together when complete. Without such a plan, there is no assurance that when the applications become operational, they will properly interconnect. For example, if a personnel system and a payroll system are developed independently at different times, they may collect data in different formats. When a decision is made to have the personnel system feed the payroll system, the data may be unexchangeable due to different formats, lengths, etc.

System Failures — Methods

The objective of reviewing system methods is to determine that the implementation confirms to the organization's policies and procedures. These policies and procedures ideally would be interpreted into standards. The causes of systems failures due to improper methods are listed in Figure 5.3 and briefly explained below.

Lack of Involvement by Users. Most organizations define responsibility by function. When users having responsibility for a function relinquish that responsibility to the data processing department, they are failing to follow the policies of their management. Top management has designated them responsible, and while they can delegate work they cannot delegate responsibility to the data processing department. This means users must be involved in the development of systems affecting their responsibility. Many organizations require by directive that users participate in the development of systems affecting their responsibility. Lack of involvement by users in systems development has frequently been called the number one cause of system failures.

Inadequate Planning. Speakers at many conferences on data processing joke that when you want to know what a system will cost you multiply the system development estimates by a factor. The only real discussion centers on whether the factor should be 3, 4, 5, etc. While many data processing managers try to substantiate their poor estimates by explaining that the product is custom made, the technology unknown, and the specifications changing, their arguments are unacceptable. The real cause is the lack of adequate planning. Planning may not produce exact costs in advance but will provide the criteria to advise management as soon as problems occur that can affect cost.

SYSTEM METHOD: Implementation conforms to the organization's policies and procedures (standards)

Causes of Methods Failures:

- Lack of involvement by users
- Inadequate planning
- Inadequate design
- Inadequate programming
- Inadequate testing
- Management unwillingness to enforce standards
- Lack of security
- Chaotic conversion

Figure 5.3 **SYSTEMS FAILURES — METHODS**

Inadequate Design. Systems analysts tend to overestimate their own abilities to solve problems at the later stages of systems development. This leads them to start programming prior to finalizing program specifications. The argument is that implementation can be facilitated, but practice has shown just the opposite. The structured top-down design approach places more attention on the design process and helps solve the problem of programming first and designing later.

Inadequate Programming. Programmers have argued that their work is an art and that to restrict them to standard programming methods lessens their creativity and performance. These arguments lead to situations in which the program logic and maintainability is dependent upon the continual employment of the programmer. Many organizations have found it easier to rewrite such programs than to understand and modify them. The use and enforcement of structured programming techniques will greatly enhance the maintainability of programs.

Inadequate Testing. Since it is impossible to test every possible condition that may be encountered in operation, testing is at best a risk situation. Also, testing is not one of the more rewarding aspects of a programmer's work. It is tedious, time consuming, and unenjoyable. Therefore, unless adequate criteria are developed to determine when a system is acceptable, this phase tends to be cut short.

Management's Unwillingness to Enforce Standards. Data processing is extremely detailed. Effective standards likewise must be detailed, and enforcement requires some detection mechanism to know when standards are not being followed. If the mechanism is ineffective, or too late in the implementation process, management may be put in a difficult position of paying to redo work to conform to standards. Coupling these factors, many data processing managers are unwilling to "bite the bullet" and enforce standards regardless of the time and effort required.

Lack of Security. Far more than keeping unauthorized personnel from the computer room, security also involves the protection of input and output data. This protection is equally necessary against honest mistakes, incompetence, negligence, lack of interest, and other similar problems on the part of employees. Failure to protect information and programs has resulted in serious problems for many organizations.

Chaotic Conversion. Detailed planning is necessary if conversions are to be properly executed. Most analysts have little experience in this systems phase. Without adequate planning and control, a series of unexpected and time-consuming problems may develop resulting in the need for special programming, extra computer time, overtime operations, and all the other things one hopes will not happen just prior to a new system going operational.

Systems Failures — Performance

The objective of systems performance review is to determine that the system is implemented and operated at a reasonable cost. Causes of systems performance failures are listed in Figure 5.4 and explained briefly below.

Ambitions of Systems and User Personnel. Systems and user personnel may design applications more for their own personal whim and desires than for the organization's needs. For example, systems personnel may utilize a new hardware concept, such as on-line terminals, even though the application does not warrant the hardware. By manipulation of costs and schedules, however, the data processing professionals are able to justify the system.

SYSTEM PERFORMANCE: System is implemented and operated at a reasonable cost.

Causes of Performance Failures:

- Ambitions of systems and user personnel
- Human resistance to change
- Inadequate performance measurements
- Operating managers do not use the information generated by the computer
- High turnover of systems personnel
- Inadequate quality of systems design and project management
- Computer system over designed
- Manual support systems are underdesigned
- System provides too much information
- Late implementation
- Cost overruns
- Frequent changes of computer hardware and software
- Inflexible systems design
- Too many changes during the design process

Figure 5.4 **SYSTEM FAILURES — PERFORMANCE**

Human Resistance to Change. There is a natural resistance to change by all people. This fact needs to be recognized and people reassured by explaining the reasons for the change and how they will be affected personally. The more that can be done to prepare people for the change, the higher the probability of success of the system.

Inadequate Performance Measurements. Unless management has developed adequate criteria, it is difficult to measure performance. Without being able to measure performance, management has little idea if and when the system is achieving even a minimal level of performance.

Operating Managers Do Not Use the Information Generated by the Computer. In the majority of computer system problems, the data to detect the problem were produced by the computer application but not acted upon by user personnel. Although this can be attributable to many causes, the fact remains that either the instructions and training were insufficient or users devoted too little time or interest. Ascertaining that error notification is causing some reaction should be made an integral part of first-line supervision's responsibility.

High Turnover of Systems Personnel. Because of the technical nature of data processing, and the extensive company background needed to develop an application, high turnover of systems personnel places any development project in jeopardy. Selection of systems personnel should take into account the stability of employment within an organization.

Computer System Overdesigned. Systems must be used by people. If the system is too complex for the mental capacity of the people who are using it, the system has problems. All systems design should take into account the caliber of personnel who will be putting data into the system and using data from the system.

Manual Support Systems Are Underdesigned. Too frequently, computer systems personnel put insufficient time and effort into the manual support systems. These include training, control, data reporting, authorization, and use of warning information produced by the system.

System Provides Too Much Information. We have all seen huge stacks of paper produced by high-speed printers. If people must have certain information to perform their function correctly, it should not be difficult for them to obtain that information from computer reports. It is essential that information be presented in a format where it is easy to locate, and in a visible format.

Late Implementation. Processing rules should be frozen during the latter parts of systems implementation; changes during the testing phase make evaluation of the system difficult. When a system implementation falls far behind scheduled implementation date, people lose interest and faith in the system. Also, continually changing conditions make it difficult to keep a system frozen for very long. Late implementation adds to the failure rate of systems.

Cost Overruns. Substantial cost overruns lessen management's faith in the project team. This loss of faith can magnify what otherwise might be minor problems in the system. However, "substantial cost overruns" may suggest existence of more than minor problems.

Frequent Changes of Computer Hardware and Software. Each change to system hardware and software has an effect on an application under development. Even where there is not a direct effect on the system (i.e., change in operating system version), there can be a ripple effect. Problems encountered with hardware and software changes can delay system implementation.

Inflexible Systems Design. Application systems in most organizations operate under a changing environment throughout the system life. The less flexible the system, the less it is able to incorporate changes necessitated by business conditions. When the series of items that cannot be incorporated into the system exceeds a certain level, the application must be replaced by a new system.

Too Many Changes During a Design Process. The system design is normally structured around and optimized for certain business characteristics (volume of business, for example). When business characteristics or the systems designers fail to recognize which business characteristics are pertinent, the design specifications must be changed. Should the number of changes become great enough, the system structure may no longer be effective. Also, when changes get too frequent, both the cost of the system and the implementation date may exceed expectations. This, in turn, causes other problems that can lead to the downfall of the system.

Top-Down Review

A systems review must begin at the highest level and work down to the lowest level. This is called a *top-down review* and its initial objective is to determine if the application system will solve the business problems according to the methods of the organization and at a reasonable cost. Without a top-down approach, the review may lose sight of that objective.

A top-down review by QA asks: What are the goals of the system? What methods need to be followed during implementation? And what level of performance is expected? Only after answers to these questions have been established should the review get into the details of systems design and programming. The review begins with a very broad scope, and then works its way down to lower and lower levels of detail.

The top-down review methodology outlined in Figure 5.5 shows each level splitting into the components it comprises. Level 1 items include reviewing, meeting goals, using methods, and achieving a reasonable level of performance. Each level 1 subdivides into a series of level 2 areas of review. In Figure 5.5 only level 1 of methods shows this breakdown, but in reality each level 1 is further divided into a group of level 2s. Each level 2, then, is further subdivided into a series of level 3 items. Thus, if we were to see Figure 5.5 broken out for each level 2 and level 3, it would be an extremely complex chart.

Level 1 of the top-down review is a very broad review of an evaluation area. This, in turn, is supported by a lower (level 2) review, which focuses on the implementation approach. The level 2 gets more specific in further subdefining what is meant by the area under review. For example, if we are reviewing methods (level 1), level 2 will involve a specific approach, such as standards for the system design phase. The third level goes into still more detail. In a review of methods, the third level review would determine if the systems designers understood the systems design standards.

Let us see how a top-down approach could be used in a court to interrogate a witness. A prosecutor is trying to establish a witness's presence at the scene of a crime. She begins by a general (level 1) question asking if anything unusual occurred on a specific date. If the witness says yes, the prosecutor proceeds to (level 2) questioning, which should lead to the location at which something occurred. The questioning would then proceed to level 3, which would get very specific about what the witness saw and heard at the location where the crime occurred. This is not to liken a computer system review to a criminal case but, rather, to illustrate that the most effective review techniques begin at the general and work down to the specific.

The remaining parts of this chapter will explain these three areas in detail. Keep in mind that this chapter is talking about "what" should be accomplished in the review. "How" the review is accomplished will be covered in Chapter 7.

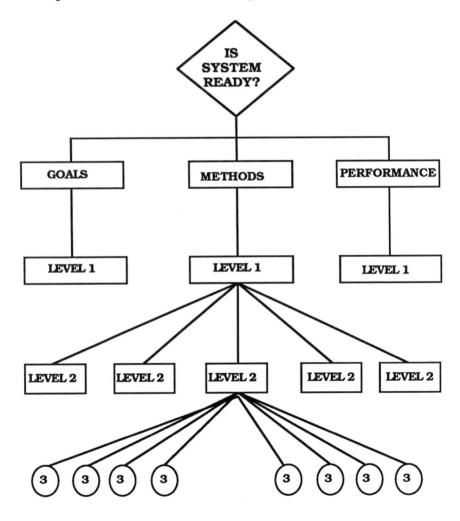

Figure 5.5 **TOP-DOWN REVIEW**

REVIEW OF GOALS

A review of systems application goals is the most valuable contribution that a QA group can make, but it may also be the most difficult work the group has to do. QA cannot establish goals. If goals are not clearly stated, QA cannot determine if they are or can be met. Thus, QA is not an all-powerful group evaluating the performance of the project team. What they are doing is reviewing whether or not preestablished goals have been met. The review items for goals are listed in Figure 5.6.

Level 1

Level 1 items for review are the broad system problems to be solved. An example previously used was ascertaining whether or not an individual is insurable. This is, perhaps, only one of the many business problems that would be solved in a systems application by an insurance company.

Each level 1 goal needs to be further reviewed by four level 2 items. Again, goal review is not meant to usurp the authority of the data processing project manager. It is intended to review what the project team is doing to ascertain that its plans are in accordance with the goals given to that project team. The four level 2 items are:

System Goals Are Realistic. This item determines that the goal is a realistic (i.e, achievable) goal for the systems designer. For example, the system's being able to answer the question "Is individual X insurable?" appears to be a realistic goal for a computer application. The quality assurance group would have to determine that there is enough quantitative data to be evaluated to ascertain if an individual is insurable. However, should the goal be to accept only good risks, and there are neither adequate rules nor enough quantitative data to define a good risk, the goal could be easily determined to be unachievable. We could define an achievable goal as one that can be accomplished with the data and rules available.

System Goals Are Achievable. The established goals should be achievable with the existing technology and resources. For example, if the system goal is to put 500 terminals on-line with an average response time of one second or less, and a maximum response time of five seconds, the QA group could readily determine if this was achievable for their organization.

Level 1

- Solves the business problem.

Level 2

- System goals are realistic.
- System goals are achievable.
- System goals are compatible with the goals of the organization.
- System goals are compatible with the goals of the user.

Level 3

- Business problem solution is compatible with system goals.
- Users can comprehend and use the system.
- User personnel want the system.
- Adequate resources are available to implement the system.
- System will be ready when needed.
- System will have a reasonable lifespan.
- Implemented system can run with existing technology for a reasonable period.
- System technology is understood by the organization.
- A plan exists to meet goals.
- Goals are achieved.

Figure 5.6 **REVIEW OF GOALS**

System Goals Are Compatible with the Goals of the Organization. This presupposes that the goals of the organization are documented. The goals of any one application system must be subservient to the goals of the organization. For example, if a goal of an organization is to compete without the use of bribes and kickbacks, then a system goal that allows for bribes and kickbacks is incompatible with the goals of the organization.

System Goals Are Compatible with the Goals of the User. The goals of the application and the goals of the user should be compatible. For example, if the user has the goal of shipping product within 24 hours after the receipt of the order, the system should be supportive of that goal. To design a system that takes more than 24 hours to process the paperwork before an order can be shipped would be incompatible with the desires of the user. Data processing personnel often make decisions affecting user goals without considering the impact of those decisions on the goal.

The third level of review is also aimed at reviewing documented established goals. It cannot be overemphasized that quality assurance is reviewing conformance to previously established criteria and statements. The more measurable those goals, statements, or criteria, the more successful quality assurance can be in the performance of its goal review function. The more subjective the judgment that has to be made by quality assurance, the more difficult the task. Bear in mind that the quality assurance function is a type of peer group review. The more objective the review, the better will be the working relationship with data processing personnel. Data processing management should want very specific systems goals, and where they exist quality assurance can do an effective job in reviewing conformance to those goals.

Each level 2 item can be further subdivided by a series of level 3 items. Let us first discuss the level 3 items and then show how they relate to the level 2 items. The level 3 items are as follows.

Business Problem Solution Is Compatible with System Goals. The project team has the task of developing a system that will solve the business problem. This is the goal of the system. The quality assurance group should look at this solution from the viewpoint of whether it does or does not solve the business problem.

Users Can Comprehend and Use the System. The solution to the business problem should be at a level comprehensible by the users of the system. The rules of the system must not be so complex that the people who have to work with them cannot understand them. Also, the data and results produced by the system should be readily understandable and usable by the users of the system. The system must not produce results that require higher competency than is available. The information in the system must be organized and presented in such a format that it is readily usable for the intended purpose.

User Personnel Want the System. The system as explained to the user is well received by the user. In other words, the user is not fighting the implementation of the system as proposed.

Adequate Resources Are Available to Implement the System. Resources refers to hardware and software, quantity of people and dollars, as well as caliber of personnel.

System Will Be Ready When Needed. The schedules as proposed are realistic within the resource constraints. The quality assurance group should also go one step further and see that the dates proposed for implementation are compatible with the needs of the user for that system.

System Will Have a Reasonable Lifespan. Based on the QA group's understanding of technology and the plans of the data processing department, the proposed system will have a life equivalent to that proposed when the project was approved by management.

Implemented System Can Run with Existing Technology for a Reasonable Period. The quality assurance group should have an appreciation of both the technological improvements in hardware and software and the plans of the organization to utilize that technology. These considerations need to be raised and evaluated by the QA group if the project team has not already contemplated these events.

System Technology Is Understood by the Organization. Technology in this instance refers primarily to that used by the system designers and programmers. If they are unfamiliar with the technology used in this application, the project is in jeopardy.

A Plan Exists to Meet Goals. In the early phases of the system development process, QA needs to examine the plan for achieving the goals. While the other items are the criteria to be included in the plan, they are not the plan itself.

Goals Are Achieved. Prior to implementation, the QA group should ascertain that the goals are actually achieved.

As you study the three levels of system review, keep in mind that each has a different impact on the project. Level 1 discusses the area itself. For example, in reviewing goals, level 1 is specific project goals. If the application has 15 goals, then there are 15 level 1 items to be covered by the QA. Level 2 discusses the approach taken by the project team for each of the level 1 items. The QA group can now begin to subdivide each goal into its review components for purposes of analysis. The level 2 questions are further subdivided by level 3 items. Some level 3 items listed in Figure 5.6 are more appropriate than others.

The Goals Evaluation Matrix (Figure 5.7) shows the relationship between level 2 items and level 3 items. The level 2 items are listed across the top and the level 3 items down the left-hand side of the matrix. The legend of the matrix shows how appropriate each level 3 item is to the level 2 items.

Examining Figure 5.7 we see the first level 3 item (Business problem solution is compatible with system goals.) is appropriate to whether the goal is realistic. A number "2" in the "realistic" column states that it is appropriate. In other words, a "realistic" goal should be compatible with the business problem solution. Thus, a number "2" in the "realistic" column indicates appropriateness of the level 2 item to the level 3 item.

On the other hand, for the goal to be achievable, it does not have to be compatible with the business problem solution. Thus, the "achievable" column is noted as inappropriate or a number "1" in the "achievable" column. However, the business problem solution must be compatible with systems goals for the level 2 items of "compatible with user goals." Each of these two are marked with a number "3" showing a very appropriate item.

Using Figure 5.6 and Figure 5.7, the QA group should be able to determine what it should accomplish in reviewing application goals.

REVIEW OF METHODS

The main part of any review will be the review of methods. (See Figure 5.8.) The one task almost universally requested of QA groups is to provide assurance that policies, procedures, and standards are being followed. This is a detailed and time-consuming but essential task.

In the case of methods, level 1 review has a single item. Project implementation conforms to the organization's policies and procedures. These policies and procedures should be incorporated into standards. Here again, as with its review goals, the quality assurance group needs objective items for review. When data processing management has adequately instructed

GOALS / REVIEW CRITERIA	Realistic	Achievable	Compatible with organization goals	Compatible with user goals	
1. Business problems is compatible with systems goals.	2	1	3	3	
2. Users can comprehend and use the system.	3	2	2	3	
3. User personnel want the system.	2	2	1	3	
4. Adequate resources available to implement the system.	3	3	1	1	
5. System will be developed when needed	3	3	3	3	
6. System will have a reasonable life.	3	1	3	3	
7. Implemented system can run with existing technology for a reasonable period.	3	1	3	3	
8. System technology is understood by the organization.	2	2	2	2	
9. A plan exists to meet goals.	3	3	3	3	
10. Goals are achieved.	2	3	3	3	

Legend:
3 = very appropriate
2 = appropriate
1 = unappropriate

Figure 5.7 **GOALS EVALUATION MATRIX**

personnel in the methods they are to utilize, adherence to those standards may be reviewed. On the other hand, if the quality assurance group is being asked to act as both judge and jury (to develop standards for each application and then review adherence to those standards), its function will be argumentative and probably ineffective.

Level 1

- Implementation conforms to the organization's policies and procedures (standards).

Level 2

- Conforms to system justification standards.
- Conforms to system design standards.
- Conforms to system program standards.
- Conforms to system test standards.
- Conforms to system conversion standards.

Level 3

- Standards are realistic for this system.
- An adequate plan is developed and followed for implementing the standards.
- The designers understand the standards.
- The standards will be in effect when the system becomes operational.
- System standards do not conflict with organization, industry, or government standards.
- Procedures are taken to assure that standards will be followed.
- Users are trained to use the system.
- System is adequately documented.

Figure 5.8 **REVIEW OF METHODS**

Level 2 items are divided among the phases of the systems development life cycle. Each of the five phases of the system development life cycle of interest to quality assurance is a level 2 item.

1. *Conforms to system justification standards.* The standards developed for the feasibility or justification phase have been or will be followed.

2. *Conforms to system design standards.* The policies and procedures of the department relating to specification of the system have been or will be followed.

3. *Conforms to system program standards.* The method by which programmers must specify and code programs has or will be followed.

4. *Conforms to system test standards.* The methods and extent to which systems and programs are to be tested have been or will be followed.

5. *Conforms to system conversion standards.* All the procedures to be followed in the conversion process have been or will be followed.

Level 3 takes on more importance in methods review because it is within level 3 that the review gets specific. Moreover, the level 3 items for a methods review apply to most of the level 2 items. In the review of methods, there are nine level 3 items, which are briefly explained below:

Standards Are Realistic for This System. Just as a law does not apply in every situation, neither does a standard. Both the project team and the review group must take a realistic approach to the application of standards. If following a standard would be detrimental to the system and not following the standard would not incur any present or future hardship on others, procedures should be available to get an exception from the standard. In many organizations, QA has the authority to waive the standard for a particular situation.

An Adequate Plan Is Developed and Followed for Implementing the Standards. People tend to do what they are instructed and that on which they are evaluated. If the project team considers following standards important to the project, standards probably will be followed. This can be made even more likely by having data processing management use adherence to standards as a criterion for review of project members.

Most Data Processing Departments Have High Personnel Turnover. This means that new members to the department must be continually instructed in the use of standards. Also, in the course of their assignments, members of the project team may come in contact with specific standards only infrequently and irregularly. Thus, an important part of the review process is to determine that the standards are known and understood by the project team.

The Standards Will Be in Effect When the System Becomes Operational. Changes to hardware, software, and implementation methodology necessitate a continual revision to standards. If a project is being developed today, and a new set of standards will be in place when the system becomes operational, the project team must work with the new standards.

Systems Standards Do Not Conflict with Organization, Industry, or Government Standards. The QA group cannot be expected to be "all knowing." However, they do have an obligation to ask questions that would indicate any potential conflict between data processing standards and other standards. This conflict might have occurred after the data processing standards were developed, or the standards may have been developed in ignorance of other standards. In either case the QA group has an obligation to be alert to trends in the literature, trade press, and organization publications regarding potential conflicts.

Procedures Are Available to Assure That Standards Will Be Followed. QA cannot be expected to look at every line of code or documentation to determine that every standard was followed. They should ascertain that the project team, through project supervision, will be performing this type of review. This then permits the quality assurance group either to evaluate only that plan or make a few tests to determine if the plan is functioning as developed.

Users Are Trained to Use the System. "Users" in this context include personnel in data processing control, operations, and input preparation, as well as the users of the system and data.

System Is Adequately Documented. Documentation requirements cover all phases of the system development life cycle. The quality assurance group requires documentation for their review;

and second, and more important, documentation is needed to protect the organization when systems problems occur.

An organization with inadequate documentation is perhaps most vulnerable during the systems development phase. Without adequate documentation, loss of one or two key people at that time can necessitate the system being completely redesigned. Once the system becomes operational, there is at least enough documentation so that the system can be run. However, during the development phase, many of the ideas approaches are within people's minds.

Figure 5.9 shows the interrelationship between the level 2 and level 3 items for methods review. Note the appropriateness of most level 3 items to the level 2 items.

REVIEW OF PERFORMANCE

The review of performance implies that there are established measurable levels of performance. Again, QA cannot be asked to be both judge and jury; it cannot be asked to establish levels of performance for each project and then review adherence to those levels of performance. What it can do is review adherence to predetermined criteria or levels of performance.

Many approaches can be taken to performance review. The level 1 criterion suggests that a realistic performance expectation is that the system is being implemented and operated at a reasonable cost. What the department or organization considers reasonable should be documented in performance standards.

Members of QA may participate in the setting of performance standards, and when this is done on department wide, it is a good assignment for them. They can still review all projects against those performance standards and not be criticized for bias against one project. It is important to emphasize that in a peer group situation the review must be made in accordance to well recognized and previously determined standards.

For review of performance, there are five level 2 items. These, plus the level 1 and level 3 items, are listed in Figure 5.10. The level 2 items are outlined below.

System Is Cost-Effective. The key element in this is that the system does the job well. It may be more costly than other means of doing the job, but in total it is more effective because of considerations such as time, customer service, or ease of use.

System Optimizes People and Machines. A total system is a combination of people effort and machine effort. The system should utilize people for what they do best and machines for what they do best. Obviously, you do not want to stop a computerized run for a small piece that can be better performed by people than machines. However, in the general context of the system, extremely cumbersome and complex routines should not be developed if that function can be readily performed by people without interruption to the system flow.

System Optimizes Hardware and Software. This is a design function focused on getting software to maximize hardware usage. On the other hand, another piece of hardware may be required to maximize a particular software package. This is a technical aspect of system design, but one that requires attention.

System Meets System Criteria. It has been said that nothing is more futile than to do a job well if the job need not be done at all. If the system does not solve the business problems, performance is irrelevant.

System Conversion Is Economical. One must not underestimate the impact of a system conversion. Many major problems have occurred in organizations because they underestimated the importance of performing the conversion well. The conversion process is a system within a system and must be so performed.

There are 10 level 3 items for review of performance. Consider as you review these that there is a continual conflict between effectiveness and economy, hardware and software utilization, and people versus machine utilization. The ideal system optimizes the tradeoffs needed to resolve each of these conflicts. The level 3 items are explained briefly below:

Standards of Performance Have Been Established. Performance cannot be evaluated unless standards of performance have been established and the people involved understand the level of performance expected of them. Performance frequently is a tradeoff between resources, time, abilities, etc. Therefore, to achieve a level of performance, the system designer must recognize these tradeoffs and work them to his advantage.

People Know What Level of Performance Is Expected. An important aspect of quality is advising people what is expected from

REVIEW CRITERIA \ GOALS	System is in conformance with					
	Justification Standards	Design Standards	Program Standards	Test Standards	Convert Standards	
1. Standards are realistic for this system.	3	3	3	3	3	
2. An adequate plan is developed and followed for implementing the standards.	3	3	3	3	3	
3. The designers understand the standards.	3	3	3	3	3	
4. The standards will be in effect when the system becomes operational.	1	2	3	1	1	
5. System standards do not conflict with organization, industry, or government standards.	3	3	3	3	3	
6. Procedures are taken to assure that standards will be followed.	3	3	3	3	3	
7. Users are trained to use the system.	1	1	1	1	1	
8. System is adequately documented.	2	3	3	2	2	

Legend:
3 = very appropriate
2 = appropriate
1 = unappropriate

Figure 5.9 **METHODS EVALUATION MATRIX**

Level 1

- System is implemented and operated at a reasonable cost.

Level 2

- System is cost-effective.
- System optimizes people and machines.
- System meets system criteria.
- System conversion is economical.

Level 3

- Standards of performance have been established.
- People know what level of performance is expected.
- Criteria are established to evaluate performance.
- Meeting performance levels will result in rewards for individuals.
- Schedules have been established.
- Budgets have been developed.
- Support systems are evaluated.
- Users are pleased with system performance.
- Design is changed frequently during design phase.
- System optimization alternatives are evaluated.

Figure 5.10 **REVIEW OF PERFORMANCE**

them. Quality is achieved by specifying quality, telling people what is expected from them, and then monitoring to be assured the expected level of quality was achieved.

Criteria Are Established to Evaluate Performance. The standards of performance must be interpreted into criteria for each specific system. These then become the level of performance the system designer tries to achieve or exceed.

Meeting Performance Levels Will Result in Rewards for Individuals. If the only criteria for evaluating project personnel is getting the system in on time and within budget, then performance will be secondary. If, on the other hand, performance is considered important, people must be evaluated and rewarded for meeting or exceeding expected levels of performance.

Schedules Have Been Established. Schedules are a category of performance in that it is an objective for the system designer to achieve.

Budgets Have Been Developed. Budgets, like schedules, are a level of performance which the system designer must meet.

Support Systems Are Evaluated. The performance of the computerized portion of a system must not degrade the performance of the total system. It is necessary to look at the total system, the computerized segment plus all the support segments. In evaluating performance, the total system needs to be considered.

Users Are Pleased with Systems Performance. There are many subtleties to be considered in performance which are difficult to quantify. One subjective judgment that should be considered is user evaluation of performance.

Design Is Changed Frequently During Design Phase. The project team should be evaluated on performing the project's tasks in an economical and effective manner. If the team's approach and plans are continually changing direction, performance must be judged as poor.

System Optimization Alternatives Are Evaluated. Effectiveness and efficiency, even with standards, can be difficult to review. Quality assurance can review adherence to standards, but cannot review whether all alternatives have been adequately evaluated. Thus, a quality assurance group has to assume the project team has considered alternatives and picked a reasonable one to implement.

The relationship between the level 2 and level 3 performance items is given in Figure 5.11. A review of this matrix begins to show some of the differences between effectiveness and economy, and optimization of people and machines, and optimization of hardware and software.

SUMMARY

In reviewing applications, the quality assurance group can consider goals, methods, and performance. Whether they review each area or some combination, this is basically a review of adherence

GOALS / REVIEW CRITERIA	System cost-effective	Optimizes people and machines	Optimizes hardware and software	Meets system criteria	Coversion economical	
1. Standards of performance have been established.	3	1	1	3	3	
2. People know what level of performance is expected.	3	1	1	3	3	
3. Criteria is established to evaluate performance.	3	3	3	3	3	
4. Meeting performance level will result in rewards for individuals.	3	3	3	3	3	
5. Schedules have been established.	3	1	1	1	3	
6. Budgets have been developed.	3	1	1	1	2	
7. Support systems are evaluated.	1	1	1	3	2	
8. Users pleased with system performance.	2	3	1	3	1	
9. Design is changed frequently during design phase.	3	3	3	3	3	
10. System optimization alternatives evaluated.	2	3	3	1	2	

Legend:
3 = very appropriate
2 = appropriate
1 = unappropriate

Figure 5.11 **PERFORMANCE EVALUATION MATRIX**

or conformance to the policies and procedures of the organization. The data processing policies and procedures must be put in

144 Effective Methods of EDP Quality Assurance

perspective with those of the entire organization. The group must also determine that the policies and procedures are reasonable and applicable to the particular application being reviewed.

The application review should be done with a top-down approach. The end result of the review is to advise the data processing manager whether to implement the application. This advice will be based on a review of such items as efficiency, economy, proper systems design, whether or not the application solves the business problems, and other factors. The top-down review approach never loses sight of the reason for undertaking the review. In other words, the means never become more important than the end.

This chapter was designed to explain "what" QA should accomplish during the review of an application. A three-level review was suggested. The first level is very broad, and related to the objectives of the review. A second level is oriented toward reviewing the approach taken by the project team to achieve its goals and objectives. The third level deals with the design and implementation of the computer system.

In this approach, levels 1 and 2 are oriented to whether or not the business problems were solved. The third level examines the implementation to the problem, which is the computerized application.

Part III

QUALITY ASSURANCE REVIEWS

Chapter 6
INITIATING SYSTEMS REVIEW

Quality assurance groups should develop a plan for utilizing their resources each year (or more frequently). The plan should identify which computer application projects will be reviewed during the planning period and must be compatible with the data processing department's plan. When changes occur in the data processing department plan, the QA plan should be modified accordingly.

The initiation of a review is important because it establishes the ground rules and sets tone of the review. Work must be completed prior to the review. This preparatory work encompasses gaining an understanding of the system and its implementation plan, determining at which point(s) in the development process reviews should be made, and developing the plan and staffing necessary to accomplish those reviews. Time expended in planning will result in a more efficient and effective review.

The review of an application begins with an entrance conference that provides an opportunity for members of the project team and the QA group to get to know one another and to discuss what will be involved during the review. The entrance conference permits QA to explain their function and objectives. They can also present the merits and advantages to the project team of having a review for their project. It is also the time to explain to the project team what is expected of them during the review process so that each group is aware of the commitment and responsibilities of the other parties.

PREPARATION FOR A QUALITY ASSURANCE GROUP

The first step in a review is authorizing the commitment of resources to conduct the review. To limit dissipation of resources on unauthorized reviews, this should be a formal step. The control over the start and stop of reviews is an important step in controlling the use of QA resources.

Preparation for a review is designed to provide the QA team with enough information to plan its review strategy. Six types of information are to be obtained.

1.   *Comprehension of the system objectives.*   QA needs to understand what the system is trying to accomplish so that it can estimate the risk the organization is subjected to by this system.

2.   *Identification of the implementors.*   The caliber and experience of the staff is an important factor in determining the depth of QA involvement.

3.   *How the system is to be implemented.*   Which techniques are to be used for implementation.

4.   *Other parties involved in reviewing this system.*   If internal or external audit is involved, that will affect the extent of the review.

5.   *Characteristics of the system.*   QA needs to know the volumes of transactions, types of master data needed, impact on other computerized applications, and so on.

6.   *Schedules and budget.*   These are evaluated to indicate the magnitude of the project together with the project team's conception of its timetable.

The aim of preparing for a review is to gain as much information about that system as possible, normally from sources other than the project team.   That does not mean information is not requested of the project team.   However, meetings, interviews, or conferences do not take place with the project team at this time.   The objective is to gather information to prepare the review team to discuss the project intelligently at the first meeting with the project team.

There are many sources of information about a new project that do not require consultation with the project team (see Figure 6.1).

System's formal documentation.   The volume of letters and memorandums and/or more formalized feasibility reports will vary greatly depending upon the point at which QA becomes involved.

- System's formal documentation
- User manuals
- Correspondence
- Budgets
- Meeting notes
- Discussions with current system users
- Discussions with current system EDP personnel
- Discussions with current third-party users
- Industry reports
- Government reports
- Current system operating statistics
- Internal auditors

Figure 6.1 **SOURCES OF INFORMATION FOR REVIEW PLANNING**

User manuals. Policies and procedures of the user department that relate to the application, but not necessarily to the computerized system.

Correspondence. These can be any type of correspondence relating to either the existing or new application. Letters may outline problems, justify the need for a new system, or discuss problems or areas of concern.

Budgets. Data processing annual budgets can contain extensive information about new projects.

Meeting notes. The project team may have had one or more meetings relating to the new system. Within these notes can be the thinking, planning, and alternatives considered.

Discussions with users of current system. Much information can be obtained from people working with the outputs of an existing system, if there is one. While this will not describe the new application, it will help describe the user's needs.

Discussions with EDP system personnel working with current system. The problems, shortcomings, and unfulfilled needs within the existing system provide background information to review the adequacy of a new application.

Discussions with current third party users. Third party users are customers of the organization as well as, staff groups and management. While not as directly associated with the system as the user having responsibility for input to the system, these third party users frequently can provide insight into the problems and needs of the system.

Industry reports. Trends in industrial problems are often reported in trade literature. This can provide quality assurance personnel with some insight into long-term considerations for the application.

Government reports. Many government agencies do in-depth studies on industries, applications, and other topics which can provide background material helpful in preparing to review an application.

Current system operating statistics. If the application being reviewed is replacing or enhancing an existing system, operating statistics are a valuable input. Systems such as IBM's System Management Facility have extensive information on transactions, number of inquiries, and so on that are helpful when hardware and software considerations are involved.

Internal auditors. Auditing continually evaluates the main operating divisions of an organization. At the end of each of these audits, the auditors prepare a report which lists in detail problems encountered during that audit. A review of those reports and discussions with the auditors who perform them, will make quality assurance personnel aware of the control weaknesses that exist in the user department(s) and/or current application.

Is it worth looking at all of this wide variety of information sources. The answer is yes. No one source can provide all the information needed. The reviewer needs to build a complete picture, and this requires examining all the individual pieces. It is like assembling a jigsaw puzzle; once the individual pieces begin to fit together, solutions become much more obvious.

During this fact-finding process, QA personnel should make notes summarizing the odd bits of information collected. These notes should contain topical headings. At the end of the preparation process, the individual can sort and then review all the notes relating to each topic. At that time, bits of isolated information begin to fit into a pattern. For example, the trade literature on electronic funds transfer systems shows problems with user acceptance. If the project team indicated high user acceptance, the QA could deduce unrealistic estimates on user acceptance.

The manager of the QA function is responsible for controlling the review process. The initial quality control review point occurs when a project is authorized for review. Authorization for review should include allocation of resources (both people and dollars), assignment of personnel, and a tentative schedule.

Figure 6.2 povides a potential project review control sheet. QA groups can use this model to prepare one sheet for each project. The sheet becomes the authorization document to review a project. It also provides some statistical data to be recorded about the review as it progresses. To complete this form, the following is necessary:

1. Project name — title used by the data processing department

2. Project number — accounting number for accumulating project costs and for control purposes

3. Date began — date on which the quality assurance review started

4. Project budget — both dollars and days allocated for the review

5. Project team — individuals assigned to the team

6. Review process — a list of estimated starting dates for all the phases of the review plus budget allocated to each of these review phases. As the project commences, the actual starting date for each review phase can be entered as well as the actual cost to complete each phase of the review. Space is provided to indicate that working documents of the review have been analyzed by a supervisor, who initializes the "reviewed by" column for each phase.

7. Review authorized by — signed and dated by the member of management who authorizes the review

Project Name: _____

Project Number: _____   Date Begin: _____

Project Budget: _____   Days: _____

Review Team: In Charge: _____

Assistant: _____

Assistant : _____

Review Process									
	Dates				Cost		Hours		
Phase	Est. Start	Card No.	Actual Start	Com- plete	Budget	Actual	Budget	Actual	Reviewed By
Preparation									
Feasibility									
Design Program									
Test									
Conversion									
Other: _____ _____									

Review Authorized by: _____

Date: _____

Figure 6.2 **PROJECT REVIEW CONTROL SHEET**

This simple form can be kept in a notebook by the manager of quality assurance. It provides a quick source of information about the work that has been, is, and will be performed.

QUALITY ASSURANCE REVIEW POINTS

The QA review process parallels the systems development process. QA will make reviews at those points during the systems development process when management will be making a decision or wants information about systems progress. On systems critical to the organization, it may be on a full-time basis. However, this is an exception rather than the rule.

Most QA groups perform reviews close to the completion of each of the five phases in a systems development life cycle:

1. Feasibility
2. System design
3. Programming
4. Testing
5. Conversion or implementation

Some systems, because of size, complexity or importance, may require more than one review at each phase. Other systems of lesser importance, complexity, or cost may only require one review for the entire development process. When one review is made, it normally occurs at the end of the design phase.

Some groups also review the system after installation. This review occurs a short time after the computer system becomes operational. In other organizations, the postimplementation review is performed by internal audit.

The value of a computerized application is the result from operations. If the application fails to produce the desired results, the design process, even though it complies with all the organization's policies and procedures, is a failure. QA can learn from problems or errors that occur in systems when they become operational and use this knowledge to prevent the same problem from occurring again. This postinstallation review may not be a formal review. It may only involve informal discussions with the project team or internal auditors.

At the end of each systems development life cycle phase, the QA group normally provides the data processing manager with an opinion as to the adequacy of the design process up to that point. Management can then use that as input in making its decision as to whether to progress to the next phase. If the next phase is not approved, the decision could involve cancelling the system, redoing the previous phase, modifying and enhancing the work done in the previous phase, or moving ahead but with extra work to be accomplished in the next phase to compensate for weaknesses in the previous phase. The five systems development phases are discussed below with the review criteria for each phase.

Feasibility Study

The primary objective of the feasibility study is to evaluate alternatives and recommend a course of action to management to solve a specific business problem. The feasibility study is a time to "blue sky" new ideas and approaches. QA may be called during this time as consultants to discuss the practicality of alternative techniques.

The feasibility study evaluates solutions to a business problem. Emphasis is placed on solving the business problem as opposed to the computer system design for solving the business problem. The individuals involved in analyzing the feasibility of various solutions may or may not be computer design personnel; however, most have a familiarity with the computer.

Cost considerations are extremely important during the feasibility phase. While management does not expect a high degree of accuracy on cost estimates, they do want reasonable estimates. These estimates and evaluations are outside the normal scope of work of QA. Again, they may be called in as a consultant, but do not have a responsibility to review cost estimates.

QA should become involved at the end of the feasibility phase. The prime concern at this point is whether the feasibility team followed the organization's procedures in developing a proposal for management. In addition, if the feasibility report proposes computerized solutions, the quality assurance group should review and comment on only those aspects of the proposal.

Design Phase

The design phase includes first the design of the solution to the business problem, and second, the design to implement the solution on a computer. In some organizations, the two design efforts are combined into one systems development life cycle phase. Unless the business system is a separate phase, it is implied that the solution to the business problem will be implemented on a computer. Other organizations treat the two design efforts as independent systems development life cycle phases. In that case, the QA group performs separate reviews on each.

The business problem systems design does not take into account *how* the problem will be resolved. It is concerned with what the system will do to solve the problem. This phase does not deal with the method of processing the data. It will deal with the information needs of a user department(s). For example, a user problem in a merchandising organization is the prompt processing of customers' orders and the collection of funds for those orders. The business problem concerns itself with shipment of the right product to the right location, invoicing on a timely basis at the right price, handling of back orders, good customer relations, efficient processing in the distribution areas, etc. The computer system design is concerned with the data contained in the customer orders, its transition to machine-readable data, the processing rules, and the master data needed to do the processing, and so forth.

The QA group has a lesser role in reviewing the solution to the business problem than with the solution to the computer system problem. The solution to the business system problem is normally not subject to the same standards as is the computer design solution. As the phases become more specific, the QA group has a greater role. They can comment on the practicality of the business solution if it is to be processed by a computer. They should not be arguing for or against the proposed solution but, rather, reviewing the procedures by which that solution was determined.

Each phase gets more specific on cost. The evaluation of cost estimates and arguments is primarily the function of management. Should the business solution problem discuss costs of computer systems, these costs can be reviewed by QA. Also, they can review the method of accumulating costs as it conforms to the policies and procedures of the organization.

The computer system design phase is an extremely critical phase for the QA group. It is at this time that they can make the greatest impact on the design. The group wants to have an impact on the design without actually participating in the design process. Many organizations divide the review of computer systems design into two phases. The first is informal, the second formal. The first occurs after a rough preliminary design has been established. This is merely a brief, "discussion only" review. Rarely are any reports forwarded to management based on this review. It requires a good working relationship to have the project team discuss its preliminary thinking; reports to management at this time could damage this relationship. In very large applications, there may be two or three reviews during the design phase.

A formal review must occur at the end of the computer systems design phase. The design is normally fixed at this point, and ensuing phases make only minor changes to that design. The quality assurance group can review conformance to systems goals, compliance to procedures, and compliance to performance criteria. From the viewpoint of data processing management, this review will provide the best input as to whether the project is meeting the objectives and the performance criteria.

Program Phase

The program phase can be broken into program design and program coding. Many organizations combine those two phases into one. By doing this, the thought process and documentation achieved through a separate program design phase may be lost. Unless program design is a distinct step, the programmer may go into the coding before carefully developing the program design. While this appears to be a shortcut, it can result in insufficient program design documentation and program design problems.

To force formal program design, the QA group should insist on a review after program design, but before program coding. This will also give them the opportunity to review compliance to program design procedures and standards before coding occurs.

The program phase review should occur at the end of the programming phase to let QA make an assessment on compliance to procedures. Operating procedures include the proper use of program code, use of operating system facilities, conformance to programming and system standards, compliance to the computer operating department requirements, etc. If the data processing department is to have compliance with its procedures and standards, this review phase must be detailed. QA must look at program code, operating system instructions (in IBM systems, this would be Job Control Language), file structures, and other aspects that affect the operation of the computer system.

System Test Phase

The project team and the user have responsibility to test the system and review the adequacy of the test results. The QA group is concerned that an adequate test plan has been prepared, that it conforms to the standards of the organization, and that it has been followed. The QA group itself is normally not involved in the detailed testing. In other words, it does not prepare test data, process it, and review the results of testing. It may examine sample results from testing, however, to determine adherence to standards.

The testing plan should be prepared during either the system design or programming phase. Ideally, the plan will be prepared during the system design phase, and modified and enhanced during the programming phase. Part of the review of system testing occurs in the previous phases.

At the completion of the system testing, QA should perform a review to determine the system has been tested adequately. This involves conformance to the organization's testing policy. QA does not try to determine that every task has been tested but, rather, that the plan which they consider to be acceptable was followed.

The users have primary responsibility for the accuracy and completeness of processed data. Therefore they must attest that the system has performed according to their specifications. During its review, QA wants to know that the users are satisfied with the system.

Conversion Phase

Conversion is the process of either replacing an existing system or installing a totally new system. The primary concern of the quality assurance group is that an adequate conversion plan has been established and is being followed. As with the testing phase, this plan should be developed during the systems design phase, and then enhanced during the programming phase. The QA will review that conversion plan during the systems design and programming phases. At that point, they will review the adequacy of the plan, and its conformance to the organization's conversion procedures.

At the completion of the conversion phase, QA will make a final review that the procedures were, in fact, followed. Again, the user has the primary responsibility for the accuracy and completeness of the data converted during the conversion process. The QA group is concerned that the necessary technical steps are performed in the proper sequence to achieve a successful conversion.

STAFFING THE QUALITY ASSURANCE REVIEW

When the manager of quality assurance has decided at which points the review will be made, the next step is to determine who will perform that review and for how long. Previous chapters have discussed methods of determining the hours to be allocated to the review. They have also discussed how to divide those hours among the system development life cycle phases. The previous section in this chapter discussed some of the considerations regarding conducting reviews during each of those phases.

The quality assurance manager needs to select individuals to perform the review at each phase. The following factors should be considered when selecting individuals for a review team

Objectivity. The reviewer should not have been involved in designing or programming the system being replaced or have a close personal relationship with key members on the project team being reviewed.

Time availability. The individual assigned should have sufficient time available to perform the review at the appropriate review points.

Background and experience. The reviewer should have sufficient technical experience to perform the review. For example, individuals should not be assigned to review an on-line data base system when all their previous experience has been with tape batched systems.

Project duration. The key individuals assigned to review the project should be available throughout the project. For example, if individuals are known to be leaving QA within two months, they should not be assigned to review a project that will be in development for an 18-month period.

PLANNING THE QUALITY ASSURANCE REVIEW

There are three types of planning involved when preparing for a review. The first is administrative and includes staffing, budgeting, and scheduling. The second is general, preparing for the tasks that occur in all application reviews. Third is application planning, which covers the steps unique to the specific application being reviewed.

Administrative Planning

The successful utilization of QA resources depends on adequate administrative planning. It is important to get the right reviewer, at the right point, at the right time. This administrative planning can be accomplished with a few simple procedures.

The information contained on the Project Review Control Sheet (Figure 6.2) can provide the manager of quality assurance with planning information. This information can be used to schedule and control the project. This involves the following steps:

1. *Transcribe information from the project review control sheet to a project tickler card* (Figure 6.3). One tickler should be made for each phase being reviewed. If the QA manager determines there should be two or more reviews during one phase, two or more tickler cards are prepared for that phase. The data that gets transcribed is:

a. Action date — the estimated start date for each phase

b. Assignment number — project number

c. Action required — brief synopsis of review objective

d. Hours allocated — the number of hours involved in the review of this phase

e. Individual assigned — staff member in charge of the review

f. Project contact — name of individual with whom the review is coordinated

g. Action resolution — brief synopsis of the results of the review (taken from the review report)

h. Next project action data — estimated starting date of next review phase (or indicate at the end that this is the last step in the review)

2. *File the cards by a reminder date one to two weeks prior to the action date.* When this reminder date arrives, someone from the quality assurance group should contact the project team to determine that the action date is still appropriate. When a review is complete, the remaining review dates should be reconfirmed with the project team and the tickler card(s) refiled under new reminder dates. The project team manager should be asked to notify quality assurance if there is a delay in a future checkpoint.

3. *Develop a chart of individual assignments for quality assurance personnel using the tickler cards.* When making the assignments consider all of the project tickler cards for the

period being scheduled, including all the cards whose action date has passed, but on which action is not yet complete. For example, if the assignment period is the last quarter of the year, October through December, then the cards wanted would be all of those with an action date of December 31 or earlier.

Sort the tickler cards by individual. The cards should now be in piles by individual. Because several names are on each card, the cards will have to be sorted as many times as there are names on the cards. The first sort is for the person in charge.

QUALITY ASSURANCE TICKLER CARD

Card No. _____
Action Date _____   Assignment No. _____
Action Required _____
_____
_____

Hours Allocated _____
Individual Assigned:
    In charge: _____
    Assistant: _____
    Assistant: _____
Project Contact: _____
Review Phase Complete   ☐ Yes
Action Resolution: _____
_____

Next Project Action Date: _____
Card No. _____

Figure 6.3 **PROJECT TICKLER CARD**

The assignments are then posted onto a Gantt assignment chart. (Figure 6.4). This chart shows the reviewer's name and each assignment for the three-month period. The person preparing the Gantt chart must use discretion when dividing the hours available over the assignment period. Generally for this type of chart, it is assumed the individual will be on the assignment full time once the assignment starts. Once the posting has been done for the person in charge, the cards can be re-sorted for the first assistant, and then again for the second assistant, etc. When the process is done, all of the assignments will be posted on the assignment chart. Next, nonreview time, such as vacation or training, must be posted on the chart. The completed chart will give the manager of quality assurance an overview of the QA group's assignments as well as individual assignments and will show overlaps and problems.

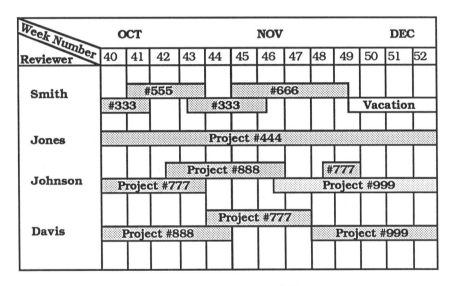

Figure 6.4 **GANTT ASSIGNMENT CHART**

Use of Gantt Chart

The Gantt chart is used to control personnel resources. When special jobs occur, or new assignments originate, the quality assurance manager can readily determine who is available and for how long. Assignment dates can change because of unexpected requests by management or users, delays or acceleration on the implementation of existing projects, and special assignments.

Using a Gantt chart, assignments are made on a realistic basis and not by chance.

For larger groups, it is helpful to have weekly status reports. These are used to track progress and update Gantt chart scheduling. Figure 6.5 shows a typical weekly status report for a quality assurance group. This report includes:

a.   Project name — name of project

b.   Week ended — the last day of the week covered by this report

c.   Project phase — the phase or subsection of that phase under review

d.   Review status — brief synopsis of the review to date

e.   Review concern — any actual or potential problem perceived by the reviewers which, in their opinion, should be brought to the attention of management at the current time

f.   Budget information — the number of hours budgeted, expended and needed to complete the review of this phase so that the quality assurance manager will know whether the project is over or under budget

---

WEEKLY STATUS REPORT

Project Name: _____   *Week Ended :* _____
Project Phase: _____
Review Status:

Review Concerns:

Budget Information:
    Budget for this phase   _____
    Actual to date for this phase: _____
    Needed to complete this phase: _____
    Estimate over (under) budget: _____

                                            _____
                                            Reviewer in Charge

---

Figure 6.5

Project Control

Some quality assurance groups maintain the status of EDP projects for the entire department. Keeping project status for QA reviews duplicates the project control administration function. This duplication can be avoided by centralizing the function within the quality assurance function.

Automating Scheduling

Quality assurance groups can obtain software to schedule computer reviews. Automating scheduling eliminates the need to hand schedule QA reviews and permits easy modification of schedules.

General Planning

The general plan covers those steps in a review that are executed on all application reviews:

1. Ascertain that all review personnel needed have been assigned to the project and will be available on the needed dates.
2. If the review is out of town, make travel and hotel arrangements.
3. If the review is conducted in another work location, make arrangements for work stations.
4. If questionnaires, procedures, etc. will be needed, obtain copies.
5. Requisition necessary supplies for the review.
6. If this is the first review for any of the group members, brief them on review procedures.
7. If assistants are assigned to the project, divide the work among the review team.
8. Obtain and review any information needed for preparatory understanding of the application.
9. Develop work schedules.

Application-Oriented Planning

Prior to commencing the review, the QA team needs to brief itself on the application. To become familiar with the application for review purposes, the team should do the following.

1.   Review information relating to the application.
2.   Make arrangements with the project team to hold an entrance conference (this will be discussed in the next section).
3.   If assistants are assigned to the review, brief them on the application.
4.   If previous phases of the project have been completed, review the results of those phases.
5.   Prepare working papers for the review (this will be covered later in this chapter).
6.   If internal auditing is involved in this review, coordinate the review with them.

ENTRANCE CONFERENCE

The entrance conference is the formal start of the review. The project team and the review team meet to discuss the review. This is one of the important parts of each review and provides an opportunity for two things to happen other than the instructions. First, QA have a chance to explain the quality assurance and promote their function. Second, they can outline their requirements. The QA group will need time, documentation, and information from the project team. These requests can be outlined so there will be no surprises, and the project team can schedule those tasks into its schedule. The planning steps previously outlined in this chapter should be completed prior to the entrance conference. It is important that QA be familiar with the project, and their needs and requirements determined before this conference.

An entrance conference is held prior to each review. Thus, if there are five review points, there will be five entrance conferences. The first entrance conference will be the most important. However, it is possible that the project team performing the feasibility study will be different from the one doing the systems design phase. People will change for other phases of the system development life cycle. New project personnel may not understand QA and its needs, so an entrance conference provides an opportunity to reestablish working relationships. If project personnel are relatively stable, the conferences after the first one can be much more informal and shorter. Where personnel change, the conferences should be more formal.

Entrance Conference Objectives

The entrance conference helps set the tone for the review and should be attended by the full review team as well as all the key people from the application project team. Ideally, the full project team should be there. The initial entrance conference should last about one hour. A second or later entrance conference can involve fewer people and be for a shorter period of time. However, if project team personnel have changed, the conference should revert to the initial meeting format.

The entrance conference should not be held until the QA group has adequately prepared for the conference. The following objectives should be accomplished at the entrance conference:

1. Review objectives and what should be accomplished by the review.

2. Explain and review the types of reports that will be prepared as a result of the review and who will receive them.

3. Determine certain aspects of the project the QA group will review.

4. Gain information from the project team about the project.

5. Discuss in detail how the review team will conduct the review.

6. Request the information the quality assurance team will need during the review.

7. Determine the role of the project team during the review.

8. Establish tentative review schedules showing the tasks for each group and the individuals involved. Discuss and agree upon key review dates.

9. Assess the competence and effectiveness of the project team.

10. Probe the project team on questions raised during their preparatory planning.

The first objective of the entrance conference is familiarization of both parties with the tasks and problems relating to the review. A second objective is to outline review requirements. The project team may not be able to commit to all requests. For uncommitted requests, an action plan needs to be developed. For example, the project team may not be able to state immediately when certain pieces of information will be available, but should be able to state on what date it can commit the availability of that information.

The review team leader should prepare an agenda for the entrance conference in order to limit the conference to about one hour. He or she should also be in charge of conducting the conference to ensure that all topics are covered.

Conducting the Entrance Conference

A typical agenda for an entrance conference would be:

1. Introduce participants of the conference.
2. Explain the objectives of QA.
3. Explain what will be the results of the review, who will see them, and how they will be used.
4. Discuss objectives of the review.
5. Outline needs and requirements of QA.
6. Have project team explain objectives of computer application.
7. Have project team ask questions of QA.
8. Discuss schedule of work.
9. Discuss housekeeping matters.

Quality Assurance Documentation

There is a need for written documentation of the review process. The complete review process will occur over a period of months. There may be gaps of several months between review points. It is possible that there will be changeover in quality assurance or on the project team during the review of a system application.

Workpapers prepared by a quality assurance group comprise a major part of its review. Most groups keep these workpapers in notebooks, by project, in order to have:

1. A chronological record of what has happened, when it has happened, and who did it
2. Reference material from which a report will be developed on the review
3. Supporting information to substantiate the conclusions in the report
4. Reference material so that the quality assurance team can review previous work

5. A means by which a supervisor can review the quality and extent of the work performed during the review.
6. A training document for new individuals assigned to the review.
7. A training document for individuals conducting similar reviews.

Workpaper Format. Workpapers should be organized for easy reference purposes. An indexing scheme enables each aspect of the review to be easily located.

There are four different types of workpapers. These are:

1. The report(s) issued as a result of the review.
2. Background and reference information collected during the review process.
3. Review programs accomplished during the review process.
4. Notes and other documents prepared by members of the review team.

The workpapers do not need to be organized in any specific manner but should be filed in the section to which they apply. In addition, each workpaper should contain the following basic identification 1) the section to which it belongs, 2) the subject of the workpaper, 3) the individual who prepared the paper, 4) the data on which it was prepared, 5) the source from which the data in the workpaper was obtained.

Contents of Workpapers. The workpapers need to be referenced for ease of location. Figure 6.6 outlines a suggested table of contents for review workpapers. Section A, which is the first section in the workpapers, is the completed report(s). Each statement in the report would be cross referenced to the detail workpaper that supports that statement. The report is the last section to be completed. However, if one looks at the workpapers as evidence to support the report, then it makes logical sense to have the report first.

Section B includes the background information on the project. Background information would include project objectives, policies, and procedures relating to the project. It might include organizational charts of the user department, background material on customers of the system, or federal regulations pertaining to the application. This is the type of information that the project review team can use to familiarize itself with the breadth and scope of the project. If data relates to one specific phase, it would be filed in that section. Data pertaining to the feasibility study is filed in the feasibility section and so forth.

Section C outlines the project approach. It is the program and instructions to the project team telling what it must do to complete the project. This will outline the key review points. This section would also include any special instructions given to the project team by the user or executive management regarding what the user or manager would like done during this review. For example, executive management may have some reservations about the hardware the project team is proposing and want a special study made on that hardware.

Section D outlines the administration of the review. It includes the plans, personnel, schedules and budgets for this project. The administrative details included in this section, are project oriented and should be in great detail.

Section E is generally a chronological filing of correspondence, including memorandums and letters both received and sent by the review team. If the correspondence is extensive, some organization of the correspondence other than chronological may be desirable. For example, it may be decided to file correspondence by addressee, department, or subject as opposed to a chronological filing.

Section F provides information on the project team. It includes the team plans, personnel, schedules, and budgets. This is the type of information the quality assurance group needs in order to plan the use of its resources.

Section G begins a series of similar sections covering the different reviews. The previous section related to the project in total. Section G relates only to the review of the feasibility study. Within the feasibility study, and all other reviews, are the following sections:

1.   Review conclusion/report — the report or conclusion issued from the feasibility study.

2.   Review questionnaire applicable to the feasibility study review. (This will be covered in Chapter 7.)

3.   Project documentation — information obtained from the project team relating to the feasibility study of the project.

4.   Correspondence — any memorandums, correspondence, or notes sent to other parties or received from them relating to the feasibility study review.

5.   Review notes — all the workpapers prepared by the quality assurance team during the feasibility study review. These should be supportive of the program/questionnaire included in this section. If notes or workpapers are developed as a result of that question asked or program step executed, it should be referenced to the question or program step.

6.   Miscellaneous — information collected during the review process not appropriate to other sections. For example, this could include information obtained from a vendor that was used as background material in this phase.

Sections H, I, J, and K all use the same format as Section G. The sections are for the systems design review, program review, test review, and conversion review. If the quality assurance group adds additional review steps, they should add more sections to the workpapers. For example, if there were two review points for the systems design phase, these would require two sections.

For larger reviews, Sections A – F are filed in one notebook. Each other section would be filed in an individual notebook. This would permit each review point to be filed separately.

Workpaper Retention.   There are no legal requirements for maintaining review workpapers. The procedures of each organization govern the length of time the documentation is maintained. Workpapers from a project should be retained throughout the life of the project and then, at a minimum, until the application has been successfully implemented.

The QA group may desire to save review workpapers as a training vehicle for new quality assurance personnel, who can refer to a full set of working papers. Workpapers are also useful as reference and background material for a postimplementation review. Internal auditors making a postimplementation audit may wish to review the workpapers. Finally, in case management disregards quality assurance advice and quality assurance suspects problems in the new system, QA may wish to save the workpapers until it is satisfied about the resolution of those problems.

SUMMARY

Planning is needed prior to a QA review. Planning includes administrative, general, and application planning. Administra-

---

WORKPAPER

Subject	*Reference*
Reference report (to workpapers)	A
Background information	B
- project objectives	B–100
- policies, procedure on project	B–200
Review program and instructions	C
Administrative (review team)	D
- plans	D–100
- personnel	D–200
- schedules	D–300
- budgets	D–400
Correspondence	E
Project team	F
- plans	F–100
- personnel	F–200
- schedules	F–300
- budgets	F–400
Feasibility study review	G
- review conclusions/report	G–100
- review program/questionnaire	G–200
- project documentation	G–300
- correspondence	G–400
- review notes (referenced to report and questionnaire)	G–500
- miscellaneous	G–600
Systems design review	H
- review conclusions/report	H–100
- review program/questionnaire	H–200
- project documentation	H–300
- correspondence	H–400
- review notes (referenced to report and questionnaire)	H–500
- miscellaneous	H–500

Figure 6.6 **WORKPAPER TABLE OF CONTENTS**

WORKPAPER (cont'd)	
Subject	*Reference*
Program Review	I
- review conclusions/report	I–100
- review program/questionnaire	I–200
- project documentation	I–300
- coreespondence	I–400
- review notes (referenced to report and questionnaire)	I–500
- miscellaneous	I-600
Test	J
- review conclusion/report	J–100
- review porgram/questionnaire	J–200
- project documentation	J–300
- correspondence	J–400
- review notes (referenced to report and questionnaire)	J–500
- miscellaneous	J–600
Conversion	K
- review conclusions/report	K–100
- review program/questionnaire	K–200
- project documentation	K–300
- correspondence	K–400
- review notes (referenced to report and questionnaire)	K–500
- miscellaneous	K–600

Figure 6.6 **WORKPAPER TABLE OF CONTENTS (Cont'd)**

tive planning includes personnel assignment, schedules, and budgets. General planning includes those aspects that relate to the application being reviewed. This planning prepares a quality assurance group for the entrance conference.

The review personnel need to gain an understanding of the system during the planning process. Once the system is understood, the group can select the points at which it wants to review the system under development. These review points normally coincide with the end of the key phases in the development process. These phases are the feasibility, systems design, test, and conversion phases. Depending on the organization's development process and the complexity of the system, there may be more or fewer review points.

The official beginning of a review is an entrance conference. At this point, QA and the project team can get together and discuss the review process and requirements. Because this entrance conference sets the tone of the review, it is essential for the QA personnel to be adequately prepared.

The entrance conference accomplishes three objectives. First, it is a mechanism for the QA group and the project team to meet. Second, it offers QA the opportunity to explain and promote its function. Third, it is the means by which QA can outline its schedule, needs, and requirements with the project team. This will enable the project team to fit those needs and requirements into its implementation schedule.

Chapter 7
CONDUCTING A QUALITY ASSURANCE REVIEW

The quality assurance review can begin when the planning and preparatory work is complete. The type, frequency, and extent of the review will be determined during the preparatory stages. The type of review will depend upon the importance of the system to the organization as well as resources available to conduct the review.

Each of the twelve points from the feasibility study to the end of conversion covers a different aspect of the application system. Many systems may not warrant all twelve reviews because they may be small or potential exposure to the organization may be minimal, or personnel are not available to conduct reviews. In those instances, two or more of the review points will be consolidated into one review.

This chapter includes a checklist for each of the recommended twelve review points. Each list concentrates on a different aspect of the application system. The reviewer should conduct tests and make evaluations based on the answers to the questions in the checklists. Chapter 8 explains how to conduct the tests. The checklists included in this chapter are cross-referenced to the tests explained in Chapter 8. Chapter 9 provides guidance on how to evaluate the results of the review and compare that evaluation to other application reviews. Chapters 7–9 provide the methodology for conducting a review.

QUALITY ASSURANCE REVIEW POINTS

The five phases of the system development life cycle are the justification phase, systems development phase, programming phase, testing phase, and conversion phase. Each of these phases normally concludes with the completion of a product. (We have discussed these phases in previous chapters.)

To assure a quality system, twelve review points have been selected during the five systems development life cycle phases. The twelve are considered to be the optimum number of reviews for a major application, so that QA can not only review but also influence system design. The twelve recommended review points are:

1.   Mid-justification phase
2.   End of justification phase
3.   Business system solution phase
4.   Computer equipment selection
5.   Computer system design
6.   Program design
7.   Testing and conversion planning
8.   Program coding and testing
9.   Detailed test plan
10.   Test results
11.   Detail conversion planning and programs
12.   Conversion results

Reviews occurring during the five system development phases should assist project personnel in the accomplishment of their task. Frequently with a few hours' consultation, quality assurance can save project personnel hours or days of wasted effort. This valuable consultation service can normally be accomplished while QA personnel are fulfilling their review requirements.

Twelve reviews do not require much more time than a smaller number of reviews. The items to be reviewed are split among several short reviews rather than consolidated into major reviews that could be held at the end of each of the five system phases.

If fewer than twelve reviews are desired, the checklists for the two or more reviews included in a phase should be consolidated in the one review. In a few cases, the same questions are included in two reviews during one system development life cycle phase, but that is the exception. The consolidation of two or more checklists is not difficult.

Review Point	Quality Assurance Review Point	Percent of QA Time Expended
1	Mid-justification review	5%
2	End of justification review	5%
3	Review of the business system solution	10%
4	Review of computer equipment selection	10%
5	Review of computer system design	20%
6	Review of program design	20%
7	Review of testing and conversion planning	5%
8	Review of program coding and testing	5%
9	Review of detail test plan	5%
10	Review of test results	5%
11	Review of detail conversion planning and programs	5%
12	Review of conversion results	5%

CONDUCTING THE REVIEW

During a review, the reviewer should maintain a helpful, cooperative attitude. Because reviews are peer group reviews, it is important to maintain a good working relationship both during and after each review. The review itself should not create tension and competition. Outstanding work performed by project personnel as well as deviations from departmental standards should be recognized.

Each review point has a checklist. The questions included on any of the checklists highlight the areas that should be addressed at that particular review. The questions included on the checklist are broad in scope. They are not meant to be answered yes or no but, rather, to indicate the degree of compliance to the departmental standards achieved by the project team. Because each organization has different standards, a general issue is raised but it must be supported by a series of very specific questions. This means that the quality assurance group will have to develop a series of questions which focus on the standards that need to be followed by the programmers.

In some cases, the degree of compliance will be a matter of judgment; in others, a more scientific approach can be taken. (Rating the quality of work of the project team will be discussed in Chapter 9.)

The amount of Time allocated to the entire review must be split among the twelve review points. Figure 2.7 suggested a breakdown of time among the five phases of the system development life cycle. Listed in Figure 7.1 is a further breakdown of those items for the twelve review points: if two or more review points are consolidated into one review, the time for the reviews should be consolidated. For example, if Review Point 11 (the review of detail conversion planning and programs) and Review Point 12 (the review of conversion results) are combined into one review point, then the total of the time for the two reviews (i.e., 5% plus 5%) or 10% of the time expended should be spent on that consolidated review. Whether the total time spent on twelve reviews is longer than the time spent on fewer reviews will depend upon the experience of the quality assurance group and the proficiency of the individual reviewers.

Each review point will be discussed in detail in this chapter. Prior to that discussion, the objectives of the project team during the system development life cycle phase will be reviewed. This should put each phase of the systems development life cycle into perspective for the reviewer.

SYSTEM JUSTIFICATION PHASE

The recognition of a business problem will lead to the organization of a study designed to develop a proposed solution. The feasibility study will result in justifying what action should occur to solve the business problem. The recommendation may be to live with the existing system, modify the existing system, or build a new system. Figure 7.1 shows the elements of this phase. Two review points are illustrated in this figure.

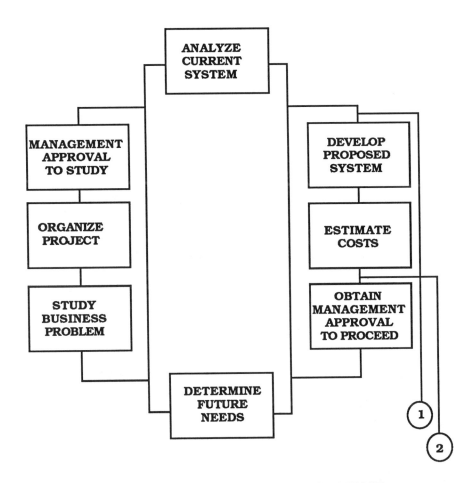

Figure 7.1 **SYSTEM JUSTIFICATION PHASE**

During the justification phase, a team will be organized to study the business problem. For example, in a merchandising organization, a business problem may be excessive stockouts of merchandise. It is this type of a business problem that needs to be solved now and not studying how the computer should be involved. The study team should examine the present system to help determine future needs.

The study team will propose a solution to the business problem based on analyzing the business problem and the needs of various users. In the example of the merchandising organization with the excessive stockouts, the proposed solution may be monitoring orders and inventory levels to determine stock replenishment points. Such a solution does not necessarily propose that the computer be involved, as it may be too early to make that determination. That aspect is normally handled in the system design phase. This does not mean that the justification study team will not recommend a computer system but, rather, the method of implementing the solution is still flexible. Cost estimates may be developed for a range of solutions giving a probable cost for each. Many organizations feel that the cost estimates produced during the justification phase need only be accurate within plus or minus 50% of actual project implementation costs.

Even though they are primarily computer oriented, QA personnel can make a contribution during this phase. The study team assigned during the justification phase may be unaware of some of the newer technology for problem solving or how to determine the costs for the use of that technology as a potential solution. Therefore, certain solutions may be overlooked without skilled technical people involved in the justification phase.

Review Point 1: Mid-Justification Phase

The basic intent of a review is to verify compliance to the standards and procedures desired by data processing management. This can be done by listing the concerns of data processing management and then verifying that appropriate action has been taken regarding those concerns. The term "concern" is used in the context of what is needed to build a well-controlled, efficient, and effective data processing system that meets the needs of the user. If the data processing department has formalized standards and procedures, the concerns should be cross-referenced to those procedures and standards.

The early phases of the systems development life cycle have less formal and demanding EDP standards and procedures. This is because there is more creativity and ingenuity during the early phases of system development than during the later phases such as programming. It is more of an art to determine which solution is best for the organization than to perform the function of programming.

The intent of the mid-justification phase review is to verify first that the appropriate fact gathering has occurred according to departmental procedures and second that the plans of the justification team will permit its work to be completed on time and within budget. Because the costs are merely low during this phase, it is normally sufficient to merely verify that there are plans and budgets which are being followed.

	QUALITY ASSURANCE CONCERN	REVIEW TECHNIQUE
1	Are there a sufficient number of capable people assigned to the justification phase?	Project documentation Fact finding Judgment
2	Have good and bad parts of the current system been determined?	System documentation Fact finding Simulation modeling
3	Have the new information needs been determined?	System documentation Fact finding Checklist
4	Have data processing procedures and standards been followed?	System documentation Fact finding Checklist
5	Are there adequate alternatives available to meet the user's needs without building a new system?	System documentation Fact finding Judgment Consultants Confirmation
6	Will justification phase be completed on time?	Project documentation Fact finding
7	Will justification phase be completed within budget?	Project documentation Fact finding
8	Are goals and objectives to be solved clearly stated?	Project documentation System documentation

Figure 7.2 **REVIEW POINT 1: MID-JUSTIFICATION PHASE REVIEW**

Figure 7.2 outlines eight concerns for the QA group to consider during the mid-justification phase review. Associated with each of the concerns are the review practices recommended to the reviewer for determining to what degree the concern has been satisfied by the project team. Note that the concerns listed are not meant to be complete but merely representative of the type of concerns that the QA group should address.

The concerns listed normally cannot be answered by a simple yes or no. For example, the first question asks if there are "a sufficient number of capable people assigned to the justification phase." The reviewer might not want to ask this question directly of the justification phase project leader. The reviewer would want to examine the project documentation to determine who had been assigned to the justification phase, then through fact finding and interviewing determine the qualifications of the individuals assigned. Once this information has been accumulated, the reviewer can judge whether a sufficient number of people have been assigned to the justification phase, and whether or not those people are capable of completing the assignments given to them. Once the review has been conducted, the reviewer is in the position to answer the concern. Concerns must be based on EDP department standards or procedures. The QA group does not probe into areas unless that area is within the QA group charter.

Review Point 2: End of Justification Phase

Management of the organization must decide at the end of the justification phase whether to adopt the recommendation of the justification phase team, reject that recommendation, or accept it in a modified form. Many organization now only approve the funding of a project one phase at a time. That means that while the recommendation for the solution is accepted, only the funds and resources to complete the next systems development life cycle phase would be approved. The process is followed for each of the phases.

The evaluation of a completed phase by QA should be an input to management for its decision-making process. It is recommended that the QA group neither approves nor disapproves the work of computer department personnel, it is merely trying to assess compliance by the project team to departmental standards and procedures. These standards and procedures can be considered in the broad sense to be the goals and objectives of the system; QA is limited to reviewing methods. Most organizations begin by reviewing methods, and then expand to goals.

The justification phase will normally have fewer standards than the later phases. Most organizations have procedures that require justification teams to consider various criteria during their study. The typical criteria include:

1. The impact of the new system on people, computer hardware and software, existing systems, supporting systems and cost

2. The expected life of the new system

3. The user reaction to the new system

4. The availability of resources, including people, to implement the new system

5. Schedules for implementation

6. Risks and exposures associated with the new system

7. Various alternatives evaluated and the reasons for rejecting the various alternative in favor of the recommended system

Figure 7.3 lists twelve concerns for the review conducted at the end of the justification phase. Associated with each of these are recommended review practices. The review should be conducted so that management has the evaluation before it must make a decision on the justification team recommendation.

SYSTEMS DESIGN PHASE

The systems design phase includes both functional specification of the business system solution and the computer system solution phase. In some organizations these are separate phases; in others they are combined. If the business system solution phase is not a separate process, all solutions will include the computer as part of the solution. Therefore, it is desirable to have a review involved in the decision regarding whether or not the computer is to be part of the solution of the business problem.

When it has been objectively determined that the computer is to be part of the solution, then the computer system should be designed. QA personnel are normally quite familiar with the processes from the point where a computer becomes part of the solution to the business problem. If the organization has a different group working on business system solutions than working on computer systems design, it may be advisable to have people with both backgrounds in the QA group.

	QUALITY ASSURANCE CONCERN	REVIEW TECHNIQUE
1	Have data processing costs been estimated?	System documentation
2	Have the user costs and benefits been estimated?	System documentation
3	Has conceptual system design been prepared	System documentation
4	Have the data processing procedures and standards been followed?	System documentation Fact finding Checklist
5	Was the proposed system selected by a reasonable method from among the various alternatives?	System documentation Fact finding Judgment Quantitative analysis
6	Are the assumptions made in arriving at a solution valid?	System documentation Fact finding Judgment Simulation modeling Consultants Quantitative analysis
7	Does the proposed solution solve the business problem?	Project documentation System documentation Judgment Simulation modeling Confirmation
8	Does the user want the proposed system?	Fact finding
9	Does the proposed system have a reasonable life expectancy?	Judgment Simulation modeling Consultants Quantitative analysis Confirmation

Figure 7.3 **REVIEW POINT 2: END OF JUSTIFICATION PHASE REVIEW**

QUALITY ASSURANCE CONCERN	REVIEW TECHNIQUE
10 Have the standards of performance for the new system been established?	System documentation Fact finding
11 Are the standards of performance documented and in the hands of the system designers?	System documentation Simulation modeling
12 Has criteria been established to evaluate performance after the system is operational?	System documentation

Figure 7.3 **REVIEW POINT 2: END OF JUSTIFICATION PHASE REVIEW (cont'd)**

At the completion of the system design phase, enough information should be documented to begin designing programs. This documentation includes the design of input data, files, and output reports. The long-range information needs of the user must be considered during the system design phase. As system designs move into distributed processing and large centralized data bases, the use of information becomes an ever-increasing part of the system design phase. In batch-oriented systems, and simple disk systems, data can be accumulated exclusively for use by that application. However, when multiple applications begin to use the same data base, the structure of the data base should be based on the needs of the information users. It is a responsibility of QA to determine that files are structured to maximize the use of information.

Figure 7.4 outlines the main parts of the system design phase. Within the system design phase are three review points. The first (Review Point 3) occurs after the business system solution has been determined. At this point, the decision on whether to use the computer as part of the solution will be made. QA should make a review prior to that. The second review point (Review Point 4) involves the computer equipment selection process. Some organizations make the decision that all applications

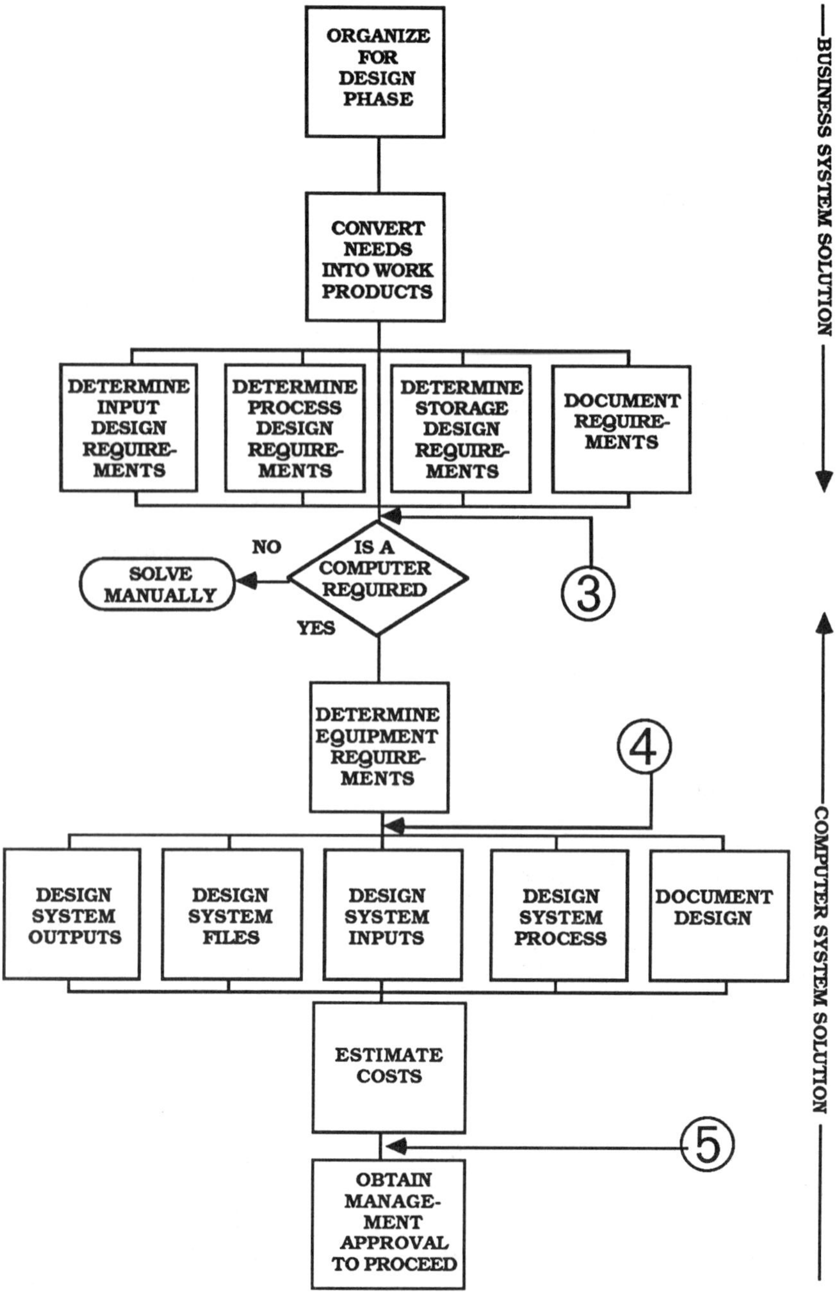

Figure 7.4 **SYSTEM DESIGN PHASE**

will run on centralized hardware. In that case, the computer equipment selection process is minimal. All the reviewer would want to do is to determine whether the available resources are sufficient to handle the new application. In other organizations, this is a very important review. The third review point (Review Point 5) comes just prior to the completion of the computer system design phase. It is the evaluation from this review that will be used by management in deciding whether to proceed to the next systems development life cycle phase.

Review Point 3: Review of the Business Systems Solutions

The business systems solutions phase determines the detailed solution to the business problem. This includes defining the information to be obtained and processed so that the desired results are obtained. The method of processing does not have to be determined, but the feasibility does. Determining the processing feasibility will decide the need for the computer. For example, certain inventory replenishment algorithms could not be hand processed on a daily basis to determine when new inventory is required. However, by using a computer, such processing becomes feasible. Similarly, in systems where interactive processing is required, it may not be feasible to solve the business problem except by computer. It is in this part of the business systems solution phase that QA can be most helpful.

As systems progress through the developmental process, flexibility for considering alternatives decreases. Therefore, it is important that as many alternative solutions as possible be considered during the justification phase. When the justification phase is complete, the system course is charted and it may be difficult to deviate from the course. Because the most maneuverability exists in the early phases, QA should be involved in those phases.

Figure 7.5 lists nine concerns to be considered during the review of the business systems solution phase. While the objective of QA is compliance to departmental standards and policies, there should be time during the review of the business systems solution phase to determine that all logical alternatives were given consideration.

Review Point 4: Review of Computer Equipment Selection

Usually project leaders build systems within restrictions designed to maximize performance on existing hardware. When applications cause either new hardware to be ordered or extensions to existing hardware, a detailed equipment evaluation process occurs. However, this may be done by computer operations personnel instead of application project personnel.

Figure 7.6 lists six concerns during the review of computer equipment selection. The questions are of a general nature and assume there is existing computer hardware. If no hardware is in place, the equipment selection process is much more extensive. With existing equipment, new hardware normally must be compatible with that existing equipment. When no equipment exists, then the process of evaluating equipment from multiple vendors increases the complexity of the review.

Review Point 5: Review of Computer Systems Design

The review of the computer systems design phase is the most time-consuming part of the review. During this phase, the QA personnel can make their greatest contribution since the computer systems design phase will determine the performance level of the computer application.

Reviewers should examine all parts of the computer system design. Look at how the system initiates transactions, transmits data from the initiation point to the computer, authorizes data, processes data, stores data, and produces reports from computerized data. It is important that the results of processing meet the needs of the user.

Most organizations have stringent standards covering the computer design phase. These standards include how data is specified, how output reports are specified, computer file specification, as well as processing specification. The reviewer must ascertain that these specifications are followed. QA personnel will be particularly interested in whether the computer system design can meet performance standards. This is critical because meeting operating cost specifications is dependent upon developing a good system design.

At the end of the computer systems design phase, traditionally there is little flexibility remaining to make major system design changes. However, the majority of the cost to implement the computerized application is yet to come, so management can still abort the system at relatively minor expense. Therefore, the quality assurance evaluation at Review Point 5 should be extremely important input to management.

Figure 7.7 lists 20 concerns to be included in this review.

The extent of these concerns illustrates the depth of the review that should be made at this point. Much of the work and time will be spent examining project and system documentation. Project documentation covers project scheduling, project organization, budgets, approaches, alternatives considered and rejected, and other information relating to managing the project. Systems documentation relates to the application being implemented. This is a permanent documentation although it needs to be updated throughout the life of the application. On the other hand, project documentation has little long-term use and probably will not be retained after the project becomes operational.

PROGRAMMING PHASE

The systems design phase provides the information necessary to design programs. If the systems design has been thoroughly documented, the individuals responsible for program design can accomplish their task with little interaction with the user.

There are three aspects of the program design phase, each of which can be associated with a review. These are program design, planning testing and conversion, and coding. If these three are not broken apart, experience has shown they will not receive the proper attention. Program design should be a step separate from coding. When it is not a separate step, much of the program design is done concurrently with coding. Experience has shown this not to be the best way to develop programs.

When a review comes after the program design is complete, but before coding, management can be assured formal program design will occur. The planning for system testing and conversion should commence when programs are being designed. This may occur prior to the completion of the program design phase. The timing is optional. However, when the programs have been designed, the steps required for conversion and system testing are known. Because changes occur between the systems design and the program design, these changes can affect system testing and conversion.

Figure 7.8 illustrates the programming phase. Included within this phase are three QA review checkpoints. The first (Review Point 6) occurs after the programs have been designed. The second (Review Point 7) occurs after the testing and conversion procedures have been planned, and the third (Review Point 8) occurs after the programs have been coded and tested.

	QUALITY ASSURANCE CONCERN	REVIEW PRACTICE
1	Have a sufficient number of capable people been assigned to the systems?	Project documentation Fact finding Judgment
2	Has the business problem been solved and are the needed work products?	System documentation Checklist
3	Has the source of the needed data been determined?	System documentation Checklist
4	Have the data storage (file) needs been determined?	System documentation Checklist
5	Has the required processing been determined?	System documentation Checklist
6	Do the various functions of the proposed system fit together?	System documentation Fact finding Judgment Confirmation
7	Does the proposed solution solve the business problem?	Judgment Simulation modeling Quantitative analysis
8	Will the system be implemented when needed?	System documentation Fact finding Judgment Simulation modeling
9	Will performance standards be achieved?	System documentation Fact finding Judgment Consultants

Figure 7.5 **REVIEW POINT 3: REVIEW OF THE BUSINESS SYSTEMS SOLUTION**

	QUALITY ASSURANCE CONCERN	REVIEW PRACTICE
1	Have the equipment requirements been determined?	System documentation Checklist
2	Has it been determined whether or not additional hardware will be required?	System documentation Fact finding
3	Has it been determined whether or not additional software will be required?	System documentation Fact finding
4	Has it been determined whether or not any special hardware or software installation will be required?	System documentation Fact finding Consultants
5	Have the EDP department and the project team determined the level of experience necessary to use the specified hardware and software?	Fact finding Judgment
6	Does the hardware provide for sufficient growth for the proposed system?	System documentation Fact finding Judgment

Figure 7.6 **REVIEW POINT 4: REVIEW OF COMPUTER EQUIPMENT SELECTION**

	QUALITY ASSURANCE CONCERN	REVIEW PRACTICE
1	Do the file specifications meet EDP standards?	System documentation Checklist
2	Do the input specifications meet EDP standards?	System documentation Checklist
3	Do the output specifications meet EDP standards?	System documentation Checklist
4	Do the process specifications meet EDP standards?	System documentation Checklist
5	Is the computer system design properly documented?	System documentation Checklist
6	Is the computer system design complete?	System documentation Judgment Consultants
7	Does the system as designed meet the needs of the user(s)?	Simulation modeling
8	Will the system as designed operate on the planned hardware and software?	System documentation Judgment Consultants
9	Have the costs been developed in accordance with EDP procedures?	System documentation
10	Does the system design provide the capacity for reasonable growth?	Judgment Simulation modeling Consultants
11	Were other design alternatives considered and rejected for valid reasons?	Project documentation Fact finding Judgment

Figure 7.7 **REVIEW POINT 5: REVIEW OF COMPUTER SYSTEM DESIGN**

	QUALITY ASSURANCE CONCERN	REVIEW PRACTICE
12	Does the system design impose undue restrictions on the user?	System documentation Fact finding Simulation modeling
13	Is the audit trail sufficient to reconstruct transactions?	System documentation Fact finding Checklist
14	Will the computer systems design phase be completed on time?	Project documentation Fact finding Judgment
15	Will the computer systems design phase be completed within budget?	Project documentation Fact finding Judgment
16	Are the EDP system standards realistic for this system?	Judgment Consultant
17	Are the current EDP system standards appropriate for the time when this system will be operational?	Judgment Simulation modeling Consultants
18	Can performance standards be achieved?	System documentation Judgment Consultants Quantitative analysis Confirmation
19	Is the system of internal control adequate to ensure the accurate and complete processing of transactions?	System documentation Fact finding Checklist
20	Is the system of internal control adequate to ensure the accurate and integrity of the computer files and/or data base?	System documentation Fact finding Checklist

Figure 7.7 **REVIEW POINT 5: REVIEW OF COMPUTER SYSTEM DESIGN (cont'd)**

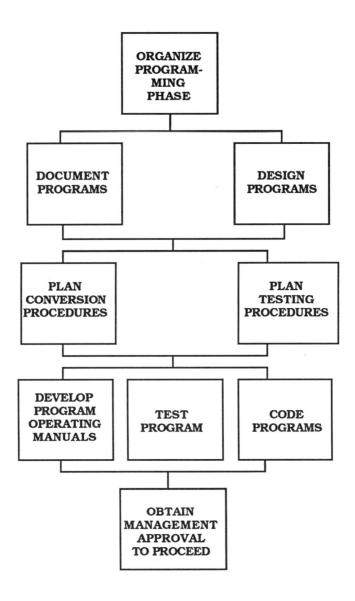

Figure 7.8 **TESTING PHASE**

Data processing management should be involved in deciding when systems are ready for system testing. Premature testing can be expensive. Therefore, a QA review prior to testing will be an important factor for data processing management to consider before they give the go-ahead on systems testing. If adequate program testing has not occurred, the cost of systems testing will be considerably higher.

Review Point 6: Program Design

QA should be sure that the program design has been executed prior to coding. Frequently systems design leaves a number of unanswered questions that do not become obvious until the programming phase. A formal program design methodology, such as structured design, will uncover these problems. It is easier to analyze program logic from design documentation than from program compiler listings. The review can be done by scanning program design documentation, or having the program designers explain briefly program logic. The reviewers should concentrate on the critical programs. Figure 7.9 lists twelve concerns for the review of program design. The program design function is one of the most standardized by organizations. Therefore, the review of program design should focus on a heavy compliance review to standards.

Review Point 7: Testing and Conversion Planning

Problems not covered during the testing phase or poor conversions can be disastrous for organizations. One large organization almost went bankrupt when the conversion of its accounts receivable system destroyed all existing copies of the accounts receivable file. These types of problems should become apparent to qualified reviewers.

Systems development may take many months or years during which individuals are writing and debugging program code. It is only at the end of these processes that systems testing occurs, and many times the user takes a lead role in systems testing. Because many data processing personnel perform system testing infrequently, they are not familiar with the types of problems that can occur.

Most data processing personnel develop test data to test the system as they wrote it. The concern of the user is to test the system for conditions as they will happen during the operational status of the system. These two types of testing may be considerably different. It is the role of QA to determine that the testing is as near "real life" as possible. Many data processing personnel fail to adequately test error conditions and unusual circumstances that will occur when the system is put in production.

Figure 7.10 lists eight concerns for the review of testing and conversion planning. Concern number 3 — "Has a plan been established to test the new system?" — is the one requiring the most investigation. It is because of concerns like this that there should be a continuity of reviewer personnel. If the same reviewers have been assigned to an application since the justification phase, they will be in a much better position to assess this concern than will someone newly assigned to the review.

Review Point 8: Program Coding and Testing

Many organizations have established program coding standards and yet fail to ensure that those standards are followed. This determination of compliance is the logical task for QA. There is a natural tendency to follow standards when they are being enforced, and QA should determine whether or not the standards are followed.

In any case, the review of program coding and testing should determine compliance to departmental standards. These standards should be put on detailed checklists so the reviewer can easily make the compliance determination. The appendix at the back of this book gives a good illustration as to the type of questions one organization asks in support of the more general list of concerns in this chapter.

Figure 7.11 lists four concerns for the reviewer of program coding and testing. This review point is one used by many QA groups to train new personnel. Less judgment is involved in review of program code than in many of the other phases. Also, many QA personnel are more familiar with coding than other aspects of the systems development life cycle.

TESTING PHASE

The testing phase should involve both data processing and user personnel. The two groups should work together as a team to design the system test plan, create test data, and develop training material for the people who will be using the system. The personnel from the data processing department should be those who were involved in the system design, program design, and coding. Personnel from the user department should be those individuals who will be involved in the use of the production system when it becomes operational.

The test data used to test the system should be normal input-type data. User personnel should fill out input forms with as many transactions as possible. Ideally, all paths through the computer application would be tested. Some organizations use test data generators in an attempt to test as many computer paths as possible.

Test data should include both valid and invalid transactions. When the various processing conditions are discussed during the systems design phase, they should be documented. This list will then serve as a guide as to the types of conditions that should be tested during the test phase. The organization's internal auditors frequently can be helpful in suggesting unusual error conditions.

System test should continue until the test team is satisfied with the results. Frequently the results of a systems test will cause modifications to be made to the systems design and programs. This necessitates going back into the systems development life cycle. Systems tests should not be conducted again until the project team is satisfied that the system design has been adequately corrected, documented, and tested.

Figure 7.12 shows the main parts of the system test phase. Within the test phase are two review points. One (Review Point 9) occurs after the test data has been created and the user has been trained. At this point, QA can make an assessment as to the adequacy of test data. The second review (Review Point 10) occurs after the tests have been run and the results evaluated. QA will then make an evaluation of test results. However, rarely does QA actually prepare, enter, and run tests.

At the conclusion of the system test phase, management must make a decision whether to put the application into production. During the previous phases, there was time to compensate for previous problems. This is not true with the testing phase. When the testing phase is over, the system may go into production, at which time systems problems become user problems. If errors are not uncovered and corrected during testing, numerous transactions initiated by users may be wrong and have to be corrected.

	QUALITY ASSURANCE CONCERN	REVIEW PRACTICE
1	Have a sufficient number of capable people been assigned to the program design phase?	Project documentation Fact finding Judgment
2	Does the program design meet EDP standards?	System documentation Checklist
3	Has the program design been properly documented?	System documentation Checklist
4	Has provision been made for restart procedures?	System documentation Checklist
5	Has provision been made for recovery procedures?	System documentation Checklist
6	Has provision been made to protect sensitive data?	System documentation Checklist
7	Is there a programming schedule?	Project documentation Fact finding
8	Will the program design phase be completed on time?	Project documentation Fact finding Judgement
9	Will the program design phase be completed within budget?	Project documentation Fact finding Judgment
10	Are the EDP program standards realistic for this system?	Judgment Consultants
11	Are the current EDP program standards appropriate for the time when this	System documentation Simulation modeling Consultants
12	Will performance standards be achieved?	System documentation Judgment Consultants Quantitative analysis Confirmation

Figure 7.9 **REVIEW POINT 6: REVIEW OF PROGRAM DESIGN**

	QUALITY ASSURANCE CONCERN	REVIEW PRACTICE
1	Has a plan been established to convert from the old to new system?	Project documentation Fact finding
2	Is the conversion plan in accordance with EDP standards?	Project documentation Fact finding
3	Has a plan been established to test the new system?	Project documentation Fact finding
4	Is the test plan in accordance with EDP standards	Project documentation Checklist
5	Have sufficient resources been allocated for the conversion?	Project documentation Judgment Consultants
6	Have sufficient resources been allocated for the system test?	Project documentation Judgment Consultants
7	Is there a testing schedule?	Project documentation Fact finding
8	Is there a conversion schedule?	Project documentation Fact finding

Figure 7.10 **REVIEW POINT 7: REVIEW OF TESTING AND CONVERSION PLANNING**

	QUALITY ASSURANCE CONCERN	REVIEW PRACTICE
1	Are programs coded in accordance with EDP standards?	Observation Checklist
2	Are programs adequately tested?	Observation Checklist
3	Is the program code maintainable by the average programmer?	Observation Judgment
4	Has the system of internal control been implemented according to specifications?	System documentation Checklist

Figure 7.11 **REVIEW POINT 8: REVIEW OF PROGRAM CODING AND TESTING**

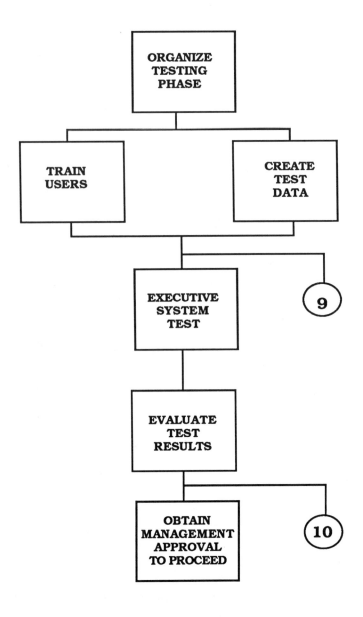

Figure 7.12 **TESTING PHASE**

along with the system when the problem is discovered. Therefore, it becomes important that the QA review is thorough and that resulting evaluation can be relied upon by management. It would be unusual for data processing management to authorize a system to go into production when QA has warned that it was not ready for that status.

Review Point 9: Detailed Test Plan

The detailed test plan includes the steps to be followed during the systems testing process. The test plan includes the criteria that must be met for the system to be acceptable for production. It identifies which tasks will be performed, who will perform them, when they will be performed, and who will verify the results.

The most important part of the test plan is the criteria which, when met, make this system acceptable. Many DP personnel fail to document these criteria and as a result incur high initial systems maintenance. Test data must be designed to test that the criteria is met. Criteria can include performance, for example, a defined response time in on-line systems or the proper handling of specified situations, such as rejecting certain types of transactions. Criteria can include the level of competence on the part of user personnel. The user should specify what criteria must be met.

Figure 7.13 lists six concerns for the review of the detailed test plan. This review depends heavily on the judgment of the QA team for five out of six concerns. This is indicative of the fact that we still have much to learn about how to test systems efficiently and effectively.

Review Point 10: Test Results

The final responsibility to determine that the system meets specifications resides with the user. The data processing department has taken the user's needs and converted them into a system. The system has been built on the understanding of the data processing personnel as to what the user said was wanted. Based on that understanding, they wrote programs and debugged them. Prior to the system going into production, the user must make an evaluation as to whether or not data processing people truly understood his needs. This is done through detailed evaluation of test results.

Systems test evaluation is a detailed, tedious, time-consuming task. There is no easy way to perform a systems test and evaluation. The results of processing normally must be manually calculated and then compared against computer-produced results. If the new and old systems have the same or similar records, the testing technique of parallel processing can be utilized. Parallel processing means running the same data through both systems and comparing results. Unfortunately this only applies to a small number of system test situations.

	QUALITY ASSURANCE CONCERN	**REVIEW PRACTICE**
1	Have a sufficient number of capable people been assigned to the system test phase?	Project documentation Fact finding Judgment
2	Will comprehensive test data be prepared?	Project documentation Checklist Judgment
3	Will users be adequately trained to evaluate test results?	Project documentation Fact finding
4	Will the planned test data test the system controls?	Project documentation Fact finding Judgment
5	Will the test phase be completed on time	Project documentation Fact finding Judgment
6	Will the test phase be completed within the budget?	Project documentation Fact finding Judgment

Figure 7.13 **REVIEW POINT 9: REVIEW ON DETAILED TEST PLAN**

Figure 7.14 lists five concerns for the review of test results. QA primarily reviews the evaluations of user and DP systems test personnel. Where additional test transactions are needed, those should have been specified by QA during the system test planning phase. QA should be more concerned with the test process than the test itself. For example, knowing how user personnel will manually calculate results and then compare them to computer-produced results is more important than QA actually making those comparisons.

	QUALITY ASSURANCE CONCERN	REVIEW PRACTICE
1	Does the system meet the needs of users as specified in the design?	Fact finding Observation Simulation modeling Testing Test data Base case
2	Does the system conform to EDP standards?	System documentation Observation Checklist
4	Is the user adequately trained to handle the day-to-day operational problems of the system?	Fact finding Observation Judgment
5	Have performance standards been achieved?	System documentation Judgment Testing Test data Base case

Figure 7.14 **REVIEW POINT 10: REVIEW OF TEST RESULTS**

CONVERSION PHASE

All systems undergo a conversion of some type. Even if there is no existing system, a conversion occurs when data processing converts from no system to a new system. This involves the building of master files, special first-run problems, and problems associated with inexperienced operating and user personnel.

The conversion of files from an old system to a new one involves all the steps in a systems development life cycle. The steps are condensed, but they all exist. The problems occur because data processing personnel frequently shortcut good systems practices during the conversion phase. For example, where special programs are needed to convert files, they are done with "quick and dirty" techniques. The normal processes of systems design, program design, and documentation do not occur. These traditional safeguards are ignored because they are not considered important. Shortcuts frequently cause serious problems.

QA must determine that the traditional good system safeguards are followed during the conversion process. When conversion standards do not exist, QA should check for compliance to normal systems development standards and procedures in the building of conversion systems and programs.

Problems occurring during the conversion phase can be more difficult to correct than normal production problems. Production systems normally have built-in procedures for correcting data, based on normal data entry procedures. Conversion systems seldom are that elaborate, and problems can occur during conversion that cannot be corrected by traditional means. For example, if a field is designated numeric, the system itself prevents other than numeric data from entering that field. If during the conversion process alphabetic data gets into that field, it may not be correctable because the new system may prevent any change in that field.

Figure 7.15 shows the major steps in the conversion phase. Within conversion are two QA review points. The first (Review Point 11) reviews the detailed conversion planning and program development step. The second (Review Point 12) is the review of the results of the conversion process.

Review Point 11: Detail Conversion Planning and Programs

QA reviewers are concerned that there are sufficient controls during the conversion phase to protect the system's data. These

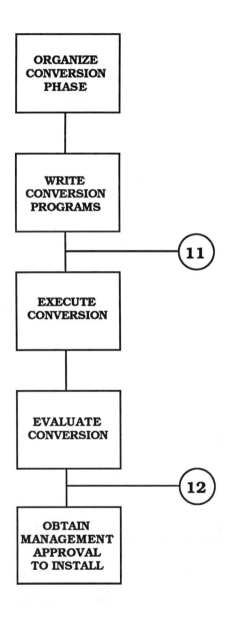

Figure 7.15 **CONVERSION PHASE**

controls may not be departmental standards and procedures. Because conversion occurs infrequently, many data processing departments have not bothered to develop conversion standards.

Figure 7.16 lists six QA concerns with the review of detailed conversion planning and program development. When conversion standards are not documented, QA should attempt to develop some general procedures and guidelines for the conversion process. When QA develops detailed checklists for reviewing the conversion process, those same checklists can be used by project personnel as they go through the process.

	QUALITY ASSURANCE CONCERN	REVIEW PRACTICE
1	Have a sufficient number of capable people been assigned to the system conversion phase?	Project documentation Fact finding Judgment
2	Are conversion programs coded and tested in accordance with EDP standards?	System documentation Observation Checklist
3	Has a contingency plan been made in case the conversion is unsuccessful?	Project documentation Fact finding
4	Will the conversion phase be completed on time?	Project documentation Fact finding Judgment
5	Will the conversion phase be completed within budget?	Project documentation Fact finding Judgment
6	Are the controls over the conversion process adequate to ensure an accurate and complete conversion	System documentation Fact finding Checklist

Figure 7.16 **REVIEW POINT 11: REVIEW OF DETAIL CONVERSION PLANNING AND PROGRAMS**

Review Point 12: Review of Conversion Results

The final step for QA is to determine that the conversion process has been successfully completed. These steps parallel very closely the steps for verifying test results. Final responsibility for the accuracy and completeness of the conversion process rests with the user, who must mandate use of tests to be sure the conversion process has been successfully completed.

If files need to be converted, or new files created, the user must examine a sufficient number of records on those files to assure themselves of the successful conversion of the data. This also includes totaling the key amount fields to assure that the totals of the old file agree to the totals in the converted file. Small errors, even in nonmoney fields, have been known to cost organizations dearly. In one example, the last digit in a post office box number was deleted on an accounts payable master file. Checks in the amount of several hundred thousand dollars were sent to the wrong post office box and cashed by the holder. The funds were never recovered.

Figure 7.17 lists two concerns for the review of conversion results. While the steps are limited, the process is difficult, time consuming, and very important. The primary responsibility will be to see that the user and data processing personnel have followed the plan in sufficient detail to be sure the conversion process is successful.

	QUALITY ASSURANCE CONCERN	REVIEW PRACTICE
1	Was the conversion performed in accordance with conversion standards?	System documentation Checklist
2	Have the results of the conversion process been verified?	Fact finding Observation Checklist

Figure 7.17 **REVIEW POINT 12: REVIEW OF CONVERSION RESULTS**

DETERMINING IF CONCERNS HAVE BEEN ADEQUATELY ADDRESSED BY THE PROJECT TEAM

A concern is normally a broad area which requires investigation to determine whether or not the project team has adequately addressed that area. For example one concern is whether or not the project team has developed an adequate test plan. To ask the question "Have you developed an adequate test plan?" would not produce a meaningful answer because the answer would be an opinion.

What is needed to evaluate a concern is a list of criteria, which if met, would mean the concern has been adequately addressed. In our test plan example some of the criteria that should be included in the test plan are:

1. Error conditions are tested.
2. Null input and 1 record file are tested.
3. Backup/recovery procedures are tested.
4. Manual interface procedures are tested.
5. File limits are tested.
6. Error correction and reentry procedures are tested.
7. Audit trails are tested.
8. Etc, etc, etc.

If all these criteria are met then the QA group could conclude the test plan was adequate. The review would provoke no argument. However these criteria must be developed and agreed upon by involved parties prior to conducting a review using those criteria.

SUMMARY

The QA review is a continuing process during the entire systems development life cycle. QA should become involved in as many points as practical for a system under development. This will provide data processing management with the continual monitoring of the health and well-being of all projects as they are being developed.

Twelve QA review points are recommended. Making reviews at these twelve points will involve quality assurance personnel at the major decision points and at the times when they can most easily influence the system design process.

QA can perform two functions during reviews. The first and most important is to provide an evaluation of the development process to data processing management. The second is to provide assistance and counsel to the project team. While the main responsibility is evaluation, the major contribution can be recommendations and suggestions to project personnel on design dilemmas.

Management of user organizations is faced with "go – no go" decisions at several points during the systems development life cycle. Depending on the point, and the value of the system, the decision may be made by executive management, user management, data processing management, or a combination thereof. Normally, the go – no go decisions during the early phases are made by executive management, during the middle phases by user management, and end phases by either data processing or user management. While QA is solely a data processing advisory group, data processing management may wish to pass the QA evaluation on to other management as an input to them in the decision making process. In other cases, data processing management may use QA input as a factor in making its decision on the advisability of continuing system application development.

This chapter has provided a list of QA concerns for each of the twelve review points. The reviewers should use these in formulating their review methodology for each of the twelve review points. With each concern is listed one or more review practices that can be used by the reviewer in determining how the project personnel or DP department handled that concern. Once the reviewers have considered each concern, they are in a position to make an evaluation of the application. The review practices are covered in the following chapter, and the evaluation methodology in Chapter 9.

Chapter 8
REVIEWING THE ADEQUACY OF APPLICATION CONTROLS

One of the major responsibilities of quality assurance groups is to review the adequacy of application controls. For many QA groups, this involves three tasks:

1. Review the controls in application systems.
2. Recommend controls in application systems.
3. Develop control standards for application systems.

A system of internal controls is a structured grouping of controls. Controls are not independent of each other but are an integrated system. Internal controls must be developed and assessed as a system. Internal control should be developed and implemented as a hierarchical structure or system. Internal control policy is established at the highest organizational level and expanded, amplified, implemented, and enforced throughout the entire organization. Control is too often viewed as an independent segment within each business system. This often leads to a duplication of controls and an excessive expenditure for control.

INTERNAL CONTROL DEFINED

Internal control can be defined in both a broad and narrow sense. When defined narrowly it usually is referred to as *internal accounting control*, and when referred to in a broad sense it is referred to as *internal control*. Quality assurance personnel should look at control in the broad sense.

An early and broad definition by the American Institute of Certified Public Accountants appears to be closely tied to management's needs:

Internal controls comprise the plan of organization and all methods and procedures that are concerned mainly with, and related directly to, the safeguarding of assets and the reliability of the financial records. They generally include such controls as the system of authorization and approval, separation of duties concerned with record keeping, and accounting reports from those concerned with operations or asset custody, physical controls over assets, and internal accounting.*

The objective of internal accounting control as defined in the Foreign Corrupt Practices Act deals with the four areas:

1. *Authorization.* Transactions are executed in accordance with management's general or specific authorization.
2. *Recording.* Transactions are recorded as necessary to permit preparation of financial statements in conformity with generally accepted accounting principles or any other criteria applicable to such statements, and to maintain accountability for assets.
3. *Access to assets.* Access to assets is permitted only in accordance with management's authorization.
4. *Asset accountability.* The recorded accountability for assets is compared with the existing assets at reasonable intervals and appropriate action is taken with respect to any differences.   Internal control is divided into environmental controls and application controls. The environmental controls govern the methods by which work is performed and apply to everybody in an organization. Examples include selected programming languages, system development life cycle, and data security systems. Application controls deal exclusively with a single applica-tion such as payroll.

Environment Control Objectives

Environmental controls are developed in support of the organization's internal control policy. Environmental controls include the plan of organization and all the methods and procedures that are concerned with operational efficiency and adherence to managerial policies. Environmental controls usually relate only indirectly to the financial records. Public ac-

---

* Section 320.10, Statement on Auditing Standard No. 1, copyright 1973, American Institute of Certified Public Accountants.

countants frequently refer to environmental controls as administrative or general controls. The internal control environment established by management has a significant impact on the selection and effectiveness of the company's application control procedures and techniques.

Application Control Objectives

More effort has gone into defining application control objectives than environmental control objectives. This is because the emphasis traditionally has been on application controls.

The three application control objectives are *accuracy, completeness,* and *authorization.* These are supplemented by other control objectives of lesser importance. The importance given to these objectives depend upon whether the evaluator's perspective is financial or operational.

Approaches to control design are as different as approaches to application design. It has been established that there are 50,000 different payroll applications in the United States. If organizations can develop that many different approaches to an application, they can develop an equal number of approaches to control.

High-volume transactions tend to be processed accurately, completely, and are authorized. It is the unusual or nonrecurring transactions that tend to cause the most problems. In many organizations the documented procedures on how to handle unusual/nonrecurring transactions are not as extensive as for high-volume transactions. Therefore, when designing application controls, attention should be paid to these unusual and/or nonrecurring transactions.

The application control objectives of the major accounting associations were studied in developing a set of application control objectives that could be used to explain application control design and assessment. The control objectives were chosen to illustrate the use of controls in applications as discussed below.

Accurate Data. Accurate data implies need for correction of inaccuracies associated with data preparation, conversion to machine-readable format, processing by the computer, or in the output preparation and delivery processes.

Complete Data. Completeness of processed data requires that data is not lost during preparation, in transit to the computer, during processing, between interrelated computer systems, and/or in transit to users of that data.

Timely Data. The timely processing of data ensures that management has the necessary information to take action in time to avert avoidable losses.

Authorized Data. Controls should ensure that any unauthorized data is detected prior to and during processing.

Processed According to GAAP. Financial data should be processed in accordance with generally accepted accounting procedures. Controls should ensure that these procedures are followed.

Compliance with Organization's Policies and Procedures. Organizations establish policies and procedures for handling transaction data. Controls should ensure that the data is processed according to those policies and procedures.

Compliance with Laws and Regulations. Regulatory agencies establish laws and regulations regarding the processing of transaction data. In today's business environment, many of these regulated transactions are highly visible, such as misuse of organizational funds on officers' expense accounts. Improper transactions can result in immediate repercussions to both individuals and their organization. Controls should ensure that laws and regulations are followed.

Adequate Supporting Evidence. Controls should ensure that sufficient evidence exists to reconstruct transactions and pinpoint accountability for processing. This evidence may also be used for restart and recovery purposes in computerized business applications. The evidence should enable tracing from source documents to control totals, and from control totals back to the supporting transactions. The methods for achieving these application control objectives are set forth in later sections of this manual.

ACCEPTABLE LEVEL OF RISK

Data processing organizations are continually subjected to the probability of loss due to risk. The primary purpose of controls is to reduce the amount of probable loss. If there is no risk, there need be no controls. Thus, in designing controls, the controls should always cost less to install than the savings achieved due to reducing losses.

Figure 8.1 illustrates the relationship of the cost of controls to the loss due to risk. At the leftmost side of the chart, we see that probable loss is maximized and there are no controls. As controls are added, the cost of controlling the risk situation increases, but the probable loss due to risk is reduced. At some point, these lines cross, which is normally the most cost-effective point for controls. On the right side of the chart we see that while the risk continues to drop, the cost of controls escalates. The total cost of any risk situation is the total of the probable loss due to the risk plus the cost of controlling that risk.

Most users of computer applications recognize that it is not cost-effective to reduce losses to zero. Therefore, application system users need to accept that there will be loss situations. For example, invoices will be mispriced, payroll will be miscalculated, checks will be processed for the wrong amount, etc., etc. The question that needs to be answered is, "How much loss is acceptable?" The answer to that question determines the level of controls to be designed.

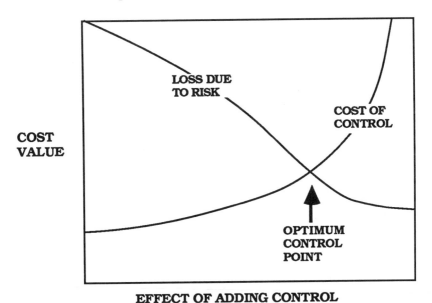

EFFECT OF ADDING CONTROL

Figure 8.1 **COST-EFFECTIVENESS CURVE OF CONTROL**

Let's look at a banking example. When a teller in a bank cashes a check, the teller is faced with two risks: first, the account holder will have insufficient funds to cover the amount of the check; and second, the individual presenting the check is doing so illegally.

The bank has several decisions to make in addressing this risk in their application systems. The system includes both manual and automated segments. The bank could reduce losses to zero by implementing controls which verify the account balance, immediately reduce the account balance, obtain positive identification that the person presenting the check is authorized, verify the signature against a signature card, and so on. Unfortunately, this level of control would be very time consuming and would substantially reduce the number of customers the bank teller could handle in a given period of time. On the other hand, without any control, the losses from bad checks may be so significant that the bank would go out of business.

The question the bank must answer is, "What is a reasonable amount of bad checks that a teller should accept?" For example, the bank might decide that each teller would be operating effectively if the bad checks he or she accepted did not exceed $500 per year. This becomes a systems requirement, and controls are designed to reduce the number of bad checks to that level.

Obviously, the effectiveness of control must be measured. If the bank managers find that with the implemented controls losses are approximately $500 per teller per year, they can be satisfied that the controls are achieving the risk requirements. On the other hand, if losses exceed $500 per teller per year, controls need to be tightened; and if losses are negligible, controls might be too tight and should be loosened.

You can see from this example that there are a lot of considerations in determining what level of loss is acceptable. This process is not followed by many organizations. This section is designed to help quality assurance analysts help systems analysts and users understand risk, and develop controls that will reduce that risk to an acceptable level.

METHODS FOR REDUCING LOSSES

Controls are designed to reduce the loss associated with risk. When the risk is high, controls should be strong, and when the risk is low only minimal controls may be needed. In some instances, the user may be willing to accept the risk, and thus no controls are needed.

The probable loss due to risk can be determined through either historical information or risk analysis. Historical information tells us what the expected losses will be in a given situation. We then use that experience in estimating losses in new situations.

Risk analysis is a methodology for determining the expected loss in a risk situation. The risk analysis algorithm involves two factors:

1. The frequency of occurrence of a loss situation
2. The average dollar loss per occurrence

The probable loss due to risk is calculated by multiplying the frequency of occurrence times the average loss per occurrence (see Figure 8.2).

There are four methods for reducing loss in a risk situation. The frequency of occurrence of loss due to risk can be reduced by reducing the frequency of occurrence of loss situations and reducing the opportunity for loss. The average loss per occurrence can be reduced by reducing the amount subject to loss and reducing the impact of the loss. Each of these four methods of reducing risk is accomplished through the implementation of controls. However, it is helpful in discussing these controls to understand how they can reduce loss. Therefore, each of the methods will be discussed individually.

REDUCE THE FREQUENCY OF OCCURRENCE

The most effective way to reduce losses is to reduce the events that lead to losses. For example, if 100 data entry errors occur per day there is probability of 100 individual losses per day. If the frequency of data entry errors can be reduced to 50 per day, the probability of loss is equally reduced.

The following are just some of the methods that are effective in reducing the frequency of occurrence of loss events.

1. Verify the correctness of input.
2. Identify problems and search them out before they occur.
3. Enter data only once into computer applications.
4. Reduce the amount of data entered (i.e., use codes rather than alphabetic descriptions).

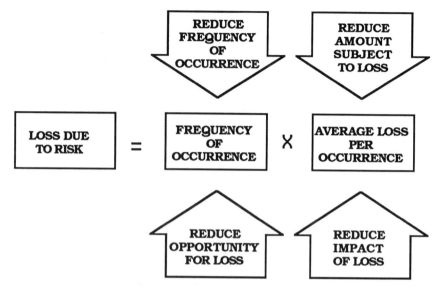

Figure 8.2 **REDUCING RISKS**

REDUCE OPPORTUNITY FOR LOSS

The conditions that lead to loss can be monitored to detect problems before they result in losses. Once the frequency of occurrences has been reduced as far as practical, monitoring of those events can help control the opportunity for error, and thus loss. Some of these controls can exist within computer applications, but many are external to the automated segment of the application.

The methods that can be used to reduce the opportunity for loss include:

1. *Manual monitoring.* People oversee events to look for errors before computer results are released for action.
2. *Anticipation audits.* Problem situations are anticipated, such as might occur when a customer orders a significantly larger amount of product than normally ordered, so that potential errors can be investigated.
3. *Authorization.* The approval process usually involves verifying compliance and reasonableness of the event.
4. *Training.* Employees are taught how to look for and anticipate problems in the normal course of their job.

REDUCE AMOUNT SUBJECT TO LOSS

Information systems can be structured so that the amount subject to loss is minimized. For example, in automated accounts payable systems, the value of a check produced by the system can be limited to a fixed amount, such as $1,000. This is imprinted on the check, and thus the loss due to any erroneously produced checks is limited to $1,000.

Two of the methods to reduce the amount subject to loss are

1. Divide property between two or more locations (e.g., backup data libraries).
2. Teach two or more people (e.g., programmers) to perform the same function.

REDUCE IMPACT OF LOSS

The impact of the loss can be reduced by recouping all or part of the loss. Minimizing the impact involves taking corrective action after the loss has occurred. Normally, the quicker the action, the more the impact can be minimized.

Among the methods that help reduce the impact of loss are

1. Insuring the loss through an insurance company or a self-insurance procedure.
2. Maintaining backup data to reconstruct processing in the event of problems, or when erroneous output is produced.
3. Creating audit trails that enable systems to substantiate and/or reconstruct processing.

TYPES OF CONTROLS

Four different methods for reducing losses through controls have been presented in this chapter. These methods use one or more of the following types of controls:

1. Preventive controls stop an undesirable event from occurring.
2. Detective controls uncover an undesirable event as it occurs.
3. Corrective controls provide the means for restoring a situation to normal after an unacceptable event.

The three types of controls can be illustrated in a fire situation. Fire is a risk that can result in loss to an organization. Preventive controls such as fire-resistant materials and firewalls stop the fire from occurring. Detective controls such as smoke detectors and fire alarms identify and announce that a fire has occurred. Corrective controls provide the means of putting out the fire; these include sprinkler system, fire department, and fire extinguishers.

The implementation and operation of preventive, detective, or corrective controls can be in one of the following two manners:

1. *Discretionary controls.* The execution and effectiveness of the control is left to the option of the implementer. For example, a guard may decide to challenge or not challenge a visitor; a supervisor may decide to verify for compliance or not to verify an event prior to approving it. Discretionary controls are normally associated with people controls. For example, an automobile seat belt is a discretionary control. People can decide whether or not they want to use the control when they get in an automobile.

2. *Nondiscretionary controls.* Controls whose use are mandatory are considered nondiscretionary controls. Normally, nondiscretionary controls are automated controls in either a manual or computerized environment. For example, air bags in an automobile activate on impact automatically, and computer system data validation routines operate on all input data. Nondiscretionary controls are dependable and consistent.

The effectiveness of the various types of control is illustrated in Figure 8.3. This figure shows that nondiscretionary controls are more effective than discretionary controls. In addition, the figure shows that the coupling of detective and corrective controls are important. Detective controls without corrective action may be of little value. For example, a fire alarm ringing serves no purpose unless corrective action is taken to put out the fire.

REVIEWING CONTROLS *

Controls should be reviewed throughout the systems development process. The control design process parallels the systems design

---

*   Audit Guide for Assessing Reliability of Computer Output, U.S. General Accounting Office, May 1978.

process. Controls are specified as needs, designed, implemented, documented, and tested.

The adequacy of control for a given application depends upon both the environmental and application controls. However, because environmental controls are common to most applications the quality assurance function may need to review environmental controls only once for all applications. Based on this review, the review of application controls may need to be increased or decreased depending upon the strength of the environmental controls.

This chapter provides quality assurance analysts with both environmental and application control checklists. In addition, a summarization form is included for both parts of control to aid the quality assurance analyst in evaluating the adequacy of the controls. Prior to presenting the questionnaires, let's review the more common system vulnerabilities.

METHOD OF IMPLEMEN-TATION	TYPE OF CONTROL		
	PREVENTIVE	DETECTIVE	
		with corresponding CORRECTIVE	without CORRECTIVE
DISCRE-TIONARY	Least effective, generally manual controls applied at front end of processing. However, moderately efficient.	Moderately effective manual controls probably least efficient controls.	Least effective and possibly dangerous since users rely improperly on them. Very inefficient.
NONDISCRE-TIONARY	Moderately effective, generally EDP controls, applied at front end of processing. Probably most efficient controls.	Most effective, generally controls which are computerized are applied before processing can take place. Moderarely efficient	May have some remote effectiveness but probably little. Highly inefficient

Figure 8.3 **EFFECTIVENESS AND EFFICIENCY OF CONTROLS**

COMMON SYSTEM VULNERABILITIES[*]

The list of risks helps explain what are the new and possibly increased risks in a computerized environment. It is presented as a tool for quality assurance to use in the identification of what may be different, from a risk perspective, in a computerized environment.

Erroneous or Falsified Data Input

Erroneous or falsified input data is the simplest and most common cause of undesirable performance by an applications system. Vulnerabilities occur wherever data is collected, manually processed, or prepared for entry to the computer.

- Unreasonable or inconsistent source data values may not be detected.
- Keying errors during transcription may not be detected.
- Incomplete or poorly formatted data records may be accepted and treated as if they were complete records.
- Records in one format may be interpreted according to a different format.
- An employee may fraudulently add, delete, or modify data (e.g., payment vouchers, claims) to obtain benefits (e.g., checks, negotiable coupons) for himself or herself.
- Lack of document counts and other controls over source data or input transactions may allow some of the data or transactions to be lost without detection— or allow extra records to be added.
- Records about the data entry personnel (e.g., a record of a personnel action) may be modified during data entry.
- Data that arrives at the last minute (or under some other special or emergency condition) may not be verified prior to processing.
- Records in which errors have been detected may be corrected without verification of the full record.

Misuse by Authorized End Users

End users are the people who are served by the EDP system. The system is designed for their use, but they can also misuse it for

---

[*]   U.S. Natural Bureau of Standard, FIPS Pub. 65, pp. 2–17 to 2–21.

undesirable purposes. It is often very difficult to determine whether their use of the system is in accordance with the legitimate performance of their job.

- An employee may convert information to an unauthorized use; for example, he may sell privileged data about an individual to a prospective employer, credit agency, insurance company, or competitor; or he may use statistics for stock market transactions before their public release.
- A user whose job requires access to individual records in a file may manage to compile a complete listing of the file and then make unauthorized use of it (e.g., sell a listing of employees' home addresses as a mailing list).
- Unauthorized altering of information may be accomplished for an unauthorized end user (e.g., theft of services).
- An authorized user may use the system for personal benefit (e.g., theft of services).
- A supervisor may manage to approve and enter a fraudulent transaction.
- A disgruntled or terminated employee may destroy or modify records—possibly in such a way that backup records are also corrupted and useless.
- An authorized user may accept a bribe to modify or obtain information.

Uncontrolled System Access

Organizations expose themselves to unnecessary risk if they fail to establish controls over who can enter the EDP area, who can use the EDP system, and who can access the information contained in the system.

- Data or programs may be stolen from the computer room or other storage areas.
- EDP facilities may be destroyed or damaged either by intruders or employees.
- Individuals may not be adequately identified before they are allowed to enter the EDP area.
- Remote terminals may not be adequately protected from use by unauthorized persons.
- An unauthorized user may gain access to the system via a dial-in line and an authorized user's password.

- Passwords may be inadvertently revealed to unauthorized individuals. A user may write his password in some convenient place, or the password may be obtained from card decks, discarded printouts, or by observing the user as he types it.
- A user may leave a logged-in terminal unattended, allowing an unauthorized person to use it.
- A terminated employee may retain access to an EDP system because his name and password are not immediately deleted from authorization tables and control lists.
- An unauthorized individual may gain access to the system for his own purposes (e.g., theft of computer service, data, or programs, modification of data, alteration of programs, sabotage, denial of services).
- Repeated attempts by the same user or terminal to gain unauthorized access to the system to a file may go undetected.

Ineffective Security Practices for the Application

Inadequate manual checks and controls to ensure correct processing by the EDP system or negligence by those responsible for carrying out these checks result in many vulnerabilities.

- Poorly defined criteria for authorized access may result in employees not knowing what information they, or others, are permitted to access.
- The person responsible for security may fail to restrict user access only to those processes and data which are needed to accomplish assigned tasks.
- Large funds disbursements, unusual price changes, and unanticipated inventory usage may not be reviewed for correctness.
- Repeated payments to the same party may go unnoticed because there is no review.
- Sensitive data may be carelessly handled by the application staff, by the mail service, or by other personnel within the organization.
- Postprocessing reports analyzing system operations may not be reviewed to detect security violations.
- Inadvertent modification or destruction of files may occur when trainees are allowed to work on live data.

- Appropriate action may not be pursued when a security variance is reported to the system security officer or to the perpetrating individual's supervisor; in fact, procedures covering such occurrences may not exist.

Procedural Errors at the EDP Facility

Both errors and intentional acts committed by the EDP operations staff may result in improper operational procedures, lapsed controls, and losses in storage media and output.

Procedures and Controls

- Files may be destroyed during data base reorganization or during release of disk space.
- Operators may ignore operational procedures; for example, by allowing programmers to operate computer equipment.
- Job control language parameters may be erroneous.
- An installation manager may circumvent operational controls to obtain information.
- Careless or incorrect restarting after shutdown may cause the state of a transaction update to be unknown.
- An operator may enter erroneous information at CPU console (e.g., control switch in wrong position, terminal user allowed full system access, operator cancels wrong job from queue).
- Hardware maintenance may be performed while production data is on-line and the equipment undergoing maintenance is not isolated.
- An operator may perform unauthorized acts for personal gain (e.g., make extra copies of competitive bidding reports, print copies of unemployment checks, delete a record from journal file).
- Operations staff may sabotage the computer (e.g., drop pieces of metal into a terminal).
- The wrong version of a program may be executed.
- A program may be executed twice using the same transactions.
- An operator may bypass required safety controls (e.g., write rings for tape reels).
- Supervision of operations personnel may not be adequate during nonworking hour shifts.

- Due to incorrectly learned procedures, an operator may alter or erase the master files.

- A console operator may override a label check without recording the action in the security log.

Storage Media Handling

- Critical tape files may be mounted without being write protected.

- Inadvertently or intentionally mislabeled storage media are erased. In a case where they contain backup files, the erasure may not be noticed until it is needed.

- Internal labels on storage media may not be checked for correctness.

- Files with missing or mislabeled expiration dates may be erased.

- Incorrect processing of data or erroneous updating of files may occur when card decks have been dropped, partial input decks are used, write rings mistakenly are placed in tapes, paper tape is incorrectly mounted, or wrong tape is mounted.

- Scratch tapes used for jobs processing sensitive data may not be adequately erased after use.

- Temporary files written during a job step for use in subsequent steps may be erroneously released or modified through inadequate protection of the files or because of an abnormal termination.

- Storage media containing sensitive information may not get adequate protection because operations staff is not advised of the nature of the information content.

- Tape management procedures may not adequately account for the current status of all tapes.

- Magnetic storage media that have contained very sensitive information may not be degaussed before being released.

- Output may be sent to the wrong individual or terminal.

- Improperly operating output or postprocessing units (e.g., bursters, decollators, or multipart forms) may result in loss of output.

- Surplus output material (e.g., duplicates of output data, used carbon paper) may not be disposed of properly.

- Tapes and programs that label output for distribution may be erroneous or not protected from tampering.

Program Errors

Application programs should be developed in an environment that requires and supports complete, correct, and consistent program design, good programming practices, adequate testing, review, and documentation, and proper maintenance procedures. Although programs developed in such an environment will still contain undetected errors, programs not developed in this manner will probably be rife with errors. Additionally, programmers can deliberately modify programs to produce undesirable side effects, or they can misuse the programs they are in charge of.

- Records may be deleted from sensitive files without a guarantee that the deleted records can be reconstructed.
- Programmers may insert special provisions in programs that manipulate data concerning themselves (e.g., a payroll programmer may alter his own payroll records).
- Data may not be stored separately from code with the result that program modifications are more difficult and must be made more frequently.
- Program changes may not be tested adequately before use in a production run.
- Changes to a program may result in new errors because of unanticipated interactions between program modules.
- Program acceptance tests may fail to detect errors that only occur for unusual combinations of input (e.g., a program that is supposed to reject all except a specified range of values actually accepts an additional value).
- Programs, the content of which should be safeguarded, may not be identified and protected.
- Code, test data with its associated output, and documentation for certified programs may not be filed and retained for reference.
- Documentation for vital programs may not be safeguarded.
- Programmers may fail to keep a change log, maintain back copies, or formalize record-keeping activities.
- An employee may steal programs he is maintaining and use them for personal gain (e.g., sale to a commercial organization, hold another organization for extortion).

- Poor program design may result in a critical data value being initialized twice. An error may occur when the program is modified to change the data value—but only changed in one place.

- Production data may be disclosed or destroyed when it is used during testing.

- Errors may result when the programmer misunderstands requests for changes to the program.

- Errors may be introduced by a programmer who makes changes directly to machine code.

- Programs may contain routines not compatible with their intended purpose, which can disable or bypass security protection mechanisms. For example, a programmer who anticipates being fired inserts code into a program which will cause vital system files to be deleted as soon as his name no longer appears in the payroll file.

- Inadequate documentation or labeling may result in wrong version of program being modified.

Operating System Flaws

Design and implementation errors, system generation and maintenance problems, and deliberate penetrations resulting in modifications to the operating system can produce undesirable effects in the application system. Flaws in the operating system are often difficult to prevent and detect.

- User jobs may be permitted to read or write outside assigned storage area.

- Inconsistencies may be introduced into data because of simultaneous processing of the same file by two jobs.

- An operating system design or implementation error may allow a user to disable audit controls or to access all system information.

- An operating system may not protect a copy of information as thoroughly as it protects the original.

- Unauthorized modification to the operating system may allow a data entry clerk to enter programs and thus subvert the system.

- An operating system crash may expose valuable information such as password lists or authorization tables.

- Maintenance personnel may bypass security controls while performing maintenance work. At such times the system is vulnerable to errors or intentional acts of the maintenance personnel, or anyone else who might also be on the system and discover the opening (e.g., microcoded sections of the operating system may be tampered with or sensitive information from on-line fields may be disclosed).

- An operating system may fail to record that multiple copies of output have been made from spooled storage devices.

- An operating system may fail to maintain an unbroken audit trail.

- When restarting after a system crash, the operating system may fail to ascertain that all terminal locations which were previously occupied are still occupied by the same individuals.

- A user may be able to get into monitor or supervisory mode.

- The operating system may fail to erase all scratch space assigned to a job after the normal or abnormal termination of the job.

- Files may be allowed to be read or written without having been opened.

Communications System Failure

Information being routed from one location to another over communication lines is vulnerable to accidental failures and to intentional interception and modification by unauthorized parties.

Accidental Failures

- Undetected communications errors may result in incorrect or modified data.

- Information may be accidentally misdirected to the wrong terminal.

- Communication nodes may leave unprotected fragments of messages in memory during unanticipated interruptions in processing.

- Communication protocols may fail to positively identify the transmitter or receiver of a message.

Intentional Acts

• Communications lines may be monitored by unauthorized individuals.

• Data or programs may be stolen via telephone circuits from a remote job entry terminal.

• Programs in the network switching computers may be modified to compromise security.

• Data may be deliberately changed by individuals tapping the line (requires some sophistication, but is applicable to financial data).

• An unauthorized user may "take over" a computer communication port as an authorized user disconnects from it. Many systems cannot detect the change. This is particularly true in much of the currently available communication protocols.

• If encryption is used, keys may be stolen.

• A terminal user may be "spoofed" into providing sensitive data.

• False messages may be inserted into the system.

• True messages may be deleted from the system.

• Messages may be recorded and replayed into the system.

REVIEWING ENVIRONMENTAL CONTROLS*

Environmental controls should be reviewed prior to reviewing application controls. The review should be performed by an individual who

1. Understands the data processing function's policies, procedures, and standards.

2. Understands how the operating environment functions.

3. Has had project management experience.

4. Understands operating system software.

5. Can identify the risks and controls in a computerized environment.

For the purpose of reviewing the environmental controls, the computerized environment has been divided into the following categories.

---

* Audit Guide for Assessing Reliability of Computer Output, U.S. General Accounting Office, May 1978.

Organizational Controls. Adequate separation of duties provides an effective check to ensure the accuracy and propriety of system and program changes and the consistency of information flowing through the computerized system. The related questions should establish the degree of job segregation within a data processing facility.

Computer Operation Controls. The related questions should help the quality assurance analyst determine whether the computer facility operates in accordance with prescribed processing procedures. An analysis of the responses should help the quality assurance analyst determine whether operating personnel could alter computer data without user knowledge.

Access Controls. These questions deal with access to the computer area, remote computer terminals, systems documentation, computer programs, and computer output. The quality assurance analyst should pay particular attention to the adequacy of documented security measures surrounding the entire system.

File Controls. These questions deal with maintenance, storage, and access to computer-processed tapes, disk packs, and other data storage media. The quality assurance analyst should pay particular attention to the adequacy of documented security measures for releasing, returning, and maintaining data files.

Disaster Recovery Controls. Disaster recovery controls are preventive procedures that help protect critical files, programs, and systems documentation from fire or other hazards. To the extent possible, the quality assurance analyst should examine the organization's preventive procedures to determine whether data processing could be continued in the event of a computer facility disaster.

The Environmental Control Review Questionnaire (see Figure 8.4) is divided into the above sections. The questionnaire is designed so that "no" answers should be considered a potential control deficiency. "No" answers require additional investigation. Space is included on the form to qualify or explain responses to the questions.

An EDP Department Controls Profile Worksheet (see Figure 8.5) should be used as a tool in assessing the adequacy of controls. The questionnaire probes a series of areas for the five environmental control characteristics (i.e., organizational, computer,

ITEM	RESPONSE			
	YES	*NO*	*N/A*	*OTHER*

Organizational Controls
 	
1. Is the EDP function independent from other operations?
2. Is each of the following functions performed by a different individual?
  a. Maintaining the operating system/ data management system, etc.
  b. Systems design
  c. Programming
  d. Acceptance testing
  e. Authorizing program changes
  f. Handling source documents (Keypunching, etc.)
  g. Hardware operations
  h. File maintenance (Librarian for data and files)
  i. Input data
 	
Computer Operation Controls
 	
1. Have documented procedures been established covering the operations of the data center? (If so, obtain copy.)
2. Are daily equipment operating logs maintained?
3. Is computer downtime shown and explained?
4. Is there an abnormal termination of job log or report for each such run?
5. Does an operator maintain a daily input/output log for each job processed?
6. Are these logs reviewed daily by the EDP operations manager?
7. Does the EDP operations manager initial each log to indicate that the review has been performed?				

Figure 8.4 **ENVIRONMENTAL CONTROL REVIEW QUESTIONNAIRE**

	RESPONSE			
ITEM	*YES*	*NO*	*N/A*	*OTHER*
Computer Operation Controls				
8. Are all operator decisions recorded in a daily log?				
9. Is the console typewriter used to list:				
a. Date?				
b. Job name and/or number?				
c. Program name and/or number?				
d. Start/stop times?				
e. Files used?				
f. Record counts				
g. Halts (programmed and unscheduled)?				
10. If the system does not have a console typewriter, does some other method afford adequate control and record the activities performed by both the computer and operator?				
11. Is all computer time accounted for from the time it is turned on each day until it is shut down?				
12. Are disposition notes entered on the console log showing corrective actions taken when unscheduled program halts occur?				
13. Are job reruns recorded on the console log?				
14. Is the reason for each rerun recorded?				
15. Are console log pages sequentially numbered?				
16. Is the console log reviewed and signed at the end of each shift by the supervisor and filed as a permanent record?				
17. Are console printouts independently examined to detect operator problems and unauthorized intervention?				

Figure 8.4 **ENVIRONMENTAL CONTROL REVIEW QUESTIONNAIRE (Cont'd)**

	RESPONSE			
ITEM	*YES*	*NO*	*N/A*	*OTHER*
18. Are provisions adequate to prevent unauthorized entry of program changes and/or data through the console and other devices?				
19. Does some form of printout indicate every operating run performed?				
20. Is there a procedure to prevent superseded programs from being used by mistake?				
21. Does the data center use a formal mechanism for scheduling jobs?				
22. Has a formal method been established for prioritizing the work schedules for operations?				
Access Controls				
A. Computer Area				
1. Is access to the computer area limited to necessary personnel?				
2. Are all employees requred to sign an agreement regarding their role and responsibility in the department and the ownership and use of processing equipment and information within the data center?				
3. Do combination locks, security badges, or other means restrict access to the computer room?				
4. Are combinations on locks or similar devices periodically changed?				
5. Are account codes, authorization codes, passwords, etc., controlled to prevent unauthorized usage?				
B. Remote Computer Terminals				
6. Are terminals adequately secured to prevent unauthorized usage?				
7. Are access passwords to remote terminals controlled to prevent unauthorized usage?				

Figure 8.4 **ENVIRONMENTAL CONTROL REVIEW QUESTIONNAIRE (Cont'd)**

	RESPONSE			
ITEM	YES	NO	N/A	OTHER
C. Systems Documentation				
8. Are operators denied access to program and system documentation?				
9. Are program listings inaccessible to computer operators?				
10. Do documented procedures exist for controlling systems documentation?				
D. Computer Programs				
11. Are programs protected from unauthorized access?				
12. Are privileged instructions in operating and other software systems strictly controlled?				
13. Does the agency use automated methods (e.g. a program management system) to restrict access to application programs?				
E. Computer Output				
14. Is access to blank stock of critical forms (i.e., negotiable instruments, identification cards, etc.) restricted to authorized individuals?				
15. Have controls been established over the issuance of critical forms for jobs being scheduled for processing?				
16. Are copies of critical output that needs to be destroyed maintained in a secure location until the destruction process can be accomplished?				
File Controls				
1. Is the responsibility for issuing and storing magnetic tapes and/or disk packs assigned to a tape librarian?				
2. Is the duty the librarian's chief responsibility?				
3. Are library procedures documented? (If so, obtain a copy.)				

Figure 8.4 **ENVIRONMENTAL CONTROL REVIEW QUESTIONNAIRE (Cont'd)**

ITEM	RESPONSE			
	YES	NO	N/A	OTHER
4. Is access to the library limited to the responsible librarian(s)?				
5. Does the agency use automated methods (e.g., a file management system) to restrict access to computerized files?				
6. Are all data files logged out and in to prevent release to unauthorized personnel?				
7. Are tape and disk inventory records maintained?				
8. Are tape and disk status records maintained?				
9. Have external labeling procedures been documented? (If so, obtain a copy.)				
10. Are external labels affixed to active tapes and/or disks? Do labels tie in with inventory records?				
11. Are work or scratch tapes or disk packs kept in a separate area of the library?				
Disaster Recovery Controls				
1. Has the computer system operated without major malfunction within the last year?				
2. Is the data center backed up by an uninterruptible power source system?				
3. Have procedures been established to describe what action should be taken in case of fire and other hazards involving the data center, data files, and computer programs?				
4. Are these procedures implemented as defined?				

Figure 8.4 **ENVIRONMENTAL CONTROL REVIEW QUESTIONNAIRE (Cont'd)**

	RESPONSE			
ITEM	*YES*	*NO*	*N/A*	*OTHER*
5. Are there provisions for retaining and/or copying master files and a practical means of reconstructing a damaged or destroyed file?				
6. Are sufficient generations of files maintained to facilitate reconstruction of records (grandfather-father-son routine)?				
7. Is at least one file generation maintained at a location other than the tape storage area?				
8. Are copies of critical files stored at a remote location and restricted from unauthorized access?				
9. Are copies of operating programs stored at outside the computer room?				
10. Are duplicate programs maintained at a remote location and restricted from unauthorized access?				
11. Have documented backup procedures been established with another compatible data center for running the agency's programs in the event of a natural disaster or other emergency situation?				
12. Are backup procedures periodically tested at the backup data center?				

Figure 8.4 **ENVIRONMENTAL CONTROL REVIEW QUESTIONNAIRE (Cont'd)**

access, file, and disaster recovery controls). You must use judgment in completing this profile. Based on the questionnaire responses relating to the control characteristics, how much risk (low, medium, high) do you believe is involved in relying on the computer-processed data? The information about controls requested on this form is designed to help you with this judgment.

PREPARER: _____   **DATE:** _____

REVIEWER: _____   **DATE:** _____

PART I

You must use judgment in completing this profile. Based on the question-naire responses relating to the control characteristics, how much risk (low, medium, high) do you believe is involved in relying on the computer-processed data? The information about controls requested on this form is designed to help you with this judgment.

CONTROL

Control Charac-teristic	Organiza-tional	Computer Operation	Access	File	Disaster Recovery
Is the control in place?					
Is the control effective?					
Is some alternate control in place?					
Is the alternate control effective?					
Level of potential risk					
COMMENTS					

Figure 8.5 **EDP DEPARTMENT CONTROLS PROFILE WORKSHEET**

PART 2

After you have assigned a potential risk assessment for each control characteristic, briefly describe your justification for assigning the various risk levels for each control characteristic noted on the previous page. This information should be used in preparing a report on the results of the control assessment.

Control Charac- teristic	Brief description of risk justification	Recommendation for further systems audit work

---

Figure 8.5 **EDP DEPARTMENT CONTROLS PROFILE WORKSHEET (Cont'd)**

After you have assigned a potential risk assessment for each control characteristic, briefly describe your justification for assigning the various risk levels for each control characteristic noted on the previous page. This information should be used in preparing a report on the results of the control assessment.

REVIEWING APPLICATION CONTROLS

The objectives of control do not change in a computerized environment. The same control objectives that are applicable to a manual system are equally applicable to a computerized system. What changes are the methods of control needed to achieve the control objectives.

The impact of the computer on the control objectives is limited to the activities that occur in a computerized environment. Many of the controls in a computerized environment occur outside the computer segment. These controls are not directly impacted by the computer. For example, an accounts receivable application system should include all the controls needed to assure that the receipt of cash and the control over those cash receipts are outside the computer system. Examples of appropriate controls within the computer system include the following.

1. The proper version of the program is in operation.
2. Data written on computer media can be fully retrieved.
3. Integrity of data is maintained as it is passed between programs. The control objectives in a computerized application are as follows
   a. Data is accurate.
   b. Data is complete.
   c. Data is authorized.
   d. Data is timely.
   e. Data is supportable.

Data Is Accurate[*]

The risk of greater reliance on a single source of information makes inaccurate data a higher concern. If data is inaccurate, it will be used inaccurately by all applications that use that particular data element. For example, if a product price is wrong, it will result in inaccurate customer billing, inventory value, credits, sales commission and bonuses, etc.

Errors affecting the accuracy of data may not be detected due to the fact that people are not monitoring the data and details may not be balanced to totals after processing. For example, if an element of information is entered as $69 as a detail record, but $89 is added to the control total, that condition will not be detected until a reconciliation has been made. At that point, the cost of correcting the inaccuracy may exceed the value of the error.

---

[*]   Draft, December 17, 1980, Guideline on Computer Security Audit for the General Auditor, Center for Programming Science and Technology, Institute for Computer Sciences and Technology, National Bureau of Standards, Washington, D.C. 20234.

The greater accessibility to data makes the possibility of intentional and unintentional manipulation greater. People interfacing with the computer may change the value of individual records, values between records, or take small amounts from many records and place them into an account under their control. All these manipulations affect the accuracy of data in the data base.

To achieve accuracy, an organization must make sure of the following.

1.   Data is not truncated.
2.   Data is entered correctly.
3.   Data is accumulated correctly.
4.   Data is identifiable to the user.
5.   Data is not misrepresented through electronic limitations such as overflow.

Data Is Complete

Because of the greater reliance on data as a source of information, the risk associated with incomplete data is increased. In a manual application, if data is incomplete only a single transaction may be affected. In a computerized environment, every application using the incomplete data is affected.

An incomplete data condition may not be detected until it is too late to take corrective action because the details may not be regularly balanced to the totals. If extended periods of time occur between reconciliations, data can be lost, and the cost of searching for that data could exceed its value.

The centralization of data in a computer provides greater accessibility to that data. This greater accessibility provides an opportunity to manipulate the data for the advantage of a particular individual. In this manipulation, data (i.e., organizational assets) can be lost.

In a data base environment, data can be lost due to simultaneous updating. Two programs may attempt to update the same element of data simultaneously. Without proper controls, one of the two updates will be lost when the data is returned to the data base. Data can also be lost if a pointer chain is broken.

To assure completeness of data, an organization would want to check the following.

1.   Transactions are not lost.
2.   All transactions are entered.

3.   Transactions are entered in the proper accounting period.
4.   Lost transactions can be identified.
5.   Detailed records support the control totals.

Data Is Authorized

The main impact of the computer on the authorization of data is the changing methods of authorization. The primary control over data authorization has been with the user level. This is not part of the computer environment. However, this is changing, as authorization is being automated. For example, inventory is being automatically replenished.

Because there is greater accessibility to data, the possibility exists that unauthorized data will be entered. Access controls in a computer system can lessen this possibility. The data in most organizations is not equally accessible to all users. Restrictions are imposed for a variety of reasons. Access to raw data is often restricted because interpretation of the raw data cannot be made without specialized knowledge or information which is not stored with the data. Some data is viewed as private and given special protection because the information could be used to the disadvantage of the person or organization. Sometimes aggregated data is viewed as worthy of protection, while the individual components are considered to have no special value (e.g., individual sales data may be accorded only minor protection, but total sales figures are severely restricted).

The authority to enter data by means of source transactions or maintenance activities is usually much more controlled than the authority to access it. To protect the organization from defalcation, the authority to enter and access data is enforced in various ways. The ability to change data is often restricted to transactions which automatically provide a complete audit trail. This is analogous to the accounting requirement that no erasures are permitted in accounting journals: corrections require an adjusting transaction in the journal of transactions, rather than a simple change to an existing entry.

The authorization of data can be controlled using security profiles of users. These profiles have the capability to control data in the following manners:

1.   Use (e.g., read only, update, delete, etc.).
2.   Control use at field level.
3.   Limit use by values (e.g., update pay rate field for fields with a value of up to $199.99).

4.   Limit rate of change (e.g., change pay rate field by no more than plus or minus 10%).

To achieve the authorized audit objective, an organization would want to make sure of the following.

1.   Improperly authorized data is not accepted.
2.   Data that is not authorized is not accepted.
3.   Authorization is verified.
4.   Practices to avoid proper authorization, such as issuing two. small purchase orders rather than one large, are identified.

Data Is Timely

Information from application systems should be available at the time of decision or action. The information needs to be available for the appropriate individual at the correct location. In many cases, failure to provide information will result in improper decisions or actions.

Timeliness is dependent on the application and type of information. In some applications, information is not critical to the process and thus the timely control objective assumes minimal importance. In other applications, such as on-line status systems, action cannot be taken until the needed information is available.

To assure timeliness of data, an organization would need to make sure that

1.   Information is sent to the right place.
2.   Information is delivered to the right person.
3.   Information is delivered on time.
4.   The needed information is identified.

Data Is Supportable

The *audit trail* is a control used for providing evidence for problems that have been detected or verifying the propriety of processing. If an authorization violation is detected and the audit trail is incomplete, the necessary corrective action may not be ascertainable. Thus, anything that affects the completeness of the audit trail has an effect on data authorization.

The adequacy of an audit trail can be viewed from two perspectives: first that it is complete; and second that the data needed is easily obtained. The computerized environment has a minor impact on the type of data retained for audit trail purposes.

In actual practice, the movement to computerized environments usually increases the amount of data available for audit trail purposes. This is because the operating environment also retains data that can be used for audit trail purposes. There is a risk that the audit trail will be split into many segments. One part of the audit trail is located with all the application data, and the second part is retained in the operating environment as part of the recovery activity. Without proper planning, it may be extremely difficult, and probably impractical, to piece together all the segments of the audit trail. Thus, while the audit trail data may exist, for practical purposes the audit trail is incomplete.

The operating environment audit trail is often destroyed within a brief time because of the extensiveness of the audit trail. Some organizations use a utility program to condense the amount of data retained for audit trail purposes. Others retain the information only as long as is needed to recover from hardware and software failures. In most organizations, the operating audit trail information is retained in a time sequence so it can be used to recover operations. This may make it impractical to locate the needed information for the more traditional purposes of substantiating processing.

To make sure data is supportable, an organization would be concerned that

1. Transaction processing can be supported.
2. The support is adequate.
3. Transactions can be traced to control totals.
4. Control totals can be supported by detailed transactions.
5. Support information is readily retrievable.

Application Control Review

For the purpose of reviewing the application controls, the application has been divided into several categories:

Application System Overview. This questionnaire should be completed for each computerized application; although the data gathered is not directly related to data reliability, it will provide the quality assurance analyst with useful systems information. This document should be kept in the permanent file and updated during subsequent reviews.

System Documentation and Program Modification. Comprehensive and current documentation is necessary to describe how a computer application operates. In assessing the adequacy of a system's documentation, the quality assurance analyst should determine not only that the documentation reflects the application's current status, but also that the documentation is complete and in accordance with established standards. Although comprehensive documentation is normally prepared when an application is initially implemented, subsequent changes may be inadequately documented and should be given special attention.

Data Input. Input controls are established to verify that data is accurately transferred from an external document into a machine-readable format. The quality assurance analyst should try to make sure that source data reaches the processing programs without loss, unauthorized additions, or error.

Data Error. Data error controls involve the detection, correction, and resubmission of erroneous data. Adequate controls over rejected data are necessary for establishing a reliable data base and reliable computer-processed products. The quality assurance analyst should carefully review the handling of data errors and rejected data to ensure that corrected data is promptly reentered into the system without loss or unnecessary manipulation.

Batch Process. Computer programs should develop control totals after processing data. These control totals should be compared with totals previously developed in the data initiating or transcribing departments. Control totals should also be compared to help make sure that data is properly processed through the entire system, i.e., run-to-run totals and trailer label checking.

Telecommunications. These questions are concerned with two remote data entry categories — remote batch systems and on-line systems. Remote batch systems permit access to the computer system at prearranged times. On-line inquiry and updating systems permit almost immediate access to the computer system. The quality assurance analyst should determine whether

• Access to the system, application programs, and files is limited to authorized personnel,

• Job scheduling procedures are used so that data is processed according to some priority, and

• Logs are maintained showing that transactions were entered into the system.

Data Output. Output controls help make sure that data processing results are reliable and that no unauthorized alterations have been made to transactions and records while they are in the custody of the data processing facility. The quality assurance analyst should make sure that output control totals are compared against those originally established and reports distributed to appropriate users.

The Application Review Questionnaire (see Figure 8.6) is divided into the categories described above. The questionnaire is designed so that "no" answers should be considered a potential application deficiency. "No" answers require additional investigation. Space is included on the form to qualify or explain responses to the questions.

A Computer Application Profile Worksheet (see Figure 8.7) should be used as a tool in assessing the adequacy of applications. The questionnaire probed a series of areas for the seven application characteristics (i.e., application system overview, system documentation and program modification, data input, data error, batch process, telecommunications, and data output).

You must use judgment in completing this profile. Based on the questionnaire responses relating to the application characteristics, how much risk (low, medium, high) do you believe is involved in relying on the computer-processed data? The information about applications requested on this form is designed to help you with this judgment.

After you have assigned a potential risk assessment for each application characteristic, briefly describe your justification for assigning the various risk levels for each application characteristic noted on the following pages. This information should be used in preparing a report on the results of the application assessment.

SUMMARY

The computer has substantially altered the methods by which data processing systems operate and are controlled and audited. The opportunities for personal review and clerical checking have declined as the collection and subsequent uses of data are changed. The changes are the result of moving from manual procedures performed by individuals familiar with both the data and

(Continued on Page 259)

ITEM	RESPONSE			
	YES	NO	N/A	OTHER
Major Application(s) System				
1. System name and agency's ID number?				
2. Date of initial implementation?				
3. Is the system a vendor-designed system or an agency-designed system?				
4. What is system type (administrative, engineering, process control, scientific, other)?				
5. Type of processing: batch or on-line?				
6. Number of programs?				
7. Size of largest program (bytes of storage)?				
8. Programming language used?				
9. Was system tested with test data, live data, or not at all?				
10. Are system test results available?				
11. Number of system modifications in the last two years?				
12. Date last modification was tested?				
13. Date of last audit or evaluation? (Obtain report.)				
14. Processing frequency?				
15. Total monthly processing hours?				

Figure 8.6 **APPLICATION REVIEW QUESTIONNAIRE**

ITEM	RESPONSE			
	YES	NO	N/A	OTHER
System Documentation and Program Modification				
A. System Documentation				
1. Does a procedures manual cover the preparation of source documents? (If so, obtain a copy.)				
2. Does this manual: a. Include control procedures? b. Define data preparation responsibility?				
3. Is there a user's data entry/conversion manual? (If so, obtain a copy.)				
4. Does this manual: a. Include instructions for entering data? b. Identify all records/fields which are subject to verification?				
5. Is there an overall narrative description of the application system?				
6. Is there an overall flowchart of the application system?				
7. Is each application program documented separately?				
8. Does program documentation include: a. Request for program development/ changes? b. General narrative description of the program? c. System specification— both original and modifications? d. Detailed narrative description of the program?				

Figure 8.6 **APPLICATION REVIEW QUESTIONNAIRE (Cont'd)**

	RESPONSE			
ITEM	*YES*	*NO*	*N/A*	*OTHER*
8. e. Detailed logic diagram or decision table?				
f. Input record formats?				
g. Input record descriptions?				
h. Output record format?				
i. Output record descriptions?				
j. Master file formats?				
k. Master file descriptions?				
l. Lists of constants, codes, and tables used?				
m. Source program listing?				
n. Object program listing?				
o. Operating instructions?				
p. Description of test plan and data used to test program?				
q. Detailed history of program failures?				
9. Do computer operators' run manuals exist?				
10. Are these run manuals provided to computer operators?				
11. Do operators' run manuals:				
a. Define input data, data source, and data format?				
b. Describe setup procedures?				
c. Characterize all halt conditions and actions to be taken?				
d. Delineate expected output data and format?				
e. Delineate output and file disposition at completion of run?				
f. Include copies of normal console sheets?				
12. Do operators' run manuals exclude:				
a. Program logic charts or block diagrams?				
b. Copies of program listings?				

Figure 8.6 **APPLICATION REVIEW QUESTIONNAIRE (Cont'd)**

	RESPONSE			
ITEM	*YES*	*NO*	*N/A*	*OTHER*
13. Is all documentation reviewed to ensure its completeness and adherence to established standards?				
14. Are copies of all documentation stored off the premises?				
15. If "yes," is the stored documentation periodically compared and updated with that being used?				
16. Is there written evidence of who performed the systems and programming work?				
B. Program Modification				
17. Are all program changes and their effective dates recorded in a manner which preserves an accurate chronological record of the system?				
18. Are programs revised only after written requests are approved by user department management?				
19. Do these written requests describe the proposed changes and reasons for them?				
20. Are changes in the master file or in program instructions authorized in writing by initiating departments?				
21. Are departments that initiate changes in master files or program instructions furnished with notices or listings showing changes actually made?				
22. Are changes reviewed to see that they were made properly?				

Figure 8.6 **APPLICATION REVIEW QUESTIONNAIRE (Cont'd)**

ITEM	YES	NO	N/A	OTHER
23. Do major users approve initial system design specifications?				
24. Is approval for each new application program supported by a cost/benefit analysis?				
25. Have program testing procedures been established?				
26. Does the test plan include cases to test: a. Mainline and end-of-job logic? b. Each routine? c. Each exception? d. Abnormal end-of-job conditions? e. Combinations of parameter cards and switch settings? f. Unusual mixtures and sequence of data (i.e., multiple transactions following deleted masters)?				
Data Input				
1. Have procedures been documented to show how all source data is entered and processed?				
2. Is there an input/output control group?				
3. Do the initiating departments independently control data submitted for processing using: a. Turnaround transmittal documents? b. Record counts? c. Predetermined control totals? d. Other? (describe) _____				

Figure 8.6 **APPLICATION REVIEW QUESTIONNAIRE (Cont'd)**

	RESPONSE			
ITEM	*YES*	*NO*	*N/A*	*OTHER*
4. Are duties separated in the initiating to make sure that one individual does not perform more than one phase of input data preparation (e.g., establishing new master records)?				
5. Are source documents retained in a manner which enables tracing all documents to related output records?				
6. Is information transcribed from the source document to some other document before being sent to the EDP department?				
7. Does the transcribing department, if separate from other offices, independently control data submitted for processing using: a. Turnaround transmittal documents? b. Record counts? c. Predetermined control totals? d. Other? (describe) _____				
8. Are control totals developed in the transcribing department balanced with those of initiating departments and are all discrepancies reconciled?				
9. Are coding, keypunching, and verifying the same document performed by different individuals?				
10. Does the transcribing department have a schedule, by application, that shows when data requiring transcription will be received and completed?				

Figure 8.6 **APPLICATION REVIEW QUESTIONNAIRE (Cont'd)**

	RESPONSE			
ITEM	*YES*	*NO*	*N/A*	*OTHER*
11. Is responsibility separated to make sure that one individual does not perform more than one of the following phases of a transaction: a. Inititating data? b. Transcribing data? c. Inputting data? d. Processing data? e. Correcting errors and resubmitting. f. Distributing output?				
Data Error				
1. Are controls in place covering the process of identifying, correcting, and reprocessing data rejected by the computer programs?				
2. Are record counts and predetermined control totals used to control these rejected transactions?				
3. Are corrections and resubmissions performed in a timely manner?				
4. Are error corrections reviewed and approved by persons outside the data processing department?				
5. Do initiating departments review error listings affecting their data?				
6. Are erroneous and unprocessable transactions (i.e., no master record corresponding to transaction record or vice versa) rejected and written to an automated suspense file?				

Figure 8.6 **APPLICATION REVIEW QUESTIONNAIRE (Cont'd)**

	RESPONSE			
ITEM	*YES*	*NO*	*N/A*	*OTHER*
7. Does the automated suspense file include: a. A code indicating error type? b. Date, time, and some sort of indicator ID?				
8. Are periodic printouts of suspense file entries produced?				
Batch Processing				
1. Does the data processing department independently control data submitted and processed using: a. Turnaround transmittal documents? b. Record counts? c. Predetermined control totals? d. Other? (describe) _____				
2. Are control totals balanced with those of the initiating department and are all discrepancies reconciled?				
3. Are run-to-run control totals used to check for completeness of processing?				
4. Do the computer operating instructions for each program identify which data files are to be used as input?				
5. Do the operating instructions for each program clearly identify output files and storage requirements?				
6. Do all programs include routines for checking file labels before processing?				

Figure 8.6 **APPLICATION REVIEW QUESTIONNAIRE (Cont'd)**

	RESPONSE			
ITEM	*YES*	*NO*	*N/A*	*OTHER*
7. Are there controls in place to prevent operators from circumventing file label routines?				
8. Are internal trailer labels containing control totals (e.g., record counts, dollars totals, hash totals, etc.) generated for all magnetic tapes and tested by the computer program to determine that all records have been processed?				
9. Do computer programs include the following type of tests for validity: a. Code? b. Character? c. Field? d. Transaction? e. Combinations of fields? f. Missing data? g. Check digit? h. Sequence? i. Limit or reasonableness test? j. Sign? k. Crossfooting of quantitative data?				
Telecommunications				
1. Are there documented procedures for using the telecommunications network? (If so, obtain a copy.)				
2. Are authorization codes required to: a. Access the computer system? b. Access the applications program? c. Perform transactions?				
3. Are different authorization codes required to perform different transactions?				
4. Are authorization codes controlled to restrict unauthorized usage?				

Figure 8.6 **APPLICATION REVIEW QUESTIONNAIRE (Cont'd)**

ITEM	RESPONSE			
	YES	NO	N/A	OTHER
5. Are authorization codes periodically changed?				
6. Is a nonprinting/nondisplaying or obliteration facility used when keying in and acknowledging authorization codes?				
7. Is a terminal identification check performed by the computer so that various transaction types can be limited to authorized data entry stations?				
8. If any answers to questions 2-7 are "yes," do these security measures work as designed?				
9. Is there a computer program used to: a. Send acknowledgements to the terminal? b. Periodically test line and terminal operating status with standardized test messages and responses?				
10. Is the message header used to identify: a. Source, including proper terminal and operator identification code? b. Message sequence number, including total number of message segments? c. Transaction type code? d. Transaction authorization code?				
11. Is the message header validated for: a. Proper sequence number from the identified terminal? b. Proper transaction code or authorization code for terminal or operator?				

Figure 8.6 **APPLICATION REVIEW QUESTIONNAIRE (Cont'd)**

ITEM	RESPONSE			
	YES	*NO*	*N/A*	*OTHER*
11. c. Number of message segments received equal to count indicated in header? d. Proper acknowledgement from terminal at end of transmission? e. Balancing of debit/credit totals derived from adding all message segments and comparing with corresponding totals in message header?				
12. Are there either accumulators in the terminal for keeping input totals or terminal-site logging procedures that record details of transactions?				
13. Are error messages returned to originating terminal, indicating type of error detected and requesting correction?				
14. Is a block of characters automatically retransmitted when an error is detected?				
15. Does an end-of-transmission trailer include: a. Message and segment counts? b. Value totals, including debit and credit? c. An ending symbol?				
16. Is a transaction log of sequence-numbered and/or time-of-day-noted transactions maintained in addition to a periodic dump/copy of the master file?				

Figure 8.6 **APPLICATION REVIEW QUESTIONNAIRE (Cont'd)**

	RESPONSE			
ITEM	*YES*	*NO*	*N/A*	*OTHER*

17. Is the transaction data log used to provide:
  a. Part of the audit trail, including originating terminal and message ID, transaction type code, time of day that the transaction is logged, and copy of transaction record?
  b. A transaction record for retrieval from terminal?				

18. At the end of the processing day, is the master file balanced, via programmed routine, by subtracting current totals from start-of-day totals and comparing the remainder to transaction log values?				
19. Are all master file records periodically processed to balance machine-derived totals against control trailer record totals?				

20. Is the master file data log used to provide:
  a. File restructuring capability?
  b. Restart points and indicators of valid data flow?
  c. Storage for partial dump of vital tables, including message queue allocation, polling table contents, transaction routine tables, etc.?				

Data Output				
1. Does the initiating department balance control totals generated during computer processing with those originally established and reconcile discrepancies?				
2. Can transactions be traced forward to a final output control?				

Figure 8.6 **APPLICATION REVIEW QUESTIONNAIRE (Cont'd)**

	RESPONSE			
ITEM	*YES*	*NO*	*N/A*	*OTHER*
3. Can transactions be traced back to the original source document?				
4. Is there some means of verifying master file contents: e.g., are samples periodically drawn from those records being printed and reviewed for accuracy?				
5. Is there an input/output control group?				
6. Is the input/output control group assigned to review output for general acceptability and completeness?				
7. Is a schedule maintained of the reports and documents to be produced by the EDP system?				
8. Are there documented control procedures for distributing reports?				
9. Is responsibility separated to make sure that one individual does not perform more than one of the following phases of a transaction: a. Initiating data? b. Transcribing data? c. Inputting data? d. Processing data? e. Correcting errors and resubmitting data? f. Distributing output?				

Figure 8.6 **APPLICATION REVIEW QUESTIONNAIRE (Cont'd)**

PREPARER: _____   DATE: _____

REVIEWER: _____   DATE: _____

You must use judgment in completing this profile. Based on the questionnaire responses relating to the following control characteristics, how much risk (low, medium, high) do you believe is involved in relying on the agency's computer-processed date?

Control Characteristic	Is the control in place?	Is the control effective?	Is some alternate control in place?	Is the alternate control effective?	Level of potential risk
Application system documentation and program modification controls					
Data input controls					
Data error controls					
Batch processing controls					
Telecommunications processing controls					
Data output controls					
COMMENTS					

Figure 8.7 **COMPUTER APPLICATION CONTROLS PROFILE WORKSHEET**

the accounting process to high-volume, automated techniques performed by individuals unfamiliar with both the data and accounting practices.

The introduction of data processing equipment frequently requires that the recording and processing functions be concentrated in departments that are separate from the origin of the data; it may, however, eliminate the separation of some of the responsibilities that previously characterized the record-keeping function. A trend toward the integration of operating and financial data into organization-wide information systems of data bases also eliminated independent records that might previously have provided a source of comparative data. At the same time, such integrated information systems can become the basis for more vital and timely management decisions.

Computerization has reduced substantially the time available for the review of transactions before their entry into the accounting records. As a result, in poorly controlled systems the opportunity for discovering errors or fraud before they have an impact on operations may be reduced, especially in the case of real-time and data base systems. This has increased the importance of internal control procedures. It also affects the work the quality assurance analyst must perform. An important aspect of this work is reviewing the adequacy of computer controls.

Chapter 9
QUALITY ASSURANCE REVIEW TECHNIQUES

Quality assurance reviews can be improved by the use of effective review techniques. These include the methods and procedures used by QA when conducting reviews, the means by which information is gathered, the techniques used to confirm and validate the accuracy of the information, and methods used to evaluate that information.

This chapter will cover thirteen QA review techniques. They are listed in Figure 9.1. Each will be described, an example provided, and an evaluation given as to where the practice can be used most effectively. The skills necessary to use the skills will show the caliber of QA reviewer needed for the different parts of the review.

Effective QA groups must conduct reviews that are consistent in approach. It is important that application A be subjected to the same rigorous review as application B. The ongoing nature of QA requires maintaining good working relationships with data processing systems and programming personnel. Knowing that all projects will be reviewed the same way helps maintain these good working relationships.

QUALITY ASSURANCE REVIEW TECHNIQUES

A quality assurance reviewer's function is broken into three segments. These are: first, gathering information about the system being reviewed; second, confirming or validating that the information gathered is correct; and third, evaluating the system based on the information gathered. Information gathering occurs both while planning for and conducting the QA review. Five vehicles are used in obtaining information about application systems. These are:

1. *Project documentation.* Use of the documentation about the management of the project, such as budgets, assignments, schedules, etc.
2. *System documentation.* All the documentation about the computer application relating to data, its processing, use, storage, operation, control, etc.
3. *Interviews.*   Interviews with appropriate, involved people.
4. *Observation.* A means of understanding a system or determining the form in which information about it exists.
5. *Checklist.* A series of questions to be asked about a topic being investigated.

Information-Gathering Techniques

- Project documentation
- System documentation
- Fact finding (interview)
- Observation (examination)
- Checklist

Confirmation/Validation Techniques

- Testing (verification)
- Test data
- Base case
- Confirmation

Evaluation Techniques

- Judgment
- Simulation modeling
- Consultants (advice)
- Quantitative analysis

Figure 9.1 **QUALITY ASSURANCE REVIEW TECHNIQUES**

If the information is erroneous, the evaluation is subjected to error. Error can occur from using false information, or using the wrong criteria in evaluating a situation. For example, a reviewer can be told that the current system has approximately 20 errors per day. The person providing this believes it to be true, but in actual practice the number of errors is closer to 100 per day. Evaluations based on this type of information will probably be erroneous. Therefore, it becomes necessary for the reviewer to confirm and validate whenever practical information is obtained and evaluations made. Some confirmation techniques are quite simple while others are time consuming. However, the value of being sure is worth the time. Reviewers use various practices:

1. *Testing.* Verify that something exists, something works, or determine what the results will be if certain conditions happen.

2. *Test data.* Prepare transactions which can be used in testing.

3. *Base case.* Prepare an exhaustive set of test data for utilization in testing.

4. *Confirmation.* Validate with the individual who knows whether or not the condition or event has, will, or can occur.

The value QA provides data processing management is in evaluating the data obtained.The data gathered will contain bias, personal opinions, one-sided viewpoints and other interpretations by the person giving or who documented that data. The QA reviewers must sift and evaluate various pieces of information to arrive at conclusions. Evaluations range from highly quantitative to intuitive. The most common techniques for evaluations used by reviewers are these four:

1. *Judgment.* Use intuition and evaluation to arrive at a conclusion based primarily on the reviewer's own training and experience.

2. *Simulation/Modeling.* Mathematically construct the system or event to study in advance the probable results.

3. *Consultant (advice).* Use the judgment and experience of "experts" in the area of concern.

4. *Quantitative analysis.* Use mathematics to assist in arriving at judgments by giving weights or scores to the criteria included in decision-making.

This list of techniques is not meant to be comprehensive but, rather, representative of the approaches used by QA in performing the function. QA reviewers can learn additional practices and techniques from auditors and visits with other QA groups.

APPLICATION OF TECHNIQUES

Each of the twelve review points requires different techniques. The early reviews rely heavily on information-gathering techniques. The middle review points use both information gathering and evaluation. The later reviews make more use of the confirmation/validation practices. This is logical because it closely parallels the system development process. Figure 9.2 shows which techniques are used for each of the review points. The most common review technique is the checklist: it is the only one used in all twelve review points. The checklist provides an organized approach to conducting a review. But the person making the review should not rely completely on the checklist; rather, he or she should use it as a guide in conducting the review. The checklist should be the initiating document for using the other review techniques.

Testing is rarely used by QA review groups. It is only in the analysis of system testing that QA gets into testing and test data practices. Testing practices are primarily utilized by the systems development team. When utilized by QA it is done mostly by piggy-backing QA tests with the project system tests. When QA needs to verify a condition or event the two most commonly used techniques are observation and confirmation.

An analysis of the review techniques matrix (Figure 9.2) shows that the majority of time spent by the QA group is in information gathering, the most common practice for making an evaluation judgment. From this we can begin to see that the ideal person for the QA group is one skilled in gathering facts who has enough experience and ability to make sound judgments about the status of application systems.

SKILLS NEEDED FOR QA REVIEW TECHNIQUES

Eight different skills and/or knowledge areas are necessary to execute effectively all the audit techniques.

1.   Project management
2.   General systems design

QA REVIEW POINT	Project Documentation	System Documentation	Fact Finding (interview)	Observation (examination)	Checklist	Testing	Test Data
1. Mid-Justification Phase	✔	✔	✔		✔		
2. End of Justification Phase	✔	✔	✔		✔		
3. Business Systems Solution Phase	✔	✔	✔		✔		
4. Computer Equipment Selection		✔	✔		✔		
5. Computer Systems Design	✔	✔	✔		✔		
6. Program Design	✔	✔	✔		✔		
7. Testing and Conversion Planning	✔		✔		✔		
8. Program Coding and Testing		✔		✔	✔		
9. Detailed Test Plan	✔		✔		✔		
10. Test Results	✔	✔	✔	✔	✔	✔	✔
11. Detail Conversion Planning and Programs	✔	✔	✔	✔	✔		
12. Conversion Results		✔	✔	✔	✔		

Figure 9.2. **QUALITY ASSURANCE REVIEW POINTS/REVIEW TECHNIQUES MATRIX**

QA REVIEW POINT	Base Case	Confirmation	Judgement	Simulation Modeling	Consultants (advice)	Quantitative Analysis
1. Mid-Justification Phase		✔	✔	✔	✔	
2. End of Justification Phase		✔	✔	✔	✔	✔
3. Business Systems Solution Phase		✔	✔	✔	✔	✔
4. Computer Equipment Selection			✔		✔	
5. Computer Systems Design		✔	✔	✔	✔	✔
6. Program Design		✔	✔	✔	✔	✔
7. Testing and Conversion Planning			✔	✔		
8. Program Coding and Testing			✔			
9. Detailed Test Plan			✔			
10. Test Results	✔	✔	✔			
11. Detail Conversion Planning and Programs			✔			
12. Conversion Results						

Figure 9.2 **QUALITY ASSURANCE REVIEW POINTS/REVIEW TECHNIQUES MATRIX (Cont'd)**

3.   Computer systems design
4.   Computer hardware
5.   Computer software
6.   Programming
7.   Computer center
8.   General business experience

It is not necessary to be a master of all eight skills. In some cases, the area in which the technique is used determines which skills are necessary. For example, to use the checklist on economic evaluations of computerized applications requires a general business experience but not a knowledge of the operation of the computer center. For some cases, the same skills are needed each time the technique is utilized. For example, to make use of auto-mated packages for simulation and modeling routines, the sys-tems analyst must have an understanding of automated packages for programming.

The eight skills and/or knowledge areas are explained be-low as is the difference between basic and advanced mastery of the skills.

Project Management. Possessing the ability to organize and su-pervise the implementation of an application system project. This includes preparation of budgets, selection of personnel, or-ganization of work, planning and scheduling the implemen-tation process, directing individuals on their assignments, and controlling and evaluating their work. Basic project manage-ment include skills involving managing one application system project. Advanced skills come after managing two or more appli-cation system projects.

General Systems Design. General systems design involves solv-ing business problems. General systems design usually occurs during the feasibility study. The system may or may not require the use of a computer. General systems design skills include the ability to make an economic evaluation of alternative solutions for the business problem. Basic skills in general systems design come from working on those systems whose obvious solution is a computerized application.   Advanced skills include general systems for which the use of the computer may or may not be all or part of the solution.

Computer Systems Design. The process of designing a computer system includes the definition of input, output, processing, and file design. A designer might have basic computer systems design skills with five years or less in computing systems and programming work. Advanced skills come with more of that kind of experience.

Computer Hardware. Computer hardware skills include the ability to select and configure computer hardware. It includes working with representatives of the computer vendors. The skill assumes a knowledge of conversion problems from one type of hardware to another, as well as economic considerations in hardware planning. Advance skills generally mean working with more than one computer vendor, or with more than one line of computers from a specific vendor. Skills include the ability to use one of the hardware evaluation manuals or services.

Computer Software. Skills in understanding the functions of computer software probably require the highest technical knowledge of all the skills. Skills include the ability to generate new versions of software systems. The features and economics of the software system must be known, as well as the control language and the means to link computer software to application systems. Basic skills include a comprehension of software packages, together with the ability to use control information to link computer software with application programs. Advanced skills include the ability to select among various software packages as well as the skill to generate the software system.

Programming. Programming knowledge and skills include the ability to design, code, and debug programs. The basic skills involve up to two years of actual programming experience. Advanced skills require over two years of programming experience.

Computer Center. Computer center skills include a knowledge of computer operations. This includes scheduling of computer runs, restart, recovery, data library and backup, telecommunication operation if applicable, as well as security of the computer center. Basic skills include an understanding of the operation of the computer center, while advanced skills can come with one year or more of experience in the operation of a computer center.

General Business Experience. General business experience means experience working in the business areas of an organization. Examples of business areas would be the payroll department, accounts receivable department, sales department, marketing, accounting or other segments of the general business operation of an organization. The experience should be that of a user of a computerized application. Basic skills include two years or less experience, advanced skills involve over two years of experience. General business experience also can be obtained in the management aspects of the data processing department. However, the experience should be other than managing the development of computer systems. An understanding of these skills and/or knowledge areas provides some additional insight into the background necessary for QA. As we examine each of the thirteen QA techniques, we will see which of these skills are needed for the various techniques.

QUALITY ASSURANCE TECHNIQUES

This section describes the thirteen QA techniques. Each write-up contains a brief overview and then a detailed description, an example of its use, and an evaluation of the future potential. Each write-up also contains a matrix showing the skills needed to use that particular technique. The skills matrix lists the eight skills described in the previous section.

Project Documentation Review Technique

One of the major sources of information is the documentation used in managing the project: the more formal the documentation, the more useful it is for QA purposes.

DESCRIPTION: Project documentation provides the reviewer with information on budgets, schedules, personnel assignments, technical decisions, user relationships, project implementation plans, project team organizational structure, as well as the current status of project implementation. Project documentation should be studied extensively during each review. Special emphasis should be placed on status of project implementation. Because many project leaders do not consolidate project documentation, it may be necessary for the reviewer to ask for some specific pieces of information.

EXAMPLE: In an effort to determine whether a phase of the project will be completed within budget, the reviewer can check both the budget status and project schedule status. If the schedule shows the phase to be 30% complete, approximately 30% of the budget should be expended. Obviously certain expenses should be excluded from the calculation such as one-time costs for purchases of software. Based on a simple analysis the reviewer can make a judgment as to whether or not the phase under review will be completed within budget. Without project documentation this evaluation could be very time-consuming.

EVALUATION: Project documentation is one of the two prime sources for gathering information. This is an essential element in QA reviews. Figure 9.3 illustrates the skills and/or knowledge needed to use project documentation in a QA review.

TECHNIQUE: Project Documentation			
Skill/Knowledge	*Skill Needed*	*Advanced Skill Needed*	*N/A*
Project Management		✔	
General Systems Design		✔	
Computer Systems Design	✔		
Computer Hardware			✔
Computer Software			✔
Programming			✔
Computer Center	✔		
General Business Experience		✔	

Figure 9.3 **SKILLS NEEDED TO USE QUALITY ASSURANCE TECHNIQUE**

Systems Documentation Quality Assurance Technique

A major segment of every QA review includes a thorough study and analysis of system documentation.

DESCRIPTION: System documentation includes all input and output documentation, processing rules, and file organization. The documentation will include control techniques, operating instructions, training instructions and manuals for the personnel who will use the system, and program listings. The reviewer studies the documentation to gain an understanding not only of what the system is supposed to accomplish, but how it functions.

EXAMPLE: To determine the adequacy of the system's file organization, the reviewer studies both the input data elements and the output reports. This will provide the reviewer with insight as to what information is in this system and how it is entered, as well as the information needs of the user as expressed in output reports. This type of information is necessary in making an assessment as to the adequacy of file structure.

EVALUATION: System documentation is, and will continue to be, the major source of information for the QA reviewer. Figure 9.4 shows the skills and/or knowledge needed by quality assurance reviewers to use and understand system documentation.

Interviewing QA Techniques

Fact finding through interviews provides raw information to the reviewer. The data collected through fact finding should be subject to further evaluation and analysis.

DESCRIPTION: Information gathered through interviews should be considered to contain personal bias and opinion. Data reported by an individual normally reflects his point of view. In medical terms, perhaps it should be considered more of a symptom rather than the true cause or result of an event. The individual doing the fact finding must make an effort to get the viewpoint of all interested parties. It is only through the accumulation of full information that the proper evaluation can be performed.

EXAMPLE: After an automobile accident involving two cars, each driver would probably present a totally different story. It is quite possible each version would show the other driver at fault. When the two versions are documented and other supportive facts collected, the true cause of the accident becomes more obvious than if all the data had been collected from only one driver.

EVALUATION: Fact-finding skills can be learned and improved. Reviewers should study fact finding and interviewing methods to improve their skills. This is one of the basic tools of a reviewer.

Figure 9.5 illustrates the skills and/or knowledge needed to use the quality assurance fact-finding (interviews) practice.

TECHNIQUE: System Documentation			
Skill/Knowledge	*Skill Needed*	*Advanced Skill Needed*	*N/A*
Project Management			✔
General Systems Design		✔	
Computer Systems Design		✔	
Computer Hardware	✔		
Computer Software	✔		
Programming			✔
Computer Center			✔
General Business Experience	✔		

Figure 9.4 **SKILLS NEEDED TO USE QUALITY ASSURANCE TECHNIQUE**

Observation (Examination) QA Technique

A picture has been said to be worth ten thousand words. This is frequently true in the case of the reviewer observing and/or examining some event or condition important to the application system.

DESCRIPTION: Observation or examination involves witnessing events as they occur, or examining documents and other physical evidence. This need not be a time–consuming process. It has proven to be much more informative than verbal explanations of a process. Frequently, observation involves going to the user's place of business and examining an operation or process from start to finish. This may be coupled with fact finding. In that case the reviewer will discuss job functions with each person as the reviewer observes a process in action. After a few hours a reviewer should have a very good understanding of how a system or process works.

TECHNIQUE: Fact Finding (Interviews)			
Skill/Knowledge	*Skill Needed*	*Advanced Skill Needed*	*N/A*
Project Management	✔		
General Systems Design	✔		
Computer Systems Design	✔		
Computer Hardware			✔
Computer Software			✔
Programming			✔
Computer Center	✔		
General Business Experience	✔		

Figure 9.5 **SKILLS NEEDED TO USE QUALITY ASSURANCE TECHNIQUE**

EXAMPLE: Assume the application system under review is a payroll system. The reviewer, in an effort to understand the system, decides to observe the entire payroll process. This would start with the addition of an individual on the payroll. Perhaps this step is done through the personnel department with a series of forms which then go to the payroll department to update the payroll master file. The QA person observes people clocking in in the morning, clocking in and out for lunch, and then out at the end of the shift. The reviewer next may observe the problems that occur with individuals trying to get to time stations to report in and out, and problems occurring because of illness or other personal problems. Observing the process of preparing the payroll and making adjustments might involve going to each individual who is part of the process in the payroll department. Once the checks have been prepared, the reviewer would want to observe the distribution methods, and perhaps the reconciliation and control procedures used to assure that the proper person receives the proper pay for that work period.

EVALUATION: Observation can be an extremely powerful technique to familiarize the reviewer with what is actually happening in the organization. Many times people describe the procedure as it should happen, or as they perceive it to happen, but only when the reviewer gets out into the user's place of business and observes the process can he or she fully understand what is actually happening. Observation is a practice that should be used by reviewers on each application reviewed. It may be possible to use observations made in early stages of a review throughout all the review point reviews. Figure 9.6 illustrates the skills and/or knowledge needed to use the observation (examination) technique.

TECHNIQUE: Observation (examination)			
Skill/Knowledge	*Skill Needed**	*Advanced Skill Needed*	*N/A*
Project Management	✔		
General Systems Design	✔		
Computer Systems Design	✔		
Computer Hardware	✔		
Computer Software	✔		
Programming	✔		
Computer Center	✔		
General Business Experience	✔		

* Varies depending on what is being observed (about 4 skills needed)

Figure 9.6 **SKILLS NEEDED TO USE QUALITY ASSURANCE TECHNIQUE**

Note: The asterisk on the skills chart indicates that all the skills checked are not needed to use the observation technique. What is implied is that the area in which the observation will occur is the skill which the reviewer should have to use the technique effectively. For example, if the computer center is being observed, the reviewer should possess the skill being monitored. It is suggested that about four skills are necessary to effectively use any practice. For example, to observe in the computer center it is helpful if the reviewer has skills in the areas of 1) computer hardware, 2) computer software, 3) programming, and 4) computer center operations. This may not always be necessary, but it is a reasonable guideline. The same logic applies to all the following skill charts where the skills are dependent on where the technique is used.

Checklist QA Review Technique

The checklist is the most commonly used of all the review techniques. It provides the reviewer an organized and standardized approach for each of the review points.

DESCRIPTION: Checklists provide a series of questions which guide the reviewer through each checkpoint review. Many organizations believe that each item on the checklist should be reviewed with data processing management to determine if it is fair, since data processing personnel should not be asked to perform at a level beyond reasonable expectations; this also helps maintain a good working relationship.

While common questionnaires can be used as a base, they should be modified to meet the standards and procedures of the data processing department conducting the reviews. The questions should be supportive of the standards and procedures of the data processing department. While questions are normally asked in a yes/no mode, the answer is seldom all yes or all no. Reviewers need to apply judgment to the answer to determine the level of adherence to the desires of data processing management.

EXAMPLE: The following questions are from a checklist for system design specifications. The questions, actually used by a QA group, deal with data validation and error messages.

1. For validation routines, have the editing rules been specified for

    a. Field format and content (data element description)?
    b. Interfield relationships?
    c. Intrafield relationships?
    d. Interrecord relationship?
    e. Sequence?
    f. Duplicates?
    g. Control reconciliation?

2.   Has the rejection criterion been indicated for each type of error situation, as follows

   a.   Warning message but transaction is accepted?
   b.   Use of the default value?
   c.   Outright rejection of record within a transaction set?
   d.   Rejection of an entire transaction?
   e.   Rejection of a batch transactions?
   f.   Program abort?

3.   Have the following validation techniques been included in the specifications

   a.   Validation of entire transaction before any processing?
   b.   Validation to continue regardless of the number of errors on the transaction unless a run abort occurs?
   c.   Provides information regarding an error so the user can identify the source and determine the cause?

Note that these questions are much more specific then those in Chapter 7. An extensive checklist may be required to support one of the concerns included in one of the review point's list of concerns included in Chapter 7.

EVALUATION: Checklists are the major technique of the reviewer. They should continually be improved through the experiences gained conducting reviews. Figure 9.7 illustrates the skills and/or knowledge needed to use the checklist technique.

Testing (Verification) QA Technique

Testing is the process of verifying that conditions are as stated. It involves performing whatever steps are necessary to verify statements or conditions are correct.

DESCRIPTION: Testing can be used to verify the existence or effectiveness of physical properties, events, conditions, and internal control, or used to verify the accuracy and completeness of both data and totals. Testing should be performed by the reviewer. If other than the QA reviewer performs the test, the technique should be confirmation of something rather than testing. Testing implies work being done by the reviewer.   In computer applications, tests can be performed with either live or fictitious data. In conducting tests the reviewer will have to calculate the results manually and then compare them to actual results.

TECHNIQUE: Checklist			
Skill/Knowledge	*Skill Needed**	*Advanced Skill Needed*	*N/A*
Project Management	✔		
General Systems Design	✔		
Computer Systems Design	✔		
Computer Hardware	✔		
Computer Software	✔		
Programming	✔		
Computer Center	✔		
General Business Experience	✔		

* Varies depending on what is being observed (about 4 skils needed)

Figure 9.7 **SKILLS NEEDED TO USE QUALITY ASSURANCE TECHNIQUE**

EXAMPLE: A project leader made a statement that the audit routines in the application being developed were so stringent that it was impossible for erroneous data to enter the system. The QA reviewer was skeptical of this statement and decided to make a test. The application under question used card input. The reviewer took two boxes of cards at random and fed them into the audit program of the application: seventeen "transactions" got through. As a result of this test additional audit routines were added in the computer application.

EVALUATION: Testing is a very valid QA technique but should be used only where necessary. QA should encourage the project team and user to do extensive testing. However, where it is concerned over the adequacy of testing or the adequacy of evaluating test results, QA may wish to make a test itself. Figure 9.8 illustrates the skills and/or knowledge needed to use quality assurance testing technique.

Test Data QA Technique

Test data is a series of transactions prepared for a computer system to see whether proper transactions are processed correctly and the improper transactions identified and rejected.

TECHNIQUE TESTING:	Testing (Verification)		
Skill/Knowledge	*Skill Needed**	*Advanced Skill Needed*	*N/A*
Project Management			✔
General Systems Design	✔		
Computer Systems Design	✔		
Computer Hardware	✔		
Computer Software	✔		
Programming	✔		
Computer Center	✔		
General Business Experience	✔		

* Varies depending on what is being observed (about 4 skills needed)

Figure 9.8 **SKILLS NEEDED TO USE QUALITY ASSURANCE TECHNIQUE**

DESCRIPTION: Test data helps to determine whether the computer programs process data accurately and whether the controls in the system can prevent improper results, such as exorbitant payroll checks. Test data should represent both expected and conceivable conditions that could happen during actual data processing operations. Before the transactions are run, expected processing results are calculated manually by the individuals conducting the tests so that actual results can be compared with these predetermined results. To design adequate test data, the reviewer must be familiar with input and output formats for all types of transactions being processed as well as the data processing system procedures. To be effective, test data should use transactions. Valid data is used for testing normal processing operations, and invalid data is used for testing programmed controls. Only one test transaction need be processed for each condition.

EXAMPLE: A payroll computer application was designed for a maximum of 99 pay hours per week. To test that condition, the reviewer entered test data which showed 90 hours of work by an employee during the week. When this was processed by the computer the 50 hours of overtime were converted into 75 pay hours. The 75 pay hours should be added to the 40 hours of regular pay equaling 115 paid hours. The system only paid the employee for 15 hours.

While the audit programs prevented over 99 hours of work from entering the application, the systems analyst did not provide for regular plus overtime pay hours that would exceed 100. Based on this test the system was modified.

EVALUATION: In most instances the reviewer will propose test transactions rather than actually prepare the test data. The experience of reviewers can help evaluate the thoroughness of the test plan. QA should concentrate test data recommendations on error conditions and unusual processing conditions. This is because data processing people tend to test for those conditions which have been provided for by the system: they do not try to think up test data for conditions which the system is not designed to process. Figure 9.9 illustrates the skills and/or knowledge needed to use test data.

Base Case QA Technique

Base case is an exhaustive group of test data designed to test all possible paths through a computer application.

DESCRIPTION: The base case test technique has proved very effective in organizations utilizing it. It is also a very costly testing technique which can cost up to 20% of the total system cost. Each organization must weigh the merits versus the cost of using the technique. It is not a QA technique per se but, rather, a technique which QA can advocate, and one in which they can participate.

TECHNIQUE: Test Data			
Skill/Knowledge	*Skill Needed*	*Advanced Skill Needed*	*N/A*
Project Management			✔
General Systems Design			✔
Computer Systems Design	✔		
Computer Hardware	✔		
Computer Software	✔		
Programming	✔		
Computer Center	✔		
General Business Experience			✔

Figure 9.9 **SKILLS NEEDED TO USE QUALITY ASSURANCE TECHNIQUE**

EXAMPLE: An organization developed an on-line entry system. This system was critical to the operation of the organization. All orders were entered and processed by this system. Thus 100% of the sales went through this system. It was determined that it was worth the cost to develop a base case testing system. The base case was also used anytime the system was modified. This double use justified the cost of the test approach.

EVALUATION: Base case is probably the most effective testing technique known to organizations. In those critical systems where processing accuracy is essential the base case should be recommended by QA. Figure 9.10 illustrates the skills and/or knowledge needed to use the base case QA technique. Confirmation Quality Assurance Technique Confirmation is the process of verifying with a knowledgeable party that a condition or event is true.

DESCRIPTION: Confirmation starts with a written or verbal request to a knowledgeable party for information. The item in question could be a policy clarification, a procedure interpretation, clarifying the accuracy of data or percentages used in processing, or the correctness of master data to be used during processing. Confirmation is used when ther eviewer has a question regarding the authenticity of a condition or data. In most instances the confirmation is made by telephone. In some instances, however, it may be advisable to document the confirmation so the reviewer will get the confirmation in writing. This is particularly true when an outside party is involved, such as a customer, a governmental agency, or a supplier.

TECHNIQUE TESTING:	Base Case		
Skill/Knowledge	*Skill Needed*	*Advanced Skill Needed*	*N/A*
Project Management			✔
General Systems Design	✔		
Computer Systems Design	✔		
Computer Hardware	✔		
Computer Software	✔		
Programming	✔		
Computer Center	✔		
General Business Experience			✔

Figure 9.10 **SKILLS NEEDED TO USE QUALITY ASSURANCE TECHNIQUE**

EXAMPLE: In a payroll application the reviewer was uncertain of the algorithm being used for pension deduction. The systems project team was using information obtained from a discussion with the personnel department of the organization. The reviewer felt there might be a misinterpretation and sent a letter explaining the deduction algorithm being used to the insurance company handling the pension plan. The confirmation asked the insurance company to state whether the algorithm was correct. In this case it was, and the program was installed with assurance on the part of all that the algorithm was correct.

EVALUATION: Confirmation is a technique available to the QA when the authenticity of an event or condition is essential. It is a seldom used technique but one that can be very valuable when needed. Figure 9.11 illustrates the skills and/or knowledge needed to use this technique.

TECHNIQUE: Confirmation			
Skill/Knowledge	*Skill Needed**	*Advanced Skill Needed*	*N/A*
Project Management	✔		
General Systems Design	✔		
Computer Systems Design	✔		
Computer Hardware	✔		
Computer Software	✔		
Programming	✔		
Computer Center	✔		
General Business Experience	✔		

* Varies depending on what is being confirmed (about 4 skills needed)

Figure 9.11 **SKILLS NEEDED TO USE QUALITY ASSURANCE TECHNIQUE**

Judgment QA Technique

Judgment is the combined use of experience, intellect, and reasoning to arrive at a conclusion based on analysis of available information. It is the reviewer's judgment that is the main ingredient in making the function successful.

DESCRIPTION: Judgment is the hardest technique to teach and yet is the most valuable. A major ingredient in judgment is extensive experience in data processing systems and programming. Many judgmental decisions are made using the experience gained by many years of practice. Knowing the pitfalls that have occurred in one's personal experience, an individual can guide others away from making the same mistake. Other judgments are more intuitive in nature. The reviewer analyzes the facts available and, mixing this with personal experience, makes a judgment as to the best course of action. Many of these judgments will involve adherence to data processing standards and procedures.

EXAMPLE: The data processing department standards state that all program modules are to be limited to 40K of computer storage. A frequently used module needs a 28K array for optimum efficiency. This will bring the total program module size to 56K. The module will be on-line frequently during the day and by including the full 28K array would substantially increase the module's performance. The reviewer must make a judgment as to whether increased performance warrants deviation from the 40K program module size standard. The reviewer should not be a policeman but, rather, apply judgment to situations.

EVALUATION: Without judgment, quality assurance is a clerical function. The prime reason organizations put senior data processing personnel into quality assurance is to gain the benefit of their judgment in problem situations. Figure 9.12 illustrates the skills needed to use this technique.

Simulation/Modeling QA Technique

When the technology is uncertain, or the application calls for some involved interrelated processing between modules, simulation/modeling provides greater assurance that the application will work when placed into production.

DESCRIPTION: Simulation or modeling is the use of one or more specially written computer programs to process data files in order to simulate normal computer application processing. A model may be built that can be used to simulate the processing of the entire application. However, in actual practice this is a very time-consuming process, and therefore modeling or simulation is used primarily on limited parts of the application. Simulation serves

TECHNIQUE: Judgment			
Skill/Knowledge	*Skill Needed*	*Advanced Skill Needed**	*N/A*
Project Management		✔	
General Systems Design		✔	
Computer Systems Design		✔	
Computer Hardware		✔	
Computer Software		✔	
Programming		✔	
Computer Center		✔	
General Business Experience		✔	

* Varies depending on what is being confirmed (about 4 skills needed)

Figure 9.12 **SKILLS NEEDED TO USE QUALITY ASSURANCE TECHNIQUE**

two purposes. First it determines how a system will function before it is built. For example, if an organization wanted to check response time in a teleprocessing system they could build a model and simulate processing. Second, simulation can be used to verify the correctness of the processing routine. The logic can be simulated in a program and the live or test data run through both the live and the simulated program. The comparison of results will determine the accuracy of the production version of the system.

EXAMPLE: If a reviewer wanted to verify the accuracy of the FICA calculation in a payroll application, a simulation program could be written to duplicate that logic. The test data used to system test the production version could be run through the simulation program. The data used by the simulation program would be extracted from an interim input file because it would come from the middle of the production system. The simulation program would only calculate the FICA deduction. The results of the two runs are compared as a means of verifying the processing logic for the FICA calculation. If the results are the same, the calculation logic would be proven correct.

EVALUATION: Simulation/modeling has limited use for the reviewer. The primary use would be in new complex data processing applications where the reviewer wanted to estimate the processing times. A more logical approach might be for the reviewer to recommend to the systems project team that they build a model to simulate the processing in question. Figure 9.13 illustrates the skills needed to use this technique.

TECHNIQUE: Simulation/Modeling			
Skill/Knowledge	*Skill Needed*	*Advanced Skill Needed*	*N/A*
Project Management	✔		
General Systems Design		✔	
Computer Systems Design		✔	
Computer Hardware	✔		
Computer Software	✔		
Programming		✔	
Computer Center	✔		
General Business Experience	✔		

Figure 9.13 **SKILLS NEEDED TO USE QUALITY ASSURANCE TECHNIQUE**

Consultants (Advice) QA Technique

It is not possible in the highly technical environment of data processing for one individual or one group to know everything.

Where the reviewers lack technical expertise they should be able to call upon outside help for advice.

DESCRIPTION: Consultants are normally called upon to answer highly technical questions. They may also be used, for example, to obtain legal advice, answer questions regarding legislation, or explain Internal Revenue Service regulations. If the reviewer suspects a problem but is uncertain of the consequences of that problem, he should take that problem to consultants. Consultants already associated with the organization such as certified public accountants or resources available from computer vendors or software firms are an excellent and normally free source of advice. Most questions can be answered very quickly and may possibly be handled with a phone call.

EXAMPLE: One QA group was uncertain about retention of computer files as outlined in the Internal Revenue Service Regulation 71-20. The reviewer called the organization's certified public accountants and obtained a quick answer regarding the Internal Revenue Service File Retention Policy. Figure 9.14 illustrates the skills needed to use consultants.

Quantitative Analysis QA Techniques

Quantitative analysis techniques provide a mathematical approach to decision-making.

DESCRIPTION: Quantitative analysis involves assigning of weights or ranking to the criteria used in the decision-making process. The individual using quantitative analysis techniques must first determine the criteria that will be used in the decision-making process, and then either rank or weight those criteria. Normally weighting is the method used. Each of the criteria will then be scored and a total score arrived at by using the weighting factors. The score can be used to state mathematically the current state of a condition or event, or it can be used to compare two or more like alternatives, conditions, statuses, or events.

EXAMPLE: The reviewer was evaluating an equipment selection decision. Discussions with the project team brought out the criteria that were to be considered. Included in the criteria were cost, available software, delivery dates, service, systems engineer support, and upward compatibility. The equipment from the various vendors considered were scored on each of these criteria and a total score for each vendor's equipment was determined. This readily showed one piece of equipment far superior to the others for that organization. The organization selected that piece of equipment.

TECHNIQUE: Consultants (Advice)			
Skill/Knowledge	*Skill Needed**	*Advanced Skill Needed*	*N/A*
Project Management	✔		
General Systems Design	✔		
Computer Systems Design	✔		
Computer Hardware	✔		
Computer Software	✔		
Programming	✔		
Computer Center	✔		
General Business Experience	✔		

* Varies depending on in what area consultants are used (about 4 skills needed)

Figure 9.14 **SKILLS NEEDED TO USE QUALITY ASSURANCE TECHNIQUE**

EVALUATION: Quantitative analysis is a very powerful practice available to reviewers. QA should be urging project teams to use quantitative analysis in their decision-making process. Chapter 10 shows how to apply this practice to quality assurance reviews. Figure 9.15 illustrates the skills needed to use this technique.

TECHNIQUE: Quantitative Analysis			
Skill/Knowledge	*Skill Needed*	*Advanced Skill Needed*	*N/A*
Project Management	✔		
General Systems Design		✔	
Computer Systems Design		✔	
Computer Hardware	✔		
Computer Software	✔		
Programming			✔
Computer Center	✔		
General Business Experience		✔	

Figure 9.15 **SKILLS NEEDED TO USE QUALITY ASSURANCE TECHNIQUE**

An analysis of skills necessary to use QA practices provides some interesting information on the makeup of QA personnel. This analysis shows which skills are the most important or members of the group and which practices should be used by the more senior QA people. The analysis also provides us some insight as to where the emphasis should be placed in reviews. Figure 9.16 is a matrix showing the relationship between QA skills/knowledge and QA techniques. This matrix is the basis for the analysis of skills.

The matrix is an accumulation of the skill charts shown for each of the thirteen quality assurance techniques. The eight skills are listed across the top and the thirteen quality assurance techniques are listed down the left-hand margin of the matrix. Within the matrix a number "1" shows a basic skill is needed for the technique listed. A number "2" indicates an advance skill is needed. A blank space indicates that the skill is not required for that particular technique. A numerical "1/2" indicates that the skill is required if it is applied in that area. For example, in the checklist technique the programming skill is required in checklists which examine programming. As previously explained, approximately 4 skills at the basic level are required to use the checklist technique effectively. The score adds to 4 using a "1/2" in each skill column. The score for all techniques in which the skill required varies by use of the technique is calculated in this manner.

By accumulating the skills/knowledge, we can see which are most needed by QA personnel. Listing them in order of importance, we find the requirements are:

Rank	*Skill/Knowledge*
1	Computer systems design
2	General systems design
3	General business experience
4	Computer center
5	Computer software
6	Computer hardware
7	Project management
8	Programming

From this, we see that the two most important are those relating to system design and general business experience. The two least important are programming and project management. This coincides with previous discussions indicating that the main area of QA involvement is in the area of compliance to systems methods, goals, and performance. While programming and project management skills are desirable, they tend to be outside the main review objectives of QA.

Analyzing the individual techniques, we see the ones that are most difficult to execute. Listing the scores from high to low, we can determine the difficulty of use. The first listed being the most difficult technically to execute, and the last, the least difficult technically to execute.

QA/TECHNIQUES	SKILL/KNOWLEDGE								
	Project Management	General Systems Designs	Computer Systems Designs	Computer Hardware	Computer Software	Programming	Computer Center	General Business Experience	Score
Information Gathering Techniques									
Project Documentation	2.0	2.0	1.0				1.0	2.0	8.0
System Documentation		2.0	2.0	1.0	1.0			1.0	7.0
Fact Finding (interview)	1.0	1.0	1.0				1.0	1.0	5.0
Observation (examination)	.5	.5	.5	.5	.5	.5	.5	.5	4.0
Checklist	.5	.5	.5	.5	.5	.5	.5	.5	4.0
TOTALS	4.0	6.0	5.0	2.0	2.0	1.0	3.0	5.0	28.0
Evaluation Techniques									
Judgment	1.0	1.0	1.0	1.0	1.0	1.0	1.0	1.0	8.0
Simulation/Modeling	1.0	2.0	2.0	1.0	1.0	2.0	1.0	1.0	11.0
Consultants (advice)	.5	.5	.5	.5	.5	.5	.5	.5	4.0
Quantitative Analysis	1.0	2.0	2.0	1.0	1.0		1.0	2.0	10.0
TOTALS	3.5	5.5	5.5	3.5	3.5	3.5	3.5	4.5	33.0
Confirmation/Validation Techniques									
Testing (verification)			1.0	1.0	1.0	1.0	1.0		5.0
Test Data			1.0	1.0	1.0	1.0	1.0		5.0
Base Case	.5	1.0	1.0	1.0	1.0	1.0	1.0		6.5
Confirmation		.5	.5	.5	.5	.5	.5	.5	3.5
TOTALS	.5	1.5	3.5	3.5	3.5	3.5	3.5	.5	20.0
GRAND TOTALS	8.0	13.0	14.0	9.0	9.0	8.0	10.0	10.0	81.0

Figure 9.16 **SKILLS/TECHNIQUES MATRIX**

Rank	Technique	Area of Technique
1	Simulation/modeling	Evaluation
2	Quantitative analysis	Evaluation
3	Judgment	Evaluation
4	Project documentation	Information gathering
5	System documentation	Information gathering
6	Base case	Confirmation/validation
7	Test data	Confirmation/validation
8	Testing	Confirmation/validation
9	Fact finding	Information gathering
10	Observation	Information gathering
11	Checklist	Information gathering
12	Consultants	Evaluation
13	Confirmation	Confirmation/validation

Analyzing this listing, we see that the techniques that require programming and analytical knowledge are the most difficult. These include simulation/modeling and quantitative analysis. This is followed quite logically by judgment and project documentation. Both of these techniques deal with management-oriented concepts and require extensive experience to perform effectively. At the bottom of the list are those that primarily involve getting information from other people. These include observation, checklists, consultants, and confirmation. In these cases the QA person is merely utilizing the knowledge and experience and information of other people.

This matrix shows us some of the intricacies of the quality assurance process. We note that the highest skills are for the techniques involved in the evaluation of application systems (i.e., simulation/modeling, quantitative analysis, and judgment). This is the main objective of QA so it should be no surprise that the most skill is needed in performing this aspect of QA. Evaluation techniques are followed in skill level by information-gathering practices. Because QA expends so much effort in gathering information, the skills are for confirmation/validation techniques. This is probably because QA does minimal tasks in this area. It does not mean that validation and confirmation techniques are necessarily easy but, rather, that these are the easier techniques in this category.

AUTOMATING THE QUALITY ASSURANCE FUNCTION

Most quality assurance groups do the majority of their work with pencil and paper. Few QA groups use the power of the computer to improve the quality of computerized applications in their organization. This appears to be an area of need.

The techniques described in this chapter are primarily manual techniques, since those are the techniques being used. However, some QA groups are using the computer to fulfill their function. The results have been rewarding, and QA groups can expect this trend to accelerate.

Use of the computer by QA groups is the key to increased productivity. For example, a QA analyst can review a program listing to determine if improper source statement or combinations of source statement have been used — in other words, standards have been violated. In this process one analyst examines one program at a time. On the other hand, the QA group could write a program to analyze the program source master library and within minutes review all the programs for violations of standards.

Examples of how quality assurance groups are using the computer to improve quality are

* Write special program to analyze
  data dictionary,
  source program library,
  object program library,
  logs.
* Use test data generator to create test data.
* Analyze programs using program analyzers to identify both highly used and unused source statements.
* Evaluate completeness of data documentation using the data dictionary analysis routines.

These types of computer analysis multiply the effectiveness of the QA function.

SUMMARY

QA groups utilize many techniques in the performance of their work. This chapter identifies thirteen, categorized into three areas. The first are techniques used for gathering information; the second are used for evaluating application systems; and the third are designed to confirm or validate information or conditions.

Different skills/knowledge are needed to effectively utilize these. Eight are identified. These result from experience in project management, general systems design, computer systems design, computer hardware, computer software, programming, computer center operations, and general business. The explanation of each of the thirteen indicates which skills/knowledge are needed to utilize that technique effectively. The skill levels needed are either basic or advanced.

We learn much about the QA function by analyzing the skills required and techniques utilized. Of the three general areas of involvement, the highest skills/knowledge were needed for evaluation. Next were those needed for information gathering with the least required for confirmation/validation. The two most valuable are general systems design and computer systems design experience. The least needed were project management and programming.

The effective QA reviewer has advanced skills in general systems design and computer systems design, as well as general business experience. In addition, that individual understands project documentation and systems documentation as well as being effective in making judgments about problems in data processing application systems. The techniques requiring the highest skill level were those involving mathematics and analysis (i.e., simulation/modeling and quantitative analysis). The lowest skills were required for the techniques aimed at gathering information and opinions from other people. The techniques that showed high skill levels were those dealing with understanding systems and projects as well as judgmental evaluations.

Chapter 10
QUANTITATIVE ANALYSIS OF SYSTEM REVIEWS

The more precise a quality assurance evaluation, the more valuable that evaluation is to data processing management. Statements like "The system looks good" or "They might have some trouble with that system" are too nebulous to be of much value to anyone. While it may be of some value to management to say that system A is better than system B, managers want to know how much better. Data processing management desires a precise measurement of the efficiency of a computer application.

This chapter provides the QA reviewer with methodology for quantifying the evaluation of computer application system review. The result will be a numerical score which can be evaluated and compared to other evaluations. Each review point can be rated and the continuum of ratings plotted to determine whether the work on the project is improving or declining. This trend evaluation can be extremely valuable to management if it has any reservation about continuing the development of a particular application. If definite improvement can be shown from one review to another, management's confidence in that project team will increase. While judgment must still be applied to any quantitative evaluation, scoring a system review is an excellent tool for describing the status of an application system and comparing current to prior status.

VALUE OF RATINGS

The concerns addressed in the checkpoint reviews should not be answered yes or no even though the concerns are worded so that it appears a yes or no answer would be appropriate. In practice, this is not practical. For example, one of the concerns stated is "whether or not the system development life cycle phase being reviewed will be completed within budget." If the answer is yes, does this mean it will be completed exactly for the budgeted amount, $1 less, $1,000 less, $10,000 less, or whatever? On the other hand, does a no answer mean it will run $1 over budget, $1,000 or $10,000 over budget? While a yes answer is comforting, and a no answer discouraging, it is possible the difference is $2 or less. Therefore, we need to be able to provide a more definitive response than yes or no.

The method given in this chapter is to answer each concern on a five-point rating scale. The midpoint on the scale is considered an average implementation or resolution of a concern. The lower end of the scale would be a poor implementation or resolution of a concern, with the bottom of the scale being very poor. The ratings on the upper end of the scale would be good and very good. This now permits the reviewer to avoid a black or white answer, and to work instead with shades of gray. The scale can be used in a variety of ways, but all are designed to provide a wider range of responses than yes/no.

The objective of the rating is to be able to accumulate the responses to the concerns to determine a total rating score for the review point. If the answer to every concern was that the EDP system project team had implemented or resolved the concern to an average degree, then the total rating for the review point would be average. However, it would be unusual if all concerns were handled at the same level.

The unweighted accumulation of the various points on the scale at first appears logical, but further analysis shows us that some of the concerns are much more important than others. For example, in the mid-justification phase review, it is important that the good and bad points of the current system have been determined, but this concern is not nearly as important as the concern that new information needs have been determined. With an unweighted system, if the reviewer were to rate the project team as very poor on determining the good and bad parts of the current system, but very good on determining the new information needs, the total rating of the work based on those two concerns would be average. That is unfair since one concern was much more important than the other. The overall rating should be above average because the more important concern scored very good.

The resolution is to weight each of the concerns by a factor of 1, 2, or 3. The weight is a measure of importance of a concern.

In our previous example, the new information needs being determined might be given a weighting factor of 3, and determining the good and bad parts of the current system is given a weighting factor of 1. The logic of this is that if you can satisfy all the current needs of the user, it is not too important whether or not you are aware of all the good and bad parts of the current system. This does not diminish the value of learning from existing experience but, rather, explains the need to compare the importance of different concerns.

The evaluation of a concern can be a very time-consuming and detailed task. QA personnel may have to develop extensive questionnaires to arrive at an evaluation for each of the concerns, and these questionnaires themselves may have to be given a rating scale so that at the conclusion of the review a quantitative score can be calculated.

RATING CONSIDERATIONS

The QA group must determine how ratings will be given for a particular concern. For example, to evaluate whether or not the project was implemented within budget, the group needs to establish guidelines for rating. Let us assume that the organization involved states that a project manager should be able to complete a project within plus or minus 5% of the stated budget amount. Since completing the project with a 5% tolerance is expected, achieving that performance can be considered average. Working with DP management,the quality assurance group could extrapolate that if the project manager can complete the project within plus or minus 15% of the stated budget, that is an acceptable performance. If costs exceed 115% of budget, performance is very poor, while if the project leader can complete it in less that 85% of the budget, the performance is very good. Using these guidelines, we can now rate the answer to the concern about implementation within the budget dollars. The rating would be as follows:

Ratings	*Criterion*
Very good	Project complete with 85% of budget or less
Good	Project complete within 85.1 – 94.9% of budget
Average	Project complete within 95 – 105% of budget
Poor	Project complete within 105.1–114.9% of budget
Very poor	Project complete for over 115% of budget

This type of evaluation must be done for each of the concerns within each review point review. Some of the concerns fit very easily into a quantitative analysis while others do not. For example, the concern that the proposed system will have a reasonable life expectancy is difficult to quantify. If we can determine what a reasonable life expectancy is, we can then develop a five-point rating for that life expectancy.

Concerns that are difficult to rate quantitatively are those that deal with subjective judgments such as feelings, preference, likings, etc. For example, consider the concern of whether or not the user wants the proposed system. Rarely will a user respond "Yes, I want it," or "No, I do not want it." Most times the response to the question if asked as stated would be "Yes, BUT ..." The interpretation of "Yes, BUT" answers can be difficult. Therefore, either the reviewer must pin down the user to a quantitative response or convert the user's response into a quantitative response.

This conversion of subjective responses into quantitative answers is not as difficult as it first appears. There are a number of methods that seem to work very well. One way is to ask the user to pick the one from the five-point scale which appears most appropriate. For example, for the question "Does the user want the proposed system?" we could give the user the following five choices and ask which is most appropriate. The five choices might be

1.   Do you very much want the proposed system to be installed?
2.   Do you want the new system to be installed?
3.   Is it unimportant to you whether or not the new system is installed?
4.   Would you prefer that the new system is not installed?
5.   Do you desire very much not to have the new system installed?

The reviewer may not feel comfortable asking user personnel to pick among five different choices. Alternatives to this are to merely discuss the general topic area, such as the user's feeling about the new system, and then let the reviewer make a judgment as to what the user has said. Obviously, this has some interpretation and bias on the part of the reviewer, but may prove to be a better method of collecting information than to have the user try to pick among five responses to a concern.

When picking a specific response is difficult for a user, or if the approach is awkward for the reviewer, another method can be used to arrive at an evaluation. Rather than ask for a specific response to a question, the reviewer can ask one or more questions related to a concern and then rate the answer on a five-point scale. In the example above, he can ask questions relating to whether the system will be easy to work with, whether the system does the job the user hoped it would do, and whether the user's job will be easier or harder after the new system is installed. For instance, in determining whether or not the user wants the new system, a good question might be "Will your job be easier when a new system is installed?" From the answer given by the user the reviewer can create a rating scale:

1.   The job will be much easier when the new system is installed. (Rate very good.)
2.   The job will be easier when the new system is installed. (Rate good.)
3.   The job will be about the same when the new system is installed. (Rate average.)
4.   The job will be harder when the new system is installed. (Rate poor.)
5.   The job will be much harder when the system is installed. (Rate very poor.)

The reviewer uses a series of questions and then, based on the totality of all the answers, makes a judgment as to the quantitative rating for that review concern.

Another method of getting quantitative opinions to subjective concerns is to probe the user's response. Again, if we wanted to determine if the user wanted the proposed system, the reviewer could ask a question such as "Do you feel that the proposed system is going to be valuable to your department?" The user would probably respond "Yes, but" and give some reasons. The reviewer can then probe the "Yes, buts" as to whether it will be helpful, very helpful, not helpful, etc. This might be done in a casual conversation that is more relaxing and easier for the user than probing for a specific answer.

REVIEW POINT EVALUATION FORMS

The QA group concerns as given in Chapter 7 become the basis for evaluating quantitatively each review point. The reviewer must make an evaluation for each of the concerns. Figures 10.1 through 10.12 are worksheets for evaluating each concern for each checkpoint.

QUALITY ASSUR-ANCE CONCERN	Factor	EDP SYSTEMS PROJECT TEAM IMPLEMENTATION/RESOLUTION OF CONCERN					
		Very Good	*Good*	*Aver-age*	*Poor*	*Very Poor*	*N/A*
1. A sufficient number of capable people have been assigned to the justificationphase.	1						
2. The good and bad parts of the current system have been determined.	1						
3. The data processing procedures and standards have been followed.	3						
4. There are no adequate alternatives available to meet the user's needs without building a new system.	2						
5. The justification phase will be completed on time.	3						
6. The justification phase will be completed within budget.	1						
7. The goals and objectives to be solved are clearly stated.	1						
8. The goals and objectives to be solved are clearly stated.	3						
Comments							

Figure 10.1 **QUALITY ASSURANCE REVIEW POINT #1: MID-JUSTIFICATION PHASE REVIEW**

QUALITY ASSUR- ANCE CONCERN	Factor	EDP SYSTEMS PROJECT TEAM IMPLEMENTATION/RESOLUTION OF CONCERN					
		Very Good	*Good*	*Aver- age*	*Poor*	*Very Poor*	*N/A*
1. The data proces- sing costs have been estimated.	1						
2. The user costs and benefits have been estimated.	1						
3. A conceptual sys- tem design has been prepared.	2						
4. The data pro- cessing proce- dures and stand- ards have been fol- lowed.	2						
5. The proposed system was sel- ected by a rea- sonable method from among the various altern- atives.	2						
6. The assumptions made in arriving at a solution are valid.	2						
7. The proposed sol- ution solves the business pro- blem.	3						
8. The user wants the proposed sys- tem.	3						
Comments							

Figure 10.2 **QUALITY ASSURANCE REVIEW POINT #2: END OF JUSTIFICATION PHASE REVIEW**

QUALITY ASSUR-ANCE CONCERN	Factor	EDP SYSTEMS PROJECT TEAM IMPLEMENTATION/RESOLUTION OF CONCERN					
		Very Good	Good	Aver-age	Poor	Very Poor	N/A
9. The proposed system has a reasonable life expectancy.	3						
10. The standards of performance for the new system have been established.	2						
11. The standards of performance is documented and in the hands of the system designers.	2						
12. Criteria has been established to evaluate performance after the system is operational.	2						
Comments							

Figure 10.2 **QUALITY ASSURANCE REVIEW POINT #2: END OF JUSTIFICATION PHASE REVIEW (Cont'd)**

| QUALITY ASSUR-ANCE CONCERN | Factor | EDP SYSTEMS PROJECT TEAM IMPLEMENTATION/RESOLUTION OF CONCERN | | | | | |
		Very Good	Good	Aver-age	Poor	Very Poor	N/A
1. A sufficient num-ber of capable people have been assigned to the systems design phase.	1						
2. The business problem has been solved and the needed work products (report, etc.) are defined.	3						
3. The source ne-eded data has been determined.	3						
4. The data storage (file) needs have been determined.	2						
5. The required pro-cessing has been determined.	2						
6. The various func-tions of the pro-posed stystem fit together.	2						
7. The proposed sol-ution solves the business prob-lem.	3						
8. The system will be implemented when needed.	2						
9. Performance standards will be achieved.	2						
Comments							

Figure 10.3 **QUALITY ASSURANCE REVIEW POINT #3: REVIEW OF BUSINESS SYSTEMS SOLUTION PHASE**

| QUALITY ASSUR-ANCE CONCERN | Factor | EDP SYSTEMS PROJECT TEAM IMPLEMENTATION/RESOLUTION OF CONCERN | | | | | |
		Very Good	Good	Aver-age	Poor	Very Poor	N/A
1. The equipment requirements have been det-ermined.	2						
2. It has been det-ermined whe-ther or not add-itional hardware will be required.	2						
3. It has been det-ermined whether or not addition-al software will be required.	2						
4. It has been det-ermined whether or not any spec-ial hardware or software instal-lation will be required.	2						
5. The EDP dep-artment and the project team have the level of experience necessary to use the specified hardware and software.	2						
6. The hardware provides for suf-ficient growth for the proposed system.	2						
Comments							

Figure 10.4 **QUALITY ASSURANCE REVIEW POINT #4: REVIEW OF EQUIPMENT SELECTION**

| QUALITY ASSUR- ANCE CONCERN | Factor | EDP SYSTEMS PROJECT TEAM IMPLEMENTATION/RESOLUTION OF CONCERN | | | | | |
		Very Good	Good	Aver- age	Poor	Very Poor	N/A
1. The file specifi- cations meet EDP standards.	2						
2. The input speci- fications meet EDP standards.	2						
3. The output speci- fications meet EDP standards.	2						
4. The process speci- fications meet EDP standards.	2						
5. The computer system design is properly docu- mented.	2						
6. The computer system design is complete.	2						
7. The system as designed meets the needs of the user(s).	3						
8. The system as designed will operate on the planned hard- ware and soft- ware.	3						
9. The costs have been developed in accordance with EDP proce- dures.	2						
Comments							

Figure 10.5 **QUALITY ASSURANCE REVIEW POINT #5:
REVIEW OF COMPUTER SYSTEM DESIGN**

| QUALITY ASSUR-ANCE CONCERN | Factor | EDP SYSTEMS PROJECT TEAM IMPLEMENTATION/RESOLUTION OF CONCERN | | | | | |
		Very Good	Good	Aver-age	Poor	Very Poor	N/A
10. The system design provides the capacity for reasonable growth.	1						
11. Other design alternatives were considered and rejected for valid reasons.	2						
12. The system design does not impose undue restrictions on the user.	2						
13. The audit trail is sufficient to reconstruct transactions.	3						
14. The computer systems design phase will be completed on time.	1						
15. The computer systems design phase will be completed within budget.	1						
16. The EDP system standards are realistic for the system.	1						
Comments							

Figure 10.5 **QUALITY ASSURANCE REVIEW POINT #5: REVIEW OF COMPUTER SYSTEM DESIGN (Cont'd)**

QUALITY ASSUR-ANCE CONCERN	Factor	EDP SYSTEMS PROJECT TEAM IMPLEMENTATION/RESOLUTION OF CONCERN					
		Very Good	*Good*	*Aver-age*	*Poor*	*Very Poor*	*N/A*
17. The current EDP systems stand-ards are approp-riate for the time when this system will be opera-tional.	1						
18. Performance standards can be achieved.	2						
19. The system of internal control is adequate to ensure the accur-ate and complete processing of transactions.	3						
20. The system of internal control is adequate to ensure the cont-inued integrity of the computer files and/or data bases.	3						
Comments							

Figure 10.5 **QUALITY ASSURANCE REVIEW POINT #5:
REVIEW OF COMPUTER SYSTEM DESIGN (Cont'd)**

QUALITY ASSURANCE CONCERN	Factor	EDP SYSTEMS PROJECT TEAM IMPLEMENTATION/RESOLUTION OF CONCERN					
		Very Good	*Good*	*Average*	*Poor*	*Very Poor*	*N/A*
1. A sufficient number of capable people have been assigned to the program design phase.	1						
2. The program design meets EDP standards.	2						
3. The program design has been properly documented.	2						
4. Provision has been made for restart procedures.	1						
5. Provision has been made for recovery procedures.	2						
6. Provision has been made to protect sensitive data.	2						
7. There is a programming schedule.	1						
8. The program design phase will be completed on time.	1						

Comments

Figure 10.6 **QUALITY ASSURANCE REVIEW POINT #6: REVIEW OF PROGRAM DESIGN**

QUALITY ASSUR- ANCE CONCERN		EDP SYSTEMS PROJECT TEAM IMPLEMENTATION/RESOLUTION OF CONCERN					
	Factor	*Very Good*	*Good*	*Aver- age*	*Poor*	*Very Poor*	*N/A*
9. The program design phase will be completed within budget.	1						
10. The EDP program standards are realistic for this system.	1						
11. The current EDP program standards are appropriate for the time when this system will be operational.	1						
12. Performance standards will be achieved.	2						
Comments							

Figure 10.6 **QUALITY ASSURANCE REVIEW POINT #6: REVIEW OF PROGRAM DESIGN (Cont'd)**

QUALITY ASSUR-ANCE CONCERN		EDP SYSTEMS PROJECT TEAM IMPLEMENTATION/RESOLUTION OF CONCERN					
	Factor	*Very Good*	*Good*	*Aver-age*	*Poor*	*Very Poor*	*N/A*
1. A plan has been established to convert from the old to the new system.	2						
2. The conversion plan is in accordance with EDP standards.	2						
3. A plan has been established to test the new system.	2						
4. The test plan is in accordance with EDP standards.	2						
5. Sufficient resources have been allocated for the conversion.	1						
6. Sufficient resources have been allocated for the system test.	1						
7. There is a testing schedule.	1						
8. There is a conversion schedule.	1						
Comments							

Figure 10.7. **QUALITY ASSURANCE REVIEW POINT #7: REVIEW OF TESTING AND CONVERSION PLANNING**

QUALITY ASSUR- ANCE CONCERN	Factor	EDP SYSTEMS PROJECT TEAM IMPLEMENTATION/RESOLUTION OF CONCERN					
		Very Good	*Good*	*Aver- age*	*Poor*	*Very Poor*	*N/A*
1. Programs are coded in accord- ance with EDP standards.	2						
2. Programs are adequately tested.	2						
3. The program code is maintain- able by the aver- age programmer.	2						
4. The system of internal control has been imp- lemented accord- ing to specifica- tions.	3						
Comments							

Figure 10.8 **QUALITY ASSURANCE REVIEW POINT #8: REVIEW OF PROGRAM CODING AND TESTING**

QUALITY ASSUR-ANCE CONCERN		EDP SYSTEMS PROJECT TEAM IMPLEMENTATION/RESOLUTION OF CONCERN					
	Factor	*Very Good*	*Good*	*Aver-age*	*Poor*	*Very Poor*	*N/A*
1. A sufficient number of capable people have been assigned to the system test phase.	1						
2. Comprehensive test data will be prepared.	2						
3. Users will be adequately train-ed to evaluate test results.	2						
4. The planned test data will test the system controls.	2						
5. The test phase will be complet-ed on time.	1						
6. The test phase will be complet-ed within budget.	1						
Comments							

Figure 10.9 **QUALITY ASSURANCE REVIEW POINT #9: REVIEW OF DETAILED TEST PLAN**

QUALITY ASSUR-ANCE CONCERN	Factor	EDP SYSTEMS PROJECT TEAM IMPLEMENTATION/RESOLUTION OF CONCERN					
		Very Good	Good	Aver-age	Poor	Very Poor	N/A
1. The system does meet the needs of the user as specified in the design.	3						
2. The system does conform to EDP standards.	2						
3. The test was performed ac-cording to EDP test standards.	2						
4. The user is ade-quately trained to handle the day-to-day pro-blems of the sys-tem.	3						
5. Performance standards have been achieved.	2						
Comments							

Figure 10.10 **QUALITY ASSURANCE REVIEW POINT #10: REVIEW OF TEST RESULTS**

QUALITY ASSUR-ANCE CONCERN	Factor	EDP SYSTEMS PROJECT TEAM IMPLEMENTATION/RESOLUTION OF CONCERN					
		Very Good	*Good*	*Aver-age*	*Poor*	*Very Poor*	*N/A*
1. A sufficient number of capable people have been assigned to the system conversion phase.	1						
2. Conversion programs are coded and tested in accordance with EDP standards.	2						
3. A contingency plan has been made in case the conversion is unsuccessful.	2						
4. The conversion plan will be completed on time.	1						
5. The conversion phase will be completed within budget.	1						
6. The controls over the conversion process are adequate to ensure an accurate and complete conversion.	3						
Comments							

Figure 10.11 **QUALITY ASSURANCE REVIEW POINT #11: REVIEW OF DETAIL CONVERSION PLANNING AND PROGRAMS**

QUALITY ASSURANCE CONCERN	Factor	EDP SYSTEMS PROJECT TEAM IMPLEMENTATION/RESOLUTION OF CONCERN					
		Very Good	*Good*	*Average*	*Poor*	*Very Poor*	*N/A*
1. The conversion was performed in accordance with conversion standards.	2						
2. The results of the conversion process have been verified.	3						
Comments							

Figure 10.12 **QUALITY ASSURANCE REVIEW POINT #12: REVIEW OF CONVERSION RESULTS**

The factor column on the worksheet shows suggested weights for every concern using a three-point scale proposed earlier. A factor of 3 is used to show the concern of most importance, and a factor of 1 to show the concern of least importance. During the evaluation process for a concern by the quality assurance reviewer, the factor is not used. However, the factor is used in arriving at a weighted score for a concern for that particular review point.

The reviewer checks the column showing his rating of how well each concern has been handled. There is also room on the worksheet to indicate if the concern is not applicable to that specific project. For example, if the organization in question does not have budgets, then the concern regarding "implementing the project within the budget" is not applicable (N/A) for that particular review point.

The worksheet includes a column for comments. For example, if the reviewer is about to begin review point 9, that individual should review the results of the previous eight reviews. Comments included can be very helpful in explaining why a particular rating was given. This is especially true if the rating could almost be determined by a toss of a coin between two categories. Therefore, a comment that indicates a borderline decision will be helpful to the next person reviewing the project.

When the reviewer has completed the entire review point review, the next step is to calculate the score for that review point.

SCORING THE QA REVIEW

There are three steps to follow in scoring each review. First, each concern must be rated by the five-point scale. Second, the rating must be translated in a quantitative score and accumulated for the review. Third is the interpretation of the score. the reviewer must rate each concern at the end of each review point. In review point 1, there are eight concerns. Assuming all eight are applicable to the application under review, each of the eight concerns would be rated within the five-point scale (i.e., very good, good, average, poor, or very poor).

The next step is to translate the rating into quantitative scores. The Review Score Sheet (Figure 10.13) is used for this purpose. The Review Score Sheet is divided into three rating sections. Each rating section is used for one of the three factor numbers. The first rating section is for factor 1 rated concerns, the second section for factor 2 rated concerns, and the third section for factor 3 rated concerns.

The best method to accumulate the total score for a review is to quantify the rating for each concern in order by its factor weight. The reviewer looks first at the concerns weighted by factor number 1. For these concerns, the reviewer adds up all the check marks in each column. This means the number of checks in the very poor column, poor column, average column, etc. In review point 1, there are 4 concerns weighted with a factor number 1. The ratings for these must now be transcribed to the factor number 1 section of Figure 10.13. For example, if 2 of those were checked not applicable, the reviewer would put a number 2 in the "number of questions rated" for the not applicable (N/A) rating. If 1 of the 4 was scored average, the reviewer would put a 1 in the "number of questions rated" column for the average rating for factor number 1. If the other concern was rated good, the reviewer would then put a 1 in the "number of questions rated" column for the good score.

Then the reviewer would move to the factor 2 and look at all the concerns that were weighted by a factor number 2. In the Review Score Sheet, this grading would be put in the factor 2

Review Point # _____   **Date Completed** _____

Reviewer's Name _____

Factor Number	Rating	Number of Questions Rated	Times This Constant	Equals This Score
1	Not Applicable (N/A)		0	
	Very Poor		1	
	Poor		2	
	Average		3	
	Good		4	
	Very Good		5	
2	Not Applicable (N/A)		0	
	Very Poor		2	
	Poor		4	
	Average		6	
	Good		8	
	Very Good		10	
3	Not Applicable (N/A)		0	
	Very Poor		3	
	Poor		6	
	Average		9	
	Good		12	
	Very Good		15	_____
	Total Score			======
	N/A Score			======

Figure 10.13 **REVIEW SCORE SHEET**

section. For review point number 1, there are three concerns weighted by factor number 3. This means in section three of the Review Score Sheet the three ratings would be transcribed to the section 3 ratings with the number of questions rated put in the "number of questions rated" column.

When the ratings for all the concerns for the review point being scored have been transcribed to the Review Score Sheet, it is time to calculate the score. To do this, the number in the "number of questions rated" column is multiplied by the constant in the"times this constant" column. For example, we said there was one question rated average for factor 1. In this example, we multiply the 1 times 3 to get a total score of 3 for the average rating for factor 1. The score of 3 is put in the "Equals this score" column. This process is continued until each number in the "Number of questions rated" column has been multiplied by the constant in the "times this constant" column to arrive at a score. The "Equals this score" column is accumulated to arrive at a total score for the review point.

Next, the not applicable (N/A) score must be calculated. This is done by multiplying the number of questions rated times the factor number for each of the three factors. The following table illustrates how this can be accomplished.

Factor Number	Number of N/A Questions Checked for Factor Number	Times This Constant	Equals the N/A Score for This Review Point
1	_____	x 1	=_____
2	_____	x 2	=_____
3	_____	x 3	=_____

Total N/A score is _____

Note: This total N/A score is put at the bottom of the Review Score Sheet (see Figure 10.13).

The review score has now been calculated for the completed review point. The top of the form should be completed, which shows the review point number, the date the review was completed, and the lead reviewer's name.

This calculation has produced a raw score which must be adjusted so that it can be compared to other reviews. The adjusted score is calculated by dividing the number of questions times their weight into the total score. This will produce an adjusted score between zero and five. Figure 10.14 is a form to be used in developing the adjusted scores. This adjusted score can then be used for comparative purposes between all twelve review points and other systems.

Assuming all concerns are applicable to the review point, the "total score" from the Review Score Sheet (Figure 10.13) is moved to the "total score" column of Figure 10.14 for the applicable review point. This "total score" is then divided by the constant in the"divided by this constant" column. The result, which is the adjusted score (should be calculated to two decimal places), is put in the adjusted score column.

If some of the concerns are not applicable (N/A) to the review point, the "Divided by this constant" constant must be adjusted. The adjustment is made by subtracting from the constant in the "Divided by this constant" (Figure 10.14) the "N/A score" calculated in the Review Score Sheet (Figure 10.13). For example, if one question with a weighting of factor 1 was not applicable, the N/A score would be 1. This is calculated by multiplying the number of not applicable questions times the factor number. If this was for review point 1, then 1 would be subtracted from the constant 15 to arrive at a new constant of 14. Fourteenwould then be divided into the total score for review point 1 to arrive at an adjusted score.

Once the adjusted score has been determined, it can then be compared to scores for the other twelve review points, and other application system reviews for the same review point number.

EVALUATING THE SCORE

At the completion of each review point, the reviewer will calculate an adjusted score. This is a score between 1.0 and 5.0 and it represents a quantitative evaluation by the reviewer for the application system for the phase under review.

The adjusted score can be compared to other review points, as well as to other application system reviews. However, like any quantitative evaluation score, it must be interpreted. The score is a very viable indicator of the health of the application system. For example, an adjusted score of 3.5 would be considered above average. This still needs interpretation. For example, a score of 3.5 that has dropped from 4.0 in the previous review point may be of more concern than a score which stayed consistent at 3.5 from review point to review point or one which has moved up from 3.0 to 3.5 at this review point.

The score can vary depending on the reviewers — some are "hard markers" and others are "easy." Some organizations assign factors to the reviewers themselves. For example, they may multiply the reviewer's score by a 1.2 for a hard marker and by a .8 for an easy marker to equate scores. A better method might be just an explanation of the mark itself. For example, an adjusted score of 3.0 from one reviewer may be equivalent to a score of 3.5 from another reviewer. This is something that must be learned from experience at each organization.

The following is a guide for interpreting adjusted scores. The final interpretation should take into account the characteristics of application systems, the caliber of people working on the system, the "hardness" or "easiness" of the individual arriving at the adjusted score, and other organization-related factors which can affect the score. The following is given as a guideline to be used on some of the early reviews.

Adjusted Score/Explanation of Adjusted Score

1.0 – 1.99 The implementation and/or resolution of concerns by the systems project team is poor. In this range, the reviewer should consider recommending substantial additional work on this systems development life cycle phase before the system is advanced. The project appears to be in trouble.

2.0 – 2.75 The project needs either additional work or more direction or both. Possibly the project should move to the next stage, but only with extra resources allocated to the project. A score in the 1.0 - 2.75 range for the final three review points flags the system as one in serious trouble.

2.76 – 3.25 The project implementation appears to be adequate. The implementation and/or resolution of concerns is at an acceptable level. Within this range, the quality assurance function can play an important role. It is important that projects in this range maintain adequate quality throughout the remaining phases of the systems development life cycle.

3.26 – 4.0 This is the ideal range for an implemented project. Projects in this range should require little attention and concern of data processing management. The caliber of implementation and/or resolution of concern is above average and should result in a cost-effective, well-controlled system that meets the needs of the user. Quality assurance personnel should be able to cut back some of their effort in reviewing application systems in this range.

4.01 – 5.0 Applications in this range should be considered superior in implementation. However, the implementation effort may be excessive and as such may not be cost-effective. Frequently, systems analysts or programmers have more time allocated than necessary to implement the project. With that time they put in the extra "bells and whistles" which make the project ideal from an implementation viewpoint, but may utilize more resources than necessary.

The trend shown by plotting the adjusted score from review point to review point is a valuable tool for analysis of the implementation process. Ideally, the adjusted score should stay within a small range (e.g., within half a point) throughout all the review points. Wide fluctuations may indicate that work is being shifted from phase to phase. For example, a score that drops during the program design can mean that the project leader is transferring that aspect of the application system development to the programming phase.

Reviewers should try to understand and explain to data processing management fluctuations in adjusted score. Whenever adjusted score fluctuates more than half a point, the difference should be investigated and explained to management. It indicates that a problem has occurred, or has been corrected, and management should be advised of this situation.

EXAMPLE OF REVIEW POINT EVALUATION

Assume that you have been assigned to review an application and that you are at the first review point.

Referring back to Figure 7.2, there are eight concerns which are listed below. The quality assurance reviewer rating for these concerns is also listed.

#	*Quality Assurance Concern*	*Rating*
1	A sufficient number of capable people have been assigned to the justification phase.	Average
2	The good and bad parts of the system have been determined.	Poor
3	The new information needs have been determined.	Good
4	The data processing procedures and standards have been followed.	Average
5	There are no adequate alternatives available to meet the user's needs without building a new system.	Very Good

#	**Quality Assurance Concern**	**Rating**
6	The justification phase will be completed on time.	N/A
7	The justification phase will be completed within budget.	N/A
8	The goals and objectives to be solved are clearly stated.	Average

The reviewer's ratings are then transcribed to the Review Score Sheet. Figure 10.15 shows a Review Score Sheet scored for this review. There are two not applicable ratings, one poor rating, three average ratings, one good rating, and one very good rating. Each of these has been transcribed to Figure 10.15 in the appropriate factor number section.Refer back to Figure 10.1 for the factor number.

After the rating from the review sheet has been transcribed, the total score can be calculated. The total score for this review point is 47. Two questions were answered not applicable (N/A). The N/A score is 2.

When the total score for the review point has been accumulated, an adjusted score needs to be calculated. From Figure 10.14, we see that the constant to divide by is 15. Because there is an N/A score, this must be adjusted. The calculation for adjusted score for this review point 1 example is shown below:

Step	**Explanation**	**Score**
1	Determine the "divided by constant" for review point one (see Figure 9.14)	15
2	Determine the "N/A score" for review point 1 (for example)	2
3	Subtract "N/A score" from constant to obtain new "divided by constant."	13
4	Determine "total score" for review point one.	47
5	Divide new "divided by constant" into "total score" for review point 1 to obtain adjusted score (i.e., 47 divided by 13 equals 3.62.)	3.62

Review Point Decimal Number	Review Point Name	Total Score	Divided By This Constant (Less N/A Score)	Adjusted Score (2 Decimal Places)
1	Mid-Justification Phase		15	
2	End of Justification Phase		25	
3	Business Systems Solution Phase		20	
4	Computer Equipment Selection		12	
5	Computer System Design		40	
6	Program Design		17	
7	Testing and Conversion Planning		12	
8	Program Coding and Testing		9	
9	Detailed Test Plan		9	
10	Test Results		12	
11	Detail Conversion Planning and Programs		10	
12	Conversion Results		5	

Figure 10.14 **ADJUSTED SCORE FOR COMPARATIVE PURPOSES**

The adjusted score is 3.62, which can be interpreted to mean this project should require little attention and concern of data processing management. The caliber of implementation is above average and should result in a cost-effective, well-controlled system.

Review Point # _____   **Date Completed** <u>November 18</u>

Reviewer's Name   <u>I.M. Reviewer</u>

Factor Number	Rating	Number of Questions Rated	Times This Constant	Equals This Score
1	Not Applicable (N/A)	2	0	—
	Very Poor		1	
	Poor	1	2	2
	Average	1	3	3
	Good		4	
	Very Good		5	
2	Not Applicable (N/A)		0	
	Very Poor		2	
	Poor		4	
	Average	1	6	6
	Good		8	
	Very Good		10	
3	Not Applicable (N/A)		0	
	Very Poor		3	
	Poor		6	
	Average	1	9	9
	Good	1	12	12
	Very Good	1	15	15
	Total Score			47
	N/A Score			2

Figure 10.15 **REVIEW SCORE SHEET**

OTHER METHODS FOR EVALUATING QUALITY

A quantitative review of project concerns produces a mathematical score representing quality. It should be used as an indicator of quality and not as a precise measurement of quality. The advantage to scoring quality is that it forces the QA analyst to make a positive statement about quality and then be prepared to defend that score. However, scoring is only one of several evaluation methods. The three most common methods of evaluating the quality of computerized applications are:

1. *Judgment.* The QA analyst, using his or her experience, draws a conclusion on the quality of the application being reviewed. This method is most successful when the reviewers are the most senior and most respected individuals in the data processing department.

2. *Missing criteria.* The QA analyst reviews the application looking for the presence of specific criteria. The evaluation then states which criteria are present and which are missing.

3. *Metrics.* The QA analyst quantitative measure of predetermined quality characteristics. Metrics are explained in Chapter 11.

SUMMARY

Determining a quantitative score for each review point serves two purposes. First, it enables both the reviewer and data processing management to evaluate the result of the review quantitatively. Second, it enables both QA and data processing management to compare different review points. These review points can be from the same or different applications. The comparison of a quantitative number enables data processing management to gain a better appreciation of the status of implementation of an application system.

To develop a comparable score, the reviewer must rate each of the QA concerns for a review point on a five-point scale. These concerns are then weighted by a factor so that the more important concerns have a greater impact on the final score. Once the concerns have been rated, a comparable adjusted score can be calculated.

The score for the quality assurance review needs to be interpreted. Variables in arriving at a score include the stringency of the individual quality assurance reviewer making the rating, the characteristics of the application system, the caliber of people working on the project, plus other unique characteristics of the project. A quantitative evaluation of an application system can be used to measure the level of success of a project implementation by all concerned parties.

Chapter 11
METRICS — A TOOL FOR DEFINING AND MEASURING QUALITY*

There has been an increased awareness in recent years of the critical problems that have been encountered in the development of large-scale application systems (i.e., application software). These problems include not only the cost and schedule overruns typical of development efforts, and the poor performance of the systems once they are delivered, but also the high cost of maintaining the systems, the lack of portability, and the high sensitivity to changes in requirements.

The potential of the metric concepts can be realized by their inclusion in quality assurance programs. Their impact on a quality assurance program is to provide a more disciplined, engineering approach to quality assurance and to provide a mechanism for taking a life cycle viewpoint of quality. The benefits derived from their application are realized in cost reductions over the life cycle of the system.

The purpose of this chapter is to present procedures and guidelines for introducing and utilizing current quality measurement techniques in a quality assurance program associated with large-scale system developments. These procedures and guidelines will explain how to identify and specify software quality requirements (set quality goals).

---

* This chapter is based on the results of research conducted in support of the United States Air Force Electronic Systems Division (ESD), Rome Air Development Center (RADC), and the United States Army Computer Systems Command's Army Institute for Research in Management Information and Computer Science (USACSC/AIRMICS).

QUALITY MEASUREMENT IN PERSPECTIVE

The evolution during the past decade of modern programming practices, structured, disciplined development techniques and methodologies, and requirements for more structured, effective documentation, has increased the feasibility of effective measurement of software quality. The metrics can be classified according to three categories: Anomaly-detecting, predictive, and acceptance.

Anomaly-detecting metrics identify deficiencies in documentation or source code. These deficiencies usually are corrected to improve the quality of the software product. Standards enforcement is a form of anomaly-detecting metrics.

Predictive metrics are measurements of the logic of the design and implementation. These measurements are concerned with attributes such as form, structure, density, and complexity. They provide an indication of the quality that will be achieved in the end product, based on the nature of the application and design and implementation strategies.

Acceptance metrics are measurements that are applied to the end product to assess the final compliance with requirements. Tests are an acceptance-type measurement.

The measurements described and used in this chapter are either anomaly-detecting or predictive metrics. They are applied during the development phases to assist in the early identification of quality problems so that corrective actions can be taken when they are more effective and economical.

The measurement concepts complement current quality assurance and testing practices. They are not a replacement for any current techniques utilized in normal QA programs. For example, a major objective of quality assurance is to assure conformance with user/customer requirements. The software quality metric concepts described in this book provide a methodology for the user/customer to specify life-cycle-oriented quality requirements usually not considered, and a mechanism for measuring if those requirements have been attained. A function usually performed by quality assurance personnel is a review/audit of software products produced during software development. The software metrics add formality and quantification to these document and code reviews. The metric concepts also provide a vehicle for early involvement in the development since there are metrics which apply to the documents produced early in the development.

Testing is usually oriented toward correctness, reliability, and performance (efficiency). The metrics assist in the evaluation of other qualities like maintainability, portability, and flexibility. A summarization of how the software metric concepts complement quality assurance activities is provided in Figure 11.1.

QUALITY ASSURANCE PROGRAM REQUIREMENTS	IMPACT OF SOFTWARE QUALITY METRIC CONCEPTS
• Assume conformance with requirements • Identify software deficiencies • Provide configuration management • Conduct Test • Provide library controls • Review computer program design • Assure software documentation requirement conformation • Conduct reviews and audits • Provide tools/techniques/methodology for quality assurance • Provide subcontractor control	• Adds software quality • Anomaly-detecting • No impact • Assist in evaluation of other qualities • No impact • Predictive metrics • Metrics assist in evaluation of documentation as well as code • Procedures for applying metrics (in form of worksheets) formalizes inspection process • This chapter describes methodology of using metrics • No impact

Figure 11.1 **HOW SOFTWARE METRICS COMPLEMENT QUALITY ASSURANCE**

IDENTIFYING QUALITY REQUIREMENTS

The primary purpose of applying software quality metrics in a quality assurance program is to improve the quality of the software product. Rather than simply measuring, the concepts are based on achieving a positive influence on the product, to improve its development.

This section addresses the problem of identifying software quality requirements or goals. These requirements are in addition to the functional, performance, cost, and schedule requirements normally specified for a software development. The fact that the goals established are related to the quality of the end product should, in itself, provide some positive influence.

The vehicle for establishing the requirements is the hierarchical model of software quality. This model, shown in Figure 11.2, has at its highest level a set of software quality factors that are user/management-oriented terms and represent the characteristics which comprise software quality. At the next level for each quality factor is a set of criteria which are the attributes that, if present, provide the characteristics represented by the quality factors. The criteria, then, are software-related terms. At the lowest level of the model are the metrics which are quantitative measures of the software attributes defined by the criteria.

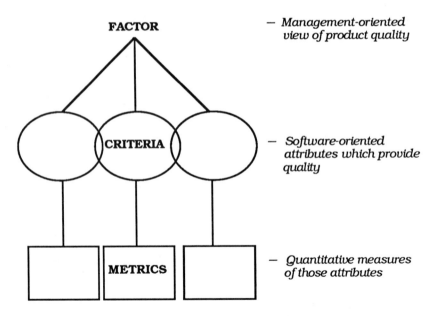

Figure 11.2 **FRAMEWORK FOR MEASURING QUALITY**

The procedures for establishing the quality requirements for a particular software system utilize this model and will be described as a three-level approach, the levels corresponding to the hierarchical levels of the software quality model. The first level establishes the quality factors that are important. The second level identifies the critical software attributes. The third level identifies the metrics which will be applied and establishes quantitative ratings for the quality factors.

Once the quality requirements have been determined by following the procedures described in the subsequent paragraphs, they must be transmitted to the development team. The quality requirements should be documented in the same form as the other system requirements and relayed to the development team. Additionally, a briefing emphasizing the intent of the inclusion of the quality requirements is recommended.

Procedures for Identifying Important Quality Factors

The basic tool to be utilized in identifying the important quality factors is the Software Quality Requirements Survey form shown in Figure 11.3. The formal definitions of each of the eleven quality factors are provided on that form.

It is recommended that a briefing be provided to the decision makers using the tables and figures which follow in this section to solicit their responses to the survey. The decision makers may include the acquisition manager, the user/customer, the development manager, and the QA manager. To complete the survey, the following procedures should be followed.

Consider basic characteristics of the application. The software quality requirements for each system are unique and are influenced by system or application-dependent characteristics. There are basic characteristics which affect the quality requirements, and each software system must be evaluated for its basic characteristics. Figure 11.4 provides a list of some of these basic characteristics. For example, if the system is being developed in an environment in which there is a high rate of technical breakthroughs in hardware design, portability should take on an added significance. If the expected life cycle of the system is long, maintainability becomes a cost-critical consideration. If the application is an experimental system where the software specifications will have a high rate of change, flexibility in the software product is highly desirable. If the functions of the system are expected to be required for a long time, while the system itself may change considerably, reusability is of prime importance in those modules which implement the major functions of the system.

With the advent of more computer networks and communication capabilities, more systems are being required to interface with other systems; hence, the concept of interoperability is extremely important. These and other system characteristics should be considered when identifying the important quality factors.

Consider life cycle implications. The eleven quality factors identified on the survey can be grouped according to three life cycle activities associated with a delivered software product. These three activities are product operation, product revision, and product transition. The relationship of the quality factors to these activities is shown in Figure 11.5. This table also illustrates where quality indications can be achieved through measurement and where the impact is felt if poor quality is realized. The size of this impact determines the cost savings that can be expected if a higher quality system is achieved through the application of the metrics. These cost savings are somewhat offset by the cost to apply the metrics and the cost to develop the higher quality software product as illustrated in Figure 11.6.

A cost to implement versus life cycle cost reduction relationship exists for each quality factor. The benefit versus cost-to-provide ratio for each factor is rated as high, medium, or low in the right-hand column of Figure 11.5. This relationship and the life cycle implications of the quality factors should be considered when selecting the important factors for a specific system.

Perform trade-offs among the tentative list of quality factors. As a result of the previous two steps, a tentative list of quality factors should be produced. The next step is to consider the interrelationships among the factors selected. Figures 11.7 and 11.8 can be used as a guide for determining the relationships between the quality factors. Some factors are synergistic while others conflict. The impact of conflicting factors is that the cost to implement will increase. This will lower the benefit-to-cost ratio described in the preceding paragraphs.

Identify most important quality factors. The list of quality factors considered to be important for the particular system compiled in the preceding three steps should be organized in order of importance. A single decision maker may choose the factors or the choice may be made by averaging several survey responses. The definitions of the factors chosen should be included with this list.

Provide explanations for choices. Document rationale for the decisions made during the first three steps.

---

1. The 11 quality factors listed below have been isolated from the current literature. They are not meant to be exhaustive, but to reflect what is currently thought to be important. Please indicate whether you consider each factor to be Very Import (VI), Important (I), Somewhat Important (SI), or Not Important (NI) as design goals in the system you are currently working on.

Response	Factors	Definition
	Correctness	Extent to which a program satisfies its specifications and fulfills the user's mission objectives.
	Reliability	Extent to which a program can be expected to perform its intended function with required precision.
	Efficiency	The amount of computing resources and code required by a program to perform a function.
	Integrity	Extent to which access to software or data by unauthorized persons can be controlled.
	Usability	Effort required to learn, operate, prepare input, and interpret output of a program.
	Maintainability	Effort required to locate and fix an error in an operational program.
	Testability	Effort required to test a program to ensure that it performs its intended function.
	Flexibility	Effort required to modify an operational program.
	Portability	Effort required to transfer a program from one hardware configuration to another.
	Reusability	Extent to which a program can be used in other applications — related to the packaging and scope of the functions that programs perform.
	Interoperability	Effort required to couple one system with another.

2. What type(s) of application are your currently involved in?

---

3. Are you currently in:
   ❑   1.   Development phase
   ❑   2.   Operations/Maintenance phase

4. Please indicate the title which most closely describes your position:
   ❑   1.   Program Manager
   ❑   2.   Technical Consultant
   ❑   3.   Systems Analyst
   ❑   4.   Other (please specify)

Figure 11.3. **SOFTWARE QUALITY REQUIREMENTS SURVEY FORM**

CHARACTERISTIC	QUALITY FACTOR
• If human lives are affected	Reliability Correctness Testability
• Long life cycle	Maintainability Flexibility Portability
• Real time application	Efficiency Reliability Correctness
• On-board computer application	Efficiency Reliability Correctness
• Processes classified information	Integrity
• Interrelated systems	Interoperability

Figure 11.4 **SYSTEM CHARACTERISTICS AND RELATED QUALITY FACTORS**

An Example of Factors Specification

To illustrate the application of these steps, consider an inventory control system. The inventory control system maintains inventory status and facilitates requisitioning, reordering, and issuing of supplies. The planned life of the system is ten years. Each step described previously will be performed with respect to the tactical inventory control system.

Consider basic characteristics of the application. Utilizing Figure 11.4 and considering the unique characteristics of the tactical inventory control system resulted in the following:

Characteristic | *Related Quality Factor*

Critical supplies | Reliability
Correctness

Long-life cycle with stable hardware and software requirements | Maintainability

Characteristic	Related Quality Factor (cont'd)
Utilized by supply personnel	Usability
Interfaces with inventory systems at other sites	Interoperability

Consider life cycle implications. Of the five quality factors identified in, all provide high or medium life cycle cost/benefits according to Figure 11.5.

Factors Cost/Benefit	Ratio
Reliability	High
Correctness	High
Maintainability	High
Usability	Medium
Interoperability	High

Perform trade-offs among factors. Using Figure 11.7, there are no conflicts which need to be considered.

Identify most important quality factors. Using the survey form, Figure 11.3, and the guidance provided in the preceding paragraphs, the following factors are identified in order of importance. The definitions are provided.

- *Correctness.* Extent to which a program satisfies its specifications and fulfills the user's mission objectives.
- *Reliability.* Extent to which a program can be expected to perform its intended function with required precision.
- *Usability.* Effort required to learn, operate, prepare input, and interpret output of a program.
- *Maintainability.* Effort required to locate and fix an error in an operational program.
- *Interoperability.* Effort required to couple one system to another.

Provide explanation for choice
- *Correctness.* The system performs critical supply function.
- *Reliability.* The system performs critical supply functions in remote environment.
- *Usability.* The system will be used by personnel with minimum computer training.
- *Maintainability.* The system life cycle is projected to be ten years and it will operate in the field where field personnel will maintain it.

- *Interoperability.* The system will interface with other supply systems.

Procedures for Identifying Critical Software Attributes

The next level of identifying the quality requirements involves proceeding from the user-oriented quality factors to the software-oriented criteria. Sets of criteria, which are attributes of the software, are related to the various factors by definition. Their identification is automatic and represents a more detailed specification of the quality requirements.

Identify critical software attributes required. Figure 11.9 should be used to identify the software attributes associated with the chosen critical quality factors.

Provide definitions. The definitions in Figure 11.10 should also be provided as part of the specification.

Example of Identifying Software Criteria

Continuing with the inventory example, the software criteria for the identified quality factors would be chosen.

Identify critical software attributes. Using the relationships provided in Figure 11.9, the following criteria would be identified:

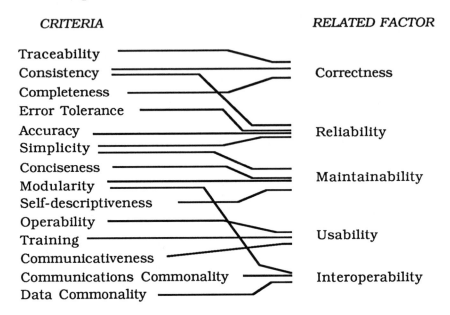

CRITERIA	RELATED FACTOR
Traceability	
Consistency	Correctness
Completeness	
Error Tolerance	
Accuracy	Reliability
Simplicity	
Conciseness	
Modularity	Maintainability
Self-descriptiveness	
Operability	
Training	Usability
Communicativeness	
Communications Commonality	Interoperability
Data Commonality	

LIFE-CYCLE PHASES / FACTORS	DEVELOPMENT			EVALUATION	POSTDEVELOPMENT			EXPECTED COST SAVED vs. COST TO PROVIDE
	REQUIRE-MENTS ANALYSIS	DES-IGN	CODE & DEBUG	SYSTEM TEST	OPER-ATION	REVI-SION	TRANS-ITION	
CORRECTNESS	Δ	Δ	Δ	X	X	X		HIGH
RELIABILITY	Δ	Δ	Δ	X	X	X		HIGH
EFFICIENCY	Δ	Δ	Δ		X			LOW
INTEGRITY	Δ	Δ	Δ		X			LOW
USABILITY	Δ	Δ		X		X		MEDIUM
MAINTAINABILITY		Δ	Δ			X	X	HIGH
TESTABILITY		Δ	Δ	X		X	X	HIGH
FLEXIBILITY		Δ	Δ			X	X	MEDIUM
PORTABILITY		Δ	Δ				X	MEDIUM
REUSABILITY		Δ	Δ				X	MEDIUM
INTEROPERABILITY	Δ	Δ		X			X	LOW

LEGEND: Δ - where quality factors should be measured   X - where impact of poor quality is realized

Figure 11.5   **THE IMPACT OF NOT SPECIFYING OR MEASURING SOFTWARE QUALITY FACTORS**

Provide definitions. The definitions for each of these criteria would be provided also.

Procedures for Establishing Quantifiable Goals

The last level, which is the most detailed and quantified, requires precise statements of the level of quality that will be acceptable for the software product. Mathematical explanations that would allow measurement at this level of precision do not yet exist for all of the quality factors. The mechanism for making the precise statement for any quality factor is a rating of the factor. The underlying basis for the ratings is the effort or cost required to perform a function such as to correct or modify the design or program. For example, rating for maintainability might be that the average time to fix a problem should be five man-days or that 90% of the problem fixes should take less than six man-days. This rating would be specified as a quality requirement. To comply with this specification, the software would have to exhibit characteristics which, when present, give an indication that the software will perform to this rating. These characteristics are measured by metrics which are inserted into a mathematical relationship to obtain the predicted rating.

In order to choose ratings such as the two mentioned above, data must be available which allows the decision maker to know what is a "good rating" or perhaps what is the industry average. Currently there is generally a lack of good historical data to establish these expected levels of operations and maintenance performance for software. The data utilized in this section is based on experiences applying the metrics to several large military command and control software systems and other experiences reported in the literature.

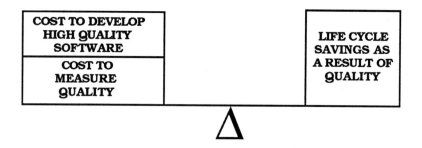

Figure 11.6 **COST VS. BENEFIT TRADE-OFF**

Specify rating for each quality factor. After identification of the critical quality factors, specific performance levels or ratings required for each factor should be specified. Figure 11.11 should be used as a guideline for identifying the ratings for the particular factors. Note that mathematical relationships have not been established for some of the factors. In those cases, it is advisable not to levy requirements for meeting a specific quality rating but instead specify the relative importance of the quality factor as a development goal. Note that the reliability ratings are provided in terms familiar to traditional hardware reliability. Just as in hardware reliability, there are significant differences between ratings of .9 and .99.

Identify specific metrics to be applied. The next step, or an alternative to the preceding step, is to identify the specific metrics which will be applied to the various software products produced during the development.

Specifications of metric threshold values. In lieu of specifying quality ratings or in addition to the ratings, specific minimum values for particular metrics may be specified. This technique is equivalent to establishing a standard which is to be adhered to. Violations to the value established are to be reported. When establishing these threshold values based on past project data, projects which have been considered successful (i.e., have demonstrated good characteristics during their life cycle) should be chosen. For example, a system which has been relatively cost-effective to maintain over its operational history should be chosen to apply the metrics related to maintainability and to establish threshold values.

Example of Metrics

Using the inventory example again the quality ratings would be specified as follows.

Specific quality factor ratings. Rating for two of the five important quality factors can be established using Figure 11.11.

Reliability	.99	Require less than one error per 100 lines of code to be detected during formal testing.
Maintainability	.8	Require 2 man-days as an average level of maintenance for correcting an error.

These ratings can also be established at each measurement period during the development as follows:

	REQ	*POR*	*CDR*	*IMPL*	*ACCEPTANCE*
Reliability	.8	.8	.9	.9	.99
Maintainability	.7	.7	.8	.8	.8

The progressively better scores are required because there is more detailed information in the later phases of the development to which to apply the metrics and more confidence in the metrics' indication of quality.   This is analogous to the concept of reliability growth.

Identify specific metrics to be applied. The metrics to be applied to assess the level of each important quality factors are chosen based on the favorable application system experiences of the organization. Some suggestions are listed below.

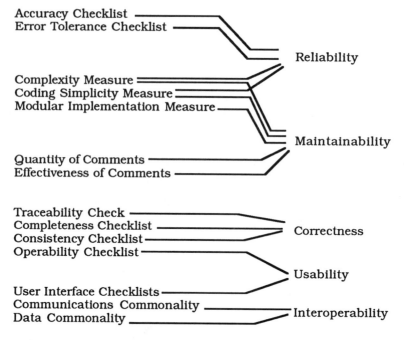

Specify threshold values. Threshold values are established based on past experience and to provide a goal for the quality factors that were not given ratings. They are derived by determining the average scores of past applications of the metrics.

FACTORS	CORRECTNESS	RELIABILITY	EFFICIENCY	INTEGRITY	USABILITY	MAINTAINABILITY	TESTABILITY	FLEXIBILITY	PORTABILITY	REUSABILITY
CORRECTNESS										
RELIABILITY	○									
EFFICIENCY										
INTEGRITY			●							
USABILITY	○	○	●	○						
MAINTAINABILITY	○	○	●		○					
TESTABILITY	○	○	●		○	○				
FLEXIBILITY	○	○	●	●	○	○	○			
PORTABILITY			●			○	○			
REUSABILITY		●	●	●		○	○	○	○	
INTEROPERABILITY		●	●					○		

LEGEND

If a high degree of quality is present for factor,
what degree of quality is expected for the other:

○ = High   ● = Low

Blank = No relationship or application dependent

Figure 11.7 **RELATIONSHIPS BETWEEN SOFTWARE QUALITY FACTORS**

INTEGRITY VERSUS EFFICIENCY	The additional code and processing required to control the access of the software or data usually lengthens run time and requires additional storage.
USABILITY VERSUS EFFICIENCY	The additional code and processing required to ease an operator's tasks or provide more usable output lengthens run time and required additional storage.
MAINTAIN-ABILITY VERSUS EFFICIENCY	Optimized code, incorporating intricate coding techniques and direct code, always provides problems to the maintainer. Using modularity, instrument-ation, and well-commented high-level code to in-crease the maintainability of a system usually in-creases the overhead, resulting in less efficient oper-ation.
TESTABILITY VERSUS EFFICIENCY	The above discussion applies to testing.
PORTABILITY VERSUS EFFICIENCY	The use of direct code of optimized system software or utilities decreases the portability of the system.
FLEXIBILITY VERSUS EFFICIENCY	The generality required for a flexible system in-creases overhead and decreases the portability of the system.
REUSABILITY VERSUS EFFICIENCY	The above discussion applies to reusability.
INTEROPERA-BILITY VERSUS EFFICIENCY	Again, the added overhead for conversion from standard data representations, and the user of inter-face routines decreases the operating efficiency of the system.
FLEXIBILITY VERSUS INTEGRITY	Flexibility requires very general and flexible data structures. The increases the data security problem.
REUSABILITY VERSUS INTEGRITY	As in the above discussion, the generality required by reusable software provides severe protection problems.
INTEROPERA-BILITY VERSUS INTEGRITY	Coupled systems allow more avenues of access to more and different users. The potential for accident-al access of sensitive data is increased as well as the opportunities for deliberate access. Often, coupled systems share data or software which compounds the security problems as well.
REUSABILITY VERSUS RELIABILITY	The generality required by reusable software makes providing error tolerance and accuracy for all cases more difficult.

Figure 11.8 **TYPICAL FACTOR TRADEOFFS**

FACTOR	SOFTWARE CRITERIA
Correctness	Traceability Consistency Completeness
Reliability	Error Tolerance Consistency Accuracy Simplicity
Efficiency	Storage Efficiency Execution Efficiency
Integrity	Access Control Access Audit
Usability	Operability Training Comm- unicativeness
Maintain-ability	Consistency
Flexibility	Modularity Generality Expandability

FACTOR	SOFTWARE CRITERIA
Testability	Simplicity Modularity Instrumentation Self-descriptive- ness
Portability	Modularity Self-descriptive- ness Machine Indep- endence Software System Independence
Reusability	Generality Modularity Software System Independence
Interopera-bility	Modularity Communication Commonality Data Common- ality

Figure 11.9 **SOFTWARE CRITERIA AND RELATED QUALITY FACTORS**

CRITERION	DEFINITION
TRACEABILITY	Those attributes of the software that provide a thread from the requirements to the implementation with respect to the specific development and operational environment.
COMPLETENESS	Those attributes of the software that provide full implementation of the functions required.
CONSISTENCY	Those attributes of the software that provide uniform design and implementation techniques and notation.
ACCURACY	Those attributes of the software that provide the required precision in calculations and outputs.
ERROR TOLERANCE	Those attributes of the software that provide continuity of operation under non-nominal conditions.
SIMPLICITY	Those attributes of the software that provide implementation of functions in the most understandable manner. (Usually avoidance of practices which increase complexity.)
MODULARITY	Those attributes of the software that provide a structure of highly independent modules.
GENERALITY	Those attributes of the software that provide breadth to the functions performed.
EXPANDABILITY	Those attributes of the software that provide for expansion of data storage requirements or computational functions.
INSTRUMENT-ATION	Those attributes of the software that provide for the measurement of usage or identification of errors.
SELF-DESCRIP-TIVENESS	Those attributes of the software that provide explanation of the implementation of a function.

Figure 11.10 **CRITERIA DEFINITIONS FOR SOFTWARE QUALITY**

CRITERION	DEFINITION
EXECUTION EFFICIENCY	Those attributes of the software that provide for minimum processing time.
STORAGE EFFICIENCY	Those attributes of the software that provide for minimum storage requirements during operation.
ACCESS CONTROL	Those attributes of the software that provide for control of the access of software and data.
ACCESS AUDIT	Those attributes of the software that provide for an audit of the access fo software and data.
OPERABILITY	Those attributes of the software that determine operation and procedures concerned with the operation of the software.
TRAINING	Those attributes of the software that provide transition from current operation or initial familiarization.
COMMUNICA-TIVENESS	Those attributes of the software that provide useful inputs and outputs which can be assimilated.
SOFTWARE SYSTEM INDEPENDENCE	Those attributes of the software that determine its dependency on the software environment (operating systems, utilities, input/output routines, etc.).
MACHINE INDEPENDENCE	Those attributes of the software that determine its dependency on the hardware system.
COMMUNICA-TION COMMON-ALITY	Those attributes of the software that provide the use of standard protocols and interface routines.
DATA COMMONALITY	Those attributes of the software that provide the use of standard data representations.
CONCISENESS	Those attributes of the software that provide for implementation of a function with a minimum amount of code.

Figure 11.10 **CRITERIA DEFINITIONS FOR SOFTWARE QUALITY (Cont'd)**

QUALITY FACTOR	RATING EXPLANATION	RATING GUIDELINES			
RELIABILITY*	Rating is in terms of the number of errors that occur after the start of formal testing. Rating = 1 - Number of Errors/Number of Lines of source code excluding comments.	RATING	.9	.98**	.99	.999
		Errors 100 LOC	10	2	1	1
MAINTAIN-ABILITY*	Rating is in terms of the average amount of effort required to locate and fix an error in an operational program. Rating = 1 - .1 (Average number of mandays per fix)	RATING	.3	.5	.7**	.9
		Average Effort (Man-Days)	7	5	3	1
PORTABILITY*	Rating is in terms of the effort required to convert a program to run in another environment with respect to the effort required to originally implement the program. Rating = 1- Effort to Transport/Effort to Implement	RATING	.25	.5**	.75	.9
		% of Original Effort	75	50	25	10
FLEXIBILITY*	Rating is in terms of the average effort required to extend a program to include other requirements. Rating = 1- .05 (Average number of mandays to change)	RATING	.3	.5**	.7	.9
		Average Effort (Man-Days)	14	10	6	2

Figure 11.11 **QUALITY FACTOR RATINGS**

QUALITY FACTOR	RATING EXPLANATION
CORRECTNESS	The function which the software is to perform is incorrect. The rating is in terms of effort required to implement the correct function.
EFFICIENCY	The software does not meet performance (speed, storage) requirements. The rating is in terms of effort required to modify software to meet performance requirements.
INTEGRITY	The software does not provide required security. The rating is in terms of effort required to implement proper levels of security.
USABILITY	There is a problem related to operation of the software, the user interface, or the input/output. The rating is in terms of effort required to improve human factors to an acceptable level.
TESTABILITY	The rating is in terms of effort required to test changes or fixes.
REUSABILITY	The rating is in terms of effort required to use software in a different application.
INTEROPERABILITY	The rating is in terms of effort required to couple the system to another system.

Figure 11.11 **QUALITY FACTOR RATINGS (Cont'd)**

Notes:

*   Data collected to date provides some basis upon which to allow quantitative ratings for these quality factors. These ratings should be modified based on data collected within a specific development environment. Data has not been collected to support ratings of the other quality factors.

**   Indicates rating which might be considered current industry average.

SUMMARY

Software developers have a tendency to view programs as static, finished products once they have gone into the operational phase of the life cycle. Most of us, however, are well aware of the fact that this is not true, that, in fact, software has a complete life cycle and goes through maintenance and enhancement phases before its final obsolescence.

Users of software systems have a different outlook. Software usually performs a service for the user, and developers then become the providers of the system that provides the needed service. Of particular importance in the MIS environment, however, is the fact that the development staff almost invariably acts as a support unit to the primary function of the organization. For the most part, the programs are not in themselves the products which the user organization ultimately produces. In this sense, the developer's staff performs a service for the rest of the organization, and so the task of the developer's staff is one of providing that service to the functional (user) components of the organization. User components are not in themselves interested in the technical aspects of programming or even in that of systems analysis; rather, they are interested in the systems provided to them and the way those systems serve their needs.

This is significant for the reason that the user will make systems decisions based on only one criterion from the developer's viewpoint. If the system adequately serves the needs of the user, even if the system is of low technical quality, the user will be hesitant to authorize expenditures for a replacement system whose quality is much higher, and which might provide better service. Similarly, if the system does not supply adequate service to the user, and will entail significant replacement costs as well as technical complexity, the user will more readily authorize the expenditure of funds in order to alleviate his immediate need for adequate service. Thus, while the developer sees the quality of the system in many lights, in terms of error rates, error tolerance, readability, ease of debugging, etc., the users perceive the system in only one way — how well it meets their needs.

To the developer, these characteristics obviously have a cumulative effect on the user's perception of the quality of the system, but for the most part users do not have this awareness since it requires that they have some experience in the technical aspects of systems development in order to be aware of the problems associated with the task. It is the responsibility of the developer to be aware of the users' needs, their perceptions of what a quality system is, and to develop the system in consonance with those perceptions. This often is not a simple task, since perceptions can change in time. Thus, a user may gain a more mature appreciation of systems if exposed to "user-friendly" systems, or may become less systems oriented after being exposed to systems which are difficult to work with.

At the highest level of our quality metric framework, some of the required translation between user and developer can be accommodated. The quality factors show relevancy of technical aspects of the software to the user's needs over the life cycle of the system. Utilizing the factors, the user can appreciate the impact of a system which is unreliable, or hard to maintain, or hard to change. The user sees this impact in terms of cost, the user's ultimate measure, and its effect on the service the system provides.

Thus, it is beneficial to organizations to view software developers as providers of services over long periods of time. Many management information systems are developed with planned life spans of ten years. The enhancement or rewrite of such systems is a large undertaking requiring the investigation of downstream processing impact. If one views software systems as services, then one can view such problems in light of their impact on the provision of service to users and customers, and thus on the entire organization, rather than on individual modules or subsystems. This enables managers to make more rational decisions based on an overall organizational viewpoint.

An important point to note, related to the nature of organizations, is that change is unavoidable. Organizations and systems change as their objectives and goals change, and it follows that information systems which they use must change with them.

A corollary to this is the fact that the tendency of software managers to engage in trying to avoid changing software systems if at all possible (while positive in some instances) can have a detrimental impact on the overall goals of the organization.

Products go away after a time. Sometimes the life span is long, as in the case of the B-52 or the Volkswagen "Beetle," but eventually they are replaced by new products. The need for specific services lasts a very long time. This long life span is a problem which an awareness of the service perspective gives in the application of quality metrics. The use of metrics throughout the life cycle gives us a method for effectively specifying and monitoring the delivery of service to the user during the operational/maintenance phase of the life cycle.

Chapter 12
REPORTING QUALITY ASSURANCE RESULTS

Effective quality assurance reviews require competent reporting of results. Reports must convince data processing personnel that their recommendations are sound and should be incorporated into the application system. The written reports prepared by QA personnel affect the function. The more professional and useful the reports, the greater the acceptance of the QA function by both management and project personnel. The reports can do a lot to help "sell" the function to DP personnel.

Effective reporting requires extensive time and effort. A rule of thumb for successful QA is for the group to spend one-third of its time on planning, one-third on fact finding, and the remaining third on analysis and report writing. While this formula will not fit all situations, it does emphasize the importance of developing and presenting conclusions.

This chapter will provide guidance on how to prepare effective QA reports from application reviews. However, many of the lessons can be utilized in preparing narratives on the objectives of quality assurance, as well as writing requirements and procedures for data processing systems personnel to follow in developing good application systems.

RESULTS EXPECTED FROM QA REVIEWS

Simply stated, the objective of quality assurance is to improve the organization's data processing applications. This theme should be included in all QA reports. The group should be a very positive force in the data processing organization; its reports should be designed to

1.   help build better data processing systems,
2.   develop a uniform approach to systems development, or
3.   share good system and control practices.

The objective of QA should become obvious to the reader of the reports. All three goals above deal with methods of building quality application systems. However, EDP goals and performance should be considered a part of these methods. Before they write a report, QA personnel must ask themselves what they want to promote as a result of writing that report.

Better data processing systems occur because better methods are used which help achieve the goals and needs of the user. Effectiveness and efficiency are attributes of a good data processing system. Thus, developing better data processing systems includes the three general quality assurance concerns, which are methods, goals, and performance.

A uniform approach to systems development has proven to be a basic building block for developing better data processing systems: it provides a methodology for data processing systems personnel to follow. Multiple review points by QA personnel give data processing management confidence that the uniform approach is being implemented. Sharing of good system and control practices can be fostered by QA personnel. They obtain this knowledge first from their own personal experience, and second from the experiences of others which are learned through performance of the quality assurance function. As they move from system to system, they can carry with them the better systems development and control practices. Good system and control practices involve both methods and performance. When good system and control practices are followed, experience has shown that performance increases.

QA personnel can convey these concepts to EDP management and project personnel by the way in which reports explain the need for incorporating quality assurance recommendations. An essential element in reporting results is the organization and presentation of findings and recommendations.

WRITING QUALITY ASSURANCE REPORTS

Writing an effective report requires the same thoroughness of planning and execution as any other aspect of data processing.

Because many data processing people dislike report writing, they tend to shortcut that aspect of a QA review. Understanding the basic aspects of any report is essential and will help to organize the material to be presented in the report. These elements are explained below:

1. *Who.* What individual or audience will receive the report? Knowing this, the report can be written in the style, language, and size appropriate for that audience.

2. *What.* What type of information does the recipient want? If the report is written for a programmer, the information should be useful in the performance of the programming function. However, if the report is written for executive managers, it should focus on the concerns of that level of management.

3. *Why.* Why is the report being written? To stop a data processing system? Shift it to other pieces of hardware or software? Or to praise the systems personnel for an outstanding job? The objective must be known before the report is written.

4. *When.* When is the report needed? A report submitted too late to be valuable in a decision-making process is a wasted report. If a recipient needs the information today, that is when the report should be ready.

5. *How.* How should the information be presented to best meet the needs of the recipient? The report can be oral (informal or formal) or written in a variety of formats. If the same individual will be receiving QA reports on a regular basis, a standard format is advisable. This will reduce the amount of time necessary by the user of the report because the format will be familiar. Personal idiosyncrasies and desires of the report recipient(s) should be considered when deciding on how the material will be presented.

Let us examine the five elements as they occur in the report writing process. First we must look at the factors to be considered prior to writing the report. This includes the "who," "why," and "when." Next we will discuss what is meant by providing information needed by the report recipient. This is primarily the information needs of management and answers the "what" question. Lastly, a report organization will be presented which answers the question "how."

PLANNING FOR WRITING A REPORT

There are many different ways to write a good report. The following approach may prove valuable:

1. Decide for whom the report will be written and when it is needed.

2. Write out the objectives you want to accomplish by writing the report.

3. Write out the recommendations you want to make as a result of the review.

4. Outline the various parts of the report and jot down brief notes of what you want to contain in those segments. (A proposed organization follows in a later part of this chapter.)

5. Cross-reference the findings and recommendations in the outline to the QA workpapers. This will provide you with the assurance that you can support each finding and recommendation. It will also show what has not been included so those items can be considered for the outline.

6. Write out a first draft of the report as quickly as possible, using the outline. If it is an oral report, rehearse the talk.

7. Read the report to see if it achieves the objectives you set out in step 2. Make any changes necessary to be sure you achieve those objectives.

8. Ask another member of the QA group, or someone else you respect, to read the report and tell you where the intent or wording is not clear.

9. Make the necessary improvements and have the report typed and presented to management. If it is to be an oral report, steps 6 through 8 will be rehearsal steps prior to presenting the report orally to management.

Step 1. For Whom and When Needed. It should be clear in the mind of the person writing the report for whom the report is being prepared. The distribution may be widespread, or to people with diverse backgrounds, but the report must be written for one person. Know the style with which that person is familiar, the concerns of the person, and then compose the report specifically for that person. Forget about all the others who will see the report.

Also, know the date when the report is needed. DON'T BE LATE. A less polished report on time is valuable; a polished report received late may be worthless.

Step 2. Objectives. For the report to be effective, the objectives must be clear in the mind of the person preparing the report. The following criteria should prove helpful:

• The report objectives should be consistent with the concerns of the person receiving the report. For example, objectives aimed at improving the computer center should not be in a report going to an application system project leader.

• The objectives covered in the report should be consistent with those of the review.

• The objectives of the report should be positive. For example, to improve a situation, increase performance, increase efficiency, etc.

Step 3. Recommendations. Recommendations included in QA reports should be presented from a management perspective. Reports which are written for the data processing manager should be written with the data processing manager's concerns addressed. A common mistake of QA groups is to write highly technical reports which the data processing manager can neither understand nor take much interest in. The data processing manager is a manager and, as such, has a manager's concern. The more the quality assurance function and its reports address those concerns, the more successful the function will be.

The data processing manager is responsible for planning, organizing, directing, and controlling the data processing function in the organization. It is on those concerns that the QA group should build its reports. Recommendations should help alleviate those concerns. Let's address these four concerns one at a time.

Planning is a management function. QA wants to determine that plans have been developed according to the organization's procedures, and not second-guess whether the plans are correct or not. Planning includes the development of detailed schedules for implementing the phase under review, and the project in total. The plans should include providing sufficient resources to perform the job. QA can make an assessment as to whether enough, too few, or too many resources have been allocated to the application system. Management is just as concerned that too many resources have been allocated as too few. Quality assessment can make some of these assessments by comparing plans, schedules, and budgets against actual usage. For example, falling behind on the schedule is indicative of either too few resources or resources of too low caliber for individuals to perform the job within the time available. Providing recommendations that address these types of management concerns can be a very valuable input to the DP manager.

Organizing the application system project team will usually be the task of the project manager, although the DP manager is responsible. The assessment as to the effectiveness of this organization by quality assurance again is compliance to the desires of data processing management. For example, if the project should be organized to include hardware and software consultants from a central group, QA should determine that that has happened. It can also make an assessment as to whether individuals are competent to perform the assignments which they have been given. While this is an argumentative part of the function, there can be no argument that it is valuable input to data processing management. Again, management has the responsibility for the successful completion of the project, and early warning of potential problems is highly appreciated by members of data processing management.

Directing the implementation of an application system implies compliance to the plans, policies, and procedures of the total organization. This must be the number one priority of quality assurance. Obviously, management is not looking for minor violations where the best interests of the company are served through a deviation from normal policies and procedures. What management is concerned about is serious violations which are not in the best interest of the organization. Recommendations should be addressed to problem areas and not to specific minor violations.

Management normally establishes *control mechanisms* to determine that the implementation process is functioning correctly. These include progress reports, time and budget reporting, and the use of accounting systems to record utilization of resources. For example, job accounting resource systems collect data on use of computer hardware and software facilities. QA wants to determine that these control mechanisms are being used. Management is also concerned that there is a reasonable control over the use of resources, so any input QA can provide management on more efficient use of resources is appreciated. This includes suggesting better ways to perform work, means of eliminating unnecessary hardware, software, or systems, as well as warning about inefficient systems design on the part of the user. Savings in the user department can be a valuable recommendation from QA reviewers.

Recommendations should encompass management concerns. Some suggestions:

- The recommendations in the report should be positively stated.
- Substantiating data to support the conclusions and recommendations should be available.
- Significant facts or events that occurred after the QA review should be contained in the report if they affect recommendations and conclusions. However, it should be clearly stated that they occurred after the report and thus were not subject to the same scrutiny as conditions that existed before and during the review.
- The desired action you want to be taken should be clearly stated.

Step 4. Report Outline. Reports from QA should be organized to make it easy for the reader to obtain the important points quickly. The size and content will fluctuate depending on the importance of the system, the extent of the review, and the frequency of reviews. But consistency of format permits management to get the essential information out of the report quickly. Quality assurance and data processing management should work together to improve upon the organization and content of quality assurance reports.

Effective QA reports can be organized as follows:

1. *Management Summary.* A one- or two-page synopsis, including summarized background information, findings, and recommendations.

2. *Background Information.* Enough data to orient the reader to the issues being discussed in the report. This includes the application under review, the phase being reviewed, the time of the review, the scope and objectives of the review, as well as other pertinent data relating to the application system.

3. *Findings.* The factual results of the review. This should include significant information only. It is specifically within the findings section that QA should present information from the perspective of the reader.

4. *Recommendations.* The specific recommendations that the QA group is recommending based on its findings. If the project team has already agreed to implement any of the recommendations, that should be noted so that the recipient of the report knows what management action is required.
5. *Effect of the Recommendation on Resources.* The anticipated effect on people, on hardware, on software, and dollar implications if the recommendations are implemented, should be clearly spelled out.
6. *Appendixes.* Include those items which are not essential to the report, but which are supportive of findings and/or recommendations, and could prove valuable to the recipient.

This organization structure is appropriate for reports of any size. The significance of the findings and recommendations will determine the size of the report. The management summary should never exceed two pages, as this provides data processing management with a quick overview of the situation, and also provides something to forward to upper management.

Listed below are some guidelines to be followed in preparing each of these sections:

1. *Management Summary*
    Is the objective of the quality assurance review clearly stated?
    Is the background information concisely summarized?
    Are the findings concisely summarized?
    Are the recommendations concisely summarized?
    Are the resource implications of the recommendations concisely summarized?

2. *Background Information*
    Is the application and review point clearly stated?
    Has the time when the review occurred as well as who made the review been stated?
    Are the objectives of the review stated?
    When personal opinions are included in the report, are they clearly identified as opinions?
    If critical comments are made about the project team, have they been put into the proper perspective recognizing that unusual circumstances may have occurred which caused the problems?
    Have the views of the project team been considered and presented in the report?

Is the material in the report factual and presented fairly?
Is sufficient information contained to explain wherever possible the causes of problems?
Has the factual material used as background information been substantiated by reviewing the contents of the review team working papers?

3. *Findings*

Have the findings been presented fairly and objectively?
Are the findings presented from a positive and not from a negative viewpoint?
Are the findings supportive of the system project personnel wherever possible? That is, if the project team is doing an outstanding job, it should be so stated.
Is enough detailed information contained in the findings to support the findings?
Are major exceptions to the organization's standards, policies, plans, and procedures noted in the findings?

4. *Recommendations*

Are recommendations clearly stated so there is no question in people's minds as to what is wanted?
Do the recommendations state who should execute the recommendations?
Are unresolved issues and questions needing further study stated as recommendations for further study, and not avoided in the report?
Are recommendations supported by the findings?

5. *Resource Implications*

Is the effect of the recommendations on people stated?
Is the effect of the recommendations on hardware and software stated?
Is the effect of the recommendations on schedules stated?
Is the effect of the recommendations on cost stated?
Is the effect of the recommendations on controls stated?
Is the effect of the recommendations on other systems stated?
Is the effect of the recommendations on the organization's plans, standards, policies, and procedures stated?

6. *Appendixes*

Do the appendixes include the information that will be helpful to the recipient of the report, but not necessary to read as support for the recommendations?

Step 5. Cross-Reference Findings to Workpapers. Working papers should be organized to reference information from detailed to general and vice versa. Problems uncovered should be summarized on lead sheets in the working papers. These lead sheets are then used by QA personnel in developing recommendations.

A copy of the report outline should be cross-referenced to the summarized lead sheets in the working papers. Each finding and recommendation should be cross-referenced. There may be several references to any one finding or recommendation.

The lead sheet should be cross-referenced to the outline. This will point out any finding uncovered or recommendation made that did not get into the report. Experience has shown this to be a very valuable exercise.

This procedure will enable QA personnel to answer questions about the report or to review it quickly. It also provides assurance that any finding or recommendation given in the report is supportable by work done during the review.

Step 6. Write a Report Draft. The quickest way to write a report is to do a rough first draft, review and modify it yourself, have it reviewed by an outside party, and then rewrite the report incorporating the review comments. The first step of this process is to complete, as quickly as possible, the first draft of the report. The draft report should be written according to the outline.

Step 7. Report Writer's Review of Report. The writer of the report should ask himself or herself:

1. Have the objectives been achieved with this report?
2. Is the report readable (i.e., do the ideas flow easily, are sentences short and words small)?
3. Is it written in a style appropriate, to the recipient of the report and does it address the concerns?
4. Is the report a professional report?
5. If I received this report, would I be moved to take action on the recommendation?

Step 8. Outside Review of Report. Once the writer is satisfied with the report, one or more outside opinions should be obtained. The outside reviewer can be the QA manager in a larger QA group. Other potential reviewers are respected friends or DP colleagues. The comments and recommendations received should be evaluated and the worthwhile ideas incorporated in the report.

If oral presentations are used, the presentation should be critiqued by giving the presentation to a small group. Because most oral presentations are not written out, they cannot be adequately reviewed by the person preparing the presentation. Therefore, the dress rehearsal is important.

Step 9. Prepare Final Report. The final report should incorporate the thinking gained from steps 1–9. The report should be the best effort possible with available resources.

The report in its physical format should be one in which the preparer can take pride. The following checklist provides suggestions to avoid some of the traps which have caused problems to other QA groups:

- The report should be neat and clean, identified, and dated.
- The preparer's name should be on the report.
- The report should not contain any grammatical or spelling errors.
- The final report should be checked before being presented to management to assure all pages are present, etc.

The reviewer's job is not complete when the report has been prepared. The contents of the report must be reviewed with the project team and then presented to management. In addition, the QA group should follow up to determine that the recommendations have been given proper consideration, and implemented wherever practical.

POSTREVIEW CONFERENCE

The best method for discussing review findings and recommendations with the project team is at an exit conference. At that time, the review personnel can discuss their findings and support them with information gathered during the review. In most cases, the recommendations would have been discussed informally during the review.

The exit conference provides the project team the opportunity to rebut, comment on, or concur with the findings and recommendations. The conference should be an open and free discussion held in an atmosphere of developing the best possible application system. Many times, when presented with findings and recommendations, the project team will have very valid arguments for not adopting certain recommendations. When arguments are valid, the quality assurance team may wish to withdraw those findings or recommendations from the final report.

The main purpose of the quality assurance report is to resolve any application system problems, and to correct any procedural misunderstandings on the part of the application system project team. This is most readily done with the cooperation of the project team. Therefore, it becomes important for the QA reviewers to review the report with the project team. Ideally, all recommendations will be resolved at the exit conference. This resolution can be that the project team has accepted the recommendation, the QA group has withdrawn the recommendation, or some compromise achieved. In these situations, the report going to management is informative rather than action oriented. Such a situation is desirable from both the viewpoint of quality assurance and the project team. QA has demonstrated that its function has provided a valuable service, and the project team has gained from that advice in a very positive professional manner by either accepting or modifying and then accepting worthwhile recommendations.

The exit conference should be conducted as soon after the review is complete as possible. Many QA groups conduct the conference on the last day of their review. This means that the report has been completed. This also has proven to be a good quality assurance practice.

Listed below are some guidelines for consideration in holding an exit conference:

1. The exit conference should be held at a time when there is sufficient time to discuss in detail the findings and recommendations.

2. The QA team leader should conduct the exit conference.

3. The quality assurance team leader should explain the objectives of the conference.

4. The project team should be given an opportunity to read the quality assurance report before the conference and to comment on it during the meeting.

5. The project team should be asked specifically if it agrees with all the findings (facts) presented in the report.

6. When a disagreement occurs regarding facts, a follow-up investigation should be made to determine if the facts presented were true and presented fairly.

7.   Differences of opinion between the project team and the quality assurance review group should be noted, and included in the final report where practical.

8.   The QA group should ask the project team if any material events have occurred or conditions changed between the end of the review and the exit conference.

9.   The QA team leader should sum up the conclusions of the conference at the end of the conference.

The review can result in many findings and recommendations. It may not be appropriate to discuss all of these with any one of the parties interested in the findings. Depending on the type of finding and/or recommendation, it may be advisable to direct that finding or recommendation to only one of the recipients of the review results. The normal recipients of information from a review are data processing management and the project team. In addition, some QA groups give copies of the report to other groups such as users, internal auditors and external auditors.

WHO GETS QUALITY ASSURANCE RESULTS?

QA personnel should direct their comments and findings to the individual in the best position to take action on those recommendations. Occasionally, it is not in the best interest of the QA group, and the organization, to present certain findings or recommendations to specific people. Comments may be critical of an individual's performance, for example. Many times these opinions are judgmental and may or may not be supported by management. In cases where the judgments are not supported, it is better for all parties concerned that the statements be kept as confidential as possible.

In those instances when a fraud or embezzlement against the organization is suspected, it should be investigated by groups knowledgeable in frauds. It is not in the best interest of the organization for quality assurance people to confront data processing personnel with these facts because they are not familiar with dealing with frauds and may adversely affect the case against the person who committed the fraud. Individuals need to have an understanding of the legal implications of confronting someone about any sort of criminal activity before they do it.

Listed below are some of the groups interested in QA reports and the types of information that should be addressed to that group:

1. *Application System Project Team*
   All findings and recommendations dealing with methods
   All findings and recommendations dealing with goals
   All findings and recommendations dealing with performance

2. *EDP Department Management*
   Significant findings and recommendations dealing with methods
   Significant findings and recommendations dealing with goals
   Significant findings and recommendations dealing with performance
   Project team member performance
   Project team management performance
   Suspected fraud or embezzlement
   Misuse of resources
   Significant under or overrun of budget
   Significant schedule deviations
   Poor working relationship with the user or other outside parties

3. *Departments Outside EDP Department*
   Full reports to internal audit when requested
   Full or extracted reports to users with EDP department agreement for areas of interest to the users
   Full or extracted reports to executive management with EDP department agreement for areas of interest to executive management.

QA personnel should have the concurrence of EDP department management before sending reports to outside groups. Sending reports to groups outside of the EDP department may reduce the effectiveness of the QA group when reviewing application projects. While quality assurance wants to maintain organizational independence of the group they are reviewing, its effectiveness is built on the belief that quality assurance is an internal EDP department function with the goal of supporting the project team. Sending negative comments about a project to the user of that application can cause hard feelings.

SUMMARY

Professional reports can greatly enhance the effectiveness of quality assurance. Management tends to judge staff groups on the quality of their reports. Quality assurance groups must spend the time and effort necessary to produce effective reports.

Effective reports to management are reports which address management concerns. Management has the responsibility for planning, organizing, directing, and controlling the data processing function. They are vitally interested in findings and recommendations which address these topics. Minor findings and recommendations should be resolved with project personnel. Findings and recommendations passed to management are those which are of interest or require the attention of management. Quality assurance personnel should discuss freely with management the organization, content, frequency, and scope of quality assurance reports.

Prior to issuing reports, quality assurance should meet with the project team to review the findings and recommendations of the report. This conference should verify the authenticity of the facts and findings stated in the report. There should be an open and frank discussion of the recommendations in an effort to reach agreement on the recommendations. It is important for the QA group to know the reactions of the project team to its findings and recommendations before presenting them to data processing management.

Chapter 13
QUALITY REQUIREMENTS FOR DEFENSE CONTRACTORS *

Purpose of Software Quality Assurance Standard. This chapter defines those requirements for software quality evaluation that are independent of a given phase of the software development cycle. Defense contractors must comply with these requirements as tailored by their contract.

This standard was developed by the Department of Defense as DOD-STD-2168 and contains requirements for evaluating the quality of software and associated documentation and activities for Mission-Critical Computer Systems, and for performing the planning and follow-up activities necessary to ensure that necessary changes are made.

Standard DOD-STD-2168 is intended to be used in conjunction with DOD-STD-2167. These standards, together with other DOD and military specifications and standards governing configuration management, specification practices, project reviews and audits, and subcontractor control provide a means for achieving, determining, and maintaining quality in software and associated documentation. This standard may be applied to software independent verification and validation (V&V) efforts if appropriately tailored.

1. **Establishment and Implementation of a Software Quality Evaluation Process.** The contractor shall establish and implement a process to evaluate the quality of software and associated documentation and activities in accordance with the requirements of this standard. Included shall be the planning and follow-up tasks specified herein that are associated with the evaluation activities. Software quality evaluation shall be an ongoing activity fully integrated

367

---

* This chapter is taken from U.S. Department of Defense STD-2168.

with each phase of the software development cycle and with the system-level integration and testing, production, acceptance, and installation and checkout that follow software development.

2.   **Independence and Qualifications of Evaluators.** Fulfillment of the requirements of this standard is not intended to be the responsibility of any single contractor organization, function, or person; however, responsibility for ensuring compliance with these requirements shall be specifically assigned and specified in the SDP, SQEP, or SVVP, as applicable. The organizations, functions, or persons performing software quality evaluations shall have sufficient resources, responsibility, authority, and organizational independence from the persons who developed the product or performed the activity being evaluated, to permit objective evaluation and to cause the initiation of corrective action. They shall also have sufficient technical expertise to permit effective technical evaluation.

3.   **Software Quality Evaluation Planning.** The contractor shall perform the following planning activities for software quality evaluation.

3.1   **Plan Development.** If planning for software quality evaluation has not been performed, the contractor shall perform this planning. The following requirements apply:

A.   The planning process shall address all requirements of this standard and shall include determination of:

1.   The organizational structure, personnel, and resources to be used for software quality evaluation.

2.   The organizational responsibilities and authorities for execution of the planned activities.

3.   The evaluation criteria to be used to perform each of the quality evaluations specified in this standard.

4.   The standards, procedures, methods, tools, and facilities to be used to meet the requirements of this standard, and the way in which they will be used to meet these requirements.

5.   Software quality evaluation activities and products, including: (a) evaluation of the software requirements, (b) evaluation of the contractor's development methodologies

as planned and as implemented, (c) evaluation of the products of software development, and (d) providing feedback and performing the follow-up actions necessary to ensure that necessary changes are made.

B.   The planning shall be documented in a quality control plan by the contract. The planning shall be consistent with other plans (e.g., configuration management plans, test plans) required by the contract and shall not unnecessarily duplicate their provisions. The planning shall be subject to contracting agency disapproval.

3.2   Plan Update. The standards, procedures, methods, tools, and facilities used for software quality evaluation shall be periodically assessed by the contractor. If the standards, procedures, methods, tools, or facilities are found to be deficient by the government or by the contractor, the contractor shall notify the contracting agency of proposed changes to the SQEP, SDP, or SVVP, as appropriate, and shall make the necessary revisions. These revisions shall be subject to contracting agency disapproval.

4.   Evaluation of Tools and Facilities. The contractor shall evaluate the tools and facilities selected for software development and support. Evaluation criteria shall be in compliance with the requirements of the contract and adequacy for the development and support of software compliant with the requirements of the contract.

5.   Evaluation of Software Configuration Management. The contractor shall evaluate the software configuration management methods applied to software, media, and documentation. The evaluation shall verify compliance with configuration management standards and procedures approved for use by the contracting agency. The evaluation shall address:

A.   *The adequacy of configuration identification, including:* (1) methods of identifying media and documentation, (2) methods of identifying each Unit and CSC of the CSCI, (3) methods of indicating the relationship between CSCI elements and the documentation for the CSCI, (4) methods of identifying the change status of software, media, and documentation.

B.   *The adequacy of configuration control, including:* (1) methods of approval for change requests and problem reports, (2) appropriateness of the management levels of approval, (3) methods for providing traceability to change requests and problem reports, (4) methods of correlating the change control process with software development library controls, and (5) effectiveness in preventing unauthorized changes.

C.   *The adequacy of configuration status accounting and reporting,* including: (1) the timeliness and appropriateness of detail of status accounting reports, (2) the visibility provided by the reports into the change control, software development library, and specification revision processes, and (3) the appropriateness of the distribution of the status accounting reports for providing management attention to the change control, software development library, and specification revision processes.

D.   *Evaluation of configuration audits.* These evaluations shall be performed in accordance with the requirements.

6.   **Evaluation of Software Development Library.** The contractor shall evaluate the software development library for compliance with standards and procedures approved for use by the contracting agency. The contractor shall verify, at a minimum, that:

a.   The library receives and maintains copies of all software, tools, and documentation relevant to the software development project.

b.   Library identification and control procedures are in compliance with standards and procedures approved for use by the contracting agency.

c.   The most recent authorized version of materials under configuration control are clearly identified and are the ones routinely available from the library.

d.   Previous versions of materials under configuration control are clearly identified and controlled to provide an audit trail that permits reconstruction of all changes made to the item.

e.   The materials contained in the library are promptly and correctly updated when a change to any of these materials is authorized.

f.   Read, write, and execute access to files are controlled in accordance with prescribed access authorizations so that no unauthorized use or modifications are made.

g.   The correct version of software is submitted for testing.

7.   Evaluation of Documentation and Media Distribution. The contractor shall evaluate controls exercised on the distribution of documentation and media for compliance with standards and procedures approved for use by the contracting agency. The contractor shall verify, at a minimum, that:

a.   Accurate distribution lists are maintained.

b.   Authorized changes are distributed to each person or organization on the distribution list with clear instructions for updating the affected documentation or media.

c.   Changes are clearly and properly marked with change bars, version numbers, and other indicators as appropriate.

d.   Controlled copies from the software development library are the only copies of documentation and media that are distributed.

8.   Evaluation of Storage and Handling. The contractor shall evaluate storage and handling of software and firmware media and documentation. The evaluation shall verify compliance with standards and procedures approved for use by the contracting agency. The contractor shall verify, at a minimum, that:

a.   Software media, firmware media, and paper products are not exposed to loss, abuse, or adverse environmental conditions such as high temperature, high humidity, magnetic forces, and dust.

b.   Classified items are appropriately marked and protected, and all applicable security requirements are met.

c.   A back-up copy of the current configuration is available in case of loss or destruction of the media.

d.   An inventory of all stored items exists to facilitate the location of items in storage areas.

e.   Retention requirements are implemented in accordance with the contract.

9.   Evaluation of Nondeliverables. The contractor shall evaluate nondeliverable software used on the software development project. The evaluation shall verify that nondeliverable items meet all applicable contractual requirements prior to their use on the software development project, and that they are maintained under configuration management throughout the time that they are in use.

10. **Evaluation of Risk Management.** The contractor shall evaluate the procedures employed and the results achieved by risk management throughout the software development cycle. This evaluation shall verify that risk factors are identified and assessed, resources are assigned to reducing risk factors, alternatives for reducing risk are identified and analyzed, and sound alternatives are selected, implemented, and evaluated.

11. **Quality of Subcontractor Products.** The contractor shall be responsible for ensuring that all software and associated documentation from subcontractors conform to contract requirements. Standards will provide details on subcontractor quality evaluation. The contractor shall:

a. Verify that a comprehensive preaward survey of prospective subcontractors is performed.

b. Verify that a complete set of requirements has been established for the software to be developed by the subcontractor, and that the requirements are maintained under configuration control.

c. Verify that the subcontractor has established and implemented a complete methodology for software development that meets all relevant requirements of the contract.

d. Monitor the subcontractor's software development activities to verify that the approved methodology is followed. Included shall be an evaluation of subcontractor methods and procedures for evaluating the quality of their software and associated documentation and activities, unless the contractor elects to perform those evaluations for the subcontractor.

e. Evaluate subcontractor products for compliance with all applicable requirements prior to accepting them.

12. **Commercially Available, Reusable, and Government Furnished Software.** The contractor shall evaluate the planning performed for the use of commercially available,

reusable, and government furnished software. The evaluation shall verify that suitability, reliability, availability, and other relevant factors have been considered in determining: (1) whether to use such software, and (2) which of several alternative software products should be used. Upon acquisition of the commercially available, reusable, or government furnished software, the contractor shall: (1) evaluate the software to determine whether it performs as documented, prior to incorporating it into the software being developed, and (2) evaluate the associated documentation to whether it meets contractual requirements.

13. **Quality Evaluation Records.** The contractor shall prepare and maintain records of each software quality evaluation performed. These records shall identify the date of the evaluation, evaluation participants, items or activities reviewed, objectives of the evaluation, all detected-problems, recommendations resulting from the evaluation, resulting software problem/change requests, and the status of changes in process. The format of these records shall be as described in the SQEP, SDP, or SVVP, as applicable. These records shall be available for contracting agency review.

14. **Corrective Action Process.** The contractor shall implement a corrective action process for all software and documentation that has been placed under contractor or government configuration control and for all software-related activities. The system shall be closed-loop, ensuring that all detected problems are promptly reported for the life of the corrected action. Specific requirements are:

a. Each problem shall be analyzed to determine extent, causes, impacts, and frequency of occurrence.

b. Each problem shall be classified by category (such as requirements, design, code, noncompliant activities, and other) and by priority (such as high, medium, and low).

c. Analysis shall be performed to identify trends in the problems reported.

d. Recommended corrective action or preventive measures for each problem, class of problems, or adverse trend shall be determined, along with a target completion date.

e. The results of steps a–e shall be documented and reported to appropriate management levels.

f.   Implementation of corrective action shall be authorized.

g.   The corrective actions that are taken shall be documented.

h.   Corrective actions shall be evaluated to verify that problems have been resolved, adverse trends have been reversed, changes have been correctly reflected in the appropriate documents, and that no additional problems have been introduced in the process.

i.   The status of all problems and adverse trends shall be tracked and reported to appropriate management levels, with overdue resolutions highlighted.

j.   The contractor shall notify the contracting agency of critical problems.

15. Quality Evaluation Reports. The contractor shall prepare and maintain reports that: (1) summarize the software quality evaluation records and serve as input to the corrective action process, (2) document the analysis performed on each problem, (3) document the corrective actions taken, and (4) document the status of all problems and trends detected. The format of these reports shall be as described in the SQEP, SDP, or SVVP as applicable (see 6.1). These reports shall be available for contracting agency review.

16. Evaluation of the Corrective Action Process. The contractor shall periodically evaluate the operation of the corrective action process. This evaluation shall determine whether each of the requirements of the corrective action process is being met.

17. Assessment of Software Quality Evaluation. The contractor shall monitor the software quality evaluations performed to ensure that they are in compliance with established standards, procedures, and methodologies.

18. Certification. The contractor shall provide evidence to the contracting agency that the software and associated documentation and activities required by the contract meet contractual requirements. Such evidence may be collected incrementally and shall include the following:

a.   Evidence that all deliverable items of software and documentation required by the contract meet the requirements of the contract.

b. Evidence that the source and object code delivered to the contracting agency or released for production correspond to one another, and that both correspond to the version described in the product baseline.

c. Evidence that the version of software delivered to the contracting agency or released for production matches the version on which CSCI testing was performed, or represents an authorized update of that software, as applicable.

d. Evidence that nondeliverable software and its documentation meet applicable requirements of the contract.

e. Evidence that commercially available and reusable software perform as documented and are documented adequately.

f. Evidence that each version of software delivered to the contracting agency or released for production is compatible with the system configuration into which it is to be installed.

g. Evidence that the physical media delivered to the contracting agency or released for production is an authorized copy of the correct version from the software development library.

h. Evidence that production copies of the media match the authorized copy from which they are made and that they are correctly marked.

19. **Interface Between Development Contractor and Software (V&V) Contractor.** The development contractor and software V&V contractor shall interface with one another as required by their respective contracts. This interface shall include the following: (1) delivery of materials to be evaluated by the software V&V contractor, (2) delivery of V&V results on these materials, (3) coordination on the status of discrepancies detected by software V&V, and (4) participation in technical interchange meetings with one another as directed by the contracting agency.

20. **Government Review at Contractor, Subcontractor, or Vendor Facilities.** The contracting agency reserves the right to review all products and activities at contractor, subcontractor, or vendor facilities to determine the conformance of products or activities with contract requirements. The contractor shall provide facilities and access to the contracting agency for these reviews.

21. **Cost of Software Quality Evaluation.** The contractor shall collect, analyze, and document data relative to the cost of detecting and correcting errors in all software and documentation that have been placed under contractor or government configuration control. The specific data to be collected, the level at which the data are to be collected, and the analyses to be performed shall be proposed by the contractor in the SQEP, SDP, or SVVP, as applicable, and shall be subject to contracting agency disapproval.

22. **Deliverable Data.** Deliverable data prepared in accordance with the requirements of sections 4 and 5 of this standard and identified on the DD Form 1423, Contract Data Requirements List, shall be prepared in accordance with the instructions in the applicable Data Item Descriptions (DIDs)

23. **Deviations and Waivers.** The contractor and, if applicable, subcontractors, shall be in compliance with this standard, as required by the contract, unless a deviation or waiver has been approved by the contracting agency in accordance with standards.

24. **Purpose.** This section defines those requirements for software quality evaluation that are specific to a particular phase of the software development cycle. The contractor shall comply with these requirements as tailored by the contract.

24.1. Software Requirements Analysis Phase

24.1.1 Activities — Software Requirements Analysis

Activities Evaluation. In addition to the evaluations specified in Section 4, the contractor shall evaluation the requirements analysis process. The contractor shall verify that: (1) all required activities are performed, (2) required approaches, tools, and techniques are used, (3) the process is in compliance with standards and procedures approved for use by the contracting agency, and (4) the process is adequate to develop software and documentation that meet all contractual requirements.

Products Evaluation. The contractor shall perform in-process reviews of the following products of the Software Requirements Analysis phase, using evaluation criteria.

a. The newly prepared or revised software development plan (SDP), Software Standards and Procedures Manual (SSPM), Software Configuration Management Plan (SGMP), and SQEP, as applicable.
b. The evolving software requirements and the Software Requirements Specification (SRS).
c. The evolving interface requirements and the Interface Requirements Specification(s) (IRS).
d. The Operational Concept Document (OCD).

Software V&V testing activities. If a software V&V contract calls for V&V testing to supplement the testing performed by the development contractor, the software V&V contractor shall identify candidate software requirements to be addressed by V&V testing. The candidate test requirements shall be subject to contracting agency disapproval.

24.1.2 Products—Software Requirements Analysis. The contractor shall produce the following software quality evaluation products during Software Requirements Analysis:

a. A newly prepared or updated version of the SQEP, software quality evaluation portions of the SDP, or the SVVP.
b. Records and reports of the software quality evaluation activities performed.
c. (Software V&V contractor only.) Documents identifying candidate software requirements to be addressed by V&V testing. The format of these documents shall be as described in the SVVP.

24.1.3 Software Specification Review. The contractor shall evaluate the preparations for the Software Specification Review (SSR) to verify that: (1) all required preparations have been made for the SSR. At the SSR, the contractor shall present a summary of all software quality evaluation findings from the Software Requirements Analysis phase. These findings shall summarize the contractor's assessment of the status and quality of each of the development products reviewed. Following the SSR the contractors shall conduct periodic evaluations to verify that all action items from the SSR have been performed. Details regarding the SSR are given in military standards.

24.2 Preliminary Design Phase

24.2.1 Activities —Preliminary Design

ITEM TO BE EVALUATED	Adherence to Required Format and Documentation Standards	Compliance with Contractual Requirements	Internal Consistency	Understandability	Technical Adequacy	Appropriate Degree of Completeness	Traceability to Indicated (Document/s)	Consistency with Indicated Document(s)	Feasibility	Appropriate Requirement, Design, Coding Technique used to prepare item	Appropriate Level of Detail	Appropriate Allocation of Sizing, Timing Resources	Adequate Test Coverage of Requirements	Adequacy of Planned Tools, Facilities, Resources, Procedures, Methods	Appropriate Content for Intended Audience	NOTES: CLARIFICATION OR ADDITIONAL CRITERIA
Software Development Plan (SDP)	●	●	●	●	●	●	SOW	SSPM SCMP SQEP	●	●				●	●	
Software Standards and Procedures Manual (SSPM)	●	●	●	●	●	●	SOW	SDP SCMP SQEP	●	●				●	●	
Software Configuration Management Plan (SCMP)	●	●	●	●	●	●	SOW	SDP SSPM SQEP	●	●				●	●	
Software Quality Evaluation Plan (SQEP)	●	●	●	●	●	●	SOW	SDP SSPM SCMP	●	●				●	●	
Evolving Software Requirements and Software Requirements Specification (SRS)	●	●	●	●	●	●	SSS	See Notes	●	●	●	●	●	●	●	Adequacy of quality factors; consistency with IRS(S) and specifications for interfacing elements
Evolving Interface Requirements and Interface Requirements Specification (IRS)	●	●	●	●	●	●	SSS	See Notes	●	●	●	●	●		●	Consistency with IRS(S) and specification for interfacing elements
Operational Concept Document (OCD)	●	●	●	●	●	●	SSS	SSS	●	●				●	●	

Figure 13.1 **EVALUATION CRITERIA FOR PRODUCTS OF SOFTWARE REQUIREMENTS ANALYSIS**

Activities Evaluation. In addition to the evaluations specified in Section 4, the contractor shall evaluate the preliminary design process. The contractor shall verify that: (1) all required activities are performed, (2) required approaches, tools, and techniques are used, (3) the process is in compliance with standards and procedures approved for use by the contracting agency, and (4) the process is adequate to develop software and documentation that meet all contractual requirements.

Products Evaluation. The contractor shall perform in-process reviews of the following products of the Preliminary Design phase, using the evaluation criteria specified in Figure 13.2 and Appendix C of DOD-STD-2168 not included here:

a. The updated SDP, SSPM, SCMP, and SQEP, and applicable
b. The evolving top-level design and the Software Top Level Design Document (STLDD)
c. The Software Test Plan (STP)
d. Preliminary versions of the Computer System Operators' Manual (CSOM), Software User's Manual(s) (SUMs), and Computer System Diagnostic Manual (CSDM)
e. The preliminary Computer Resources Integrated Support Document-(CRISD)

Software V&V Testing Activities. If a software V&V contract calls for V&V testing to supplement the testing performed by the development contractor, the software V&V contractor shall develop test plans for both informal and formal V&V tests.

A. Informal V&V tests shall test individual Units during Coding and Unit Testing and aggregates of Units during CSC Integration and Testing. For V&V Unit testing, the software V&V contractor shall identify: (1) the test requirements applicable to V&V Unit testing, and (2) test responsibilities and schedule information. For V&V CSC integration testing, the software V&V contractor shall identify: (1) the test requirements applicable to V&V CSC integration testing, (2) test responsibilities and schedule information, and (3) different classes of V&V CSC integration tests. Although informal test documentation does not require Government approval, it shall be made available for Government review.

B. Formal V&V tests shall test the fully implemented CSCI. For V&V CSCI testing, the software V&V contractor shall identify: (1) the test requirements applicable to the V&V

CSCI testing, (2) information concerning the V&V CSCI test organization, responsibilities, and schedule, (3) classes of V&V CSCI testing to be performed, (4) plans for data recording, reduction, and analysis, and (5) the purpose of each V&V CSCI test planned.

C. The software V&V contractor shall identify all of the resources (facilities, personnel, hardware, and software) required for informal and formal V&V testing.

24.2.2 Products — Preliminary Design. The contractor shall produce the following software quality evaluation products during Preliminary Design:

a. An update version of the SQEP, software quality evaluation portions of the SDP.

b. Records and reports of the software quality evaluation activities performed.

c. (Software V&V contractor only.) An V&V Software Test Plan for each CSCI to describe the plans for both informal and formal V&V testing of the CSCI.

24.2.3 Preliminary Design Review. The contractor shall evaluate the preparations for the Preliminary Design Review (PDR) to verify that: (1) all required products will be available and ready for government review, and (2) all required preparations have been made for the PDR. At the PDR, the contractor shall present a summary of all software quality evaluation findings from the Preliminary Design phase. These findings shall summarize the contractor's assessment of the status and quality of each of the development products reviewed. Following the PDR the contractor shall conduct periodic evaluations to verify that all action items from the PDR have been performed. Details regarding the PDR are given in military standards.

24.3 Detailed Design Phase

24.3.1 Activities — Detailed Design

Activities Evaluation. In addition to the evaluations of specified in Section 4, the contractor shall evaluate the detailed design process. The contractor shall verify that: (1) all required activities are performed, (2) required approaches, tools, and techniques are used, (3) the process is in compliance with standards and procedures approved for use by the contracting agency, and (4) the process is adequate to develop software and documentation that meet all contractual requirements.

Products Evaluation. The contractor shall perform in-process reviews of the following products of the Detailed Design phase, using the evaluation criteria.

a.   The update SDP, SSPM, SCMP, and SQEP, as applicable.

b.   The evolving detailed design and the Software Detailed Design Document (SDDD), Interface Design Document (IDD), and Data Base Design Document (DBDD), as applicable.

c.   A representative subset of the software development files (SDFs), including the Unit test cases.

d.   The CSC integration test cases.

e.   The Software Test Description (STD) for each CSCI.

f.   The Software Programmer's Manual (SPM) and the Firmware Support Manual (FSM).

g.   The update CSOM, SUM(9), and CSDM.

h.   The completed CRISD.

Software V&V Testing Activities. If a software V&V contract calls for V&V testing to supplement the testing performed by the development contractor, the software V&V contractor shall:

1.   Formulate test cases for each V&V Unit test to be conducted. Each test case shall be defined in terms of inputs, expected results, and evaluation criteria.

2.   Formulate test cases for each V&V CSC integration test to be conducted. Each test case shall be defined in terms of inputs, expected results, and evaluation criteria.

3.   Formulate test cases for each CSCI test identified in the V&V Software Test Plan. The test case descriptions shall include (1) initialization requirements, (2) input data, (3) expected intermediate test results, (4) expected output data, (5) criteria for evaluating results, and (6) assumptions and constraints.

24.3.2 Products — Detailed Design. The contractor shall produce the following software quality evaluation products during Detail Design.

a.   An updated version of the SQEP, software quality evaluation portions of the SDP, or the SVVP, as applicable

b.   Records and reports of the software quality evaluation activities performed.

ITEM TO BE EVALUATED	Adherence to Required Format and Documentation Standards	Compliance with Contractual Requirements	Internal Consistency	Understandability	Technical Adequacy	Appropriate Degree of Completeness	Traceability to Indicated Document(s)	Consistency with Indicated Document(s)	Feasibility	Appropriate Requirement, Design, Coding Technique, used to prepare item	Appropriate Level of Detail	Appropriate Allocation of Sizing, Timing Resources	Adequate Test Coverage of Requirements	Adequacy of Planned Tools, Facilities, Procedures, Methods, Resources	Appropriate Content For Intended Audience	NOTES: CLARIFICATION OR ADDITIONAL CRITERIA
Updated EDP, SSPM, SCMP, SQEP	•	•	•	•	•	•	SOW	Each Other	•	•				•	•	All plans (updated and non updated) reflect current approaches and plans
Evolving Top Level Design and Software Top Level Design Document (STLDD)	•	•	•	•	•	•	SRS IRS		•	•	•	•				
Software Test Plan (STP)	•	•	•	•	•	•	SRS IRS	SDP	•	•			•	•	•	
Preliminary Computer System Operator's Manual (CSOM)	•	•	•	•	•	•	SRS IRS	STLDD SUM CSOM		•				•	•	
Preliminary Software User's Manual (SLUM)	•	•	•	•	•	•	SSS	STLDD CSDM CSOM		•				•	•	
Preliminary Computer System Diagnostics Manual (CSLUM)	•	•	•	•	•	•	SRS IRS	STLDD CSOM SUM		•				•	•	
Preliminary Computer Resources Integrated Support Document (CRISD)	•	•	•	•	•	•	SSS	See Notes	•	•				•	•	Consistency with government support concept

Figure 13.2 **EVALUATION CRITERIA FOR PRODUCTS OF PRELIMINARY DESIGN**

ITEM TO BE EVALUATED	Adherence to Required Format and Documentation Standards	Compliance with Contractual Requirements	Internal Consistency	Understandability	Technical Adequacy	Appropriate Degree of Completeness	Traceability to Indicated Document(s)	Consistency with Indicated Document(s)	Feasibility	Appropriate Design, Coding Technique, Requirement, used to prepare item	Appropriate Level of Detail	Appropriate Allocation of Sizing, Timing Resources	Adequate Test Coverage of Requirements	Adequacy of Planned Tools, Facilities, Procedures, Methods, Resources	Appropriate Content For Intended Audience	NOTES: CLARIFICATION OR ADDITIONAL CRITERIA
Updated SDP, SSPM, SCMP, SQEP	●	●	●	●	●	●	SOW	Each other	●	●				●	●	All plans (updated and non updated) reflect current approaches and plans
Evolving Detailed Design and Software Detailed Design Document (SDDD)	●	●	●	●	●	●	SRS IRS STLDD	IDD DBDD	●	●	●					Consistency between data definition and data use
Evolving Interface Design and Interface Design Document (IDD)	●	●	●	●	●	●	SRS IRS STLDD	SDDD DBDD	●	●	●					
Evolving Data Base Design and Data Base Design Document (DBDD)	●	●	●	●	●	●	SRS IRS STLDD	SDDD IDD	●	●	●				●	Consistency between data definition and data use accuracy and required precision of constants. Adequacy of backup procedures and mechanisms
Software Development Files (SDFS)	●	●	●	●	●	●	SRS IRS STP	SDDD IDD DBDD		●	●	●	●	●	●	Adequacy of status and schedule information, Adequacy of unit test cases— see separate entry
Unit Test Cases	●	●	●	●	●	●	STP	SDDD IDD DBDD		●	●	●	●	●	●	Adequate detail in specifying test inputs, expected results, evaluation criteria

Figure 13.3   EVALUATION CRITERIA FOR PRODUCTS OF DETAILED DESIGN

Evaluation Criteria	CSC Integration Test Cases	Software Test Description (STD)	Software Programmer's Manual (SPM)	Firmware Support Manual (FSM)	Updated CSOM, SUM, CSDM	Completed CRISD
NOTES: CLARIFICATION OR ADDITIONAL CRITERIA	Adequate detail in specifying test inputs, expected results, evaluation criteria	Adequate detail in specifying CSCI test inputs expected results, evaluation criteria			Consistency with updated SDDD, IDD, DBDD; consistency with each other	Consistency with government support concept
Appropriate Content For Intended Audience	•	•	•	•	•	•
Adequacy of Planned Tools, Facilities, Procedures, Methods, Resources	•	•	•	•	•	•
Adequate Test Coverage of Requirements	•	•				
Appropriate Allocation of Sizing, Timing Resources						
Appropriate Level of Detail	•	•	•	•	•	•
Appropriate Requirement, Design, Coding Technique used to prepare item						
Feasibility	•	•	•	•		•
Consistency with Indicated Document(s)	SDDD IDD DBDD	SDDD IDD DBDD	SDDD IDD DBDD	SDDD IDD DBDD	See Notes	See Notes
Traceability to Indicated Document(s)	SRS IRS STP	STP SRS IRS			SRS IRS	
Appropriate Degree of Completeness	•	•	•	•	•	•
Technical Adequacy	•	•	•	•	•	•
Understandability	•	•	•	•	•	•
Internal Consistency	•	•	•	•	•	•
Compliance with Contractual Requirements	•	•	•	•	•	•
Adherence to Required Format and Documentation Standards	•	•	•	•	•	•

Figure 13.3 **EVALUATION CRITERIA FOR PRODUCTS OF DETAILED DESIGN (Cont'd)**

c. (Software V&V contractor only) Documents that identify each V&V Unit test and describe the corresponding test cases. The format of these documents shall be as described in the SVVP.

d. (Software V&V contractor only) Documents that identify each V&V CSC integration test and describe the corresponding test cases.

e. (Software V&V contractor only) An V&V Software Test Description for each CSCI to undergo V&V testing, to define test cases for each V&V CSCI test described in the V&V Software Test Plan.

24.3.3 Critical Design Review. The contractor shall evaluate the preparations for the Critical Design Review (CDR) to verify that: (1) all required products will be available and ready for Government review, and (2) all required preparations have been made for the CDR. At the CDR, the contractor shall present a summary of all software quality evaluation findings from the Detailed Design phase. These findings shall summarize the contractor's assessment of the status and quality of each of the development products reviewed. Following the CDR the contractor shall conduct periodic evaluations to verify that all actions items from the CDR have been performed.

24.4 Coding and Unit Testing Phase

24.4.1 Activities — Coding and Unit Testing

Activities Evaluation. In addition to the evaluations, the contractor shall evaluate the coding and unit testing process. The contractor shall verify that: (1) all required activities are performed, (2) required approaches, tools, and techniques are used, (3) the process is in compliance with standards and procedures approved for use by the contracting agency, and (4) the process is adequate to develop software and documentation that meet all contractual requirements.

Products Evaluation. The contractor shall perform in-process reviews of the following products of the Coding and Unit Testing phase, using the evaluation criteria specified.

a. The updated SDP, SSPM, SCMP, and SQEP, as applicable.

b. The evolving and completed source code for each software Unit.

c. The object code for each software Unit.

d.   A representative subset of the updated software development files including Unit test procedures and Unit test results.

e.   The updated STLDD, SDDD, IDDD, and DBDD, as applicable.

f.   The informal CSC integration test procedures.

g.   The preliminary CSCI Software Test Procedure (STPR)

h.   The updated CSOM, SUM(s), and CSDM.

Software V&V Testing Activities. If a software V&V contract calls for V&V testing to supplement the testing performed by the development contractor, the software V&V contractor shall:

a.   Prepare test procedures for conducting each V&V Unit test identified in the previous phases.

b.   Prepare test procedures for conducting each V&V CSC integration test identified in the previous phases.

c.   Prepare a preliminary version of the formal test procedures for conducting each V&V CSCI test identified in the previous phases. The procedures shall include: (1) test schedule, (2) pretest procedures, including equipment preparation and software preparation, (3) each step of the procedure, (4) applicable data reduction and data analysis procedures, and (5) assumptions made and constraints imposed on the V&V CSCI test procedures.

d.   Test Units as called for in the V&V Unit test cases and test procedures. V&V test results shall be documented in the contractor's own format.

24.4.2 Products — Coding and Unit Testing. The contractor shall produce the following software quality evaluation products during Coding and Unit Testing:

a.   An updated version of the SQEP, software quality evaluation portions of the SDP, or the SVVP, as applicable.

b.   Records and reports of the software quality evaluation activities performed.

c.   (Software V&V contractor only.) Documents describing the V&V Unit test procedures. The format of these documents shall be as described in the SVVP.

d.   (Software V&V contractor only.) Documents describing V&V CSC integration test procedures. The format of these documents shall be as described in the SVVP.

e.   (Software V&V contractor only.) A preliminary version of the V&V Software Test Procedure for each CSCI to undergo V&V testing.

f. (Software V&V contractor only.) Documents describing the V&V Unit test results. The format of these documents shall be as described in the SVVP.

24.5 CSC Integration and Testing Phase

24.5.1 Activities — CSC Integration and Testing

Activities Evaluation. In addition to the evaluations, the contractor shall evaluate the CSC integration and test process. The contractor shall verify that: (1) all required activities are performed, (2) required approaches, tools, and techniques are followed, (3) the process is in compliance with standards and procedures approved for use by the contracting agency, and (4) the process is adequate to develop software and documentation that meet all contractual requirements.

Products Evaluation. The contractor shall perform in-process evaluations of the following products of the CSC Integration and Testing phase, using the evaluation criteria specified.

a. The updated SDP, SSPM, SCMP, and SQEP, as applicable
b. The informal test results of CSC integration testing
c. The updated STLDD, SDDD, IDD, and DBDD, as applicable
d. The updated source code, as applicable
e. The updated object code, as applicable
f. A representative subset of the updated software development files
g. The completed STPR
h. The updated CSOM, SUM(s), and CDSM

Software V&V Testing Activities. If a software V&V contract calls for V&V testing to supplement the testing performed by the development contractor, the V&V contractor shall:

a. Complete the procedures for conducting each V&V CSCI test and for analyzing V&V CSCI test results.
b. Test aggregates of integrated Units in accordance with the V&V CSC integration test cases and test procedures. V&V test results shall be documented in the software V&V contractor's own format.

24.5.2 Products — CSC Integration and Testing. The contractor shall produce the following software quality evaluation products during CSC Integration and Testing:

EVALUATION CRITERIA \ ITEM TO BE EVALUATED	Updated SDP, SSPM, SCMP, SQEP	Evolving and completed source code for each unit	Object code for each unit	Updated SDFS	Unit test procedures
NOTES: Clarification or Additional Criteria	All plans (updated and non updated) reflect current approaches and pland	Compliance with language and coding standards; compliance with maintainability requirements; compliance with unit requirements	Compliance with size and other constraints; correspondence with source version placed under control	Adequacy of status and schedule information; adequacy of unit test procedures – see separate entry; adequacy of unit test result – see separate entry	
Appropriate Content For Intended Audience	●			●	●
Adequacy of Planned Tools, Facilities, Procedures, Methods, Resources	●				●
Adequate Test Coverage of Requirements					●
Appropriate Allocation of Staff, Timing Resources					●
Appropriate Level of Detail		●			
Appropriate Requirement, Design, Coding Technique, used to prepare item	●			●	●
Feasibility		●			
Consistency with Indicated Document(s)	●				●
Traceability to Indicated Document(s)	Each other				STDDD IDD DBDD
Appropriate Degree of Completeness	SOW	SDDD IDD DBDD		SDDD IDD DBDD	STP Unit Test Cases
Technical Adequacy	●	●		●	●
Understandability	●	●		●	●
Internal Consistency	●	●		●	●
Compliance with Contractual Requirements	●	●		●	●
Adherence to Required Format and Documentation Standards	●	●		●	●

Figure 13.4 **EVALUATION CRITERIA FOR PRODUCTS OF CODING AND UNIT TESTING**

Evaluation Criteria \ Item to be Evaluated	Unit Test Results	Updated STLDD, SDDD, IDDD, DBDD	CSC Integration test procedures	Preliminary software test procedure (STPR)	Updated CSOM, SUM, CSDM
NOTES: CLARIFICATION OR ADDITIONAL CRITERIA	Conformance to expected results in unit test cases; completeness of unit testing; adequacy of unit to enter developmental configuration	Consistency with updated code; consistency with each other	Adequate detail in specifying test procedures schedules, constraints	Adequate detail in specifying test procudures, schedules, constraints	Consistency with updatad SDDD, IDD, DBDD; consistency with each other
Appropriate Content for Intended Audience	•	•	•	•	•
Adequacy of Planned Tools, Facilities, Resources, Procedures, Methods			•	•	•
Adequate Test Coverage of Requirements			•	•	•
Appropriate Allocation of Sizing, Timing Resources	•		•	•	
Appropriate Level of Detail	•	•			
Appropriate Requirement, Design, Coding Technique used to prepare item	•	•	•	•	•
Feasibility		•			
Consistency with Indicated Document(s)		•	•	•	
Traceability to Indicated Document(s)		See Notes	SDDD IDD DBDD	SDDD IDD DBDD	See Notes
Appropriate Degree of Completeness	See Notes	SRS IRS	STP CSC Test Cases	STP STD SRS IRS	SRS IRS
Technical Adequacy	•	•	•	•	•
Understandability	•	•	•	•	•
Internal Consistency	•	•	•	•	•
Compliance with Contractual Requirements	•	•	•	•	•
Adherence to Required Format, and Documentation Standards	•	•	•	•	•

Figure 13.4 EVALUATION CRITERIA FOR PRODUCTS OF CODING AND UNIT TESTING (Cont'd)

a.   An updated version of the SQEP, software quality evalua-
     tion portions of the SDP, or the SVVP, as applicable.
b.   Records and reports of the software quality evaluation ac-
     tivities performed.
c.   (Software V&V contractor only)   The completed V&V
     Software Test Procedures for each CSCI.
d.   (Software V&V contractor only)   Documents describing the
     V&V CSC integration test results.

24.5.3 Test Readiness Review. The contractor shall evaluate the
preparations for the Test Readiness Review (TRR) to verify that:
(1) all required products will be available and ready for
Government review, and (2) all required preparations have been
made for the TRR. At the TRR, the contractor shall present summary of all software quality evaluation findings relevant to: (1)
the status and quality of each of the development products reviewed at TRR, and (2) the contractor's readiness to begin CSCI
testing. Following the TRR the contractor shall conduct periodic
evaluations to verify that all actions items from the TRR have
been performed. A separate TRR may be conducted for V&V CSCI
testing.

24.6 CSCI Testing Phase

24.6.1 Activities — CSCI Testing

     Activities Evaluation.   In addition to the evaluations, the
contractor shall evaluate the CSCI testing process. The contractor shall evaluate the CSCI testing process. The contractor shall
verify that: (1) all required activities are performed, (2) required
approaches, tools, and techniques are used, (3) the process is in
compliance with standards and procedures approved for use by
the contracting agency, (4) the process is adequate to develop
software and documentation that meet all contractual requirements. In particular, the contractor shall verify that: (1) CSCI
tests are conducted in accordance with the approved STP, STD,
and STPR, (2) recorded test results are the actual findings of the
tests, (3) test-related media and documentation are maintained to
allow repeatability of tests, and (4) adequate retesting is performed on corrections to problems found during CSCI testing.
     Products Evaluation.   The contractor shall perform in-
process evaluations of the following products of the CSCI Testing
phase, using the evaluation criteria.

a.   The updated SDP, SSPM, SCMP, and SQEP, as applicable.
b.   The CSCI Software Test Reports (STRs).
c.   The updated STLDD, SDDD, IDD, and DBDD, as applicable.
d.   The updated source code, as applicable.
e.   The updated object code, as applicable.
f.   A representative sample of the updated software development files.
g.   The Software Product Specification (SPS).
h.   The Version Description Document (VDD).
i.   The completed CSOM, SUM(s), and CSDM.

Software V&V Testing Activities. If a software V&V contract calls for V&V testing to supplement the testing performed by the development contractor, the V&V contractor shall:

a.   Perform formal V&V CSCI tests in accordance with the V&V Software Test Plan, Test Description, and Test Procedure developed in previous phases.
b.   Document the results of V&V CSCI testing. The report shall include: (1) Summary and detail of test results, (2) detailed test history, (3) evaluation of test results, and recommendations resulting from these results, and (4) description of test procedure deviations.

Products — CSCI Testing. The contractor shall produce the following software quality evaluation products during CSCI Testing:

a.   An updated version of SQEP, software quality evaluation portions of the SDP, or the SVVP, as applicable.
b.   Records and reports of the software quality evaluation activities performed.
c.   (Software V&V contractor only.) V&V Software Test Reports (STRs), which document the results of V&V CSCI tests, test data analysis, and any deviations or discrepancies discovered in the testing.

Configuration Audits. The contractor shall evaluate the preparations for the Functional Configuration Audit (FCA, and the Physical Configuration Audit (PCA). The contractor shall verify that: (1) all required products will be available and ready for government review, and (2) all required preparations have been made for the FCA and PCA. At the FCA and PCA, the contractor shall present a summary of all software quality evaluation findings from the CSCI Testing phase. These findings shall summarize the contractor's assessment of the status and quality of each of the development products audited. Following the FCA and PCA the contractor shall conduct periodic evaluations to verify that all action items from the FCA and PCA have been performed. Details regarding the FCA and PCA are given in military standards.

24.7 Evaluations Following the CSCI Testing Phase

24.7.1 Evaluations Associated with System-Level Testing. If System Integration and Testing, Development Test and Evaluation, and Operational Testing and Evaluation result in software changes, the contractor shall:

a. Evaluate the category, priority, and class assigned to each software problem/change report to verify their appropriateness.

b. Evaluate proposed change requests and specification change notices (SCNs) to determine whether they fully respond to the software problem/change report or software change request, are consistent with software requirements, and are in conformance with applicable standards and data item descriptions.

c. Conduct in-process reviews to evaluate whether the methods and procedures established for software changes are being followed.

d. Evaluate modified documentation and code to verify that: (1) the modifications are in agreement with approved SCNs, (2) the modified documents accurately describe the current version of the software, and (3) the documents are in conformance with applicable standards and requirements.

e. Evaluate test plans, test descriptions, and test procedures for software modifications to verify that the testing to be performed will adequately test both the modifications made and continued conformance of the software to requirements that have not changed.

f. Monitor formal testing of software modifications to verify that the testing is performed in accordance with test plans, test descriptions, and test procedures.

g. Evaluate test reports to verify that they accurately reflect the testing performed.

h.   Conduct in-process reviews of configuration management to verify that all changes are handled in accordance with established configuration management procedures

24.7.2   Evaluations Associated with Software or Firmware Production. The contractor shall evaluate the controls exercised on software or firmware production. The contractor shall verify that:

a.   The correct version(s) of each CSCI are released for production.

b.   Production copies of the CSCI match the original controlled version(s), are properly marked, and are correctly correlated with the system configuration to which they belong.

24.7.3 Evaluations Associated with Acceptance Inspection and Preparation for Delivery. The contractor shall support software acceptance inspection and preparation for delivery. The contractor shall ensure that all required products are available and ready for government inspection, all required procedures have been performed, and evidence of satisfactory completion of these procedures is available for government inspection. The contractor shall verify that all software and documentation to be delivered have been updated to reflect any changes that may have occurred since the completion of FCA and PCA, if approved by the government and scheduled for inclusion in the items to be delivered.

24.7.4 Evaluation of Software Installation and Checkout. The contractor shall evaluate installation and checkout of the software at government-designated facilities, if installation and checkout is a requirement of the contract. The contractor shall monitor and evaluate the installation and checkout activities to ensure that: (1) the installation and checkout is performed in accordance with government-approved procedures, (3) any deviations therefrom are noted and explained to the satisfaction of the government, (4) any changes required to the installation and checkout procedures are documented, and (5) the installed software is performing properly in its operational environment.

NOTES: CLARIFICATION OR ADDITIONAL CRITERIA (per item column):

- Updated SDP, SSPM, SCMP, SQEP — All plans (updated and non updated) reflect current approaches and plans
- CSC Integration test results — Conformance to expected results in CSC test cases; completeness of testing; acceptability of deviations; adequacy of retesting; adequacy of integrated CSCI to enter CSCI testing
- Updated STLDD, SDDD, IDD, and DBDD — Consistency with updated code; consistency with each other
- Updated source code listings — Compliance with language and coding standards; compliance with maintainability requirements; consistency with updated design documentation
- Updated object code — Compliance with size and other constraints correspondence with source version placed under control.

EVALUATION CRITERIA (ITEM TO BE EVALUATED →)	Updated SDP, SSPM, SCMP, SQEP	CSC Integration test results	Updated STLDD, SDDD, IDD, and DBDD	Updated source code listings	Updated object code
Appropriate Content For Intended Audience	•	•	•		
Adequacy of Planned Tools, Facilities, Procedures, Methods, Resources	•				
Adequate Test Coverage of Requirements		•			
Appropriate Allocation of Sizing, Timing Resources			•	•	
Appropriate Level of Detail			•	•	
Appropriate Requirement, Design, Coding Techniques used to prepare item	•	•	•		
Feasibility			•	•	
Consistency with Indicated Document(s)	Each other		See Notes		See Notes
Traceability to Indicated Document(s)	SOW	See Notes	SRS IRS	See Notes	See Notes
Appropriate Degree of Completeness	•	•	•	•	
Technical Adequacy	•	•	•	•	
Understandability	•	•	•	•	
Internal Consistency	•	•	•	•	
Compliance with Contractual Requirements	•	•	•	•	
Adherence to Required Format and Documentation Standards	•	•	•	•	

Figure 13.5 **EVALUATION CRITERIA FOR PRODUCTS OF CSC INTEGRATION AND TESTING**

EVALUATION CRITERIA \ ITEM TO BE EVALUATED	Updated SDFS	Completed STPR	Updated CSCM, SUM, CSDM
NOTES: CLARIFICATION OR ADDITIONAL CRITERIA	Consistency with updated code, SDDD, IDD, DBDD; adequacy of updated unit test cases procedures; adequacy of updated unit test results	Adequate detail in specifying test procedures schedules constraints	Consistency with SDDD, IDD, DSDO, Consistency with each other
Appropriate Content For Intended Audience	●	●	●
Adequacy of Planned Tools, Facilities, Procedures, Methods, Resources		●	●
Adequate Test Coverage of Requirements	●	●	
Appropriate Allocation of Sizing, Timing Resources			
Appropriate Level of Detail	●	●	●
Appropriate Requirement, Design, Coding Techniques used to prepare Item			
Feasibility		●	
Consistency with Indicated Document(s)	Each other	SDDD IDD DBDD IRS	See Notes
Traceability to Indicated Document(s)	See Notes	STP STD SRS	SRS IRS
Appropriate Degree of Completeness	●	●	●
Technical Adequacy	●	●	●
Understandability	●	●	●
Internal Consistency	●	●	●
Compliance with Contractual Requirements	●	●	●
Adherence to Required Format and Documentation Standards	●	●	●

Figure 13.5 **EVALUATION CRITERIA FOR PRODUCTS OF CSC INTEGRATION AND TESTING (Cont'd)**

Evaluation Criteria	Updated SDP, SSPM, SCMP, SDEP	Software test report (STR)	Updated STLDD, SDDD, IDD, and DBDD	Updated source code	Updated object code
NOTES: CLARIFICATION OR ADDITIONAL CRITERIA	All plans (updated and non-updated) reflect current approaches and plans	Conformance to STP and expected results in STD; completeness of testing; acceptability of deviations; adequacy of retesting; adequacy of tested CSCI	Consistency with updated code; consistency with each other	Compliance with language and coding standards; compliance with maintainability requirements; consistency with updated SDDD, IDD, DBDD	Compliance with size and other constraints; correspondence with source version placed under control
Appropriate Content For Intended Audience	•	•	•		
Adequacy of Planned Tools, Facilities, Procedures, Methods, Resources	•				
Adequate Test Coverage of Requirements		•			
Appropriate Allocation of Sizing, Timing Resources		•	•	•	
Appropriate Level of Detail	•	•	•		
Appropriate Requirement, Design, Coding Techniques used to prepare item			•	•	
Feasibility	•		•		
Consistency with Indicated Document(s)	Each other		See Notes		See Notes
Traceability to Indicated Document(s)	SOW	See Notes	SRS IRS	See Notes	
Appropriate Degree of Completeness	•	•	•	•	
Technical Adequacy	•	•	•	•	
Understandability	•	•	•	•	
Internal Consistency	•	•	•	•	
Compliance with Contractual Requirements	•	•	•	•	
Adherence to Required Format and Documentation Standards	•	•	•	•	

Figure 13.6 **EVALUATION CRITERIA FOR PRODUCTS OF CSCI TESTING**

Evaluation Criteria \ Item to be Evaluated	Updated SDFS	Software Product Specification (SPS)	Version description document (VDD)	Completed CSOM, SUM, CSDM
Appropriate Content For Intended Audience	•	•	•	•
Adequacy of Planned Tools, Facilities, Procedures, Methods, Resources				•
Adequate Test Coverage of Requirements				
Appropriate Allocation of Sizing, Timing Resources				
Appropriate Level of Detail				
Appropriate Requirement, Design, Coding Technique used to prepare item			•	•
Feasibility	•			
Consistency with Indicated Document(s)		See Notes	See Notes	SPS Each other
Traceability to Indicated Document(s)	See Notes	SRS IRS		SRS IRS
Appropriate Degree of Completeness	•	•	•	•
Technical Adequacy	•	•	•	•
Understandability	•	•	•	•
Internal Consistency	•	•	•	•
Compliance with Contractual Requirements	•	•	•	•
Adherence to Required Format and Documentation Standards	•	•	•	•
NOTES: CLARIFICATION OR ADDITIONAL CRITERIA	Consistency with updated code, SDDD, IDD, DBDD; adequacy of updated unit test cases procedures; adequacy of updated unit test results	Incorporated of STLDD, SDDD, DBDD, IDD and software listings consistent with the updated source code	Accuracy in identifying the exact version of the CSCI, SRS, IRS, and SPS, including all incorporated ECPS and SCNS	

Figure 13.6 **EVALUATION CRITERIA FOR PRODUCTS OF CSCI TESTING (Cont'd)**

Part IV

RELATIONSHIPS TO OTHER QA TASKS

Chapter 14
SPECIAL QUALITY ASSURANCE GROUP TASKS

QA groups are frequently asked by data processing management to undertake special assignments, covering all aspects of data processing. Examples are developing standards, evaluating software and hardware, and performing special cost/benefit analyses for the data processing manager.

Rarely will postponing a QA review impact on meeting schedules for implementing application systems. The quality of systems might be affected, but rarely the schedule. This permits the data processing manager to pull QA groups from their normal work to handle special assignments.

Quality assurance groups should welcome special assignments. They do not substantially affect the members' performance of their regular reviews and the experience gained in the special assignments may well assist the individual in the performance of later (QA) application review.

The different types of assignments should be considered and prioritized by QA groups so that if and when assignments occur, the group has developed a position. Some assignments are very supportive of QA functions while others may best be done by other groups or other people in data processing.

QA groups have the obligation to inform the data processing manager of the consequences of undertaking a special assignment. If in their opinion a special assignment will adversely affect the review function of the group, this should be brought to the attention of the data processing manager.

Undertaking special assignments makes maximum use of quality assurance experience. In conducting reviews, personnel have the opportunity to see many systems. They are able to discuss a variety of approaches with various members of the data processing department. They are involved in the newer technology, as it is normally first used by systems under development. QA personnel have the time and opportunity to study problems and look for solutions. They approach evaluation from a management viewpoint. When special assignments occur, this background, experience, and approach are what data processing management wants in the individual conducting the special task.

Because they do not have any application systems line responsibility, QA personnel can approach a special assignment from an independent viewpoint. They are not biased by special needs that will make "their" application more efficient. QA group members are charged with maintaining and improving quality on all application systems. This perspective makes them ideal candidates for special assignments.

Many special assignments are a result of a departmental problem, a user request, or an inquiry by a member of executive management of the organization. Answering these needs and requests permits QA personnel to delve into problems and potential solutions to those problems. This type of experience can prove very beneficial when they are evaluating the goals, methods, and performance of application system implementation.

Executing special assignments is a vehicle for training QA personnel. This adds a new dimension and a new challenge for a group member. Having to conduct these assignments will broaden one's background and experience. Many times the assignments will involve new technology and will help prepare the QA person to review applications that use that technology at a later time.

In most cases the QA group is performing the review function that a data processing manager would do in a smaller organization. The administrative challenge of a larger department does not permit the data processing manager to do quality assurance type assignments. From this perspective, special assignments are an extension of the QA function. Those tasks that the data processing manager does not have time to undertake are logical tasks for quality assurance personnel.

There are some strong reasons why QA personnel should reject some assignments. These should be weighed heavily because the primary responsibility of quality assurance is to assure quality on installed application systems. The major disadvantage for a QA group to undertake a special assignment is that it dilutes their primary tasks. If a review effort is reduced, delayed, or consolidated due to special assignments, the effectiveness of the group may suffer. Project leaders will begin to view QA as a group organized to do special assignments for the DP manager. When this happens, the function will be viewed as less important in the eyes of the project personnel.

Conducting many special tasks can also cause groups to lose objectivity in conducting reviews. Many special assignments involve the setting of standards and procedures to be followed by project personnel. Because QA has established those procedures, they may not be able to view them from an independent viewpoint when conducting a review. For example, when project personnel argue that a procedure or standard is unrealistic because of unique circumstances to that application, the person who developed that procedure or standard may be blinded by his or her own logic in developing it.

Some special assignments can lead to conflict with project personnel. The type of assignment that can lead to conflict is one in which the QA is making judgments about the performance and competency of project personnel. When quality assurance takes on the role of a supervisor, it no longer is a peer group review and a cooperative attitude on the part of project personnel will probably be lost.

The advantages and disadvantages discussed for the tasks may not apply to any given assignment involving that task. The group must examine the types of assignments that may be offered to quality assurance. During this examination, each of the above advantages and disadvantages must be put into the perspective of their own data processing department. If the group is given an option of whether or not to accept an assignment, they will have a position because of having previously analyzed the advantages and disadvantages of that assignment. This will enable them to present a very logical reason to the data processing manager as to why they want to accept or reject that assignment.

TYPICAL QUALITY ASSURANCE SPECIAL TASKS

The number and broad range of tasks quality assurance groups are asked to do indicates that there are gaps in many data processing organizations. There appears to be a need for a group in data processing to conduct special studies and no such group exists, so the assignments go to QA.

When the assignments given to a QA group begin to occupy a significant amount of resources — more than 20% of available time, for example — the group should rethink those assignments.

When special tasks become an integral part of the QA function, management might consider revising the charter of the group and adding personnel to undertake those tasks. Many assignments are recurring; for example, developing systems and programming standards. The group should be adequately staffed to perform those recurring functions.

Developing Control Standards

The single most beneficial step that most data processing departments could undertake is formalizing control standards. Many of the problems occurring in data processing occur because technology has outpaced the ability to control applications. Data processing departments work on technology years in advance of its use, but they only worry about control after problems have occurred. Development of control standards may be one of the most fruitful areas for quality assurance involvement.

Controls can be subdivided into those that prevent problems, those that detect problems, and those that provide information to correct problems once they occur. Controls are further organized by system functions such as recording, authorizing, transmitting, processing, storage, and output. Control standards include both the type of control the organization believes necessary for an application system and the process to select the controls. Many organizations include in their control standards a list of actual controls to select from.

Most controls used by organizations are there due more to happenstance than to planning. Many project leaders select controls based on their own personal experience rather than on training. For example, one of the major problems in data processing is control of the accounting period cutoff. This involves synchronizing manual and computerized operations. In many organizations, they use a different control mechanism. Quality assurance personnel having experience in reviewing and working with many applications are in the best position in data processing to develop a control standard for a procedure such as the accounting period cutoff procedure.

Hardware Selection Analysis

Hardware analysis involves comparing hardware alternatives in order to obtain the best piece of equipment for the job and may range from selecting major pieces of equipment to minor upgrading or downgrading of existing hardware. The assignment usually involves working with representatives of hardware vendors.

Quality assurance groups can maintain manuals that provide comparison between various hardware units. Even when quality assurance does not do the actual selection, they can provide material to the group doing it and then review the selection process.

Because quality assurance personnel are continually reviewing new applications, they are in a good position to make an assessment of future hardware needs. Quality assurance should be involved in the hardware selection process, either doing the selecting or reviewing the selection process.

Software Selection Analysis

Software selection analysis involves determining which piece of software optimizes both the hardware and the application systems. Software analysis can occur for both new and existing software packages. Frequently features of existing software are not properly utilized. Packages and/or features must be analyzed using a knowledge of the hardware, the software package, and the application system. Few people have a knowledge of all three.

Selecting and generating software systems is a highly technical function. In most organizations, the individuals performing that function have only a minimal appreciation of the goals and objectives of application systems. This is because their specialty does not permit the time to work on applications from a user viewpoint. Therefore, they tend to optimize hardware and software without regard for the needs of the application system. Quality assurance personnel involved in this process bring to the selection process a wide background in application systems.

Involving quality assurance personnel in software selection benefits systems programmers as well since they gain an appreciation of the needs of both current and future application systems. This will put software in a better perspective for them. Quality assurance personnel become more familiar with the capabilities of software, and are then better able to advise application systems and programmers on the capabilities and shortcomings of software systems.

Develop Systems and Programming Practices

Systems and programming practices are the methods by which application systems are implemented. Systems practices include the process for developing systems, documentation procedures, organization of project teams, data documentation, and progress reporting procedures. Programming practices include program documentation, programming conventions, testing procedures, program change procedures, and status reports.

The major responsibility of QA is to review compliance with systems and programming practices. In this review, weaknesses in the practices are readily discernable. Areas where systems and programming practices should be strengthened become apparent. Quality assurance people are in an ideal position to develop and/or improve systems and programming practices because they have seen them used over many applications.

Training EDP Personnel in Control, System, and Programming Practices

New personnel and changing technology make it essential to train data processing personnel continually. Vendors provide training in their hardware and software packages. However, organizations must train their personnel in their own systems and control practices. It is not enough to develop standards and procedures; these must be taught to the people who will use them during systems implementation.

Quality assurance experience in review of application systems puts them in an ideal position to conduct these training sessions. From the reviews, they become aware of the problems systems and programming personnel are having in using the organization's control and systems practices. This enables them to emphasize the areas that are causing trouble. Also, by having reviewed many diverse applications, QA personnel have the experience necessary to answer questions in terms of applications familiar to the students.

By teaching, QA personnel learn themselves. In order to teach control and systems practices, personnel must have a thorough understanding of those practices. This teaching experience also makes them better reviewers because the classroom teaching experience has shown them the students' areas of concern and areas where misunderstandings are most likely to occur.

Providing Systems Consultant Services

In today's complex technology, it is unrealistic to expect a project team to possess all the knowledge and disciplines necessary to adequately implement a computer application. A successful project team requires the combined experiences of many data processing specialists. In addition to technological problems, the project team may need advice in organizational policies and procedures, general business advice, government or industry regulations, plus other business disciplines.

In forming a QA group, data processing management should try to draw from diverse backgrounds. For example, the group may include software specialists, hardware specialists, telecommunication specialists, programming specialists, etc. When a project team member has need for expertise in one of these areas, it is logical to call upon quality assurance to help them with a particular difficult system problem.

QA personnel keep their skills up-to-date by working with project personnel on real-life problems. There is value in reading manuals and attending sessions in an area of skill, but the real value comes in applying those skills to an application problem. It is also to the advantage of the data processing department to make as many uses of specialized skills as possible.

Resolving the Technical Problems of Application Systems

Many application systems run into technical problems during the implementation phases of an application system. The project personnel decide on an approach, may or may not discuss it with consultants, and then begin implementing that approach. When they begin to move from the general specifications to the specific implementation, problems arise. In the latter stages of implementation, this may be a hang-up on the computer. In earlier stages, they can reach a point where they cannot work out the details for a general solution.

Technical problems can occur because of the lack of planning or because people are too close to the problem to see an obvious solution. Other times people cause their own problem. For example, a programmer may misuse a program language instruction but be convinced the misinterpretation is correct. The use of an outside party to make an assessment may save project personnel considerable time.

QA personnel are in an ideal position to make this independent assessment. Working with multiple systems, they may have seen the same technical problem previously, and either have solved the problem or been aware of the solution to the problem. The experience gained in working out technical problems can be used by them in solving similar problems when they occur in other systems.

Bridging the Gap Between Systems and Operations Personnel

One of the major problems which has plagued data processing from its inception is the language barrier. One group develops one set of jargon and another group adopts another set. When they begin discussing a problem, not only do the different perspectives cause problems, but so does terminology. For example, application systems personnel tend to use the jargon of their application and user, while operations personnel will use the jargon of the hardware and software vendors.

Without a full appreciation of the other group's needs and problems, operations and systems groups can develop procedures which are not mutually supportive. For example, operations personnel can select operating systems options which make systems work more difficult. On the other hand, systems personnel can build systems which are ineffective to operate. Neither group may be aware of the impact of their work on the other.

Quality assurance groups working with both systems personnel and operations personnel can gain a good understanding of the concerns and problems of each group. Using quality assurance personnel as mediators to resolve differences of opinions between the two groups is a valuable service. Because of its independent position in data processing, QA's opinions and recommendations will not be taken to be self-serving in most situations.

Developing More Effective EDP Methods

Data processing management continually looks for new and better ways of performing that data processing function. These methods can be better ways to develop systems, more effective programming techniques, better use of hardware and software, or better training and use of personnel. Because data processing is a production environment, it is frequently difficult for project personnel and data processing management to step back and objectively view the department, its policies and procedures.

Quality assurance is in the unique position of independently reviewing the implementation of application systems. During these reviews, they observe the good and bad points of different implementation methods. After several reviews, they begin to determine which methods are the most efficient and which are the least efficient. They also begin to get an appreciation between methods and the caliber of people using those methods.

Charging QA with the responsibility for developing more effective EDP methods is a logical assignment for the group. As an ongoing special assignment, they can transfer the knowledge gained from the better implemented systems to the less skilled systems and programming personnel. This special assignment is highly recommended as one which quality assurance should seek, and one which should be assigned to them by data processing management.

Reviewing Data Center Operations

Data center operations include input preparation, job scheduling, computer operations, data storage, security, and output distribution. If telecommunications are used, data processing has a responsibility for the outlying terminals. The operations responsibility includes making sure that the right program is run at the right time using the right data.

QA can review the data center operations for compliance to procedures, as well as effectiveness, efficiency, and economy of operations. The review can be concentrated in one area (for example, the data library), or it can be broad in nature and cover all facets of the data center.

A review of data center operations is also beneficial to QA in its application systems review process. Having a better appreciation of the problems and procedures in the data center equips QA better to assess implementation plans on new applications. This provides sufficient background information to make an adequate evaluation as to whether or not the planned implementation of an application system will cause operating difficulties.

Evaluation of Operational Application Systems

After the system has become operational, it is advisable to compare the actual systems results against the planned systems results. For example, if the system specifications called for responding to a user terminal request within three seconds, it should be determined whether or not the system in production meets that three-second response as specified.

QA personnel have the application background needed to conduct such a review. This is because they have worked throughout the systems development life cycle. They have built up an extensive background about the project and know its strengths and weaknesses. By having quality assurance personnel make an evaluation of an operational system, they can provide data processing management with a judgment based on full knowledge of the application, and do it more efficiently than probably any other group could.

Few QA groups perform evaluations of application systems once they are operational. This function is normally done by internal auditors. Evaluation of operational systems normally is done for executive management and user departments. This would put quality assurance in the position of evaluating data processing for outside departments. While quality assurance may be in a good position to do it, it tends to undermine their relationships with data processing personnel.

Advantages and Disadvantages of Special Assignments

The unique situations and needs of each organization make accepting or rejecting special assignments by QA a very personal decision. The actual decision may be based on factors unique to that organization such as utilizing one individual's extensive personal experience. There are some general guidelines a QA group can use in evaluating special assignments and these are illustrated in Figure 14.1, the Special Assignment/Advantages-Disadvantages Matrix.

The matrix lists the advantages and disadvantages of special assignments. Checkmarks in the rows beside each special assignment indicate which advantages and disadvantages are appropriate for that special assignment. Organizations may wish to change some of these based on unique situations.

The two columns on the right-hand side of the matrix state whether or not the quality assurance group should undertake that special assignment. The four assignments not recommended are:

1. *Hardware selection analysis.* While this is a good training assignment, it does take a lot of time. Also, it may require more specialized knowledge than possessed by quality assurance personnel. This assignment may be done by QA in smaller organizations because no one else is better qualified.

2. *Software selection analysis.* Again, while this is a good training assignment, it does take a lot of time. Also, it may require more specialized knowledge than possessed by quality assurance personnel. This assignment may be done by QA in smaller organizations because no one else is better qualified. If the QA group is included, software selection is more appropriate than hardware selection.

Special Assignment	Maximizes Experience	Independent Viewpoint	Implementation Schedule Not Affected	Increases QA Awareness of Needs	QA Training Vehicle	Helps DP Manager	Dilution of QA Effort	Loss of Objectivity	Causes Conflict With Project Personnel	Yes	No
	Advantages to QA						Disadvantages to QA			Quality Assurance Should Perform This Special Assignment	
Developing control standards	✓	✓	✓			✓	✓	✓		✓	
Hardware selection analysis	✓		✓	✓	✓	✓	✓	✓			✓
Software selection analysis	✓		✓	✓	✓	✓		✓			✓
Develop system and programming practices	✓	✓	✓			✓		✓		✓	
Training EDP personnel in control and systems programming practices	✓		✓	✓	✓	✓	✓			✓	
Providing systems consultant services	✓		✓	✓		✓		✓		✓	

Special Assignments Has These

Figure 14.1 **SPECIAL ASSIGNMENT/ADVANTAGES-DISADVANTAGES MATRIX**

Special Assignment	Maximizes Experience	Independent Viewpoint	Implementation Schedule Not Affected	Increases QA Awareness of Needs	QA Training Vehicle	Helps DP Manager	Dilution of QA Effort	Loss of Objectivity	Causes Conflict With Project Personnel	Yes	No
			Advantages to QA				Disadvantages to QA			Quality Assurance Should Perform This Special Assignment	
Resolving the technical problems of application systems	✓		✓	✓	✓	✓				✓	
Bridging the gap between systems and operations personnel	✓	✓	✓	✓	✓	✓				✓	
Developing more effective EDP methods	✓	✓	✓		✓	✓		✓		✓	
Reviewing data center operations	✓		✓	✓	✓	✓	✓		?		✓
Evaluation of operational application systems	✓		✓	✓	✓	✓			✓		✓

Figure 14.1   **SPECIAL ASSIGNMENT/ADVANTAGES-DISADVANTAGES MATRIX (Cont'd)**

3.   *Reviewing data center operations.* When done by QA, as opposed to auditing, this tends to become more of a performance review and as such can cause personality conflicts.

4.   *Evaluation of operational application systems.* This assignment is best done by auditing because it is more of a performance review than a compliance review unless system
performance has been specified in detail. Most organizations leave this assignment for auditing. A major reason is
that reports should go outside data processing to the user
and executive management.

The other assignments are supportive of quality assurance and
should be done by them unless it interferes too much with their
regular reviews.

EVALUATING THE MERITS OF SPECIAL TASKS

Each special assignment should be evaluated on its own merits.
Given the choice, QA needs a method of determining whether or
not to undertake a special assignment. There will be some special
assignments that most QA groups would like to do, and others
that would be preferable not to perform. However, rather than
making the choice on personal preference, some logic should be
applied to the decision.

Listed below are questions that QA should be asking about
each of the special assignments. An honest and fair evaluation of
the special assignment based on these questions will determine
the merits of doing or not doing the special assignment. The
questions are:

1.   Is there a choice about doing the special assignment? If not,
do it.

2.   If QA performs the special assignment, will it have an effect
on the regularly scheduled reviews? If the answer is yes,
then a judgment must be made as to which is the most important for the department and the organization.

3.   Will performing the special assignment help the QA in either reviews or in developing QA procedures? If the answer
is yes and the assignment will not adversely affect review
schedules, the assignment probably should be undertaken.

4.   Will the special assignment provide some needed training
      for one or more of the people in QA? If the answer is yes and
      the special assignment will not adversely affect the review
      schedules, the assignment probably should be performed.

5.   Will conducting the special assignment cause QA personnel
      to lose objectivity in future reviews? This question implies
      that the assignment would bias the quality assurance re-
      viewer's opinion on a future review. For example, an in-
      depth study of a special piece of hardware might convince a
      person that all systems should use that piece of hardware. If
      conducting a review on a system where the project team se-
      lected an alternative piece of hardware, it may be difficult
      for that reviewer to accept the project team's judgment as the
      best choice.

SUMMARY

The quality assurance group is in a unique position to receive
special assignments from the data processing manager. Their experience is broad, they become involved in most of the new applications in the data processing department, and they are frequently the more senior people in the data processing department. In addition, they are not tied to a strict production schedule, where a week or two on a special assignment would adversely
affect that schedule.

This chapter was designed to alert QA to the types of assignments being given their counterparts in other organizations.
Quality assurance groups should do some planning as to which
types of assignments are valuable and which are not prior to being asked about special assignments. Making assessments as to
the worth of conducting each of these types of assignments puts
quality assurance in a very strong position to try to obtain assignments which would be helpful to the group, and to avoid assignments which would dilute their primary responsibility.

Chapter 15
RELATIONSHIP TO INTERNAL AUDITING

Executive management has recognized the importance of data processing to its day-to-day operation. The proper functioning of data processing applications is becoming increasingly important in the ongoing functioning of an organization. Management, in exercising its control responsibility, is establishing groups to provide assurance that data processing systems are adequately implemented and controlled.

Both internal and external audits avoided heavy involvement in data processing until about 1970. Since then, auditing review of data processing has been increasing. A major study in systems auditability and control concluded that not enough emphasis was being placed on control. In that study, it was recommended that greater involvement by the internal audit function should occur in all phases of data processing.

In some organizations, internal audit had tried to fill the control gap by designing controls for computer applications, but this is a function that should be done by the data processing department and the user. The user has primary responsibility for application controls, and data processing for data center related controls. Internal audit should review controls, but not design them.

The establishment of the QA function in data processing permits internal audit to exercise its normal independent review function. Many internal audit groups are strongly recommending the establishment of a QA function in data processing. Where one is established, it should develop a close working relationship with internal auditing.

INTERNAL AUDIT RESPONSIBILITIES

With more than 15,000 members, the Institute of Internal Auditors is the only international organization dedicated to the

415

advancement of the individual internal auditor and the profession. The Institute issued a Statement of Responsibility of the internal auditor in 1947 and three revisions in 1957, 1971, and 1978. The current statement embodies the concepts previously established and includes such changes as are deemed advisable in the light of the present status of the profession. It reads:

Nature

Internal auditing is an independent appraisal activity within an organization for the review of operations as a service to management. It is a managerial control which functions by measuring and evaluating the effectiveness of other controls.

Objectivity and Scope

The objective of internal auditing is to assist all members of management in the effective discharge of their responsibilities by furnishing them with analyses, appraisals, recommendations and pertinent comments concerning the activities reviewed. Internal auditors are concerned with any phase of business activity in which they may be of service to management. This involves going beyond the accounting and financial records to obtain a full understanding of the operations under review. The attainment of this overall objective involves such activities as:

1. Reviewing and appraising the soundness, adequacy, and application of accounting, financial, and other operating controls, and promoting effective control at reasonable cost.
2. Ascertaining the extent of compliance with established policies, plans, and procedures.
3. Ascertaining the extent to which company assets are accounted for and safeguarded from losses of all kinds.
4. Ascertaining the reliability of management data developed within the organization.
5. Appraising the quality of performance in carrying out assigned responsibilities.
6. Recommending operating improvements.

Responsibility and Authority

The responsibility of internal auditing in the organization should be clearly established by management policy. The related authority should provide the internal auditor full access to all of the organization's records, properties, and personnel relevant to the subject under review. The internal auditor should be free to review and appraise policies, plans, procedures, and records.

The internal auditor's responsibilities should be:

1. To inform and advise management, and to discharge this responsibility in a manner that is consistent with the Code of Ethics of the Institute of Internal Auditors.
2. To coordinate internal audit activities with others so as to best achieve the audit objectives of the organization.

In performing their functions, internal auditors have no direct responsibilities for nor authority over any of the activities review. Therefore, the internal audit review and appraisal does not in any way relieve other persons in the organization of the responsibilities assigned to them.

Independence

Independence is essential to the effectiveness of internal auditing. This independence is obtained primarily through organizational status and objectivity.

1. The organizational status of the internal auditing function and the support accorded to it by management are major determinants of its range and value. The head of the internal auditing function, therefore, should be responsible to an officer whose authority is sufficient to assure both a broad range of audit coverage and the adequate consideration of an effective action on the audit findings and recommendations.
2. Objectivity is essential to the audit function. Therefore, internal auditors should not develop and install procedures, prepare records, or engage in any other activity which they would normally review and appraise and which could reasonably be construed to compromise the independence of the internal auditor. The internal auditor's objectivity need not be adversely affected, however, by determining and recommending standards of control to be applied in the development of the systems and procedures being reviewed.

CONTROL IN AN EDP ENVIRONMENT

One of the primary responsibilities of an auditor is to evaluate the adequacy of control. Over the past several hundred years control in a business environment has been slowly revolving. Prior to the advent of the computer, auditors understood good control practices. The computer changed control. Let's review what has happened to control in computerized business environment.

Most EDP departments are organized into two groups. One group runs the computer, while the other group designs and writes programs. Generally the EDP department takes direction for new assignments from prospective users who have little, if any, real knowledge of how to use or control a computer. In the old days when the computer read a card, sorted some data, and printed a report, the user could somehow relate to the data even though the user did not totally understand what was being done to it. The accepted control philosophy was that the user was responsible for defining the needs and controlling the data that flowed through the user's system. In small companies where minicomputers are being installed, we can still find this basic pattern of organization and control.

In larger companies, with large computer installations, we are finding increasing sophistication employing such new concepts as distributed network processing, data base systems, virtual storage, transaction processing, and a whole lot of other buzzwords. Although the technology of computers and systems design has been changing at an unbelievable rate, many companies still retain the same organization they had in the early days of the computer or, worse, in the days of the unit record tab equipment.

To illustrate quickly what can happen, a bank recently installed an on-line teller systems linking a number of branches into a centrally controlled system. Prior to the change, each bank had a head cashier who was directly responsible for the direction and control of each teller. After the change, the computer performed most of the tasks previously performed by the head cashiers. The head cashiers, operating independently at each bank, did not design the system nor could they, as a group, direct or control the system effectively. Nor did they fully understand all that the computer was doing. Organizationally, the head cashiers were still held responsible for teller operations, but no one realized until later that the administrative responsibility for all of the bank's normal cash-handling functions had passed over to a programmer/analyst, who seized the opportunity to get rich. As a postscript, an auditor had approved the controls built intothe system but failed to realize that no one was organizationally responsible for using them.

There is generally lack of control within many EDP installations, but the auditing profession may be trying to solve the wrong problem. Very little has been researched, written, or discussed relative to the impact the computer is having on traditional organization structures. Yet, weaknesses in the organizational structure may very well be the primary cause for the lack of control that exists in many EDP systems. To illustrate the situation, a president of a large corporation asked the payroll manager if he would do anything differently if he knew he would be fired if anyone connected with the EDP installation were found defrauding the company through the payroll system. His immediate response was a very audible "yes!" The president wanted to know why he wasn't presently doing those other things. The manager's response was "Today, I am not responsible if something goes wrong in there." The payroll manager's job description has since been rewritten and there have been dramatic improvements in control.

In many cases the technological advances in computers and their associated systems have outstripped the ability of the rest of the organization to keep up. As an illustration, there was a medium-sized company where many normal administrative procedures went from manual mode to a small card handling computer to a large mainframe transaction processing data base-oriented computer within three years. Managers were just realizing the need for adequate batch controls when they had to start learning all over again. In this same company, the manual mode never worked well even before the computer made a mess of things. This situation created an environment where, admittedly, the organization was unable to change fast enough to keep up with the changing computer technology. Rather than slow down or change the organization, the attitude shifted to one of making the users look incompetent with the end result being a total takeover of most administrative responsibilities by the EDP group! Control almost disappeared. This company was, at one time, virtually being run by the EDP organization.

Control is management function that requires an appropriate organization to be effective. To have control, one must be assigned a responsibility for control and be vested with appropriate authority which will assure getting it. The breakdown of control can usually be traced to an organizational efficiency where a responsibility was not spelled out or the person responsible was not granted sufficient authority to carry out his responsibilities. As in the earlier example of the president and payroll manager, the absence of control in EDP systems is often traceable to improperly defined responsibility.

THE AUDITOR AND CONTROL

In many companies, the EDP auditor has stepped into the breach, recognizing the lack of control, user ignorance, and a certain apathy toward control on the part of EDP personnel. He has chosen to improve the situation by demanding that certain basic controls be established and performing certain tests which proved assurance that the absence of these basic controls and not created as yet an undetected problem. There is little, if any, question that the auditor's input was both necessary and desirable. However, auditors who jump into the breach have often been so busy trying to "plug holes" they have not stepped back to determine what is causing the problem. If the cause can be identified, then it can be dealt with is such a way that the solution should reduce or eliminate the undesirable effects.

Internal auditing, through the EDP auditor, is trying to fill an organizational void by assuming the responsibility for control. Obviously, the responsibility has been properly defined in the organization and there is lack of control in most EDP systems. The lack of an assigned responsibility for control should be dealt with. However, the assumption of responsibility for control by an auditor, any auditor, is an impossible and illogical solution. Responsibility and authority must be granted in equal shares, organizationally. To be effective as an independent and object observer, an auditor, by definition, must be denied, organizationally, any authority. Without authority there can be no responsibility. If auditors assume the responsibility, they must be granted or must seize the authority — at which point, they cease to be effective as auditors. This represents a very real "catch-22" and one which has not been faced up to very well.

The first step in improving the overall control of the computer resource is to recognize that there is probably no defined organizational responsibility for control. A lot of people probably recognize the need for control and are no doubt involved in some way in providing controls. This is not the same thing as being responsible for control.

The second step is to recognize that sophisticated systems require integration of function which, in most cases, involves the horizontal linkage of many organizational components. Historically, control, responsibility, authority, and communication were all channeled in a vertical organization structure. The imposition of a horizontal structure by the computer results in an absence of an organizational entity that is responsible for the system as a whole even though a number of persons may be assigned some responsibility for control of a portion of the total system.   Internal auditing's role is not to provide the missing control elements on an ongoing basis but, rather, to apprise management that this defect in control exists and to request that it be remedied.   The near absence of any written research or other material on organization structure indicates that the cause and effect relationship between the computer-imposed horizontal organization and an attendant lack of assigned responsibility for control of "The System" has not yet been widely recognized.

CONTROL AND EDP ORGANIZATION

It has been recognized that no one in an organization has an assigned responsibility for control of "The System" and that to be effective large, integrated systems must be based on a horizontal integration of function which imposes a strain on traditional vertical organization structures by complicating the assignment of a responsibility for control.   Then what is the answer?   In many companies there is an awareness that the installation of large-scale computers with highly integrated systems does, in fact, force the traditional organization structure to change.   Many managers have the feeling that things are coming unglued and that they are no longer "in control."   However, most of them can't define why they feel as they do.   There is also a perception that the EDP group is increasingly gaining a bigger piece of the management pie.   However, in most companies the change away from traditional concepts is not necessarily a planned change toward something better.   The change just happens and out of the confusion something that works emerges.   The something that works most often seems to be an assumption of responsibility by the EDP group for "The System" and an assumption of responsibility by the EDP auditor for control of "The System." This is an assumption of responsibility because there is no assignment of appropriate authority, and it works only until disaster occurs, at absence of an organizational entity that is responsible for the which time it is quickly learned that no one is responsible for anything.   This is not necessarily the only or best solution.   In most cases it is, in reality, the default solution which occurs because the effect of the computer-dictated horizontal integration of function on the corporate organization structure is not well understood in advance and management responsibility assignments are not appropriately planned or made in advance to support the change.

The solution to the problem must lie in creating new and different organizational structures, ones more suited to the horizontal structure imposed by the computer. There are two sides to the organizational question, the corporate organization itself which must relate to the conditions imposed by computer systems and the organization of the EDP group so that it can relate more effectively with the corporate organization.

Using the example of the on-line teller systems noted earlier, the bank could have created the position of "Vice President for On-Line Teller System" and assigned him total responsibility and authority for the planning, direction, organization, and control of the entire system. This course would have resulted in all head cashiers, tellers, and some EDP personnel reporting to this newly created position. In other words, he would have been given all the tools he needed to do the job. Recognizing that a horizontal integration-of-function type system does cross normal organization boundaries, then one answer might be to create a new organizational entity within the traditional vertical framework which is suitably chartered so that it has complete control over all of the entities that are horizontally connected by "The System." Quite obviously, to maintain appropriate management control via segregation of duties, this person would be part of the line organization and outside the EDP group.

Another way of assigning responsibility and authority might entail nothing more than amending a job description or providing some form of incentive-related control. The payroll manager is an example of what might happen just by expanding a job description and giving the manager more authority. Another example concerns a case where it was merely a case of oversight. A plant manager for a $20 million brass casting plant was allowing some of the inventory to be piled next to the fence which separated the storage yard from the parking lot. Many of the mill hands drove pickup trucks which were parked against the fence. Inventory write-offs were common but not of a material nature. The plant manager had argued, successfully, that the write-offs were small and that a lack of storage capacity, budget constraints, poor systems, and a whole lot of other problems prevented him from doing things differently. The auditors were never able to really prove that a problem existed or that the risk was greater than the cost of the control. The president toured the plant one day and saw the situation which the plant manager dutifully explained. Upon returning to his office the president learned that the plant manager's job description did not list as one of his responsibilities that he "... shall have responsibility for the security and protection of corporate owned assets." This was added to the plant manager's job description and along with it the incentive system was changed so that inventory write-offs caused a direct reduction of the manager's bonus. Suddenly, controls that had always been too difficult or expensive in the past became feasible almost overnight. In many large corporations, job descriptions, manager contracts, and policy charters do not make any reference to responsibility control, protection, or security.

The rapid growth in the complexity of computer systems has outpaced the ability of many organizations to alter their organizational structure into new forms required by these technical advances. Recognizing this, there needs to be a similar growth in the state of the art of management theory and organization structure. Little has been done or written in this area. New or different ideas should be explored such as managers or directors of systems. A careful evaluation of job descriptions and incentive systems should be made to determine if responsibilities for control of computer systems have been appropriately defined.

The absence of usable alternatives has resulted in many companies relying on the default solution whereby responsibility for "The System" is assumed by EDP auditing. The first area of worthwhile exploration lies in finding improved methods for restructuring the organization to improve areas within the EDP group itself.

Historically, neither the DP group responsible for writing the programs nor the group responsible for running the programs on the computer has been given any responsibility for control or authority to direct the installation of controls. As a point of fact, most controls are counterproductive to the whole idea behind using computers in the first place in that they create inefficiency, redundancy, and a lot of extra work. Whatever control does exist in most EDP installations has been forced upon them by outsiders such as internal auditors, CPA firms and executive management personnel who have become terrified by the horror stories in leading business publications.

NEED FOR QUALITY ASSURANCE

Establishing a quality assurance group is an approach to the organization of various functions to achieve a responsibility for the control of computer systems. This is not the only alternative, but it may be the best. It is almost a written law that the cashier cannot be general ledger bookkeeper. Auditors can identify with this element of internal control and have no difficulty expressing their concern in an audit report. However, most auditors, including the specialized breed of EDP auditors, run right past the fact that there is no independent responsibility in most EDP organizations for the control of computer systems. There is copious material on the appropriate organizational splits that are effective in achieving control over the accounting records, but very little has been written on how to organize functions within EDP organizations. Therefore, most EDP installations are organized to produce and run programs with an emphasis on volume or production. Controls, or any other administrative overhead, that tend to reduce the production rate are not going to be installed willingly by the EDP organization.

Somewhere along the line during the evolution of computer technology, the auditing profession went astray of its mission. Historically, if the organization structure did not provide for a sufficient segregation of duties a recommendation was made to correct the deficiency. However, if the deficiency was present, the auditor would not put himself into the position of chief accountant for an indefinite period in order to make sure everything was being done properly. With computer systems, however, EDP auditors have sensed an absence of control, have been unable to trace the problem to organizational weaknesses, and have put themselves into the middle of things as they assume the responsibility for instituting control. There is something very wrong about this, but for some reason the profession has not been particularly vocal about letting EDP auditors throw away their objectivity and independence.

One of the very real myths that exist in some aspects of EDP auditing may be in confusing a test of properly designed controls with providing control as a function. Test decks, for example, are a very necessary part of getting a new program released into production. Someone within the EDP group should be assigned specific responsibility for making sure any new program or program change is adequately tested before it can become operational. An EDP auditor should verify that this testing was done and done properly, but if the EDP auditor does it, the EDP auditor is, in fact, assuming a responsibility for executing a control procedure which the EDP auditor has not been authorized to do. In this latter case where test decks are a necessary control to make sure programs are functional before they are released, the auditor, if he creates or uses the test deck himself, is in reality providing the control rather than determining if an appropriate control is actually operational.

Auditors appear to be so busy concentrating on the detailed minutiae of EDP that they have overlooked the bigger picture. They keep checking for check digits, running test decks, bench tracing, checking logic loops, trying to defeat passwords, and testing a zillion other specific controls. When problems are noted, auditors have a tendency to take over and install control mechanisms or assume a responsibility for proving the control themselves. Admittedly, the conclusion, almost universally quoted by EDP auditors, is that there is an appalling lack of control in most EDP systems. Similarly, EDP auditors have been instrumental in providing some basic level of control to prevent abuses. However, the cause of the problem in the first place is not being adequately addressed.

Organizations have not recognized that the installation of sophisticated computer systems has substantially altered the traditional organizational structure. This has resulted in numerous breakdowns in the traditional management control systems primarily because of an absence of assigned responsibilities for control of computer systems. This problem of organizational structure obsolescence should be studied and dealt with in three different but related ways.

1. Attempt to define new acceptable organizational structures which reestablish the more traditional vertical lines of authority and responsibility by reaching out in unique ways to reconfine the horizontal integration of function that results from sophisticated computer systems.

2. Redefine the organization structure within the data processing group to establish a separate quality assurance activity which is held responsible for the control of the quality of the computer product and which, appropriate design, will also strengthen the overall management control of the function by improving the segregation of duties within the EDP organization.

3. Reinforce the essential mandate of the auditing profession, which is objectivity through independence.

WORKING RELATIONSHIPS WITH INTERNAL AUDITORS

Quality assurance and internal audit have different but overlapping functions. It is in the best interest of both groups to coordinate their efforts to avoid overlap. Internal audit is primarily concerned with the system of internal control that assures accurate and complete processing of financial transactions. They're also interested in protecting the assets of the organization, which includes the proper use of assets. While quality assurance is concerned with the financial accuracy of data, its concern is limited to processing within the computerized application. This perspective is considerably different that that of internal audit.

In an application review, the quality assurance responsibility is much broader than that of internal audit. Some organizations have had an internal auditor participate as a member of the quality assurance review team. In this capacity, the internal auditor can concentrate on the adequacy of internal control to assure accuracy and completeness of processing financial data. In a review in which the internal auditor does not participate, the quality assurance group may wish to get a checklist from the internal auditors to be used in reviewing the control aspect of the application system.

Internal auditing and quality assurance use many of the same practices in performing their respective functions. One group can learn from the experiences and techniques of the other. It may be advisable to hold joint meetings where the practices and problems of each can be openly discussed. This sharing of experiences will also promote a better working relationship between the groups.

Organizations having both a quality assurance group and internal audit department have developed practices which help their joint working relationship. These practices are in the following areas:

1. Working with auditors to perform the audit function
2. Using auditors on the quality assurance review team
3. Reliance by auditors on QA reviews
4. Cross-training
5. Exchange of reports
6. Internal audit support of quality assurance

The discussion of these experiences provided below should prove helpful in building good working relationships with internal auditors.

Working with Auditors to Perform the Audit Function

Many audits in the data processing department are conducted by auditors with minimal data processing experience. Obtaining internal auditors with sufficient data processing experience has been a major problem for internal audit departments. Recently internal audit departments have been using large numbers of data processing professionals in auditing. This has proven to be a stopgap measure and is not regarded as a long-term solution to the problem.

Quality assurance personnel have an objective outlook on the data processing function. This outlook makes them candidates to assist internal auditors in fulfilling their internal audit function. Internal audit assignments include audits of specific applications, developing extract programs to obtain data for audit purposes, participation in systems design, audits of security, and audits of the data center. Auditors frequently desire to have some party other than the one being audited to discuss some of the technical data processing problems. Quality assurance personnel can fill this need.

Quality assurance should initiate a policy to "Take an auditor to lunch." This provides an informal opportunity to discuss mutual problems and alternative solutions.

Using Auditors on the Quality Assurance Review Team

Many internal audit groups are involved in reviewing the systems during the development phase. Current internal auditing literature is strongly recommending audit involvement during systems development. This is based on the premise that if controls are not built in during the developmental phase the cost to add them after the system is live may be prohibitive. Thus, internal audit's involvement becomes a matter of economics, as well as control evaluation.

There are no standards of control in the data processing industry. Control of each computer application must be handcrafted. Some organizations have general guidelines, but very few state specific programming control standards. Without control standards, many internal audit groups spend much of their time working with data processing personnel to build controls into data processing applications. Most data processing people do not understand control from an accounting viewpoint and, therefore, much of the internal auditor's time must be spent on persuasion and instruction.

It may be advisable to have the internal auditor participate as a member of the quality assurance review group rather than have a project team work separately with both the internal audit group and the quality assurance group. Because the internal auditors must maintain an independent attitude, they cannot work under the direction of a quality assurance review team leader. However, it is reasonable to expect an internal auditor to work very closely with the QA team during a review.

When participating on the quality assurance team, the internal auditor will still need to prepare an independent report. This report may be attached to the quality assurance group's report, or it might be incorporated into the quality assurance report. Regardless of the method of distribution, the audit report will probably be seen by the same people who receive the quality assurance report.

Reliance by Auditors on QA Reviews

Quality assurance reviews properly performed can be used by internal auditors in the performance of their work. By relying on quality assurance, audit costs can be reduced two ways. First, there is the elimination of duplication of work by having two groups performing the same review. Second, quality assurance personnel will probably be more proficient in the data processing than the average internal auditor and, therefore, can perform the review more efficiently.

Internal auditors will tend to rely more on the work of quality assurance when the quality assurance review procedures are formalized. The use of a quality assurance approach similar to that outlined in Chapters 7, 8, and 9 gives the proper assurance to internal auditing that an adequate review has been performed. A standardized approach, plus good working relationships with internal auditors, will enable internal auditing to reduce their effort in review systems under development. This reduction may also be extended to external audit costs as they, too, may rely on the quality assurance group.

Cross-Training

One of the dilemmas facing both quality assurance and internal audit is how to keep the members of their department current on technological developments. In addition, the problem of maintaining proficiency in data processing poses another problem. Cross-training the two groups can be helpful in staying current technically and in maintaining the proficiency of personnel in both groups.

Cross-training of the groups can be conducted in one of the

following manners:

1. Assign a quality assurance member to work with auditing during one or more audits.
2. Assign an internal auditor to work with quality assurance during one or more reviews.
3. Hold joint meetings to discuss practices and problems.
4. Conduct joint training sessions for members of both groups.
5. Both groups participate in data processing training sessions.
6. Members of either group attend professional seminars and conferences and the report back to both groups.

Exchange of Reports

Quality assurance should make all its reports available to internal audit excluding from this distribution only special reports that deal with individual performance as distinct from the review of an application system. By receiving the quality assurance reports regularly, internal audit will be more willing to rely on the quality assurance work. This will help reduce audit costs.

Conversely, internal audit should make available to quality assurance reports and workpapers relating to applications under review. For example, if quality assurance is reviewing a new payroll system, workpapers of the internal audit department for the past few audits of payroll could prove very beneficial. As with the QA reports dealing with personnel performance, it may be necessary for internal audit to do some screening of confidential data in audit reports and workpapers, but most of the data should be accessible to QA personnel. If internal audit does not offer quality assurance its workpapers, QA should ask for them.

Internal Audit Support of Quality Assurance

Quality assurance is one of the best methods of assuring adequately controlled data processing applications, and most internal audit departments will support establishing the function. Quality assurance not only makes the internal audit function in data processing easier, but adds control that would not be possible with internal audits alone.

The data processing departments should solicit the support of the internal audit function regarding quality assurance. Strong recommendations by internal audit to executive manage ment urging the formation of the group, strengthening the group, expanding the scope and responsibility of the group, and urging more independence within the data processing department for the group, are all supportive of effective quality assurance. The concept of "taking an internal auditor to lunch" may do more for quality assurance than any other single use of a lunch hour.

SUMMARY

It is advantageous to both internal audit and quality assurance to develop a good working relationship. Quality assurance personnel can help internal auditors perform their function. Internal auditors can participate in quality assurance reviews. They should work with each other to cross-fertilize practices and experiences. Quality assurance personnel should have access to internal audit workpapers and reports, where practical, to assist them in reviewing an application. The background information provided in the internal audit workpapers can prove very helpful in conducting quality assurance reviews.

Quality assurance and internal audit personnel can help each other with training. Training can be done by having personnel of one group participate in the work of another. There can be joint training sessions. Also, the exchange of reports and other information is a training mechanism.

Internal audit support of quality assurance can be very helpful in promoting quality assurance in an organization. It is advantageous to both groups to work for a strong quality assurance group. The quality assurance group, by performing its function diligently, can reduce audit effort and costs. Auditors should be able to reduce the number of data processing reviews conducted for systems under development by relying on the work of the quality assurance group.

APPENDIXES

Appendix A
SAMPLE QUALITY
ASSURANCE MANUAL

Included in this appendix is a manual developed and used by a quality assurance group in a large organization. The QA group had been in existence for about two years when they developed this manual. The material comes from their actual review experiences and was developed by the manager of the QA group. Note that most of the material in this manual is quality control (i.e., an application system review process).

The text of this book discusses the reasons for establishing QA, how to establish it, areas to be reviewed by quality assurance, and methods of conducting those reviews. The scope of the book is broad and covers all the functions that are attributable to a mature QA group. In actual practice, there is probably no group whose scope is as broad as to encompass all the areas covered in this book. For this reason, it is felt that a "real-world" example would be helpful to organizations contemplating establishing a QA function.

The manual included in this appendix should be used as a guide to developing a manual for your organization. The topics included in the manual are those which need to be addressed. A major factor in the success of QA is performing consistent reviews. Manuals offer the standardized procedures which help ensure that the consistency of reviews is maintained. Also, the existence of a review manual will show project leaders the level of performance expected by their management.

Organization's Computer Philosophy

The organization which contributed this manual uses a structured approach to system design. The process begins with the examination of the general business problem. The philosophy of

433

organization is that they solve business problems; their goal is not to develop computer systems. The solution to the business problem may or may not result in development of a computer application.   Each step is completed and reviewed with management approval obtained prior to going to the next phase in the systems development life cycle.   Management then allocates resources sufficient to complete the phase of the systems development life cycle and then reviews progress again. In such an environment, QA is a very valuable aid to management in making this phase-by-phase evaluation.

The organization is an IBM shop, using IBM hardware and software. The programming languages used are primarily COBOL and PL/1. Throughout the manual there will be references to these languages, as well as IBM software products. The abbreviations used throughout the manual (e.g., ISAM, DDNAME, etc.) are terms associated with the IBM operating system and its associated program products including compilers. These IBM terms are not defined in the appendix.

Abbreviations Used

MSP — Management Systems and Programming Department: The department responsible for all systems designs and programming.
BSD — Business System Design: Those aspects of system design that relate to solving the business problem.
CSD — Computer System Design: Those aspects of design work that relate to the development of the computer system.
QA — Quality Assurance: Abbreviation for quality assurance.
SAPP — Systems and programming Practices: The data processing department manual that includes system design and programming standards.
SDM — System Development Methodology: The step-by-step approach used by the organization during the systems development life cycle to develop new applications.

Quality Assurance Philosophy

The QA group that developed this manual was established primarily to verify compliance to the system development methodology and systems and programming procedures for the Management Systems and Programming Department of the organization. All questions included in the manual were reviewed by the management of the Management Systems and Programming Department. The questions have been judged by management to the fair questions. The systems analysts and programmers in the Management Systems and Programming Department have access to this manual. The general philosophy of the QA group is to be helpful to the systems analysts and programmers in fulfilling their function, while at the same time reviewing compliance to the systems and programming procedures.

How the Manual Is Used

Each question of the manual is cross-referenced to a paragraph or section within the Management Systems and Programming Department's system and programming procedural manual and system development methodology manuals. The development of the manual required a thorough review of all Management Systems and Programming Department procedures. quality assurance helps assure the level of quality specified by the management of the Management Systems and Programming Department.

QUALITY ASSURANCE MANUAL

CONTENTS

I.   INTRODUCTION

A.   Purpose
      The purpose of the Quality Assurance Program (QA) is to
      provide MSP management with another tool to assure that
      systems comply with existing MSP standards and guide-
      lines.

B.   Assumptions
      The Quality Assurance program will establish formal QA
      reviews to be conducted subsequent to these discrete phases
      of SDM:
      -    Feasibility Study
      -    Business System Design
      -    Computer System Design
      -    Programming
      -    Installation

      The tuned versions of the SDM phase being reviewed would
      be the standard against which the review would be made.

      Projects would not be delayed entering a subsequent phase
      pending the results of a QA review of the prior phase.

      The QA function will be a separate activity within MSP, re-
      porting to the manager of the support group.

      The checklists for each phase must represent a consensus of
      views and be acceptable to all functional areas prior to their
      inclusion in the program.

C.   Quality Assurance — Philosophy
      1.   Manufacturing and Other Disciplines
           Within Manufacturing as well as within other environ-
           ments, the quality assurance of products has been con-
           sidered a proper and normal procedure. It is commonly
           referred to as quality or production control. Products
           are tested in toto or by using statistical acceptance sam-
           pling techniques to measure performance to specifica-
           tions.

      2.   MS Functions
           MS functions can be compared to manufacturing and
           other disciplines in that products (systems) are pro-

duced. Since systems are developed according to established standards and procedures, the role of quality assurance within MS becomes analogous to that of QA for manufacturing, namely assuring that the systems (products) produced have adhered to these standards and guidelines.

D.   Benefits

The QA Function would yield benefits to MSP as follows:

- Provide management with a mechanism that will monitor adherence to existing standards and procedures.
- Ensure a uniform approach to phase reviews.
- Assure resolution of differences of interpretation by providing for more than one review.

II.   SUMMARY

In order to begin the Quality Assurance Program within MSP, the following tasks have been approved for implementation after reviews with management and/or their representatives from each functional area:

- The scope, objectives, and constraints fo the QA program as it will be implemented.
- QA review and evaluation procedures.
- Project selection procedures.
- Checklists for the BSD, CSD, and programming phases of SDM.
- Feasibility and installation.

The Quality Assurance Team will include:
- QA project leader (from MSP Support).
- Analysts from each functional area who will not be permanent team members at this time.

The mechanics of the QA review and evaluation procedure are described in detail in Chapter IV.

Checklists will be used for all reviews and they have been geared to those tasks and activities within a particular SDM phase. Provision has been made to indicate to the QA team any task or activity for the phase that was not addressed by the project team.

III. MSP QUALITY ASSURANCE PROGRAM (QA) SCOPE,
      OBJECTIVES, CONSTRAINTS

A. Introduction
    The purpose of this write-up is to outline the MSP Quality
    Assurance (QA) program that will be established within
    MSP. The program provides MSP management with control
    information regarding adherence to established standards
    and guidelines for project development work within MSP.

B. Scope
    1. The Quality Assurance Program would be applicable to
        all projects being developed within MSP.
    2. The Quality Assurance Program will be structured ac-
        cording to various phases of the established systems de-
        velopment methodology (SDM).

C. Objectives
    1. To establish a Quality Assurance Program for MSP
        compatible with the aims and goals of the department
        using current standards and guidelines.
    2. Develop a core of analysts capable of performing QA re-
        views across a wide range of systems.
    3. To assure that all projects which are budgeted over a
        stipulated amount, which impact profit or which in-
        volve a substantial risk factor are subject to Quality
        Assurance Review. In addition, to make sure that pro-
        jects not included in the preceding groupings would be
        subject to a QA review.

D. Constraints
    1. Projects will not require a QA signoff in order to proceed
        to the next stage of development.
    2. QA team personnel (other than the QA project leader
        from the Support Group) will not be permanently as-
        signed to the QA function.

IV. QA REVIEW AND EVALUATION PROCEDURE

A. Purposes
    To establish guidelines and procedures to govern the con-
    duct of Quality Assurance Reviews during various discrete
    phases of the system development cycle.

B. Definition
    A Quality Assurance Review is, by definition, a periodic and

systematic review of system development efforts and their products to determine the adherence to existing standards or guidelines in use within the MSP community.

C.   Objective
The aim of the Quality Assurance Review is to assure that the system is being developed according to established policies, procedures, and standards.

D.   Scope
This procedure applies to selected system development efforts across the spectrum of MSP. Quality Assurance may be done on any project selected as a result of the Project Selection Procedure.

E.   Responsibilities
  1.   Functional Area
Each functional area has the primary responsibility for the quality of its systems.
  2.   Management — MSP
The manager of MSP has overall responsibility (using QA as a tool for assuring that existing standards have been adhered to during the development of systems by each functional area).
  3.   The manager of MSP Support has staff responsibility for the Quality Assurance Program as well as the Quality Assurance Reviews.

F.   Concept
Quality Assurance is founded on the principle that a peer review of a project based upon agreed standards or guidelines will lead to a better product. It is not to be construed as a restrictive procedure or an attempt to direct department efforts. Quality Assurance should be approached with a spirit of assistance relying ultimately upon close cooperation and mutual professional confidence.

G.   Procedure

Responsibility	*Action*
QA Project Leader (Group Support)	1. Under the Direction of Manager of MSP Support:
	a. Develop and maintain sets of Quality Assurance checklists suitable for various systems

	and geared to discrete phases of systems development.
	2. Provide copies of checklists to the MSQ QA team as directed by the Manager of MSP support.
Manager MSP Support	1. Notifies Functional Managers of a scheduled Quality Assurance Review for a particular SDM phase and indicates the documentation required for the Quality Assurance Review Team.
Functional Manager	1. Acknowledges the notification of the QA Review; may suggest different date.
	2. Provides the required documentation and indicates any tasks and/or activities within tasks that have not been included and sends the requisite number of copies to the QA Project Leader.
QA Project Leader (Support Group)	1. Sets up and maintains QA project file.
	2. Notifies members of the QA review team that a review has been scheduled and distributes the phase documentation to each team member.
	3. Schedules each QA review meeting.
QA Team	1. Individually review phase documentation using the appropriate checklist. (The checklist may have been modified depending upon whether all tasks and activities are to be reviewed.)
	2. In session, prepare the first version of the QA Evaluation Form(s).
QA Project Leader (Support Leader)	Schedules the second QA review to be held jointly with the project team.

QA Team Review	1. Discuss and review the QA evaluation with the project team.
	2. Complete and distribute Quality Review Evaluation Form(s) for the phase reviewed to the Functional Department. The Evaluation Form(s) are cross-referenced to the QA phase checklist.
QA Project Leader	If required, informs Functional Manager and schedules the third and final QA review. Attendees would be the QA Team, the project team members, and the Functional Manager.
QA Team, Project Team, Function Manager	Discuss, review, and resolve outstanding items from the evaluation forms.
QA Project Leader	1. Prepares final version of the QA Evaluation Form(s).
	2. Prepares a QA report to management summarizing the findings of the review.
	3. Places all forms and reports in the QA project file.

V. QUALITY ASSURANCE: PROJECT SELECTION

The purpose of this phase is to set forth the criteria that will be used for selection of projects for QA review. In addition, a proposed procedure stating the mechanics is included for your consideration. Also included is a definition of the principles that would be considered standard for QA purposes.

A. Criteria
1. Effect on Financial Results

Definition:
Those projects which by their nature impact the financial results of the corporation. These would include such projects as modeling, cost minimization, profit maximization, allocation of raw materials, facilities planning, and inventory, among others.

2. Exposure to Fraud

    Definition:
    Those projects which by their classification are prone to
    fraud. These would encompass such projects as accounts
    payable, general ledger, purchasing payroll, petty cash,
    as well as some other peripheral applications.

3. Scope of the System

    Definition:
    Those projects which, because of their cost or by virtue
    of interfacing with or impacting many other systems,
    can be defined as being large in scope.

4. Risk to the Company

    Definition:
    Those projects which influence decisions regarding
    large capital expenditures or because of the confidential
    nature of the data may require unique security consid-
    erations.

5. Impact on Future Systems

    Definition:
    Those projects that because they utilize new technology
    (Data Base Management Systems) may affect the design
    considerations of others which may interface with
    them.   In addition, projects using "Improved
    Programming Techniques" (LPT's) would be in this cate-
    gory since they would influence other systems being de-
    veloped.

6. Workload of the QA Team

    Because of the large number of systems being developed,
    modified, and expanded throughout MSP, coupled with
    the fact that the QA team will only have one permanent
    full-time member, these criteria should be evaluated on
    a prioritized basis.

B. Proposed Selection Procedures

1. Priorities
    Following for your consideration is the suggested rank-
    ing of priorities for project selection in descending se-
    quence of priority.

a. Effect on Financial Results
b. Exposure to Fraud
c. Scope of System
d. Risk to Company
e. Impact on Future Systems

2. Procedure

Person(s) Responsible   *Action Required*

Person(s) Responsible	Action Required
MGR, MSP Support and QA Team Leader	1. Review projects from various Functional Areas and based upon the priorities established select a project for Quality Assurance Review.
QA Team Leader	2. Inform Functional Manager of the project and SDM phase to be reviewed.
	3. Inform Project Manager of the QA review and the SDM phase to be reviewed.
	4. Inform the rotating members of the QA team of the project and SDM phase to be reviewed.
	5. Set up a QA file for the project.
Project Manager	6. Acknowledge notification of QA review notification and set up QA file for the project.

VI. PHASE DESCRIPTIONS

A. Feasibility Study
   The intent of a Feasibility Study is to determine whether or not a solution or set of solutions can be applied to solve a business problem or to enhance an opportunity. In order to accomplish this, the following objectives should be pursued.
   1. Identify solution alternatives considering business, operational, environmental, technical, and economic factors including costs.
   2. Recommend a best alternative.
   3. A clear definition or statement of the business problem and/or opportunity.
   4. A description of the current system.

5. A clear statement regarding the viability of the solution(s) in light of the factors mentioned previously.

The primary and singularly most important deliverable of the Feasibility Study is the final report with supporting detail that would be used by management to decide whether or not to make the commitments required to proceed to the next phase.

B.   Business System Design
     The objectives of the Business System Design phase are to:
     1. Furnish the user with a comprehensive functional description the system proposed to solve the business problem or enhance the business opportunity. It should describe the components to be performed either by clerical or automated processes.
     2. Provide a basis for orderly development of a technical solution by defining the requirements for the resolution.
     3. Develop a test strategy which will assure that the requirements of the system can be met.
     4. Provide reasonable assurance that the solution can be developed and put into operation.
     5. Distill the financial analysis and time projections to a level where they can be construed as firm for the duration of the project.

C.   Computer System Design
     The aim of the Computer System Design is to translate the set of requirements put forth in the BSD into a computer system which satisfies those requirements.
     The key objectives of the Computer System Design are to:
     1. Develop the physical files (and/or data base records).
     2. Develop the set of programs to process the data to produce the output.
     3. Develop the specifications for the programs by showing what each has to accomplish rather than how to achieve that.

D.   Programming
     The computer system defined and subsequently designed during the Computer System and Program Design phases is programmed according to specific test plans during this phase.

NOTIFICATION OF QUALITY ASSURANCE REVIEW

To: _____ From: _____ Date: _____

Project Name: _____

Project Mgr./Leader: _____

An: _____ Review has been scheduled:

The review is scheduled tentatively for Date: _____ Time: _____

Room #: _____

Indicate here a more convenient date if required: _____

Please send a copy of the phase document to _____ MSP Support

Indicate tasks and activities omitted by three-digit SDM Reference #:

_____

Please return this form (or copy) to the manager of MSP Support:

MSP representatives assigned to the Quality Assurance Review Team for this project:

Team Member	*Extension*
_____	_____
_____	_____
_____	_____
_____	_____
_____	_____

Mgr. MSP Support: _____ Date: _____

_____

_____

_____

QUALITY ASSURANCE REVIEW
NOTIFICATION TO PROJECT TEAM

To: _____ From: _____ Date: _____

Project Name: _____

Project Mgr./Leader: _____

A Quality Assurance Review for the: _____

Phase of this project has been completed _____

The project team review is scheduled for: _____

Indicate here a more convenient date if required: _____

Please assign project team member(s) to take part:

QA Team, Member(s)	Ext.	Project Team Member(s)	Ext.
_____	_____	_____	_____
_____	_____	_____	_____
_____	_____	_____	_____
_____	_____	_____	_____
_____	_____	_____	_____
_____	_____	_____	_____
_____	_____	_____	_____

Mgr. MSP Support: _____ Date: _____

_____

_____

_____

MSP QUALITY ASSURANCE REVIEW
EVALUATION FORM

Project Name: _____   QA Review #: _____

Project #: _____   QA Proj. Ldr.: _____

Functional area: _____

Development Phase: _____

Checklist reference #: _____ QA Comment/Analysis: _____

_____

_____

Date prepared: _____

_____

_____

_____

_____

Recommendation: _____

_____

_____

_____

_____

Date prepared: _____

_____

Response: _____

_____

Date: _____

E.   Installation
      The purpose of this phase is to shift the system from test to
      production mode in the user and operations areas. Some of
      the objectives are:
      1. Where necessary, transform files and implement user
          operating procedures.
      2. Conduct user and Computer Operations acceptance tests
          and analyze the results.
      3. Ensure that user and operations documentation has
          been reviewed and update, if appropriate.

VII.   BUSINESS SYSTEM DESIGN CHECKLIST

	YES	NO	N/A	REF. #
Systems Overview:				
1. Is there a brief description of interfaces with other systems?				
2. Is there an outline of the major functional requirements of the system?				
3. Are the major functions defined into discrete steps with no boundary overlapping?				
4. Have manual and automatic steps been defined?				
5. Has the definition of what data is required to perform each step been indicated of how the data is obtained?				
System Descriptions:				
6. Has a system structure chart been developed, showing the logical breakdown into subsystems and interfaces with other systems?				

	YES	NO	N/A	REF. #

7. Have the major inputs and outputs been defined as well as the functional processing required to produce the output?

8. Is there a narrative description of the major functions of the system?

9. Have subsystem functional flow diagrams been developed showing the inputs, processing, and outputs relevant to the subsystem?

10. Has a subsystem narrative description been developed?

11. Do the functional outlines follow the logical structure of the system?

12. Are they hierarchical in nature, that is, by function and by steps within function?

13. Has the data been grouped into logical categories (i.e. customer product, accounting, marketing, sales, etc.)?

Design Input and Output Data:

Data Structure:

14. Has the data been categorized as follows:
   a. Static
   b. Historical data likely to be changes
   c. Transaction related?

	YES	NO	N/A	REF. #
15. Have standard data names (if possible) been used?				
16. Has the hierarchical relationship among data elements been defined and described?				

Design Output Documents:

	YES	NO	N/A	REF. #
17. Are there headings?				
18. Do the headings include report titles, department, date, page, number, etc.?				
19. Are the output dates, system identification, titles and page numbers shown?				
20. Are processing dates, system identification, titles and page numbers shown?				
21. Has consideration been given to COM or other output devices?				
22. Is each data column identified?				
23. Where subtotals are produced (e.g. product within customer) are they labeled by control break?				
24. Are the date elements clearly indicated?				
25. Has the source of the data been defined (department and individual)?				
26. Have input requirements been documented?				

	YES	NO	N/A	REF. #

27. Is the purpose of the input document clear (e.g., enter orders, process salary action)?

28. Is the sequence (if applicable) indicated?

Design Computer Processing:

29. Has each function been described using functional terminology (e.g., if salary exceeds maximum, print message)?

30. Has validity checking been defined with reference to the Data Element Dictionary?

31. In cases where the same data may be coming from several sources, have the sources been identified as to priorities for selection by the system?

32. Has processing been classified according to type of function (e.g., transaction, calculation, editing etc.)?

Define Non-Computer Processing:

33. Has the preparation of input been described?

34. Has the distribution of output been described?

35. Has an error correction procedure been described?

36. Have organizational controls been established?

	YES	NO	N/A	REF. #

37. Have controls been established across department lines?

38. Have the control fields been designed?

39. Are there control validation procedures prior to proceeding to the next step?

Overall System Controls:

40. Have controls been designed to reconcile data received by the computer center?

41. Have controls for error correction and re-entry been designed?

42. Have controls been designed that can be reconciled to those of another system (e.g., accounting transactions whose various categories should equal General Ledger totals)?

Input Controls:

43. Have some or all of the following criteria been used for establishing input controls?
    a. Sequence numbering
    b. Prepunched cards
    c. Turnaround documents
    d. Batch numbering
    e. By type of input
    f. Predetermined totals
    g. Self-checking numbers
    h. Field length checks
    i. Limit checks
    j. Reasonability checks

	YES	NO	N/A	REF. #

    k. Existence/nonexistence
        checks

Processing Controls:

44. Do controls and totals exist
     for:
     a. Each value column
     b. Where appropriate, cross-
         foot totals
     c. Counts of input trans-
         actions, errors, accepted
         transactions
     d. Input transactions, old
         master, new master?

45. Are the results of all updates
     listed for each transaction
     showing the before and
     after condition?

46. As the result of an update are
     the number of adds, deletes,
     and changes processed shown?

47. If relationship tests have
     been used, are the grouped
     and defined?

48. If used, have control total
     records been utilized to
     verify that all records have
     been processed between runs?

Output Controls:

49. Have output controls been
     established for all control
     fields?

50. Is there a separate output
     control on errors rejected
     by the system?

	YES	NO	N/A	REF. #

BSD System Test Plan:

51. Have acceptance criteria (user-defined conditions) been identified?

52. Has a tentative User Acceptance Strategy been identified?

53. Have test data requirements been defined?

Complete BSD:

54. Have Data Element Dictionary forms been completed?

55. Have organizational changes been defined (if required)?

56. Have new organization charts or new positions been required?

57. If required, have areas for special user procedures been identified?

58. Has a timetable for operating the system been developed?

59. Were separate timetables developed for different cycles (weekly, monthly)?

60. Has the documentation been gathered and organized?

Evaluate BSD:

61. Has a financial analysis been performed?

62. Have the scope, objectives and constraints for the CSD been developed?

	YES	NO	N/A	REF. #

63. Has a plan for CSD, user pro-
    cedures, and conversion
    phases been completed?

64. Has the plan been broken
    down into approximate "work
    units" (days) to serve as a
    basis for a schedule for
    the other phases?

65. Have the resources and res-
    ponsibilities been arranged
    (who is doing what?)?

66. Have schedules been pre-
    pared for the next phases?

67. Have appropriate budgets
    for the next phases been
    prepared?

68. Has a project authorization
    been properly prepared for
    remaining phases?

VIII. COMPUTER SYSTEMS DESIGN
    (CSD) CHECKLIST

Develop Outline Design:

1. Has a detailed review of the
   BSD resulted in requiring
   additional information or
   changes?

2. Have revisions been reviewed
   by the analyst (BSD) and the
   user and used to update the
   BSD or the CSD?

3. Have existing sources of data
   been identified?

	YES	NO	N/A	REF. #

4. Has a data management alternative been considered because of the nature of the system?

5. Have the data elements been grouped by category of data?

6. Have the record layout forms been used for listing the data elements?

7. Has the file description form been used to show the characteristics of each file?

8. Have the access methods been determined?

9. Has use been made of blocking factors to reduce access for a sequential file?

10. If a data base has been used, has the relationship between segments (views of the data base) been included?

11. If new data elements have been required, have they been included as part of the data dictionary?

12. Has the description of processing (BSD) been translated into system flowcharts showing programs and their relationships as well as reports?

13. Has the processing been isolated by frequency as well as function?

	YES	NO	N/A	REF. #

14. Does each file requiring updating have an associated unique transaction file?

15. Does each main file have a separate validation and update function?

16. Have the following been addressed in order to reduce excessive passing of files:
    a. Sort verbs (statements)
    b. Input procedure
    c. Output procedure
    d. Random updating?

17. Has a matrix been prepared showing which programs create, access, and update each file?

18. Has a separate program section been set up for each program in the system showing:
    a. Cover page showing the program name, systems and/or subsystem name, run number, and a brief description of the program
    b. Input/Output diagram
    c. processing description?

19. Does the processing description contain a brief outline of the processing that the program is going to perform?

20. Has the content and format of each output been defined?

	YES	NO	N/A	REF. #

21. Conversely, has the same been completed for each input?

22. Have data items been checked out to the rules specified in the data dictionary?

23. Have transactions that update master files been assigned record types?

24. For multirecord transactions have the following been done:
    a. Identifying the record types that define the records comprising one transaction
    b. Developing a sequence number if required
    c. Defining mandatory and optional records?

Hardware/Software Configuration:

25. Has the hardware configuration been defined showing:
    a. CPU
    b. Minimum Core Storage
    c. Number and type of peripherals
    d. Special Hardware
    e. Numbers of tapes and/or disk packs
    f. Terminals, minicomputers, microfilm, microfiche, optical scanning, etc.?

26. Has the software been defined specifically:
    a. Operating system

	YES	NO	N/A	REF. #

26. b. Telecommunications (CICS, TSO, etc.)

27. If telecommunications equipment is involved, has a communications analyst been consulted regarding type, number, speed, etc.?

File Conversion Computer System:

28. If applicable, have the file conversion requirements been specified (task 10.2 in BSD)?

29. If required, have program specifications for the file conversion programs been completed?

30. If applicable, can the main program(s) be utilized to perform the file conversion?

31. Has a schedule been established?

Design System Tests:

32. Has the user's role for testing been defined, namely:
    a. Has the user described what he expects from the system output?
    b. Has the user agreed to provide system test data and to check system output?

33. Have responsibilities and schedules for preparing test data been agreed to by the user?

	YES	NO	N/A	REF. #

34. Has the input medium been agreed to (cards, on-line entry, other)?

35. Is special hardware/software required, and if so, will programmers and/or users require additional training?

36. Have turnaround requirements been defined?

37. Have testing priorities been established?

38. If an on-line system, has an investigation of required space as opposed to available space been made?

39. Has an analysis of the impact upon interfacing systems been made and have arrangements been made for acquiring required information and data?

Design System Test:

40. Have testing control procedures been established (logs, tapes, disks, etc.)?

41. Has the possibility of utilizing existing code (prewritten subroutines) been investigated?

42. Has a System Test Plan been prepared consisting of a description of each run (program or a number or programs) to be made and specifically does each show:
    a. Test run identification

	YES	NO	N/A	REF. #

42. b. Test run description (program/job title)

    c. Programs and utilities required for the test

    d. Dependencies (runs which must be completed prior to testing)

    e. Inputs and their sources

    f. Outputs: content and destination

    g. List of conditions to be tested (e.g., validation rules)

43. Has the user prepared the system test data ad defined by the conditions to be tested in the System Test Plan?

44. Has Computer Operations been consulted regarding key-punching and/or verification?

Revise and Complete Design:

45. Have all required forms from previous phases as well as previous tasks/ activities in this phase been completed?

46. Has the processing description for program specifications been categorized by function (e.g., validation, error handling, reports, updating end of file)?

47. For validation routines have the editing rules been specified for:

	YES	NO	N/A	REF. #

47. a. Field format and content
        (data element descrip-
        ions)
     b. Interfield relationships
     c. Intrafield relationships
     d. Interrecord relationships
     e. Sequence
     f. Duplicates
     g. Control reconciliation

48. Have the rejection criteria
     been indicated for each type
     of error situation, as fol-
     lows:
     a. Warning message but
         transaction is accepted
     b. Use of the default value
     c. Outright rejection of re-
         cord within a transac-
         tion set
     d. Rejection of an entire
         transaction
     e. Rejection of a batch of
         transactions
     f. Program abort

49. Have the following valid-
     ation techniques been in-
     cluded in the specifica-
     tions:
     a. Validation of entire
         transaction before any
         processing
     b. Validation to continue
         regardless of the number
         of errors on the trans-
         action unless a run
         abort occurs
     c. Provide information re-
         garding an error so the

	YES	NO	N/A	REF. #

user can identify the source and determine the cause?

Revise and Complete Design:

50. If applicable, has a procedure been developed for correction of rejected input either by deletion, reversal or re-entry?

51. Do the specifications for each report (output) define:
    a. The origin of each time including the rules for the selection of optional items
    b. The rules of governing calculations
    c. The rules for printing and/ or print suppression?

52. Have the following been defined for each intermediate (work) file:
    a. Origins or alternative origins for each element
    b. Calculations
    c. Rules governing record types, sequence, optional records as well as inter and intra-record relationships?

53. Have the following audit controls been built in where applicable:
    a. Record counts (in and out)
    b. Editing of all source input
    c. Has totals on selected fields

	YES	NO	N/A	REF. #

53.　d.　Sequence checking of input files
　　e.　Date checking
　　f.　Listing of errors and review
　　g.　Control records?

Determine Tentative Operational Requirements:

54.　Has the impact of the system upon existing computer resources been evaluated?

55.　Have the computer processing requirements been discussed with Computer Operations (e.g., volumes, timeframes, turnaround, etc.)?

56.　Have backup procedures been developed?

On-Line Systems:

57.　Have testing plans been discussed with Computer Operations to ensure that required resources (core, disk space) for "sessions" will be available?

58.　Have terminal types been discussed with appropriate Technical Support personnel?

59.　Have IMS considerations (if applicable) been coordinated with Computer Operations. Technical Support and DBA representatives?

60.　Has a user training program been developed?

	YES	NO	N/A	REF. #

61. Have run schedules been prepared to provide Computer Operations with the basic information necessary to schedule compute usage?

62. Have run flowcharts including narrative (where required) been prepared?

63. Have "first cut" estimates of region sizes, run times (using SAPP 15.02.13) etc. been provided on the flowcharts or some other documentation?

64. Has the following information been shown for either input or output tapes and disks:
   a. DDNAME, DSNAME, LABEL, UNIT, DCB, RECFM, BLKSIZE, DISP, RETPD, estimated volumes of records, concatenation, source, destination

On-Line Systems:

   b. In addition to the above, for disk files:
      1. Input, output or input/output
      2. Space (number of blocks)

65. Where appropriate, have restart procedures been described for each step of the job?

	YES	NO	N/A	REF. #

66. If appropriate, have restart procedures been appended to the Security and Backup section of the CSD documentation?

Plan Program Design:

67. Has all relevant documentation for each program been gathered?

68. Has the sequence in which programs are to be developed been defined in accordance to the System Test Plan?

69. Has the number of user and personnel (including outside vendors) required been ascertained?

70. Has computer time required for program testing (compiles, test runs) been established?

71. Have data preparation requirements been discussed with Computer Operations regarding data entry?

72. Has a development cost worksheet been prepared for the next phase or phases?

73. Have personnel been assigned and project work schedules been prepared?

74. Has the project schedule and budget been reviewed and updated if required?

	YES	NO	N/A	REF. #

Prepared Project Authorization:

75. If required, has a Project Authorization Form been com-
pleted?

IX. PROGRAMMING CHECKLIST

A. COBOL Checklist

General Principles:
1. Does the program accomplish
everything specified in the
acceptance criteria?

2. It is maintainable, i.e.,:
a. It is clearly written
b. Is it formatted according to standards
c. Does each procedure/
paragraph contain
comments regarding
function and purpose?

Identification Division:

3. Have the following standards
been incorporated into the
program:
a. Program identification
using the Panvalet nam-
ing standard
b. Has the name(s) been
entered for AUTHOR
c. Has the data upon which
coding commenced been
entered for date written?

4. Are there remarks to indicate:
a. Function of the program
b. The name of the system
of which it is a member

	YES	NO	N/A	REF. #

    c. Date and author of any revisions?

Environment Division:

5. Do the source and object computer statements state the model number of any computer?

6. Has the IBM-370 been specified for the object computer?

7. For the Input/Output section have the following been adhered to:
    a. Does the DDNAME used in the SELECT clause adhere to standards set forth in SAPP Data Dictionary Procedures?

8. For class:
    a. Has UT been used for all QSAM data sets?
    b. Has DA been used for only ISAM/VSAM and BDAM?
    c. Has UR been used?

9. Has the use of RESERVE NO ALTERNATIVE AREAS been eliminated?

10. Has the APPLY WRITE-ONLY clause been used for variable mode files that use standard sequential organization?

	YES	NO	N/A	REF. #

11. Has APPLY CORE-IN-DEX clause been used for ISAM/VSAM files accessed randomly?

Data Division — General:

12. Do all record names begin with an 01 level?

13. Do all subsequent record fields begin with 05 and are they in turn incremented by factors of 05?

14. Have all level number greater than the preceding level number been indented four spaces?

15. Do the same level numbers appear in the same columns?

16. Where applicable, have COPY Techniques been used in instances when at least two modules are utilizing identical record descriptions?

Data Division — File Section:

17. Do the file and record names follow Data Dictionary specifications?

18. Has the LABEL RECORDS clause been used?

19. Has BLOCK CONTAINS 0 RECORDS been coded for all sequential files?

	YES	NO	N/A	REF. #

20. Do FD's for files containing spanned records indicate BLOCK CONTAINS 0 RECORDS?

21. Has BLOCK CONTAINS n RECORDS been specified for all ISAM/VSAM files?

22. Had BLOCK CONTAINS (n^1 TO n^2) CHARACTERS clause been used for documentation purposes, where applicable?

Working Storage Section:

23. Has the use of "77" levels been eliminated?

24. Have 01 levels and levels within the 01 groups been utilized to aggregate data?

25. Wherever possible (codes, conditions) have 88 levels been used?

26. Have meaningful data names been used consistent with Data Dictionary procedures?

27. Has DISPLAY been specified for numeric data not being used for computation or subscripting?

28. Has COMPUTATIONAL been used for subscripting and has the filed been signed and synchronized?

29. Has COMPUTATIONAL-3 been used to designate numeric fields used for compari-

	YES	NO	N/A	REF. #

sons and calculations, and have the fields been signed?

30. Has the VALUE clause been used to establish initial values?

31. When the REDEFINES clause has been used does the re-defined data name have an R suffix?

Procedure Division:

32. Is the program modular; i.e., does it consist of routines which can be:
    a. Performed paragraphs through an exit
    b. Performed sections
    c. Separately compiled cal-led modules?

33. Is the program arranged in such a manner that it com-prises blocks of code that accomplish specified func-tions (main line, initial-ization, input, match, out-put, etc.)?

34. Do the modules have one entry point and one exit?

35. Do the blocks comprise a reasonable amount of lines of code averaging 30–50 over the course of the program?

36. Are the section and para-graph names on separate lines?

37. Has the program been form-atted for readability?

	YES	NO	N/A	REF. #
38. Has the use of literals been generally restricted to the working storage section of the data division?				
39. Have GOTO's been restricted to forward movement within a paragraph or section or at most back to the immediate paragraph name?				
40. Has the use of "called" separately compiled subprograms been kept to a minimum?				
41. Have overlays and/or segmentation been avoided?				
42. With the exception of performed sections, have all performs been written through exits?				
43. Has all reference to the ALTER verb been eliminated?				
44. Have all verbs used for debugging purposes been removed?				
45. Has the COMPUTE verb been used for all calculations above the most rudementary level?				
46. If arithmetic verbs have been used, has the GIVING option been specified?				
47. If applicable, have COPY techniques been used when				

	YES	NO	N/A	REF. #
at least two modules are using identical procedures?				

48. Does the use of IF statements correspond to suggested standards regarding:
    a. Negative IF statements
    b. Complicated compound statements
    c. Number of levels of nesting
    d. Column alignment?

49. Has the program been terminated using the GOBACK rather than STOP RUN?

Program Logic Structure:

50. Does the program consist of a main block and a series of CALLED procedures,DO groups and BEGIN blocks?

51. Do each of the blocks (procedures) contain only one entry and one exit?

52. Does each block (sub-blocks may be nested within blocks) perform one function?

53. Have the blocks been coded according to the principles of structuring, namely using the constructs CALL, DO, WHILE, IF THEN ELSE, and implied CASE?

54. Have other ON units been used primarily for trapping I/O conditions (ON ENDFILE, ON

	YES	NO	N/A	REF. #

ENDPAGE) or workspace overflow (ON AREA)?

55. Have other ON units (ZERO-DIVIDE, SUBSCRIPTRANGE, ERROR) been used and documented in the program?

56. Has the use of GOTO been minimized as follows:
   a. Restricted to forward use
   b. Raising error conditions
   c. As an aid for implementing the structured CASE facility?

57. Are standard PL/1 error features being utilized?

Formatting of Code:

58. Does each line of code within a block contain one statement?

59. Has use been made of indentation to indicate logic flow?

60. Have sub-blocks been indented within each higher level block?

61. Does the program contain initial comments specifying its name, purpose, function, inputs, outputs, program author, revision information, and a brief description of program flow?

62. Does each block of code contain comments regarding its purpose and function?

	YES	NO	N/A	REF. #

63. Have comments been used preceding CALLS describing the purpose and function?

64. Whenever possible, has the use of label variables been eliminated?

65. Are the variable and procedure (block) names meaningful?

66. Have all statements used as debugging aids been removed from the program?

67. Where "Built-in Functions" have been utilized, have they been adequately documented by comments?

68. Does the program contain the following comments:
    a. Program identification, including the Panvalet name, program name, system name, department number, project number, and CASE number
    b. Author(s) responsible
    c. Date written
    d. A brief description of what the program is to accomplish along with the I/O requirements and general logic
    e. Revision information showing the requester and the date along with a brief description of the revision

	YES	NO	N/A	REF. #

    f.   External references show-
ing the list of subroutines
or CALLED functions

    g. A glossary showing a list
of important variables
along with a brief description of each?

69.   For each subroutine within
the program, have comments
been included describing how
subroutine was called along
with the parameters?

70.   Have the parameters been
broken down and described?

71.   Do the comments give an
understanding of what the
programming intended to accomplish?

Variable Names:

72.   Do the selected variable
names best identify the
symbolic quantities they
represent?

73.   Has the use of variables in
different contexts been eliminated within the pro-
gram?

74.   Has the use of the Fortran
Standard comments as
variable names been eli-
minated?

Statement Formatting:

75.   Have parentheses been used
to clarify mathematical expressions and/or to simplify

	YES	NO	N/A	REF. #

the reading of a compound
IF statement?

76. Has the use of splitting variable names over two lines
been avoided?

77. Does the variable name
appear subsequent to an
operator?

78. Are blanks included in statements to enhance readability?

79. Have the lists in specification statement (INTEGER,
REAL, DIMENSION, etc.)
been arranged in alphabeti-
cal order?

80. Has the program been written
in a neat, logical manner?

Statement Ordering:

81. Has the following pattern of
statements been followed as
closely as possible?

    a. TYPE statements
    b. EXTERNAL statements
    c. DIMENSION statements
    d. COMMON statements
    e. EQUIVALENCE state-
       ments
    f. DATA statements
    g. Statement function state-
       ments
    h. Executable statements
    i. END Line?

82. Are the statement numbers
in ascending order?

	YES	NO	N/A	REF. #
83. Have FORMAT statements been grouped together at the end of the program with numbers in the 9000 level?				

Subscripting:

84. Has the use of subscripting adhered to SAPP standards?				
85. Have scalars been used in lieu of vectors wherever possible?				
86. Have N dimensional arrays been eliminated when an array of N-1 dimensions will suffice?				

Subroutines:

| 87. Have subroutines been used to repeatedly execute common blocks of code? | | | | |
| 88. If available, has use been made of vendor and corporate library subroutines? | | | | |

Fortran Statements:

89. Have COMMON statements been stored to the source library and brought into the program using ++ INCLUDE statements?				
90. Have verbs used primarily for debugging purposes been removed from the program?				
91. Have separate statements for each DEFINE FILE been used?				

	YES	NO	N/A	REF. #
92. Does every DO statement refer to a CONTINUE as the end of its range and does each DO refer to a different CONTINUE?				
93. Has the use of GOTO's been minimized or, at the least, been restricted to forward references?				
94. Has FORMAT been used to read cards, write to the printer, produce a print tape, and create files for input to non-Fortran programs?				
95. Has the use of FORMAT been excluded for all other input/output transmissions?				
96. Has the ERR = and END = option been used to transfer control upon an error or end-of-file condition?				
97. Has the use of implied DO loops been avoided I/O statements?				

X. FEASIBILITY STUDY CHECKLIST

Review Scope, Objectives and Constraints

	YES	NO	N/A	REF. #
1. Have the scope, objectives and constraints been specifically defined?				
2. If applicable, have the Project and Personnel Work schedules been established?				

	YES	NO	N/A	REF. #

3. Have personnel assigned to the project been briefed about the system to be developed?

Analyze Business Functions and Environments

4. Have the relevant business functions been identified?

5. Has the purpose of each function and the interrelationships between functions been described?

6. Has an estimate of the volume of business transactions and the personnel required to process them been made?

7. Have system interfaces been defined?

8. Have the "key leverage points" (those impacting profits, costs, sensitivity) been analyzed with a view toward isolating those that are not affected by the objectives of the project?

9. Has the management environment been described functionally and administratively?

Describe Current Information Systems:

10. Has the information required to accomplish each function been described?

11. Has the output created by each function been described?

	YES	NO	N/A	REF. #

12. Has the source of information and the destination of output been described?

13. Have each of the functions been divided into component processes showing dependencies?

14. Has the flow of data been described and linked to either an input, process, or output function?

15. Have the existing controls been identified and categorized as follows?
    a. Management Controls (1)
    b. Data Security Controls (2)
    c. Organizational Controls (3)
    d. System Controls (4)
       1. Management Controls would include statistical information, such as average times to process transactions, peak load periods, etc.
       2. Data Security Controls would consist of those procedures required to protect confidential and sensitive data.
       3. Organizational Controls are those concerned with checks and balances required to safeguard assets (separation of duties).
       4. System Controls are those used to control input (batch controls);

	YES	NO	N/A	REF. #

control processing (checkpoints, cross-footing, etc.); file controls (pre-determined totals); output controls (total logs) and overall controls (trial balance).

16. Have interfaces with other systems been described showing data flow medium and scheduling?

17. Have transaction characteristics been defined showing anticipated volume by type, complexity and frequency?

18. Has an analysis been made of the possible growth of transaction volume?

Analyze Current Operating Costs:

19. Has the pattern of work been defined to reflect personnel costs as well as to serve as a basis for estimating operating costs and benefits of alternative solutions (if applicable)?

20. If the function is clerical, have standard rates been used to arrive at a unit cost per hour?

21. If the function is automated have the machine costs been shown?

	YES	NO	N/A	REF. #

22. Have Operating Cost Worksheets been completed showing time and cost per function.

23. Has an estimate been made of the cost to maintain the system?

Develop Alternative Solutions:

24. Have alternative solutions been developed on the business and technical levels?

25. Have the alternatives considered:
    a. The capability to satisfy system "musts" and "desirables"
    b. The probable cost of developing and, in turn, operating the system
    c. Time constraints
    d. Control requirements
    e. Risk factors
    f. Hardware/software requirements
    g. The impact on the users of other operations?

26. Have the broad system requirements been ascertained and described showing:
    a. Major input transactions
    b. Major output(s)
    c. Major functional processing elements
    d. A description of the data (not to include attributes or editing considerations)

	YES	NO	N/A	REF. #
e. Timing and/or response time requirements				
f. Controls, security, and backup requirements				
g. Interfaces with existing or planned systems?				
27. Have the high-volume, high-cost functions been isolated?				
28. Have alternatives for getting information into and out of the system been described?				
29. In the event new hardware/software or packages may be required, have the following questions been considered for further study and action:				
a. Has the equipment been thoroughly tested?				
b. Has the technology group been made aware of their possible consulting role?				
c. Have, or will estimates be increased to reflect the learning curve?				
d. Does the package require modification prior to installation?				
e. Are there other sources of supply?				
f. Is the equipment (package) compatible with existing in-house equipment?				
g. Is there anyone within the organization experienced with the technology?				
h. Is the vendor reliable and capable of providing support?				

	YES	NO	N/A	REF. #

30. Has a Development Cost Worksheet been prepared for the subsequent phases? (NOTE: This is only a guide.)

31. Has an estimate been made of the cost to run or modify the new solution(s)?

32. Has the user indicated the benefits to be accrued including such items as:
    a. Increased profits
    b. Reduction of costs
    c. Better data for strategic planning (site selection, demand forecasting, seasonality factors, etc.)
    d. Improved customer service (new order entry system)
    e. More effective and timely reporting to management and governmental authorities
    f. Improvement in data security
    g. Better cost control?

Evaluate Alternative Solutions:

33. Has the solution been shown to be technically feasible?

34. If appropriate, has Computer Operations indicated that the proposed solution(s) is compatible with the existing or planned environment?

35. If appropriate, have cash flow worksheets been prepared for

	YES	NO	N/A	REF. #

the current and proposed
solution(s) using the Net
Present Value (NPV) calculation formula as the criterion
for economic evaluation?

36. If applicable, has an asses-
ment of risks been made for
considerations such as:
a. Changing business environment
b. Fluctuating volumes
c. Organization changes
d. Changing product lines?

37. Has a solution been recommended?

Plan Subsequent Phases

38. Have the scope, objectives,
and constraints for the next
phase(s) been stated?

39. Have the tasks and activities
to be done during the next
phase(s) been selected?

40. Has a logical network or PERT
network been developed for the
next phase(s)?

41. Have the resources required
for the next phase(s) tasks
and activities been estimated?

42. Have work schedules and a
budget for the next phase(s)
been prepared?

43. Has a Development Cost
Worksheet been prepared
for the next phase(s)?

	YES	NO	N/A	REF. #

XI.   INSTALLATION CHECKLIST

Prepare for Acceptance Test:

1.   Have success criteria for system performance been stated
specifically by the user?

2.   Has agreement been reached
on how the acceptance test
will be evaluated?

3.   When comparing old and new
system results as a part of
acceptance testing, has agreement with the user been obtained regarding the following:
a.   The number of cycles to
be run and the definition
of what constitutes a
cycle
b.   Correctness of results?

4.   If current data is required for
acceptance testing, has an
alternative for that testing
that may require cyclical processing been discussed with
the user?

5.   If applicable, has all equipment to be installed at the
user's location been put into
place?

6.   If prior system procedures are
to be eliminated by installation
of the new system, has a backup procedure been provided
in the event of system failure?

	YES	NO	N/A	REF. #

7. Is input to the acceptance test based upon rules set forth in the BSD System Design Test Plan?

8. If required, have the appropriate files been converted?

9. Have the files been checked to verify counts, totals, etc?

10. Have listings of the old and new files been prepared for comparison, if required?

Conduct Acceptance Test:

11. Have the system outputs been verified according to the acceptance test plan and the user's criteria?

12. Has a checklist of problems encountered during acceptance testing been maintained?

13. If problems were encountered and corrected, was the documentation of appropriate prior phases changed?

14. If problems were uncovered, was a schedule prepared to estimate the amount of time required to make the appropriate changes?

15. If applicable, has Computer Operations tested the system?

16. Has Computer Operations evaluated the system for conformance to Computer

	YES	NO	N/A	REF. #
Operations requirements, if applicable?				

Documentation:

17. Is the documentation organized for ease of reference?				
18. Have COM procedures for source program listings been included as a separate portion of documentation?				

Hand Over New System:

19. Has the user signed off on the system by approving the documentation?				
20. Has Computer Operations signed off on the system?				

XII. STAFFING THE QUALITY ASSURANCE FUNCTION

The Quality Assurance Program will be administered by the MSP Support Department. The team, initially, will consist of one permanently assigned QA Project Leader with other team members participating as defined by MSP management. Team members, either permanently assigned, on rotation for a defined period of time, or assigned by project should possess the appropriate training and systems experience to achieve maximum acceptance from their peer group.

Obviously, participation in terms of time (assuming the absence of a permanent group) of team members reviewing a phase of a project would vary depending upon the size of the project.

Appendix B
REPORT BY THE NATIONAL BUREAU OF STANDARDS ON QA, TESTING, VERIFICATION AND VALIDATION*

TABLE OF CONTENTS

---

* Reprinted from Powell, Patricia B., ed., "Planning for Software Validation, Verification and Testing," NBS Publication 500-98. Washington, D.C., 1982.

Chapter 1
QUALITY ASSURANCE THROUGH VERIFICATION

The National Bureau of Standards (NBS) has a mission under Public Law 89-306 (Brooks Act) to develop standards to enable the "economic and efficient purchase, lease, maintenance, operation, and utilization of automatic data processing equipment by Federal Departments and agencies." As part of its current standards initiative, NBS is studying methods to ensure the quality of software procured by the Government and software developed within the Government.

Testing is the traditional technique used to determine and assure the quality of products. For many items procured by the Government, the definition or description of a quality product and the testing methods used to ensure that quality are well established. These tests are usually physical tests based on both industry and Government standards (such as dimensions for fittings, strength for materials, power for motors, etc.). The success of these methods depends upon the definition of what constitutes a quality product, the determination of measurable properties that reflect the quality, the derivation of meaningful test criteria based on the measurable quantities, and the formulation of adequate tests to ensure the quality.

Unfortunately, software does not fit into the traditional framework of quality assessment. One reason is that software, in general, is a "one of a kind" product especially tailored for a particular application. There is often no standard product or specification to use as a model to measure against. Secondly, analogies to physical products with applicable dimensional, strength, etc. standards do not exist. Of greatest importance, the concept of what constitutes quality in software is not as well formulated. There is no universally accepted definition of software quality.

1.1 Attributes of Quality Software

There have been many studies directed toward the determination of appropriate factors for software quality. A number of attributes have been proposed; the set given by Figure 1.1 [of this Appendix] is representative. Most of these factors are qualitative rather than quantitative.

In Figure 1.1, the top level characteristics of quality software are reliability, testability, usability, efficiency, transportability, and maintainability. In practice, efficiency often turns out to be in conflict with other attributes, e.g. transportability, maintainability, and testability. As hardware costs decrease, efficiency of machine use becomes much less an issue and consequently a less important attribute of software quality. At present, a reasonable software development methodology will support the creation of software with all these qualities. While a piece of code may not be locally as efficient as a skilled programmer can write it disregarding all other factors, it must be designed to be as efficient as possible while still exhibiting the other desired qualities.

For the purpose of this document, two qualities stand out, reliability and testability. The others are equally important, but less related to testing and verification issues, and perhaps more qualitative than quantitative. Reliable software must be adequate; that is, it must be correct, complete, consistent, and feasible at each stage of the development life cycle. An infeasible set of requirements will lead to an inadequate design and probably an incorrect implementation. Given that the software meets these adequacy requirements at each stage of the development process, to be reliable it must also be robust. Robustness is a quality which represents the ability of the software to survive a hostile environment. We cannot anticipate all possible events, and we must build our software to be as resilient as possible.

At all stages of the life cycle, software should be testable. To accomplish this it must be understandable. The desired product (the requirements and design) and the actual product (the code) should be represented in a structured, concise, and self-descriptive manner so that they can be compared. The software must also be measurable, allowing means for actually instrumenting or inserting probes, testing, and evaluating the product of each stage.

Emphasis on particular quality factors will vary from project to project depending on application, environment, and other considerations. The specific definition of quality and the importance of given attributes should be specified during the requirements phase of the project.

Even if good quality is difficult to define and measure, poor quality is glaringly apparent. Software that is error prone or does not work is obviously poor quality software. Consequently, discovery of errors in the software has been the first step toward quality assurance. Program testing, executing the software using representative data samples and comparing the actual results with the expected results, has been the fundamental technique used to determine errors. However, testing is difficult, time consuming, and inadequate. Consequently, increased emphasis has been placed upon insuring quality through the development process.

The criticality of the problem determines the effort required to validate the solution. Software to control airplane landings or to direct substantial money transfers required higher confidence in its proper functioning than does a carpool locator program since the consequences of malfunction are more severe. For each software project not only the product requirements but also the validation requirements should be determined and specified at the initiation of the project. Project size, uniqueness, criticality, the cost of malfunction, and project budget all influence the validation needs. With the validation requirements clearly stated, specific techniques for verification and testing can be chosen. This document surveys the field of verification and testing techniques. The emphasis is upon medium and large size projects but many of the individual techniques have broader applicability. Verification and testing for very small projects are discussed elsewhere.

Although a glossary is included as an appendix to this document, the following terms are sufficiently important to warrant

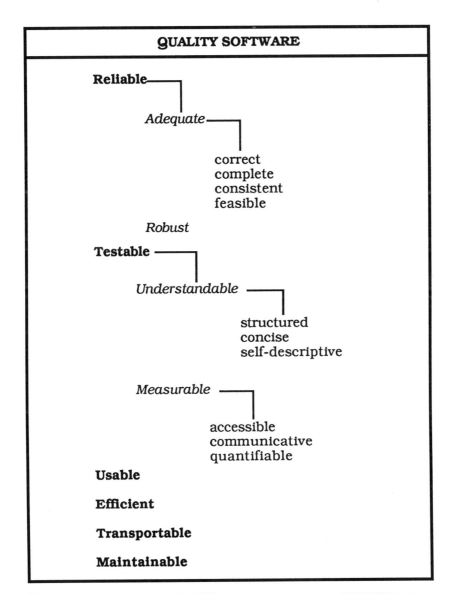

Figure 1.1 **A HIERARCHY OF SOFTWARE QUALITY ATTRIBUTES**

definition in the test. It should be noted that some of these terms may appear with slightly different meanings elsewhere in the literature.

1.   VALIDATION: Determination of the correctness of the final program or software produced from a development project with respect to the user's needs and requirements. Validation is usually accomplished by verifying each stage of the software development life cycle.

2.   CERTIFICATION: Acceptance of software by an authorized agent usually after the software has been validated by the agent, or after its validity has been demonstrated to the agent.

3.   VERIFICATION: In general the demonstration of consistency, completeness, and correctness of the software at each stage and between each stage of the development life cycle.

4.   TESTING: Examination of the behavior of a program by executing the program on sample data sets.

5.   PROOF OF CORRECTNESS: Use of techniques of logic to infer that an assertion assumed true at program entry implies that an assertion holds at program exit.

6.   PROGRAM DEBUGGING: The process of correcting syntactic and logical errors detected during coding. With the primary goal of obtaining an executing piece of code, debugging shares with testing certain techniques and strategies, but differs in its usual ad hoc application and local scope.

1.2 Verification Throughout Life Cycle

Figure 1.2 presents a traditional view of the development life cycle with testing contained in a stage immediately prior to operation and maintenance. All too often testing is the only verification technique used to determine the adequacy of the software. When verification is constrained to a single technique and confined to the latter stages of development, severe consequences can result. It is not unusual to hear of testing consuming 50% of the development budget. All errors are costly but the later in the life cycle that the error discovery is made, the more costly the error. Consequently, of lower cost and higher quality are the goal, verification should not be isolated to a single stage in the development process but should be incorporated into each phase of development. Barry Boehm has stated that one of the most prevalent and costly mistakes made on software projects today is to defer the activity of detecting and correcting software problems until late in the project. The primary reason for early investment in verification activity is that expensive errors may already have been made before coding begins.

Figure 1.3 presents an amended life cycle chart which includes verification activities. The success of phasing verification throughout the development cycle depends upon the existence of a clearly defined and stated product at each development stage. The more formal and precise the statement of the development product, the more amenable it is to the analysis required to support verification. Many of the new software development methodologies encourage a firm product from the early development.

REQUIRE-MENTS	DESIGN	CODE	INTEGRATE	TEST	OPERATION & MAINTEN-ANCE

Figure 1.2 **THE SOFTWARE DEVELOPMENT LIFE CYCLE**

We will examine each stage of the life cycle and discuss the relevant activities. The following activities should be performed at each stage:

1. Analyze the structures produced at this stage for internal testability and adequacy.
2. Generate test sets based on the structures at this stage.

In addition, the following should be performed during design and construction:

3. Determine that the structures are consistent with structures produced during previous stages.
4. Refine or redefine test sets generated earlier.

Throughout the entire life cycle, neither development nor verification is a straightline activity. Modifications or corrections to structures at one stage will require modifications and reverification of structures produced during previous stages.

Requirements

The verification activities that accompany the problem definition and requirements analysis stage of software development

Life Cycle Stage	Verification Activities
Requirements	Determine verification approach Determine adequacy of requirements Generate functional test data
Design	Determine consistency of design with requirements Determine adequacy of design Generate structural and functional test data
Construction	Determine consistency with design Determine adequacy of implementation Generate structural and functional test data Apply test data
Operation & Maintenance	Retest

Figure 1.3 **LIFE CYCLE VERIFICATION ACTIVITIES**

are extremely significant. The adequacy of the requirements must be thoroughly analyzed and initial test cases generated with the expected (correct) responses. Developing scenarios of expected system use may help to determine the test data and anticipated results. These tests will form the core of the final test set. Generating these tests and the expected behavior of the system clarifies the requirements and helps guarantee that they are testable. Vague or untestable requirements will leave the validity of the delivered product in doubt. Late discovery of requirements inadequacy can be very costly. A determination of the criticality of software quality attributes and the importance of validation should be made at this stage. Both product requirements and validation requirements should be estimated.

Some automated tools to aid in the requirements definition exist. Examples include Information System Design and Optimization System, The Software Requirements Engineering Program, Structured Analysis and Design Technique, and Systematic Activity Modeling Method. All provide a disciplined frame work for expressing requirements and thus aid in the checking of consistency and completeness. Although these tools provide only rudimentary validation procedures, this capability is greatly needed and it is the subject of current research.

Design

Organization of the verification effort and test management activities should be closely integrated with preliminary design. The general testing strategy, including test methods and test evaluation criteria, is formulated; and a test plan is produced. If the project size of criticality warrants, and independent test team is organized. In addition, a test schedule with observable milestones is constructed. At this same time, the framework for quality assurance and test documentation should be established.

During the detailed design, validation support tools should be acquired or developed and the test procedures themselves should be produced. Test data to exercise the functions introduced during the design process as well as test cases based upon the structure of the system should be generated. Thus as the software development proceeds, a more effective set of test cases is built up.

In addition to test organization and the generation of test cases to be used during construction, the design itself should be analyzed and examined for errors. Simulation can be used to verify properties of the system structures and subsystem interaction, design walk throughs should be used by the developers to verify the flow and logical structure of the system while design inspection should be performed by the test team. Missing cases, faulty logic, module interface mismatches, data structure inconsistencies, erroneous I/O assumptions, and user interface inadequacies are items of concern. The detailed design must be shown internally consistent, complete, and consistent with the preliminary design and requirements.

Although much of the verification must be performed manually, the use of a formal design language can facilitate the analysis. Several different design methodologies are in current use. Top Down Design proposed by Harlan Mills of IBM, Structured Design introduced by L. Constantine, and the Jackson Method are examples. These techniques are manual and facilitate verification by providing a clear statement of the design. The Design Expression and Configuration Aid, the Process Design Language, High Order Software and SPECIAL are examples of automated systems or languages which can also be used for analysis and consistency checking.

Construction

Actual testing occurs during the construction stage of development. Many testing tools and techniques exist for this stage of system development. Code walk-through and code inspection are effective manual techniques. Static analysis techniques detect errors by analyzing program characteristics such as data flow and language construct usage. For programs of significant size, automated tools are required to perform this analysis. Dynamic analysis, performed as the code actually executives, is used to determine test coverage through various instrumentation techniques. Formal verification or proof techniques are used to provide further quality assurance. These techniques are discussed in detail in [Appendix] Chapter 3.

During the entire test process, careful control and management of test information is critical. Test sets, test results, and test reports should be catalogued and stored in a data base. For all but very small systems, automated tools are required to do an adequate job, for the bookkeeping chores alone become to large to be handled manually. A test driver, test data generation aids, test coverage tools, test results management aids, and report generators are usually required.

Maintenance

Over 50% of the life cycle costs of a software system and spent on maintenance. As the system is used, it is modified either to correct errors or to augment the original system. After each modification the system must be retested. Such retesting activity is termed *regression testing*. The goal of regression testing is to minimize the cost of system revalidation. Usually only those portions of the system impacted by the modifications are retested. However, changes at any level may necessitate retesting, reverifying and updating documentation at all levels below it. For example, a design change requires design reverification, unit retesting and subsystem and system retesting. Test cases generated during system development are reused or used after appropriate modifications. The quality of the test documentation generated during system development and modified during maintenance will affect the cost of regression testing. If test data cases have been catalogued and preserved, duplication of effort will be minimized.

We will emphasize testing, verification, and validation during software development. The maintenance and operation stage is very important, but generally outside the scope of this report. The procedures described here for software development will if followed correctly, make the task of maintaining, upgrading, evolving, and operating the software a much easier task.

Chapter 2
AN OVERVIEW OF TESTING

2.1 Concepts

The purpose of this section is to discuss the basic concepts and fundamental implications and limitations of testing as a part of software verification. There are many meanings attributed to the verb "to test" throughout the technical literature. Let us begin by looking at the Oxford English Dictionary definition:

Test — *That by which the existence, quality, or genuineness of anything is, or may be, determined.*

The objects that we test are the elements that arise during the development of software. These include modules of code, requirements and design specifications, data structures, and any other objects that are necessary for the correct development and implementation of our software. We will often use the term "program" in this document to refer to any object that may be conceptually or actually executed. A design or requirements specification can be conceptually executed, transforming input data to output data. Hence, remarks directed toward "programs" have broader application.

We view a program as a representation of a function. The function describes the relationship of an input (called a *domain element*) to an output (called a *range element*). The testing process is then used to ensure that the program faithfully realizes the function. For example, consider the function $1/x$. Its domain is the set of all floating point numbers excluding 0. Any program that realizes the function $1/z$ must, when given a floating point value r (r nonzero), return the value $1/r$ (given the machine dependent precision). The testing problem is to ensure that the program does represent the function.

Elements of the function's domain are called *valid inputs*. Since programs are expected to operate reasonably on elements outside of a function's domain (called "robustness"), we must test the program on such elements. Thus any program that represents $1/x$ should be tested on the value 0 and perhaps also on meaningless data (such as strings) to ensure that the program does not fail catastrophically. These elements outside of the function's domain are called *invalid inputs*. How to choose these and other test input values is discussed in detail in 3.3.

The essential components of a program test are a description of the functional domain, the program in executable form, a description of the expected behavior, a way of observing program behavior, and a method of determining whether the observed behavior conforms with the expected behavior. The testing process consists of obtaining a valid value from the functional domain (or an invalid value from outside the functional domain to test for robustness), determining the expected behavior, executing the program and observing its behavior, and finally comparing that behavior with the expected behavior. If the expected and the actual behavior agree, we say the test instance succeeds, otherwise we say the test instance fails.

Of the five necessary components in the testing process, the most difficult to obtain is a description of the expected behavior. Often ad hoc methods must be used to determine expected behavior. These methods include hand calculation, simulation, and other less efficient solutions to the same problem. What is needed is an *oracle*, a source which for any given input description can provide a complete description of the corresponding output behavior. We will discuss this process throughout [Appendix] Chapter 3.

2.2 Dynamic Testing

We can classify program test methods into *dynamic* and *static analysis* techniques. Dynamic analysis requires that the program be executed and, hence, involves the traditional notion program testing; i.e. the program is run on some test cases and the results of the program's performance are examined to check whether the program operated as expected. Static analysis does not usually involve actual program execution. Common static analysis techniques include such compiler tasks as syntax and type checking. We will first consider some general aspects of dynamic analysis within a general discussion of program testing.

A complete verification of a program, at any stage in the life cycle, can be obtained by performing the test process for every element of the domain. If each instance succeeds, the program is verified; otherwise an error has been found. This testing method is known as *exhaustive testing* and is the only dynamic analysis technique that will guarantee the validity of a program. Unfortunately, this technique is not practical. Frequently functional domains are infinite, or if not infinitive very large, so as to make the number of required test instances infeasible.

The solution is to reduce this potentially infinite exhaustive testing process to a finite testing process. This is accomplished by finding criteria for choosing representative elements from the functional domain. These criteria may reflect either the functional description or the program structure.

The subset of elements used in a testing process is called a *test data set* (test set for short). Thus the crux of the testing problem is to find an adequate test set, one that "covers" the domain and is small enough to perform the testing process for each element in the set. The paper of Goodenough and Gerhart presents the first formal treatment for determining when a criterion for test set selection is adequate. In their paper, a criterion C is said to be *consistent* provided that test sets T1 and T2 chosen by C are such that all test instances of T2 are successful. A criterion C is said to be *complete* provided that it produces test sets that uncover all errors. These definitions lead to the fundamental theorem of testing which states:

If there exists a consistent, complete criterion for test set selection for a program P and if a test set satisfying the criterion is such that all test instances succeed, then the program P is correct.

Unfortunately it has been shown to be impossible to find consistent, complete test criteria except for the simplest cases. The above just confirms that testing, especially complete testing, is a very difficult process. Examples of criteria that are used in practice for the selection of test sets include:

1. The elements of the test set reflect special domain properties such as extremal or ordering properties.

2.   The elements of the test set exercise the program structure such as test instances ensuring all branches or all statements are executed.

3.   The elements of the test set reflect special properties of the functional description such as domain values leading to extremal function values.

2.3 Structural vs. Functional Testing

The properties that the test set is to reflect are classified according to whether they are derived from a description of the program's function or from the program's internal structure. Test data generation based on *functional analysis* and on *structural analysis* is described in 3.3 and 3.4. Classifying the test data inclusion criteria given above, the first and the third are based on functional analysis criteria while the second is based on structural analysis criteria. Both structural and functional analysis should be performed to ensure adequate testing. Structural analysis-based test sets tend to uncover errors that occur during "coding" of the program, while functional analysis-based test sets tend to uncover errors that occur in implementing requirements or design specifications.

Although the criterion for generating a structure-based test set is normally simple, the discovery of domain elements that satisfy the criterion is often quite difficult. Test data are usually derived by iteratively refining the data base on the information provided by the application of structural coverage metrics. Since functional analysis techniques often suffer from combinatorial problems, the generation of adequate functional test data is no easier. As a result, ad hoc methods are often employed to locate data which stress the program.

2.4 Static Testing

The application of test data and the analysis of the results are dynamic testing techniques. The class of static analysis techniques is divided into two types: techniques that analyze consistency and techniques that measure some program property. The consistency techniques are used to ensure program properties such as correct syntax, correct parameter matching between procedures, correct typing, and correct requirements and specification translation. The measurement techniques measure properties such as error proneness, understandability, and well-structuredness.

The simplest of the consistency checking static analysis

techniques is the syntax checking feature of compilers. In modern compilers, this feature is frequently augmented by type checking, parameter matching (for modules), cross-reference tables, static array bounds checking, and aliasing. Two advanced static analysis techniques are symbolic execution and program proving. The latter proves the consistency of stated relations between program variables before and after program segments. Symbolic execution performs a "virtual" execution of all possible program paths. Since an actual execution does not occur, the method is considered a static analysis technique. Both are described in detail in [Appendix] Chapter 3.

2.5 Manual vs. Automated Testing

A final classification of methods can be made upon the basis of whether the method is a *manual* method such as structured walk through or code inspection, or whether the method is *automated.*

In Table 2.1 we list the verification methods that will be discussed throughout the rest of this report. We provide a classification according to whether the method is dynamic or static, structural or functional, manual or automated. We also provide a reference to where the method is discussed in the body of the report.

Technique	*Section*	*Manual/ Automatic*	*Static/ Dynamic*	*Structural/ Functional*
Correctness proof	3.1	both	static	both
Walk throughs	3.1	manual	dynamic	both
Inspections	3.1	manual	static	both
Design Reviews and Audits	3.1	manual	static	both
Simulation	3.1	automated	dynamic	functional
Desk Checking	3.1	manual	both	structural
Peer Review	3.1	manual	both	structural

Table 2.1 **SUMMARY OF TESTING TECHNIQUES**

Technique	Section	Manual/ Automatic	Static/ Dynamic	Structural/ Functional
Executable Specifications	3.2	automated	dynamic	functional
Exhaustive Testing	3.3	automated	dynamic	functional
Stress Testing	3.3	manual	dynamic	functional
Error Guessing	3.3	manual	dynamic	functional
Cause-Effect Graphing	3.3	both	dynamic	functional
Design-Based Functional Testing	3.3	manual	dynamic	functional
Coverage-Based Metric Testing	3.4	automated	both	structural
Complexity-Based Metric Testing	3.4	automated	both	structural
Compiler Based Analysis	3.6	automated	static	structural
Data Flow Analysis	3.6	automated	static	structural
Control Flow Analysis	3.6	automated	static	structural
Symbolic Execution	3.6	automated	static	structural
Instrumentation	3.7	automated	dynamic	structural
Combined Techniques	3.8	automated	both	both

Table 2.1 **SUMMARY OF TESTING TECHNIQUES (Cont'd)**

Chapter 3
VERIFICATION TECHNIQUES

A description of verification, validation, and testing techniques can be arranged in several different ways. In keeping with the emphasis on verification throughout the life cycle, we first present general techniques which span the stages of the life cycle. The remaining sections are organized along the lines of the usual testing plan, providing discussion of test data generation, test data evaluation, testing procedures and analysis, and the development of support tools. Each procedure will be briefly discussed, with emphasis given to its role in the validation process and its advantages and limitations.

3.1 General Verification Techniques

Techniques that can be used throughout the life cycle are described here. The majority of the techniques involve static analysis and can be performed manually. They can be utilized without a large capital expenditure, although for analysis of large systems automated aids are advised. These include traditional informal methods of desk checking and review, disciplined techniques of structured walk throughs and inspections, and formal methods of proof of correctness. In addition, the role simulation plays in validation and verification is described.

Desk Checking and Peer Review

Desk checking is the most traditional means for analyzing a program. It is the foundation for the more disciplined techniques of walk throughs, inspections, and reviews. In order to improve the effectiveness of desk checking, it is important that the programmer thoroughly review the problem definition and requirements, the design specification, the algorithms and the code listings. In most instances, desk checking is used more as a debugging technique than a testing technique. Since seeing one's own errors is difficult, it is better if another person does the desk checking. For example, two programmers can trade listings and read each other's code. This approach still lacks the group dynamics present in formal walk throughs, inspections, and reviews.

Another method, not directly involving testing, which tends to increase overall quality of software production is peer review. There are a variety of implementations of peer review, but all are based on a review of each programmer's code. A panel can be set up which reviews sample code on a regular basis for efficiency, style, adherence to standard, etc. and which provides feedback to the individual programmer. Another possibility is to maintain a notebook of required "fixes" and revisions to the software and indicate the original programmer or designer. In a "chief programmer team" environment, the librarian can collect data on programmer runs, error reports, etc. and act as a review board or pass the information on to a peer review panel.

Walk throughs, Inspections, and Review

Walk throughs and inspections are formal manual techniques which are a natural evolution of desk checking. While both techniques share a common philosophy and similar organization, they are quite distinct in execution. Furthermore, while they both evolved from the simple desk check discipline of the single programmer, they are very disciplined procedures aimed at removing the major responsibility for verification from the developer.

Both procedures require a team, usually directed by a moderator. The team includes the developer, but the remaining 3–6 members and the moderator should not be directly involved in the development effort. Both techniques are based on a reading of the product (e.g. requirements, specifications, or code) in a formal meeting environment with specific rules for evaluation. The difference between inspection and walk through lies in the conduct of the meeting. Both methods require preparation and study by the team members, and scheduling and coordination by the team moderator.

Inspection involves a step-by-step reading of the product, with each step checked against a predetermined list of criteria. These criteria include checks for historically common errors. Guidance for developing the test criteria can be found elsewhere. The developer is usually required to narrate the reading of the product. Many errors are found by the developer just by the simple act of reading aloud. Others, of course, are determined as a result of the discussion with team members and by applying the test criteria.

Walk throughs differ from inspections in that the programmer does not narrate a reading of the product by the team, but provides test data and leads the team through a manual simulation of the system. The test data are walked through the system, with intermediate results kept on a blackboard or paper. The test data should be kept simple given the constraints of human simulation. The purpose of the walk through is to encourage discussion, not just to complete the system simulation on the test data. Most errors are discovered through questioning the developer's decisions at various stages, rather than through the application of the test data.

At the problem definition stage, walk through and inspection can be used to determine if the requirements satisfy the testability and adequacy measures as applicable to this stage in the development. If formal requirements are developed, formal methods, such as correctness techniques, may be applied to insure adherence with the quality factors.

Walk throughs and inspections should again be performed at the preliminary and detailed design stages. Design walk throughs and inspection will be performed for each module and module interface. Adequacy and testability of the module interfaces are very important. Any changes which result from these analyses will cause at least a partial repetition of the verification at both stages and between the stages. A reexamination of the problem definition and requirements may also be required.

Finally, the walk through and inspection procedures should be performed on the code produced during the construction stage. Each module should be analyzed separately and as integrated parts of the finished software.

Design reviews and auditors are commonly performed as stages in software development. The Department of Defense has developed a standard audit and review procedure based on hardware procurement regulations. The process is representative of the use of formal reviews and includes:

1. *System Requirements Review* is an examination of the initial progress during the problem definition stage and of the convergence on a complete system configuration. Test planning and test documentation are begun at this review.

2. *System Design Review* occurs when the system definition has reached a point where major system modules can be identified and completely specified along with the corresponding test requirements. The requirements for each major subsystem are examined along with the preliminary test plans. Tools required for verification support are identified at this stage.

3. The *Preliminary Design Review* is a formal technical review of the basic design approach for each major subsystem or module. The revised requirements and preliminary design specifications for each major subsystem and all test plans, procedures and documentation are reviewed at this stage. Development and verification tools are further identified at this stage. Changes in requirements will lead to an examination of the test requirements to maintain consistency.

4. The *Critical Design Review* occurs just prior to the beginning of the construction stage. The complete and detailed design specifications for each module and all draft test plans and documentation are examined. Again consistency with previous stages is reviewed, with particular attention given to determining if test plans and documentation reflect changes in the design specifications at all levels.

5. Two audits, the *Functional Configuration Audit* and the *Physical Configuration Audit* are performed. The former determines if the subsystem performance meets the requirements. The latter audit is an examination of the actual code. In both audits, detailed attention is given to the documentation, manuals and other supporting material.

6. A *Formal Qualification Review* is performed to determine through testing that the final coded subsystem conforms with the final system specifications and requirements. It is essentially the subsystem acceptance test.

Proof of Correctness Techniques

Proof techniques as methods of validation have been used since von Neumann's time. These techniques usually consist of validating the consistency of an output "assertion" (specification) with respect to a program (or requirements or design specification) and an input assertion (specification). In the case of programs, the assertions are statements about the program's variables. The program is "proved" if whenever the input assertion is true for particular values of variables and the program executes, then it can be shown that the output assertion is true for the possibly changed values of the program's variables. The issue of termination is normally treated separately.

There are two approaches to proof of correctness: formal proof and informal proof. A formal proof consists of developing a mathematical logic consisting of axioms and inference rules and defining a proof either to be a proof tree in the natural deduction style or to be a finite sequence of axioms and inference rules in the Hilbert-Ackermann style. The statement to be proved is at the root of the proof tree or is the last object in the proof sequence. Since the formal proof logic must also "talk about" the domain of the program and the operators that occur in the program, a second mathematical logic must be employed. This second mathematical logic is usually not decidable.

Most recent research in applying proof techniques to verification has concentrated on programs. The techniques apply, however, equally well to any level of the development life cycle where a formal representation or description exists. The GYPSY and HDM methodologies use proof techniques throughout the development stages. HDM, for techniques throughout the development stages. HDM, for example, has as a goal the formal proof of each level of development.

Heuristics for proving programs formally are essential but are not yet well enough developed to allow the formal verification of a large class of programs. In lieu of applying heuristics to the program, some approaches to verification require that the programmer provide information, interactively, to the verification system in order that the proof be completed. Such information may include facts about the program's domain and operators or facts about the program's intended function.

A typical example of a program and its assertions is given below. The input assertion states that the program's inputs are respectively a non-negative integer and a positive integer. The output assertion states that the result of the computation is the smallest non-negative remainder of the division of the first input by the second.

Input Assertion $\{ a >= 0 \text{ and } d > 0 \text{ and integer } (a) \text{ and integer } (b) \}$

Program   integer r, dd;

                               $r := a$; $dd = d$;

                               while $dd <= r$ do $dd := 2 * dd$;

                               while $dd \sim = d$ do

                                     begin $dd = dd/2$;

                                           if $dd <= r$ do $r := r - dd$

                               end

Output Assertion $\{0 <= r < d \text{ and } a \text{ congruent to } r \text{ modulo } d \}$

Informal proof techniques follow the logical reasoning behind the formal proof techniques but without the formal logical system.   Often the less formal techniques are more palatable to the programmers.   The complexity of informal proof ranges from simple checks such as array bounds not being exceeded, to complex logic chains showing noninterference of processes accessing common data.   Informal proof techniques are always used implicitly by programmers.   To make them explicit is similar to imposing disciplines, such as structured walk through, on the programmer.

Simulation

Simulation is most often employed in real-time systems development where the "real world" interface is critical and integration with the system hardware is central to the total design. There are, however, many non-real-time applications in which simulation is a cost effective verification and test data generation technique.

To use simulation as a verification tool several models must be developed.   Verification is performed by determining if the model of the software behaves as expected on models of the computational and external environments using simulation.   This technique also is a powerful way of deriving test data.   Inputs are applied to the simulated model and the results recorded for later application to the actual code.   This provides an "oracle" for testing.   The models are often "seeded" with errors to derive test data which distinguish these errors.   The data sets derived cause errors to be isolated and located as well as detected during the testing phase of the construction and integration stages.

To develop a model of the software for a particular stage in the development life cycle a formal representation compatible with the simulation system is developed.   This may consist of the formal requirement specification, the design specification, or separate model of the program behavior.   If a different model is used, then the developer will need to demonstrate and verify that the model is a complete, consistent, and accurate representation of the software at the stage of development being verified.

The next steps are to develop a model of the computational environment in which the system will operate, a model of the hardware on which the system will be implemented, and a model of the external demands on the total system.   These models can be largely derived from the requirements, with statistical representations developed for the external demand and the environmental interactions.   The software behavior is then simulated with these models to determine if it is satisfactory.

Simulating the system at the early development stages is the only means of determining the system behavior in response to the eventual implementation environment. At the construction stage, since the code is sometimes developed on a host machine quite different from the target machine, the code may be run on a simulation of the target machine under interpretive control.

Simulation also plays a useful role in determining the performance of algorithms. While this is often directed at analyzing competing algorithms for cost, resource, or performance trade-offs, the simulation under real loads does provide error information.

3.2 Test Data Generation

Test data generation is the critical step in testing. Test data sets must contain not only input to exercise the software, but must also provide the corresponding correct output responses to the test data inputs. Thus the development of test data sets involves two aspects: the selection of data input and the determination of expected response. Often the second aspect is most difficult. As discussed previously, hand calculation and simulation are two techniques used to derive expected output response. For very large or complicated systems, manual techniques are unsatisfactory and insufficient.

One promising direction is the development of executable specification languages and specification language analyzers. These can be used, as simulation is used, to act as an oracle providing the responses for the test data sets. Some analyzers such as the REVS system include a simulation capability. An executable specification language representation of a software system is an actual implementation of the design, but at a higher level than the final code. Usually interpreted rather than compiled, it is less efficient, constructed with certain information "hidden." This implementation would be in Parnas' terms an "abstract program," representing in less detail the final implementation. The execution of the specification language "program" could be on a host machine quite different from the implementation target machine.

Test data can be generated randomly with specific distributions chosen to provide some statistical assurance that the system, when tested, is error free. This is a method often used in high density LSI testing. Unfortunately, while errors in LSI chips appear correlated and statistically predictable, this is not true of software. Until recently the domains of programs were far more intractable than those occurring in hardware. This gap is closing with the advances in VLSI.

There is another statistical testing procedure for hardware that applies to certain software applications. Often integrated circuits are tested against a standard "correct" chip using statistically derived test sets. Applications of this technique include testing mass produced firmware developed for microcomputers embedded in high volume production devices such as ovens, automobiles, etc. A second possibility is to use this concept to test "evolving" software. For the development of an upwardly compatible operating system, some of the test sets can be derived by using a current field tested system as an oracle. Compiler testing employs a similar test set for each different compiler tested. However, since most software is developed as a "one of a kind" item, this approach generally does not apply.

Due to the apparent difficulty of applying statistical tests to software, test data are derived in two global ways, often called "black box" or functional analysis and "white box" or structural analysis. In functional analysis, the test data are derived from the external specification of the software behavior. No consideration is usually given to the internal organization, logic, control, or data flow in developing test data sets based on functional analysis. One technique, design-based functional analysis, includes examination and analysis of data structure and control flow requirements and specifications throughout the hierarchical decomposition of the system during the design. In a complementary fashion, tests derived from structural analysis depend almost completely on the internal logical organization of the software. Most structural analysis is supported by test coverage metrics such as path coverage, branch coverage, etc. These criteria provide a measure of completeness of the testing process.

3.3 Functional Testing Techniques

The most obvious and generally intractable functional testing procedure is exhaustive testing. As was described in [Appendix] Chapter 2, only a fraction of programs can be exhaustively tested since the domain of a program is usually infinite or infeasibly large and cannot be used as a test data set. To attack this problem, characteristics of the input domain are examined for ways of deriving a representative test data set which provides confidence that the system will be fully tested.

As was stated in [Appendix] Chapter 2, test data must be

derived from an analysis of the functional requirements and include representive elements from all the variable domains. These data should include both valid and invalid inputs. Generally, data in test data sets based on functional requirements analysis can be characterized as *extremal*, *non-extremal*, or *special* depending on the source of their derivation. The properties of these elements may be simple *values*, or for more complex data structures they may include such attributes as *type* and *dimension*.

Boundary Value Analysis

The problem of deriving test data sets is to partition the program domain in some meaningful way so that input data sets which span the partition can be determined. There is no direct, easily stated procedure for forming this partition. It depends on the requirements, the program domain, and the creativity and problem understanding of the programmer. This partitioning, however, should be performed throughout the development life cycle.

At the requirements stage a coarse partitioning is obtained according to the overall functional requirements. At the design stage, additional functions are introduced which define the separate modules allowing for a refinement of the partition. Finally, at the coding stage, submodules implementing the design modules introduce further refinements. The use of a top down testing methodology allows each of these refinements to be used to construct functional test cases at the appropriate level.

Once the program domain is partitioned into input classes, functional analysis can be used to derive test data sets. Test data should be chosen which lie both inside each input class and at the boundary of each class. Output classes should also be covered by input which causes output at each class boundary and within each class. These data are the extremal and non-extremal test sets. Determination of these test sets is often called *boundary value analysis* or *stress testing*.

The boundary values chosen depend on the nature of the data structures and the input domains. Consider the following FORTRAN example:

INTEGER X
REAL A(100,100)

If X is constrained, a<X<b, then X should be tested for valid inputs a+1, b−1, and invalid inputs a and b. The array should be tested as

a single element array A(1,1) and as a full 100 x 100 array. The array element values A(I,J) should be chosen to exercise the corresponding boundary values for each element.

Error Guessing and Special Value Analysis

Myers suggests that some people have a natural intuition for test data generation. While this ability cannot be completely described nor formalized, certain test data seem highly probable to catch errors. Some of these are in the category Howden calls special, others are certainly boundary values. Zero input values and input values which cause zero outputs are examples. For more complicated data structures, the equivalent null data structure such as an empty list or stack or a null matrix should be tested. Often the single element data structure is a good choice. If numeric values are used in arithmetic computations, then the test data should include values which are numerically very close and values which are numerically quite different. Guessing carries no guarantee for success, but neither does it carry any penalty.

Cause-Effect Graphing

Cause-effect graphing is a technique for developing test cases for programs form the high level specifications. A high level specification of requirements states desired characteristics of behavior for the system. These characteristics can be used to derive test data. Problems arise, however, of a combinatorial nature. For example, a program that has specified responses to eight characteristic stimuli (called causes) given some input has potentially 256 "types" of input (ie. those with characteristics 1 and 3, those with characteristics 5,7, and 8, etc.). A naive approach to test case generation would be to try to generate all 256 types. A more methodical approach is to use the program specifications to analyze the program's effect on the various types of inputs.

The program's output domain can be partitioned into various classes called effects. For example, inputs with characteristic 2 might be subsumed by those with characteristics 3 and 4. Hence it would not be necessary to test inputs with just characteristic 2 and also inputs with characteristics 3 and 4, for they cause the same effect. This analysis results in a partitioning of the causes according to their corresponding effects.

A limited entry decision table is then constructed from the directed graph reflecting these dependencies (i.e., causes 2 and 3 result in effect 4, causes 2, 3, and 5 result in effect 6, etc.). The decision table is then reduced and test cases chosen to exercise each column of the table. Since many aspects of the cause effect graphing can be automated, it is an attractive tool for aiding in the generation of functional test cases.

Design-Based Functional Testing

The techniques described above derive test data sets from analysis of functions specified in the requirements. Howden has extended functional analysis to functions used in the design process. A distinction can be made between requirements functions and design functions. Requirements functions describe the overall functional capabilities of a program. In order to implement a requirements function it is usually necessary to invent other "smaller functions." These other functions are used to design the program. If one thinks of this relationship as a tree structure, then a requirements function would be represented as a root node. All functional capabilities represented by boxes at the second level in the tree correspond to design functions. The implementation of a design function may require the invention of other design functions. The successive refinement during top down design can then be represented as levels in the tree structure, where the *n+1st* level nodes are refinements or subfunctions of the *n*th level functions.

To utilize design based functional testing, the functional design trees as described above are constructed. The trees document the functions used in the design of the program. The functions included in the design trees must be chosen carefully. The most important selection feature is that the function be accessible for independent testing. It must be possible to apply the appropriate input values to test the function, to derive the expected values for the function, and to observe the actual output computed by the code implementing the function.

Each of the functions in the functional design tree, if top down design techniques are followed, can be associated with the final code used to implement that function. This code may consist of one or more procedures, parts of a procedure, or even a single statement. Design-based functional testing requires that the input and output variables for each design function be completely specified. Given these multiple functions to analyze, test data discussion above. Extremal, non-extremal, and special values test data should be selected for each input variable. Test data should also be selected which results in the generation of extremal, non-extremal, and special output values.

3.4 Structural Testing Techniques

Structural testing is concerned with ensuring sufficient testing of the implementation of a function. Although used primarily during the coding phase, structural analysis should be used in all phases of the life cycle where the software is represented formally in some algorithmic, design, or requirement language. The intent of structural testing is to stress the implementation by finding test data that will force sufficient coverage of the structures present in the formal representation. In order to determine whether the coverage is sufficient, it is necessary to have a structural coverage metric. Thus the process of generating tests for structural testing is sometimes known as *metric-based test data generation.*

Metric-based test data generation can be divided into two categories by the metric used: complexity-based testing or coverage-based testing. In the latter, a criterion is used which provides a measure of the number of structural units of the software which are fully exercised by the test data sets. In the former category, tests are derived in proportion to the software complexity.

Coverage-Based Testing

Most coverage metrics are based on the number of statements, branches, or paths in the program which are exercised by the test data. Such metrics can be used both to evaluate the test data and to aid in the generation of the test data.

Any program can be represented by a graph. The nodes represent statements or collections of sequential statements. The control flow is represented by directed lines or edges which connect the nodes. A node with a single exiting edge to another node represents a sequential code segment. A node with multiple exiting edges represents a branch predicate or a code segment containing a branch predicate as the last statement.

On a particular set of data, a program will execute along a particular *path*, where certain *branches* are taken or not taken depending on the evaluation of branch predicates. Any program path can be represented by a sequence, possibly with repeating sub-sequences (when the program has backward branches), of edges from the program graph. These sequences are called *path expressions.* Each path or each data set may vary depending on the number of *loop iterations* caused. A program with variable loop control may have effectively an infinite number of paths. Hence, there are potentially an infinite number of path expressions.

To completely test the program structure, the test data chosen should cause the execution of all paths. Since this is not possible in general, metrics have been developed which give a measure of the quality of test data based on the proximity to this ideal coverage. Path coverage determination is further complicated by the existence of *infeasible paths.* Often a program has been inadvertently designed so that no data will cause the execution of certain paths. Automatic determination of infeasible paths is generally difficult if not impossible. A main theme in structured top down design is to construct modules which are simple and of low complexity so that all paths, excluding loop iteration, may be tested and that infeasible paths may be avoided.

All techniques for determining coverage metrics are based on graph representations of programs. A variety of metrics exist ranging from simple statement coverage to full path coverage. There have been several attempts to classify these metrics; however, new variations appear so often that such attempts are not always successful. We will discuss the major ideas without attempting to cover all the variations.

The simplest metric measures the percentage of statements executed by all the test data. Since coverage tools supply information about which statements have been executed (in addition to the percentage of coverage), the results can guide the selection of test data to insure complete coverage. To apply the metric, the program or module is instrumented by hand or by a preprocessor. A post processor or manual analysis of the results reveal the level of statement coverage. Determination of an efficient and complete test data set satisfying this metric is more difficult. Branch predicates that send control to omitted statements should be examined to help determine input data that will cause execution of omitted statements.

A slightly stronger metric measures the percentage of *segments* executed under the application of all test data. A segment in this sense corresponds to a *decision-to-decision path (dd-path)*. It is a portion of a program path beginning with the execution of a branch predicate and including all statements up to the evaluation (but not execution) of the next branch predicate. Segment coverage guarantees statement coverage. It also covers branches with no executable statements; eg., an IF-THEN-ELSE with no ELSE statements still requires data causing the predicate to be evaluated as both true and false. Techniques similar to those need for statement coverage are used for applying the metric and deriving test data.

The next logical step is to strengthen the metric by requiring separate coverage for both the exterior and interior of loops. Segment coverage only requires that both branches from a branch predicate be taken. For loops, segment coverage can be satisfied by causing the loop to be executed one or more times (interior test) and then causing the loop to be exited (exterior test). Requiring that all combinations of predicate evaluations be covered requires that each loop be exited without interior execution for at least one data set. This metric requires more paths to be covered than segment coverage requires. Two successive predicates will require at least four sets of test data to provide full coverage. Segment coverage can be satisfied by two tests, while statement coverage may require only one test for two successive predicates.

Implementation of the above metric is again similar to that for statement and segment coverage. Variations on this metric include requiring at least "k" interior iterations per loop or requiring that all 2**n combinations of Boolean variables be applied for each n variable predicate expression. This latter variation has led to a new path testing technique called *finite-domain testing*.

Automated tools for instrumenting and analyzing the code have been available for a few years. These tools are generally applicable to most of the coverage metrics described above. Automation of test data generation is less advanced. Often test data are generated by iterating the use of analyzers with manual methods for deriving tests. A promising but expensive way to generate test data for path testing is through the use of symbolic executors. More on the use of these tools will be discussed in a later section.

Complexity-Based Testing

Several complexity measures have been proposed recently. among these are cyclomatic complexity, software science, and Chapin's software complexity measure. These and many other metrics are designed to analyze the complexity of software systems. Most, although valuable new approaches to the analysis of software, are not suitable, or have not been applied to the problem of testing. The McCabe metrics are the exception.

McCabe actually proposed three metrics: *cyclomatic, essential,* and *actual complexity.* All three are based on a graphical representation of the program being tested. The first two are calculated from the program graph, while the third is a runtime metric.

McCabe uses a property of graph theory in defining cyclomatic complexity. There are sets of linearly independent program paths through any program graph. A maximal set of these linearly independent paths, called a basis set, can always be found. Intuitively, since the program graph and any path through the graph can be constructed from the basis set, the size of this basis set should be related to the program complexity. From graph theory, the cyclomatic number of the graph, V(G), is given by:

$$V(G) = e - n + p$$

for a graph G with number of nodes n, edges e, and connected components p. The number of linearly independent program paths though a program graph is V(G) + p, a number McCabe calls the cyclomatic complexity of the program. Cyclomatic complexity, CV(G), where:

$$CV(G) = e - n + 2p$$

can be easily calculated from the program graph.

A proper subgraph of a graph, G, is a collection of nodes and edges such that if an edge is included in the subgraph, then both nodes it connects in the complete graph, C, must be in the subgraph. Any flow graph can be reduced by combining sequential single entry, single exit nodes into a single node. Structured constructs appear in a program graph as a proper subgraph with only one node which is single entry and whose entering edge is not in the subgraph, and with only one node which is single exit and whose exiting edge is not included in the subgraph. For all other nodes, all connecting edges are included in the subgraph. This single entry, single exit subgraph can then be reduced to a single node. Essential complexity is based on counting these single entry, single exit proper subgraphs of two nodes or greater. Let the number of these subgraphs be m, then essential complexity EV(G) is defined:

$$EV(G) = CV(G) - m$$

The program graph for a program built with structured constructs will obviously have all proper subgraphs as single exit, single entry. The number of proper subgraphs of a graph G of more than one node is CV(G) - 1. Hence the essential complexity of a structured program is one. Essential complexity is then a measure of the "unstructuredness" of a program.

Actual complexity, AV, is just the number of paths executed during a run. A testing strategy can be based on these metrics. If for a test data set, the actual complexity is less than the cyclomatic complexity and all edges have been executed, then either there are more paths to be tested or the complexity can be reduced by CV(G) - AV by eliminating decision nodes and reducing portions of the program to in-line code. The cyclomatic complexity metric gives the number of linearly independent paths from analysis of the program graph. Some of these paths may be infeasible. If this is the case, then the actual complexity will never reach the cyclomatic complexity. Using a tool which derives the three complexity metrics, both a testing and a programming style can be enforced.

3.5. Test Data Analysis

After the construction of a test data set it is necessary to determine the "goodness" of that set. Simple metrics like statement coverage may be required to be as high as 90% to 95%. It is much more difficult to find test data providing 90% coverage under the more complex coverage metrics. However, it has been noted that methodologies based on the more complex metrics with lower coverage requirements have uncovered as many as 90% of all program faults.

Statistical Analyses and Error Seeding

The most common type of test data analysis is statistical. An estimate of the number of errors in a program can be obtained from an analysis of the errors uncovered by the test data. In fact, as we shall see, this leads to a dynamic testing technique.

Let us assume that there are some number of errors, E, in the software being tested. There are two things we would like to know, a maximum likelihood estimate for the number of errors and a level of confidence measure on that estimate. The technique is to insert known errors in the code in some way that is statistically similar to the actual errors. The test data is then applied and errors uncovered is determined. If one assumes that the statistical properties of the seeded and original errors is the same and that the testing and seeding are statistically unbiased, then

$$\text{estimate } E = IS/K$$

where S is the number of seeded errors, K is the number of discovered seeded errors, and I is the number of discovered unseeded errors. This estimate obviously assumes that the proportion of undetected errors is very likely to be the same for the seeded and original errors.

How good is this estimate? We would like to ascertain the confidence level for the various predicted error levels. Assuming that all seeded errors are detected (K = S), the confidence that number of errors is less than or equal to E is given by:

$$0 \qquad ; I > E$$

$$\frac{S}{S + E + 1} \qquad ; I <= E$$

Note that when E = 0 and no errors are detected other than seeded errors (I <=E) when testing, the confidence level is very high (for S=99, confidence = 99%). Testing for the error free case can be accomplished with high confidence as long as no errors are uncovered. On the other hand, if nonseeded errors are discovered and the estimate for E is higher, our confidence in the estimate also decreases. If the E = 10, then with S = 100, our confidence drops to 90%. When the number of actual errors approaches or exceeds the number of seeded errors, then the confidence in our estimates decreases dramatically. For example, if E = 10 and S = 9, then the confidence is only 45%.

A strategy for using this statistical technique in dynamic testing is to monitor the maximum likelihood estimator, and perform the confidence level calculation as testing progresses. If the estimator gets high relative to the number of seeded errors, then it is unlikely that a desirable confidence level can be obtained. The errors should then be corrected and the testing resumed. If the number of real errors discovered remains small or preferably zero as the number of seeded errors uncovered approaches the total seeded, then our confidence level for an error-free program increases.

Tausworthe discusses a method for seeding errors which has some hope of being similar statistically to the actual errors. He suggests randomly choosing lines at which to insert the error, and then making various different modifications to the code introducing errors. The actual modifications of the code are similar to those used in mutation testing as described below.

Mutation Analysis

A relatively new metric developed by DeMillo, Lipton, and Sayward is called mutation analysis. This method rests on the *competent programmer hypothesis* which states that a program written by a competent programmer will be, after debugging and testing, "almost correct." The basic idea of the method is to seed the program to be tested with errors, creating several mutants of the original program. The program and its mutants are then run interpretively on the test set. If the test set is adequate, it is argued, it should be able to distinguish between the program and its mutants.

The method of seeding is crucial to the success of the technique and consists of modifying single statements of the program in a finite number of "reasonable" ways. The developers conjecture a *coupling effect* which implies that these "first order mutants" cover the deeper, more subtle errors which might be represented by higher order mutants. The method has been subject to a small number of trials and so far has been successfully used interactively to develop adequate test data sets. It should be noted that the method derives both branch coverage and statement coverage metrics as special cases.

It must be stressed that mutation analysis, and its appropriateness, rests on the competent programmer and coupling effect theses. Since neither is provable, they must be empirically demonstrated to hold over a wide variety of programs before the method of mutations can itself be validated.

3.6 Static Analysis Techniques

As was described in [Appendix] Chapter 2, analytical techniques can be categorized as static or dynamic. The application and analysis of test data is usually described as dynamic activity, since it involves the actual execution of code. Static analysis does not usually involve program execution. Many of the general techniques discussed in 3.1, such as formal proof techniques and inspections are static analysis techniques. In a true sense, static analysis is part of any testing technique. Any analysis to derive test data, calculate assertions, or determine instrumentation breakpoints must involve some form of static analysis, although the actual verification is achieved through dynamic testing. As was mentioned earlier, the line between static and dynamic analysis is not always easily drawn. For example, proof of correctness and symbolic execution both "execute" code, but not in a real environment.

Most static analysis is performed by parsers and associated translators residing in compilers. Depending upon the sophistication of the parser, it uncovers errors ranging in complexity from ill-formed arithmetic expressions to complex type incompatibilities. In most compilers, the parser and translator are augmented with additional capabilities that allow activities such as code optimization, listing of variable names, and pretty printing, all such activities being useful in the production of quality software. Preprocessors are also frequently used in conjunction with the parser. These may perform activities such as allowing "structured programming" in an unstructured programming language, checking for errors such as mismatched common areas, and checking for module interface incompatibilities. The parser may also serve in a policing role. Thus software shop coding standards can be enforced, quality of code can be monitored, and adherence to programming standards can be checked.

Flow Analysis

Data and control flow analysis are similar in many ways. Both are based upon graphical representation. In control flow analysis, the program graph has nodes which represent a statement or segment possibly ending in a branch predicate. The edges represent the allowed flow of control from one segment to another. The control flow graph is used to analyze the program behavior, to locate instrumentation breakpoints, to identify paths, and in other static analysis activities. In data flow analysis, graph nodes usually represent single statements, while the edges still represent the flow of control. Nodes are analyzed to determine the transformations made on program' variables. Data flow analysis is used to discover program anomalies such as undefined or unreferenced variables. The technique was introduced by Cocke and Allen for global program optimization.

Data flow anomalies are more easily found than resolved. Consider the following FORTRAN code segment.

```
SUBROUTINE HYP (A,B,C,)
U = 0.5
W = 1/V
Y = A ** W
Y = E ** W
Z = X + Y
C = Z ** (V)
```

There are several anomalies in this code segment. One variable, U, is defined and never used while three variables, X, V and E, are undefined when used. It is possible that U was meant to be V, E was meant to be B, and the first occurrence of Y on the left of an assignment was a typo for X. The problem is not in detecting these errors, but in resolving them. The possible solution suggested may not be the correct one. There is no answer to this problem, but data flow analysis can help to detect the anomalies, including ones more subtle than those above.

In data flow analysis, we are interested in tracing the behavior of program variables as they are initialized and modified while the program executes. This behavior can be classified by when a particular variable is *referenced, defined,* or *undefined* in the program. A variable is referenced when its value must be obtained from memory during the evaluation of an expression in a statement. For example, a variable is referenced when it appears on the right-hand side of an assignment statement, or when it appears as an array index anywhere in a statement. A variable is defined if a new value for that variable results from the execution of a statement, such as when a variable appears on the left-hand side of an assignment. A variable is unreferenced when its value is no longer determinable from the program flow. Examples of unreferenced variables are local variables in a subroutine after exit and FORTRAN DO indices on loop exit.

Data flow analysis is performed by associating, at each node in the data flow graph, values for tokens (representing program variables) which indicate whether the corresponding variable is referenced, unreferenced, or defined with the execution of the statement represented by that node. If symbols, for instance u, d, r, and l (for null), are used to represent the values of a token, the *path expressions* for a variable (or token) can be generated beginning at, ending in, or for some particular node. A typical path expression might be drlllllrrlllllldllrllu, which can be reduced through eliminating nulls to drrrdru. Such a path expression contains no anomalies, but the presence of ... dd ... in an expres sion, indicating a variable defined twice without being referenced, does identify a potential anomaly. Most anomalies, ... ur ..., r ..., etc. can be discovered through analysis of the path expressions.

To simplify the analysis of the flow graph, statements can be combined as in control flow analysis into segments of necessarily sequential statements represented by a single node. Often, however, statements must be represented by more than one node. Consider,

$$\text{IF } (X\,.GT.\,1)\,X = X - 1$$

The variable X is certainly referenced in the statement, but it may be defined only if the predicate is true. In such a case, two nodes would be used, and the graph would actually represent code which looked like

```
          IF (X .GT. 1) 100,200
    100   X = X - 1
    200   CONTINUE
```

Another problem requiring node splitting arises at the last statement of a FORTRAN DO loop after which the index variable becomes undefined only if the loop is exited. Subroutine and function calls introduce further problems, but they too can be resolved.

Symbolic Execution

Symbolic execution is a method of symbolically defining data that force program paths to be executed. Instead of executing the program with actual data values, the variable names that hold the input values are used. Thus all variable manipulations and decisions are made symbolically. As a consequence, all variables become string variables, all assignments become string assignments and all decision points are indeterminate. To illustrate, consider the following small pseudocode program;

```
        IN a,b;
        a := a*a;
        x :=a + b;
        IF x=0 THEN x :=0 ELSE x :=1;
```

The symbolic execution of the program will result in the following expression.

if a*a + b = 0 then x :=0 else if a*a + b~=0 then x :=1

Note that we are unable to determine the result of the equality test, for we only have symbolic values available.

The result of a symbolic execution is a large, complex expression. The expression can be decomposed and viewed as a tree structure where each leaf represents a path through the program. The symbolic values of each variable are known at every point within the tree and the branch points of the tree represent the decision points of the program. Every program path is represented in the tree, and every branch path is effectively taken.

If the program has no loops, then the resultant tree structure is finite. The tree structure can then be used as an aid in generating test data that will cause every path in the program to be executed. The predicates at each branch point of the tree structure for a particular path are then collected into a conjunction. Data that causes a particular path to be executed can be found by determining which data will make the path conjunction true. If the predicates are equalities, inequalities, and orderings, the problem of data selection becomes the classic problems of trying to solve a system of equalities and orderings.

There are two major difficulties with using symbolic execution as a test set construction mechanism. The first is the combinatorial explosion inherent in the tree structure construction. The number of paths in the symbolic execution tree structure may grow as an exponential in the length of the program leading to serious computational difficulties. If the program has loops, then the symbolic execution tree structure is necessarily infinite. Usually only a finite number of loop executions is required enabling a finite loop unwinding to be performed. The second difficulty is that the problem of determining whether the conjunct has values which satisfy it is undecidable even with restricted programming languages. For certain applications, however, the method has been successful.

Another use of symbolic execution techniques is in the construction of verification conditions from partially annotated programs. Typically, the program has attached to each of its loops an assertion, called an invariant, that is true at the first statement of the loop and at the last statement of the loop (thus the assertion remains "invariant" over one execution of the loop). From this assertion, an assertion true before entrance to the loop and assertions true after exit of the loop can be constructed. The program can then be viewed as "free" of loops (i.e., each loop is considered as a single statement) and assertions extended to all statements of the program (so it is fully annotated) using techniques similar to the backward substitution method described above for symbolic execution.

3.7 Dynamic Analysis Techniques

Dynamic analysis is usually a three-step procedure involving static analysis and instrumentation of a program, execution of the instrumented program, and finally, analysis of the instrumentation data. Often this is accomplished interactively through automated tools.

The simplest instrumentation technique for dynamic analysis is the insertion of a turnstyle or a counter. Branch or segment coverage and other such metrics are evaluated in this manner. A preprocessor analyzes the program (usually by generating a program graph) and inserts counters at the appropriate places. Consider

```
            IF (X) 10,10.15
              •
              •
10          Statement i
              •
              •
15          Statement j
              •
              •
            DO 20 I = J,K,L
              •
              •
20          Statement k
```

A preprocessor might instrument the program segment as follows:

```
            IF (X) 100,101,15
              •
              •
100         N(100) = N (100) + 1
            GO TO 10
101         N(101) = N(101) +1
            Statement i
```

```
            •
            •
         I = J
         IF ( I .GT. K) THEN 201
    20   N(20) = N(20) + 1
            •
            •
         Statement k
         I = I + L
         IF (I .LE. K) THEN 20
   201   N(201) = N(201) +1
```

For the IF statement, each possible branch was instrumented. Note that we used two counters N(100) and N(101) even though the original code branches to the same statement label. The original code has to be modified for the DO loop in order to get the necessary counters inserted. Note that two counters are used, N(20) for the interior execution count and N(201) for the exterior of the loop.

Simple statement coverage requires much less instrumentation than branch coverage or more extensive metrics. For complicated assignments and loop and branch predicates, more detailed instrumentation is employed. Besides simple counts, it is interesting to know the maximum and minimum values of variables (particularly useful for array subscripts), the initial and last value, and other constraints particular to the application.

Instrumentation does not have to rely on direct code insertion. Often calls to runtime routines are inserted rather than actual counters. Some instrumented code is passed through a prepocessor/compiler which inserts the instrumentation only if certain commands are set to enable it.

Stucki introduced the concept of instrumenting a program with *dynamic assertions*. A preprocessor generates instrumentation for dynamically checking conditions often as complicated as those used in program proof techniques [STUC77]. These assertions are entered as comments in program code and are meant to be permanent. They provide both documentation and means for maintenance testing. All or individual assertions are enabled using simple commands and the preprocessor.

There are assertions which can be employed globally, regionally, locally, or at entry and exit. The general form for a local assertion is:

ASSERT LOCAL (extended-logical-expression)[optional qualifier] [control]

The optional qualifiers are ALL, SOME, etc. The control options include LEVEL, which controls the levels in a block structured program; CONDITIONS, which allows dynamic enabling of the instrumentation; and LIMIT, which allows a specific number of violations to occur. The logical expression is used to represent an expected condition to be dynamically verified. For example:

ASSERT LOCAL (A(2:6,2:10) .NE. 0) LIMIT 4

placed within a program will cause the values of array elements A(2,2),A(2,3),...,A(2,10),A(3,2),...,A(6,10) to be checked against a zero value at that locality. After four violations during the execution of the program, the assertion will become false.

The global, regional, and entry-exit assertions are similar in structure. Note that similarity with verification conditions, especially if the entry-exit assertions are employed. Furthermore, symbolic execution can be employed to generate the assertions as it can be used with proof techniques. Some efforts are currently underway to integrate dynamic assertions, proof techniques, and symbolic evaluation. One of these is described below.

There are many other techniques for dynamic analysis. Most involve the dynamic (under execution) measurement of the behavior of a part of a program, where the features of interest have been isolated and instrumented based on a static analysis. Some typical techniques include expression analysis, flow analysis, and timing analysis.

3.8 Combined Methods

There are many ways in which the techniques described above can be used in concert to form a more powerful and efficient testing techniques. One of the more common combinations today is the merger of standard testing techniques with formal verification. Our ability, through formal methods, to verify significant segments of code is improving, and moreover there are certain modules, which for security or reliability reasons, justify the additional expense of formal verification.

Other possibilities include the use of symbolic execution or formal proof techniques to verify segments of code, which through coverage analysis have been shown to be most frequently executed. Mutation analysis, for some special cases like decision tables, can be used to fully verify programs. Formal proof techniques may be useful in one of the problem areas of mutation analysis, the determination of equivalent mutants.

Osterweil addresses the issue of how to combine efficiently powerful techniques in one systematic method (combining dataflow analysis, symbolic execution, elementary theorem proving, dynamic assertions, and standard testing) As has been mentioned, symbolic evaluation can be used to generate dynamic assertions. Here, paths are executed symbolically so that each decision point and every loop has an assertion. The assertions are then checked for consistency using both dataflow and proof techniques. If all the assertions along path are consistent, they they can be reduced to a single dynamic assertion for the path. Theorem proving techniques can be employed to "prove" the path assertion and termination, or the path can be tested and the dynamic assertions evaluated for the test data.

The technique allows for several tradeoffs between testing and formal methods. For instance, symbolically derived dynamic assertions are more reliable than manually derived assertions, but cost more to generate. Consistency analysis of the assertions using proof and dataflow techniques adds cost at the front end, but reduces the execution overhead. Finally there is the obvious tradeoff between theorem proving and testing to verify the dynamic assertions.

3.9 Test Support Tools

Testing, like program development, generates large amounts of information, necessitates numerous computer executions, and requires coordination and communication between workers. Support tools and techniques can ease the burden of test production, test execution, general information handling, and communication. General system utilities and test processing tools are invaluable for test preparation, organization, and modification. A well organized and structurable file system and a good text editor are a minimum support set. A more powerful support set includes data reduction and report generation tools. Library support set includes data reduction and report generation tools. Library support systems consisting of a data base management system and a configuration control system are as useful during testing as during software development since data organization, access, and control are required for management of test files and reports. Documentation can be viewed as a support technique. In addition to the general purpose support tools and techniques, specific test support tools exist. Test drivers and test languages are in this category. The following paragraphs will discuss these test specific support tools and techniques.

Test Documentation

The NBS guideline for software documentation during the development phase recommends test documentation be prepared for all multipurpose or multiuser projects and for other software development projects costing over $5000. It recommends the preparation of a test plan and a test analysis report. The test plan should identify test milestones and provide the testing schedule and requirements. In addition, it should include specifications, descriptions, and procedures for all tests; and the test data reduction and evaluation criteria. The test analysis report should summarize and document the test results and findings. The analysis summary should present the software capabilities, deficiencies, and recommendations. As with all types of documentation, the extent, formality, and level of detail of the test documentation are functions of agency ADP management practice and will vary depending upon the size, complexity, and risk of the project.

Test Drivers

Unless the module being developed is a stand-alone program, considerable auxiliary software must be written in order to exercise and test it. Auxiliary code which sets up an appropriate environment and calls the module is termed a *driver* while code which simulates the results of a routine called by the module is a *stub*. For many modules both stubs and drivers must be written in order to execute a test.

When testing is performed incrementally, an untested module is combined with a tested one and the package is then tested. Such packaging can lessen the number of drivers and/or stubs which must be written. When the lowest level of modules, those which call no other modules, are tested first and then combined for further testing with the modules that call them, the need for writing stubs can be eliminated. This approach is called *bottom-up testing*. Bottom-up testing still requires that test drivers be constructed. Testing which starts with the executive module and incrementally adds modules which it calls, is termed *top-down testing*. Top-down testing requires that stubs be crated to simulate the actions of called modules that have not yet been incorporated into the system. The testing order utilized should be coordinated with the development methodology used.

Automatic Test Systems and Test Languages

The actual performance of each test requires the execution of code with input data, an examination of the output, and a comparison of the output with the expected results. Since the testing operation is repetitive in nature, with the same code executed numerous times with different input values, an effort has been made to automate the process of test execution. Programs that perform this function of initiation are called *test drivers*, *test harnesses*, or *test systems*.

The simplest test drivers merely reinitiate the program with various input sets and save the output. The more sophisticated test systems accept data inputs, expected outputs, the names of routines to be executed, values to be returned by called routines, and other parameters. These test systems not only initiate the test runs but compare the actual output with the expected output and issue concise reports of the performance. TPL/2.0 which uses a test language to describe test procedures is an example of such a system. In addition to executing the tests, verifying the results and producing reports, the system helps the user generate the expected results.

PRUFSTAND is an example of a comprehensive test system. It is an interactive system in which data values are generated automatically or are requested from the user as they are needed. The system is comprised of a:

- preprocessor to instrument the code
- translator to convert the source data descriptors into an internal symbolic test data description table.
- test driver to initialize and update the test environment
- test stubs to simulate the execution of called modules
- execution monitor to trace control flow through the test object
- result validator
- test file manager
- post processor to manage reports

A side benefit of a comprehensive test system is that it establishes a standard format for test materials, which is extremely important for regression testing. Currently automatic test driver systems are expensive to build and consequently are not in widespread use.

Chapter 4
SUMMARY

In the previous sections we have surveyed many of the techniques used to validate software systems. Of the methods discussed, the most successful have been the disciplined manual techniques, such as walk throughs, reviews, and inspections, applied to all stages in the systems life cycle. Discovery of errors within the first stages of development (requirements and design) is particularly critical since the cost of these errors escalates significantly if they remain undiscovered until construction or later. Until the development products at the requirements and design stages become formalized and hence amenable to automated analysis, disciplined manual techniques will continue to be key verification techniques.

For the construction stage, automated techniques can be of great value. The ones in widest use are the simpler static analysis techniques (such as type checking), automated test coverage calculation, automated program instrumentation, and the use of simple test harnesses. These techniques are relatively straightforward to implement and all have had broad use. Combined with careful error documentation, they are effective validation methods.

Many of the techniques discussed in [Appendix] Chapter 3 have not seen wide use. The principal reasons for this include their specialization (simulation), the high cost of their use (symbolic execution), and their unproven applicability (formal proof of correctness). Many of these techniques represent the state of the art in program validation and are in areas where research is continuing.

The areas showing the most commercial interest and activity at present include automated test support systems and increased use for automated analysis. As more formal techniques are used during requirements and design, an increase in automatic analysis is possible. In addition, more sophisticated analysis techniques are being applied to the code during construction. More complete control and automation of the actual execution of tests, both in assistance in generating the test cases and in the management of the testing process and results, are also taking place.

We re-emphasize the importance of performing validation throughout the life cycle. One of the reasons for the great success of disciplined manual techniques is their uniform applicability at requirements, design, and coding phases. These techniques can be used without massive capital expenditure. However, to be most effective they require a serious commitment and a disciplined application. Careful planning, clearly stated objectives, precisely defined techniques, good management, organized record keeping, and strong commitment are critical to successful validation. A disciplined approach must be followed during both planning and execution of the verification activities.

We view the integration of validation with software development as so important that we suggest that it be an integral part of the requirements statement. Validation requirements should specify the type of manual techniques, the tools, the form of project management and control, the development methodology, and acceptability criteria which are to be used during software development. These requirements are in addition to the functional requirements of the system ordinarily specified at this stage. Thus embedded within the project requirements would be a contract aimed at enhancing the quality of the completed software.

A major difficulty with a proposal such as the above is that we have neither the means of accurately measuring the effectiveness of validation methods nor the means of determining "how valid" the software should be. We assume that it is not possible to produce a "perfect" software system; the goal is to try to get as close as required to perfect. In addition, what constitutes perfection and how important it is for the software to be perfect may vary from project to project. Some software (such as nuclear reactor control systems) needs to approach perfection more closely than other software (such as an address labeling program). The definition of "perfect" (or quality attributes) and its importance should be part of the validation requirements. However, validation mechanisms written into the requirements do not guarantee high quality software, just as the use of a particular development methodology does not guarantee high quality software. The evaluationof competing validation mechanisms will be difficult.

A second difficulty with specifying as collection of validation methods in the requirements is that most validation tools do not exist in integrated packages. This means that the group performing the verification must learn several tools that may be difficult to use in combination. This is a problem that must receive careful thought. For unless the combination is chosen judiciously, their use can lead to additional costs and errors. The merits of the tool collection as a whole must be considered as well as the usefulness of any single tool.

Future work in validation should address the above issues. One possible course of action is to integrate the development and validation techniques into a "programming environment." Such an environment would encompass the entire software development effort and include verification capabilities to:

1. Analyze requirements and specifications
2. Analyze and test designs
3. Provide support during construction (e.g. test case generation, test harnesses)
4. Provide a data base sufficient to support regression testing

The use of such environments has the potential to improve greatly the quality of the completed software and also to provide a mechanism for establishing confidence in the quality of the software. At present the key to high quality remains the disciplined use of a development methodology accompanied by verification at each stage of the development. No single technique provides a magic solution.